THE
FUNDAMENTAL
INSTITUTION

THE
FUNDAMENTAL
INSTITUTION

POVERTY, SOCIAL WELFARE, AND AGRICULTURE IN AMERICAN POOR FARMS

MEGAN BIRK

UNIVERSITY OF ILLINOIS PRESS
Urbana, Chicago, and Springfield

Library of Congress Cataloging-in-Publication Data
Names: Birk, Megan, 1979- author.
Title: The fundamental institution: poverty, social
    welfare, and agriculture in American poor farms /
    Megan Birk.
Description: Urbana: University of Illinois Press, [2022] |
    Includes bibliographical references and index.
Identifiers: LCCN 2021046459 (print) | LCCN 2021046460
    (ebook) | ISBN 9780252044380 (hardback) | ISBN
    9780252086458 (paperback) | ISBN 9780252053375
    (ebook)
Subjects: LCSH: Almshouses—United States—History.
    | Rural poor—Government policy—United States.
    | Rural poor—United States—Social conditions. |
    Agriculture—Social aspects—United States. | United
    States—Rural conditions. | United States—Social
    conditions—1865–1918. | United States—Social
    conditions—1918–1932. |
BISAC: HISTORY / United States / State & Local / Midwest
    (IA, IL, IN, KS, MI, MN, MO, ND, NE, OH, SD, WI) |
    SOCIAL SCIENCE / Human Services Classification:
    LCC HV63.U6 B57 2022 (print) | LCC HV63.U6 (ebook)
    | DDC 353.53/320973—dc23/eng/20211208
LC record available at https://lccn.loc.gov/2021046459
LC ebook record available at https://lccn.loc.gov/
    2021046460

Contents

Acknowledgments

Across the country genealogists and local historians are doing the tedious and underappreciated task of preserving their local institutional histories by transcribing, digitizing, and writing about poor farms. I owe them a great debt toward making this project possible. Those working to preserve the physical sites of this history also have my thanks.

My University of Texas Rio Grande Valley colleagues Linda English and Friederike Bruehoefener read various chapters, and their friendship is a great gift. Dan Knight and David Danbom made time to read the manuscript, and their thoughtful feedback has strengthened this book. Kara, Chris, Eric, and the world's best librarian Sara Morris have allowed me to talk at length through the variations and implications of poor farm history. Moriah McCracken and my sister Abbey graciously copyedited earlier versions, and Trace Christenson located and photographed institutions he found in his travels. The team from the University of Illinois Press is amazing, and I appreciate their support and the feedback from outside reviewers. Friends across the country opened their homes and schedules for me: Peg and Jim Wolfe, Patty and Ken Cramer, Betsy Knott, our door is always open.

Other scholars and friends gave freely of their own research; Leah Tookey generously provided me with her thesis materials from Iowa; Jenny Barker Devine clued me in to some wonderfully fruitful Illinois records; Melissa Walker shared a memoir she received during her research. My gratitude to the community of scholars of agricultural and rural history is abundant. Pamela Riney-Kehrberg continues to be the best mentor her former students could ask for, and I owe her no small thanks for her encouragement, expertise, and enthusiasm. It was a pleasure to meet with Gina Wysocki, Heather Bigcek, and photographer Jeffrey Hall during my research travels. Claudia Hunt, Elaine Burrus, and I connected working on genealogy, and I am thankful for the information on their own family histories, which deeply enriched this book. Photographs from Steven Mizer's family collection illustrate the humanity and family nature of poor farm life.

I benefitted from support at UTRGV from Tom Britten and College of Liberal Arts Dean Walter Diaz, who helped me secure a Faculty Research Award that provided academic leave. Additionally, the College of Liberal Arts and Department of History provided financial support. Thanks to those I saw and presented with at conferences who provided insights and feedback. Components of this work were published in *Food, Culture, and Society* and presented in an Intervals podcast for the Organization of American Historians, and at meetings for the Midwestern History Association, the OAH, the Agricultural History Society, and the Rural Women's Studies Association.

It was impossible to complete this book during the COVID pandemic without acknowledging the vulnerability of the institutionalized and the historical importance of their experiences.

Joe has seen poor farms from the air, the trail, and the highway. Gratitude does not begin to explain how fortunate I am to have his support. My dad, Jim Birk, was not able to see this book completed, so it is dedicated to his memory.

THE
FUNDAMENTAL
INSTITUTION

Introduction

"I am bound to say I find myself damning with faint praise the mixing of agriculture and the care of the indoor poor."
—Francis Bardwell, "Standards of Almshouse Administration," *NCSW Proceedings*, 1917, 364

In 1884, Emma Love arrived at her local poor farm with her one-year-old son, Leroy. The farm superintendent noted that "bastardy" was the cause of admission. When Emma left three days later, Leroy stayed behind. It was rare for a child of that age to be at a poor farm alone. In the years that followed, Emma married, and in 1900 the census listed her as the mother of six living children, a total that did not include Leroy. Glimpses of his life appear in the poor farm ledger.[1] In 1890, a six-year-old named Lee Hardin was admitted to the poor farm. He had no parents listed, and the cause of admission was startling but sparse on detail: "poverty and hunger." Lee remained there for three years, and the farm register gives no explanation for his departure. He came back at age eleven and stayed another three years. A decade later, he stayed for a single night, coming from the Illinois Asylum for Feeble-Minded Children, which eventually housed adults as well. Lee does not appear in the ledger again until 1914, having been released from the asylum, which had a large farm where he may have learned agricultural skills, enabling him to sometimes find work with local farmers.

The case of the missing Leroy Love circles back in August 1916, when the ledger listed an intake as "Frisby, Leroy or Hardin, Lee" with his parents as Emma Wagner (the married name at that time for Emma Love Frisbee Wagner) and George Frisbee (her first husband). Someone at the poor farm knew Lee Hardin's history: the boy left at the farm by his mother in 1884 and the child found starving in 1890 were the same person. Over the next forty years, Lee moved in and out of the poor farm. In the final record he was fifty-seven years old, had lived at the farm since at least 1935, and had no education. One of his draft registrations named the farm superintendent as his contact person. He signed with a mark. It appears that Emma Love gave birth to a child she either could not or did not want to raise, perhaps because of his disability. The poor farm became his place of refuge, a home of sorts, as he bounced between place-ments, institutions, and occasional jobs. The record dries up after 1942, with no evidence of when he died or how he spent his final years.[2] Lee and his mother used the poor farm in ways common to the late nineteenth and early twentieth centuries: to provide shelter for a single mother, care for a disabled person, or harbor someone aging and unable to work. It appears to be the closest thing to a home Lee experienced.

It is sometimes said that each generation rediscovers its poor. Trite as that may be, the United States had at least one multigenerational institution with memory: the poor farm. The story of the Loves illustrates not just the variety of reasons people went to the poor farm, but the changing demographics over time—from a younger woman with a child in the 1880s to an older, single man by the 1930s. Only one type of institution in the United States supported, at public expense, such a wide variety of people for such a long period of time. In each ledger, intake file, and census enumeration of the nation's poor farms, there are unique stories of individuals and families facing untold struggles.

Renowned social worker Amos G. Warner called the almshouse the "funda-mental institution in American poor relief" and referred to its residents as "the most sodden driftwood from the social wreckage of the time." He believed it was "ordinarily a depressing experience to visit an almshouse, and accordingly we find it an institution that even the benevolent willingly forget."[3] Forgetting that poor farms served for generations as the backbone of localized social wel-fare is surprising given their former ubiquity, but unsurprising given their bad reputation. The term *almshouse* summons the image of a Dickensian urban prison for the poor, but in the United States a majority of almshouses for the poor were on farms, located in rural areas, and did not resemble the hulking workhouses of Victorian England or urban America. When Francis Bardwell gave it "faint praise," he highlighted the deep but often overlooked connections between the agrarian ideal and social welfare, which focused on the notions of healthiness in bucolic surroundings and the ability of farms to provide food and funds for the poor. Despite the common affiliation of farming and relief, much of the existing historical analysis of social welfare has concentrated on antebellum almshouses, or urban poorhouses, which provide an important but different perspective from the farm-based institutions of the late nineteenth and early twentieth centuries. There were, moreover, substantive differences in poor farms between the early and late nineteenth centuries. Not only did they increase dramatically in number, but their population changed as well, with poor farms increasingly serving as refuges for the older and unemployed instead of the younger and temporarily dependent. The advancing organizational structure of state and local government and their more prominent role in public assistance made poor farms a visible aspect of communities across the country.

What did not change was that each state created its own rules and regulations about indigent provisions, leaving the responsibility to townships, towns, or counties. Rules on paper about providing aid differed widely from the chaotic local environment.[4] Municipalities that were required by state law to care for their dependents did so through a combination of indoor and outdoor relief depending on the circumstance. The impetus to build institutions sprang from a desire to save money by reducing aid costs for the poor and sick—thrift, not compassion, was the motive. In a primarily rural nation, it is not surprising that towns and counties located their institutions on farms: that land represented an investment. Caring for people in a group setting seemed fiscally responsible, especially as it seemed there would be no abatement of the need. While there was initially hope that residents might provide the labor for these institutional farms, that notion was usually quickly discounted by those who managed them.

Exploring the proliferation of poor farms after the Civil War until the Great Depression, a period marked by institutional expansion—how they functioned, who lived there and why, and what role the farm played in providing aid—adds to a significant understanding of social welfare. There is no question that many poor farms were dilapidated places that people did not choose lightly. Notions about destitute people as unworthy of help were reflected in the fact that some early poorhouses were log cabins designed to keep people alive, but little else. One author called them "a groping attempt to deal with community failure to care for a growing underclass."[5] Poor farms did not necessarily shelter a growing underclass, but anyone for whom direct aid was not useful. There was no easy solution to help people unable to help themselves. The story of poor farms encompasses good and bad institutions tasked with the care of a remarkably diverse group of people. The elderly, the sick, single mothers, and abused wives stayed alongside transients, disabled people, orphans, and families who were victims of illness or disaster. Frequently people left of their own volition, needing help for short periods of time—days, weeks, or months.

Despite the commonality of relief institutions in the past, Amos Warner was right about the historical amnesia that plagues welfare policy in the United States. The oft-repeated mantra that relief came exclusively from private charity, or that people worked for their assistance, has had damaging implications for generations of aid recipients. It has framed them as opportunistic, lazy, and entitled—unwilling to work like those who preceded them—and posits that their problems and crises are less a product of circumstance and more a lack of personal responsibility. These ideas are also historically and boldly wrong: hundreds of thousands of people in the United States—a majority of them white and native born—received shelter, food, health care, burial, and even cash or store credit from public funds, without being means tested or forced to labor. Historically, welfare in the United States was locally managed and publicly funded, and based on necessity not deservedness.

Some of the responsibility for these misunderstandings falls on scholars. There seems to be a disconnect between what historian Ruth Wallis Herndon identified as the "face-to-face nature" of relief in the colonies and early nation, and an impersonal, rationally driven type of relief associated with the Progressive Era. For a place that was the "fundamental institution" of poor relief, historians usually speak in generalizations about almshouses and rely heavily on studying urban institutions as the measure for understanding aid and relief. Urban almshouses held hundreds of people, which required different governance; they lacked agricultural space, which led to subpar provisions; they housed more immigrants; and the poor in cities had a greater number of charities to which they could turn. At their most numerous in the early 1900s, there were at least 2,400 relief institutions operating in the United States, most of which were farm-based and serving fewer than 100 residents. To understand social welfare in US history, it is necessary to understand poor farms.

Earlier scholarship about almshouses framed them as intentionally degrading. Historian Robert Brenmer said they "had a tendency to transform temporary misfortune into permanent poverty."[6] Those assertions, however, invert cause and effect. People facing temporary misfortune left the institution as soon as possible while those mired in permanent poverty stayed. Much of the relief given was personal and gave "the poor some latitude in designing their own relief."[7] Many poor farms were revolving doors as people came and went at will, a type of flexibility not found in penitentiary-style institutions designed to contain and isolate. It was not unusual for poor farms to be considered homes of sorts, where management was expected to foster a familylike environment. Most of the poor farms in the United States opened after the Civil War, but the dreadful conditions in the antebellum period created an indelible reputation of harsh, cold places that wielded punishments liberally. Historian Walter Trattner noted those problems, using New York's 1824 Yates Report and an 1850s New York legislative report, which described pauper auctions and institutional residents dressed in rags and starving.[8] Trattner is not alone among historians trying to assess the confusing array of conditions and what higher goals these institutions served. Viewing poor farms simply as mechanisms of control and containment overshadow the human details about what daily life was like and what drove people to use poor farms.

Previous histories of the development of state-managed social welfare systems have focused on the failings of poor farms as they relate to the trajectory of welfare in the United States. But poor farms, as a bastion of local control, have a deeper, richer story to tell about the importance and longevity of localized relief. Efforts during the Progressive Era to professionalize aid or shift it from public to private did not, as historian Thomas Krainz has demonstrated, prove successful in most places. State efforts to systematize care, records, and policies and procedures met with failure. Communities may have been burdened by the expense of the poor, but it allowed them to retain power. This contributed to the variable conditions of poor farms; while some contained and isolated, others were points of local pride and demonstrations of community compassion.[9]

Sources, too, created confusing ideas about life in poor farms. Some of the worst and oft-repeated descriptions of them came from Harry C. Evans's 1926 screed, which has been used ever since as a guidepost to discuss poor farm conditions. Evans's eugenics propaganda showed a clear obsession with interracial sex and appeared supportive of forced sterilization for poor and disabled people. His researchers, in partnership with the pro-eugenic Committee on Mental Hygiene and following in the pattern of earlier eugenics studies, were committed to revealing the ways in which publicly supported facilities were breeding a dangerous subclass of Americans. The aim of the report was to urge centralized state institutional care to advance eugenics policies.[10]

Evans was certainly not the first to criticize recipients of aid or suggest their unworthiness. Having imported large numbers of prisoners, prostitutes, orphans, and vagrants, the British colonies in North America began with the intent of making people work for their bread. Historian Nancy Isenberg uses the colonial term "rubbish" to explain how some in Europe viewed the New World as "one giant workhouse" and the poor as "an alien race." The habit of indenturing people to labor for their support caused confusion about what was expected of those receiving relief. The most well known institutions for the poor were also the most notorious, emphasizing the criminality, isolation, and misery of poverty. Blackwell's Island in New York City contained both the poorhouse and a workhouse described as "most detrimental to the moral being of the individual." Having criminal institutions share the same property and management as poor farms and referring to residents as inmates reinforced this idea. High-profile locations such as Blackwell's, which appeared regularly in national newspapers, helped cement conclusions about institutional care for the poor and the character of those receiving it.[11]

However, categorizing poor farms as places of confinement or criminality is not an accurate depiction of what they eventually became. Sometimes the simplest explanation is the correct one. As historians Glenn C. Altschuler and Jan M. Saltzgaber point out, poor farms were designed not necessarily to "mold dangerous and disruptive classes into docile and dutiful individuals," but were instead intended to save as much money as possible on relief needs. Poor farms did not try to reform residents, nor were they always as cost effective as county personnel might have liked. They did not usually worsen the fates of their residents, who were in fairly bad circumstances already, but they did provide comfort to a great many.[12] Being dependent on strangers, not being able to manage one's own schedule, having nothing of tangible value—all of these combined to make "reception at the Poor Farm represent the ultimate in degradation to the hard-working farmers, the artisans and merchants, the unskilled but self-respecting day laborers. The urge to avoid that degradation with its attached stigma was enormously strong."[13] This is not a disadvantage attached solely to poor farms, it is a natural reaction to losing one's independence and a recognition that "shame or humiliation" comes from believing that others hold you in contempt or disgust.[14]

Historian Michael Katz advanced the idea that "fear of the poorhouse became the key to sustaining the work ethic of 19th century America."[15] However, as Joan Marshall asserted in her study about antebellum poor relief practices in the Midwest, "social control, the motivation behind changes in poor relief posited by some scholars, is not germane to an indigent population composed not of the unemployed able-bodied but of the sick, aged, and infirm, as was the group of poor relief recipients in rural agrarian America." Silvia Marina Arrom, a scholar of Mexican poor relief, agrees that narratives detailing either control or intentional degradation of the poor miss significant details about the social obligation of communities to their poor. People who could self-support did not stay long in poor farms, and when they did, it was frequently during times of the year where no work was available.[16]

People *were* afraid of the poorhouse, not because of intentional institutional misery, but because people could labor diligently and still face illness, injury, and abandonment that left them destitute. Katz believed that supporting a strong work ethic for wage-earners was a driving motivator in relief planning, or, "what poorhouses were all about."[17] But records demonstrate that almost as many people came and left poor farms during the year as stayed there regularly; they did not all lack for a work ethic, they lacked opportunities or the ability to make a living wage. Despite discriminatory perceptions about sloth and hereditary laziness among immigrants, paupers, and people of color, Americans did not need much prodding on the part of an institution to be independent, which is why most poor farm residents were already physically incapable of paid labor when they arrived. If they were not, they left in short order to resume their lives as working people.[18] To surmise otherwise is to continue a dangerous narrative that the chief sin of people in need is sloth. The changing nature of labor and resource allocation left many people behind or incapable of the type of labor required to earn a living or build savings. Despite that, a vast majority of people living in poverty never entered an institution. Issues of health care also played a role, because many poor farm residents arrived ailing from a variety of conditions. Being poor is expensive; it compounds problems, turning an untreated toothache into a debilitating infection, or an unhealthy diet into diabetes. People often came to poor farms suffering from conditions related to a lifetime of being poor or with bodies broken by hard work.[19]

Part of the reason people believed poor farms were designed to scare people into work is the erroneous idea that they were "full of able-bodied men." Statistically, both wintertime transients and children were regularly counted as "able-bodied," especially during the antebellum period.[20] By the 1920s, however, only 7 percent of the poor farm population was considered able-bodied, and only 12 percent of those people stayed a year or longer.[21] The goal of poor farms was not to terrify people out of using them: the goal was simply to keep people sheltered and fed, which became increasingly important as kinship networks broke down and extended family played a diminished role in caring for relatives. Institutions were not made fearful for effect; rather, the fear of them was a reaction to the loss of autonomy that came with circumstances out of one's control. Poor farms created an institutional patriarchy, organized somewhat like a household with a male figurehead and female helpmate, that required residents to surrender a certain amount of power. This struck at the core of basic American principles related to self-sufficiency, citizenship, and a dislike of paternalism and condescension, especially as it related to the privileges of whiteness.[22] Poor farms tended to be white spaces, managed by white people for other white people: based on the community temperament, sometimes nonwhites might also be admitted.

Forcing people to work—especially white people who made up the vast majority of poor farm residents—would have degraded their racial standing and criminalized poverty in a way that did not fit with the management and operation of poor farms.[23] Over time, a better understanding developed of the ways in which poverty and crises drove people to the poor farm in the first place. By the 1880s, rarely did anyone involved with a poor farm discuss the merits of resident labor. The opposite was often true, with superintendents complaining that overseeing residents' work took more effort than it was worth. Many of the transient, temporary residents were injured, sick, or briefly incapacitated. For the stable population there was little hope of "reform, rehabilitation, and education."[24] Those who most often labored on poor farms were frequently those classified as mentally ill or disabled. The true purpose of having a farm as part of a relief institution was not to be like a workhouse where care was tied to labor, but as an investment that contributed to the financial stability of the county as well as the institution.[25]

The success of a poor farm as both an investment and a residence depended on several factors. The quality of the land needed to be good; the management needed to be competent and stable; the county officials needed to be conscientious in their duties. These components could compensate for ills such as a rundown building, distance from town, or an ailing population. The type of relief provided to the poor varied wildly, with counties deciding what to spend and how to allocate funds. There were counties that provided no relief at all, others only direct aid, a few only institutional, and many blended the two; levels of generosity were entirely dependent on the finances and feelings of county officials and voters. Few people were forced into poor farms: they arrived on their own, were too sick to protest, or accepted an offer of institutional care from a county official. Historian Monique Bourque aptly described almshouses as "porous in both physical and administrative terms," because of the number of people who moved fluidly in and around the institutions.[26] Instead of a penal atmosphere, most poor farms resembled a large, strange household.[27] Communities did not necessarily look down on their poor farm residents. People visited with food and entertainment, newspapers recorded deaths and events, and many people felt more sympathy than loathing for their less fortunate neighbors.

Poor farms were also reflections of their counties. Counties struggling with poverty where people lived in rough cabins that lacked basic necessities were more likely to operate rundown and decrepit poor farms; economically successful counties wanted their prosperity reflected in the quality of the institution, farm, and management. Rarely would a county that prided itself on modernity besmirch its own reputation by keeping its needy in a hovel. Newspapers sometimes exaggerated institutional problems to sell papers, and county officials sometimes downplayed issues to improve their election prospects. Poor farms and local relief played an important economic role in communities. Ruth Wallis Herndon discusses a pipeline for local profit that came from relief spending, some of which went to people who provided care in their own homes for the indigent, while other expenditures linked institutions with their surrounding communities, giving local people roles such as supplying the poor farm with labor, selling supplies, providing transportation to residents, and a host of other opportunities.[28]

As the example of Lee Hardin and Emma Love demonstrates, demographics in poor farms changed noticeably over time.[29] In the late nineteenth century people were more likely to leave the institution on their own accord, but by the twentieth century the chief cause of departure was death. This gradual aging of the institutional population had much to do with direct relief and a continued lack of public healthcare services. Younger people, especially those with families, were ultimately encouraged to stay in their own homes with assistance, instead of moving to the institution. In contrast, the elderly and infirm for whom direct aid did not solve the basic problem of care increasingly came to institutions.[30] The removal of children from almshouses in favor of placement in families or children's institutions also increased the median age of residents. In the West and Midwest, allowing transient men to spend the winter supplemented spring labor needs and ensured farmers who needed seasonal hands would have a ready share, but the age of these men increased over time as did their need for more long-term care.[31] In the South where transients could be jailed, laborers were meant to be stable and captive, and local relief was viewed by landowners as a threat to their autonomy and power.[32] This limited institutional use by seasonal workers and increased the likelihood that poor farm residents in that region were unable to work.

The intent here is to examine poor farms as institutions made up of people— not policies—where design and function were intimately tied to agriculture.[33] It mattered less whether people needed a safe place to recover or a safe place to die: both of these were accomplished in the same institution. These goals may seem as though they are at cross purposes, but because poor farms served both chronic and acute cases of poverty, disease, and disability, they were both custodial and temporary—poor farms served many masters. They "reformed" people not through labor but in the sense that if people recovered, they could leave; they "contained" people not by locking them up, but insofar as they kept people from starving in the streets or becoming the responsibility of neighbors, villages, and employers. There was no high-minded idealism. Poor farms were there to be used by those in need—they were institutions where people might start, spend, or end their lives.[34]

The connection of farm to institution began as early as the 1820s, when Josiah Quincy of Massachusetts suggested that attaching a farm to an almshouse harbored the best chance for financial savings. His belief that residents could work to offset the expense of their care persevered as one of the great myths of social welfare in the United States. He articulated the connection between farming and poverty by saying "of all modes of employing the pauper, agriculture affords the best, the most healthy, and the most certainly profitable."[35] His position can be traced back further, to Jeffersonian ideals about agrarianism. Thomas Jefferson inextricably linked self-sufficiency and farming, writing that the "corruption of morals in the mass of cultivators is a phenomenon of which no age nor nation has furnished an example." He continued this line of reasoning by claiming that "dependence begets subservience and venality." Jefferson expressed these opinions during a time of preindustrial growth in the United States and was himself a man who did no farm labor, relegating those tasks to people whose bodies he owned and sold at will. By standing firmly on the side of agriculture, he created an indelible connection between farming, self-sufficiency, and the health of the nation.[36] The seeming abundance of land available for cultivation in the nineteenth century, however, did not prevent poverty. The fluidity with which urban and rural economies affected each other, workers, and the growth of wage labor coincided with the post–Civil War building boom of poor farms across the country.

The connection of agriculture and poverty opens a new avenue of social welfare history; it also helps explain what types of provisions existed outside the scope of private charities. The poor farms that dotted the landscape of the United States served as one of the last vestiges of institutionalized Jeffersonian agrarianism. This connection was so intense that many counties experiencing urban expansion managed to keep acreage for their poor farm, relocating institutions when cities encroached. States such as Tennessee and South Carolina mandated institutions have tillable land.[37] This book focuses on the connection between agriculture, provisions for the poor, and the daily realities of life at poor farms. In so doing, it avoids some of the better-known almshouses in the nation, namely those that served thousands of people each year in cities.[38] While this is not a story about urban poverty, it is impossible and unwise to disregard the influences urban reformers had on rural institutions, and vice versa, and the entwined agricultural and industrial economies. Assumptions about caring for the poor generally harken back to "the community" as an undefined but helpful unit of charity that came "discreetly" in the form of food, medical aid, and clothing. Relief services are often assumed to mean charities, which rural areas lacked. While some did participate in aid efforts outside cities, the "community" was the county poor relief system, which used public funds for direct and institutional aid.[39] The margin between county officials providing direct aid that allowed poor people to stay in their home or admitting them to the poor farm instead could be razor thin and subjective. The South lagged, especially in direct aid, and aid budgets were smaller. Historian Cybelle Fox demonstrates that race affected the spending and development of state and local welfare provisions. The sparse numbers of people of color in poor farm records supports that assertion.[40]

A huge trove of records exists for thousands of counties across the country. Many of the most numerous and comprehensive can be found in the midwestern states, where farms were almost always a part of the institution and where county officials openly discussed the acquisition of a farm as an investment. As such, this is not an exhaustive compilation but a concerted effort to sample institution records to better understand how poor farms worked and for whom.[41] Although I relied heavily on midwestern records I have attempted here to broaden the institutional representation as much as possible to provide a fuller national picture, using records spanning multiple years. Poor farms were highly localized institutions, and significant regional distinctions existed, but the premise that poor farms were critical parts of the welfare system and that their links to agriculture were meaningful is true nationwide. Research opportunity abounds for regional, microhistories, and comparative studies in relief practices. Where relevant I draw attention to the ways in which regionalism created distinct contrasts.

Because these records are public, I have used people's names unless the record was obscured in some way, included medical records, or was from the last seventy-five years. Ledgers, farm record books, superintendent diaries, census enumerations, newspapers, and county meeting minutes are included in those materials. In addition to relying on census reports for special populations, I have also utilized the census for the purposes of gaining a better understanding of what life was like for poor farm residents before and after institutionalization. This is a challenging method not without pitfalls, not the least of which is ensuring that the correct individual or family has been found.[42] Using institutional records provides the opportunity to consider, as suggested by historian Sowande' M. Mustakeem, that the human body is a source. Poor farm records routinely remarked on the physical attributes of residents. Those people whose bodies contributed to their dependency made up a substantial portion of institutionalized people. Although they left few personal sources behind, the information recorded about their physical condition helps us better understand their experiences.[43]

The people who used poor farms were a varied group. As historian James T. Patterson asserts, the poor "have never been an undifferentiated mass." Some counties had poor farm residents of diverse backgrounds while others recorded large numbers of a specific group of people.[44] As an example, Ontonagon County, Michigan, experienced a large influx of men from Poland, and as a result had more Polish men in its poor farm during the 1870s, but by the 1890s when the Finnish were the largest ethnic group in the county, they outnumbered everyone else in the poor farm.[45] California records, too, show small numbers of Indigenous, Mexican, and Asian residents in addition to white migrants. The same racism and discrimination that kept African Americans from using a variety of public services were reflected in their relative absence from poor farm registers. The reservation system intended to contain Native Americans resulted in a lack of localized institutions. Local economies and geographies also affected the processes of relief: coal- and timber-producing counties had more men and fewer women with children than counties reliant on agriculture.[46] Many people, like Lee Hardin, used the poor farm repeatedly. Children were most likely to be there with at least one parent.[47] Poor farms did not separate the worthy from unworthy, which is how they came to be mixed institutions with the sick, drunk, orphaned, widowed, and unemployed under one roof.[48]

The quality and conditions inside poor farms were also profoundly inconsistent, not just between regions, but from county to county and state to state. While every county in Ohio had a poor farm, not a single county in New Mexico did; only one-fourth of Texas's 254 counties opened one; Pennsylvania and Virginia had county, district, and township institutions; New England states featured town farms in addition to other jurisdictional almshouses. In counties with smaller populations, officials knew many relief recipients and frequently determined what was best. Those they did not know well could be met with suspicion and sometimes transferred to another location where they had more recent residency.[49]

The terminology I have chosen to describe people, relief, and institutions is significant. In addition to "indigent," which was a historically common term for the poor, I will use the term "dependent" to describe those who received relief in any form from a public source. That word is laden with meaning, as established by historians Nancy Fraser and Linda Gordon and philosopher Eva Feder Kittay. In the context of county-level relief, dependency is not a term reserved only for poor women and children, nor should it be confused with modern contextualizations related to "welfare dependency." As Kittay asserts, dependency is part of the lifecycle and includes a wide range of vulnerabilities: being young, being old, being sick, having a disability. Historically, the use of "dependent" replaced the long-time use of "pauper" to describe those in need.[50] I have not assumed to diagnose anyone with a disease or other condition that was not noted in historical documentation. Likewise, I have tried to police my use of the words pauper, disability, feebleminded, insane, etc. carefully. I employ "disability" to connote a condition that might fit into a range of diagnoses. Current use of disability refers to a bodily configuration, and a handicap is a "set of social relations or meanings assigned to a particular bodily configuration." Disability occurs through disease, accident, or congenital circumstances.[51] When the records referred to someone as an idiot, or imbecile, insane, or feebleminded, I have used the historical terminology but have used appropriate modern terms where possible, while being mindful that I cannot always determine what term would be most appropriate for that individual.

I have tried to reserve the terms pauper and pauperism to describe only those people who were labeled as such, because as Oscar Craig, former president of the New York Board of Charities said in 1893, "poverty and pauperism are words which should not be used as equivalents, or even as synonyms." Pauperism was considered a personal fault and a degeneracy, a product of a person's "vicious indulgence." Social Gospel leader Oscar McCulloch believed paupers to be immoral and weak, which connected to ideas about heredity, environment, and eventually eugenics.[52] This lack of dignity and shame marked them as paupers.[53] There was a criminality attached to pauperism that was not true of poverty or those labeled as poor or unfortunate. Pauperize is also a verb, indicating people ruined by relief and made lazy.

Early use of the term "almshouse" often evoked ideas of incarceration, and the institutions themselves have been called "dreary, lifeless, and degrading," and a "dumping ground."[54] In 1911, reformer Alexander Johnson decided to use the term as his catchall for the variety of titles used in the United States, although he preferred "Home for the Aged and Infirm" as "the most free from disagreeable connotations" and indicative of the population in poor farms by that time.[55] By the early twentieth century, reformers wanted to remove the stigma of the word "poor" for the residents. As a result, some counties and states including Ohio and New York referred to their poor farms as infirmaries or county homes, placing an emphasis on the purposes of providing a home and health care to the sick and destitute.[56] Carl Johnston, who for a time lived at the Allen County, Indiana, Infirmary, remembered that his superintendent grandfather required his family to always say infirmary, not poor farm.[57] I will use the terms poor farm and almshouse interchangeably, as was common. When discussing a specific institution, I will use its proper name.

When places dropped the word "poor" from names, they were making a concerted effort to change the reputations and clarify the functions of the institutions themselves. Kossuth County, Iowa, specifically declared its institution a county farm, because "there are those there who are infirm at times to whom those words [poor] have an insulting significance. Some of these inmates are not poor but are simply unfortunate and in need of just such a home." Removing the stigma was difficult, since some institutions were still located on "Poor Farm Road" or known locally by old terminology.[58] The 1890 US Census summarized the diversity of names this way: "In Arizona, California, Colorado, and Nevada they are termed 'hospitals,' in Ohio, 'infirmaries,' in Indiana, 'asylums,' and in North Carolina the names of most almshouses were changed by a recent act of the legislature to 'homes for the aged and infirm.'"[59] In 1910, the census recorded the Barbour County Almshouse, Bullock County Poorhouse, Cleburne County Paupers Home, Dallas County Old Folks Home, Etowah County Farm, Mobile County Asylum for the Poor, and Randolph County Pauper Farm—and those are just from Alabama.[60]

The trajectory of this book begins by tracking the evolution of aid from boarding out, to direct aid, to institution building, where local control eventually intersected with state efforts at inspection. Chapter 2 explains in clearer detail what economic conditions drove people to poor farms, who those people were, and the conditions inside poor farms. Management affected the conditions inside poor farms, and chapter 3 highlights the role of the superintendent in the operation of the farm. While political patronage sometimes played a part in the hiring of superintendents, some positions were held for decades by the same person or by members of the same family, largely avoiding political interference. Long-term superintendents were often a marker of a well-run institution and a productive farm.[61]

In chapter 4, the roles of women as employees and residents are examined. Women not only made up a critical part of the staff of institutions, but also used them for reasons related to abuse, pregnancy, and abandonment. Chapter

5 describes the connections between poor farms and long-term care for those people classified as mentally ill or intellectually disabled. While the lack of specialized care they received caused criticism, these residents were relied on as workers and for additional funds from states. Chapter 6 builds on the idea of specialized populations to discuss the aged population of poor farms, an important and large segment that came to dominate what people thought of, and feared, about the poor farm. Chapter 7 expands on the healthcare needs of residents to evaluate how the sick and ailing were treated, using doctors' records and the physical bodies of the residents themselves as sources to discuss poor farms as sites of public health care. State and federal programs eventually drove local governments out of the aid business, shuttering poor farms or turning them into nursing facilities, which is the subject of chapter 8. The Depression and federal intervention in social services played a critical role in the rapid decline of poor farms nationwide.

Local provisioning of the poor is a policy as old as the country itself, and poor farms were fundamental staples of local, public social welfare. While the earliest iterations existed in the 1700s, the number of institutions and people using them grew rapidly after the Civil War, alongside the population of the nation. The focus here is on that period of institutional proliferation between 1870 and 1930, decades in which poor farm populations were at their greatest and attention paid to those populations also peaked. But because the story of poor farms does not simply stop in 1930 when the problems of poverty ignited national discussions that culminated in the New Deal, I have chosen to consult records until institutions closed their doors, and discuss the transition to state and federal welfare. Before that transition, when people relied most heavily on local resources, the poor farm represented a community's responsibility to its dependent population. The quality of care varied just like the architecture, farm productivity, and management. Although a cultural sense of fear and foreboding existed around the institution, for hundreds of thousands of people the poor farm represented their best option in a time of need.

1 The Founding of Community Institutions

"Government has been forced to become the protector of the poor."
—Albert O. Wright, "The New Philanthropy,"
    NCCC Proceedings, 1896, 3

In August 1870, Buchanan County, Missouri, paid P. L. King \$21 for fees associated with five days "keeping and nursing" Thomas Hindrek. When he died after his brief convalescence the county provided a coffin and burial. P.L. is most likely an abbreviation for recently widowed Purlina King, who, at thirty-nine years old, had six children at home. She would have been a good candidate to earn extra money by nursing a sick man at a time when the county was between poor farms. Officials had recently sold their original farm and were keeping poor farm residents in private homes until a new institution could be acquired. Contracting with King gave her a way to earn money for her family while ensuring a respectful death for Hindrek.[1]

This chain of events details the difficulties of poor relief after the Civil War. Boarding out people who were sick and incapable of self-support put money into the local economy by paying for care, but it was expensive. Having a poor farm consolidated those expenses and made relief more efficient, provided that the farmland and management were both of good quality. Chroniclers of Polk County, Iowa, explained their decision in loftier terms, articulating exactly what financial circumstances drove them to decide that a poor farm should be the "protector of the poor" in the county:

> In early days few persons were very rich, and it is likewise true that there were very few poor. As the country settled up, farms were improved, elegant farm houses erected, and the various natural resources of the country developed, the more industrious, economical, and fortunate became richer, and those who had less enterprise, business sagacity, or were unfortunate grew poorer. Not only had the number of paupers increased rapidly, but exorbitant prices were frequently demanded for maintaining such, and when accommodations could not be procured elsewhere, the authorities were compelled to pay the prices demanded. It is said

that as much as six dollars per week have been paid for the maintenance of a single pauper. Under these circumstances the people began to inquire after some plan whereby the poor could be more economically cared for.[2]

As states were settled and counties formed, legislatures tasked local government with care of their poor, concentrating "authority in the hand of the directors of the poorhouse," and creating local variants with no systematic approach.[3] Local officials led the push to more effectively use tax dollars to fulfill their obligation to the poor, whose numbers increased as did the population of the nation.[4] Including a farm in to the institutional planning represented not just the realities of life in a mostly rural nation, but also the hope that farm profits might offset relief expenses.[5] This possible infusion of funds was important, since direct aid was still used in many places because local officials learned that "removal to an almshouse breaks up the home and all its associations," potentially increasing poverty instead of mitigating it and extending the length and expense of stays at the poor farm.[6] Instead of poor farms completely eliminating direct aid, both frequently operated in tandem.

Generally, the administration of local aid followed a pattern in which "the oldest States have copied, or rather imitated, the English methods, the new States have imitated the methods of the old States, and all have improvised alterations and additions as circumstances seemed to call for them."[7] In practice, this meant that counties transitioned through a period of expending cash or in-kind items on individual cases before determining that the acquisition of a poor farm would help with expenses and management of the poor, especially those who could not take care of themselves or had no home. This evolution in local aid increased after the Civil War because of economic downturns and a changing labor market. Once officials made that determination, details such as farm purchases, institution building, funding, and other concerns became paramount and a matter of public record for the review of the taxpayers footing the bills. What resulted was an assortment of locally administered relief practices that included poor farms, but which eventually ran counter to evolving Progressive Era ideals of rationalized, centralized control that could be studied and improved through consolidated power. This set up a battlefront in which poor farms played a pivotal role between local welfare management and state and national attempts to rationalize aid.

Boarding and Leasing

The practice of paying people like Purlina King to care for a dependent person was popular before the Civil War because it required little infrastructure. The process could include county officials finding someone willing, having a notoriously shameful pauper auction, or taking bids to care for the poor, but these practices led to neglect and fraud. When communities auctioned off the poor, sometimes those perceived to be mentally ill but harmless or intellectually disabled were most sought after because they were able to contribute labor to a household. Boarding was most expensive for the chronically ill because it could drag out for weeks or months. Officials had no real way of budgeting how much money they would spend on any one case or how many times a doctor would be needed.[8]

Eliminating this system in favor of a poor farm was not always a popular choice because boarding the poor could be a boon to those who received the county's stipends. Massac County, Illinois, records provide a clear window into their antebellum pre–poor farm expenditures. Depending on the severity of the case, county officials paid approximately $4 a week during the 1840s and 1850s, generating payments to locals as high as $45 for a single individual's care. Chronic cases, like that of Thomas Hobbs, "a free man of colour a poor person and pauper," proved to be expensive. For at least two years multiple people were paid approximately $4 a week to take care of him, and that he bounced between households suggests he was not an easy houseguest. At a poor farm his care would have cost between fifty cents and $2 a week. Even strangers were provided for; in 1854 Mary and Willis Gurley housed, and then buried, an unknown man after his illness led to death, for which they were paid and given his shotgun. The county also paid direct relief to keep people in their own homes, helping with burial expenses and doctor's bills. Sometimes the practice backfired and resulted in fraud, as was the case in 1871 when George Steele received $19 and a reprimand for overspending his budget to bury a man. The cashmere pants and coat, a fine shirt, gloves, socks, and a tie probably did not make it into the walnut coffin.[9] Records indicate that these methods of relief drained antebellum county coffers of cash at alarming rates.[10] Dubuque County, Iowa, justified the purchase of its first farm in 1848 because aid costs were the county's largest expense.[11] Options used elsewhere that put relief funds into the hands of local people included renting houses for the poor, renting rooms for them in hotels and boardinghouses, leasing a log cabin from a local man, and using a roadside saloon.[12] It is little wonder that counties believed a farm-based institution could help offset their costs for food, shelter, doctor's visits, and burials. The justification was widely shared.

Given that one goal of poor farms was to consolidate relief expenses, it is noteworthy that their founding did not always eliminate boarding out. Calhoun, Iowa, ran out of room at its poor farm and continued boarding out until 1900. Counties with small populations continued to do so too, believing it cheaper than the overhead for an institution. This was the case during the 1910s in Pope County, Illinois, which paid a local farmer and his wife $10 a month to care for two incapacitated people. This type of boarding created an ad hoc type of poor-house/boardinghouse harkening back to colonial and early nineteenth-century notions of keeping the poor.[13] Counties in Ohio, Kansas, and Oregon are just some of the places that prolonged the practice, with Oregon officials asserting that the payments also helped the family finances of those providing the care.[14] Using this seemingly outdated method of relief was an issue of population density and cost. More populous counties had greater relief needs, and keeping the poor together reduced expenses.[15] Other states used boarding for special cases. Massachusetts, despite having a large state-level institutional system for indoor relief and local almshouses, continued to do some boarding of poor people with disabilities. So regular was this habit that in 1897 the state mandated quarterly visitations be made to the more than 700 people being boarded.[16]

The practice of auctioning off the poor, although rarer, also quietly contin-ued. In 1872, Appling County, Georgia, auctioned off its poor, both Black and white, and spent around $100 a person. Beginning in 1871, Grace Sellers, an African American woman estimated to be near 100 years old, was auctioned off in three consecutive years for $75, $99, and $150—the cost increasing as she aged, indicating that she required more care and contributed little or no labor.[17] Auctions continued in Virginia as well, and an 1876 state law allowed for the lowest bidder to provide essentials to the poor; the auctions ended because of accusations of abuse.[18] Texas listed a total of 1,851 people as dependent in the late 1880s; thirty-five counties had poor farms containing 835 residents, but almost as many people, 716, had been let out to the lowest bidder.[19] Scott County, Arkansas, officials still allowed people to bid on the poor during the 1890s, and later estimated that the poor farm saved approximately half the cost of auctions.[20]

The construction of poor farms did not discontinue direct aid, either. The practice of providing direct aid to those in need was commonplace, controver-sial, and misunderstood. County officials frequently noted that some forms of direct aid played an important role in treating people with dignity, saving money on long-term cases, and keeping families intact. Historian Jenny Barker-Devine located records showing a brief but interesting pattern in Illinois of requiring aid recipients to repay their aid through work for local merchants who provided them with goods including shoes and fabric. Most of the beneficiaries of this 1850s program were local women who needed employment but not institutional-ization.[21] This unique arrangement appears to have applied only to those people who were perceived as capable of laboring in exchange for temporary assistance. A crisis had befallen them, but they did not need institutional care. County officials across the country consistently used direct aid, usually without a work requirement, to support those people who were in acute distress but not home-less or helpless. Relief records show the variety of direct aid expenses, including coffins, medicine, food, and fuel, which were frequently given to families and women with children as an alternative to the poor farm. One pregnant woman, for example, received a dollar a day for nine days during her "confinement"; doctors' bills were paid for those with typhoid and broken bones. Removing people from their homes was not always the best long-term solution to their distress, so direct aid helped keep families together and in their own homes if possible. Deciding the right course of action for specific cases exemplified the particularly personal nature of relief in many areas of the country.[22] Many counties reported that they spent as much, if not more, on direct aid as they did the poor farm.

Building the Poor Farm

Official permission authorizing counties to begin the institution building process came from state legislatures. The timing for permission varied—Illinois passed an 1839 authorization to establish county poorhouses, but Texas waited until 1869.[23] Most states did not mandate institutions, instead requiring local provisions for the poor and codified limits on expenditures. Kansas legislation included an acreage limit seeking to avoid giant, tax-free public farms, and a Pennsylvania law allowed for district poor farms shared between counties.[24] County officials did not always agree on a farm-based institution. During the Civil War, Wayne County, Michigan, officials debated whether a farm was an appropriate part of a poorhouse. The representative from Detroit believed it a waste, and the two rural township officials dissented. A proposal to sell all but thirty acres of their existing farm was circulated, but stopped when the county auditors stepped in, noting that while 280 acres seemed like a lot, 58 were in cultivation, others served as pasturage and timber stands, and the farm more than paid for itself each year. The city faction lost the debate, and eventually this farm and its sister farm for the county asylum had over 900 acres, making it possibly the largest county farm in the country.[25]

When county officials determined that an institution for poor relief was desirable, they typically began by buying land. Far from being limited to private land sales, they purchased from railroad companies, acquired a ghost town at a tax auction, and St. Joseph, Michigan, foreclosed on the tavern and farm of an escaped felon for its institution. Counties also purchased existing farms from locals, making alterations to the existing structures to suit their needs. In Iowa buying land required voter approval. In Mills County, the 1875 vote to build a poor farm passed by more than 800 votes, but the "no" votes drew criticism, with a county chronicler recording, "it is a matter of deep regret that so many were to be found in the county so occupied with their own schemes that they not only took no interest in, but actually tried to defeat the will of more liberal minded and more humane men."[26] Voters in Howard County, Iowa, held off on a farm for twenty years after it was first proposed, justifying the delay by noting that "many of the taxpayers are poor, and in view of this fact relief should be granted only in cases of extreme destitution."[27] In some cases, the land preceded the actual institution by years. Pratt County, Kansas, officials reported that they had no poor farm residents but were looking forward to a strong wheat harvest from their farm, with the money helping to offset direct relief costs. A report filed with the state claimed that the land "has proven a good investment anyway . . . very few people make application for aid when told we have a poor farm and they can go there."[28] Dodge County, Nebraska, bought land in 1872 but did not build on the site, five miles from the county seat, until 1884. One Minnesota newspaper believed that purchasing land before a poor farm was necessary and a benefit to all involved: "as the population of the county increases it will grow larger and larger. Money invested in land in this county cannot be a bad investment, and if a farm of 621 acres is bought, and judiciously managed, it will be but a short time before our poor will be able to pay their own way."[29] Despite this initial enthusiasm, the county did not purchase such a large farm, believing it to be too big to manage successfully.

The cost, location, and quality of land purchased were scrutinized by local taxpayers. Scott County, Arkansas, citizens were displeased when they learned in 1909 that the farm for which the county paid $1,000 was "not worth $250." The newspaper reported that "someone is to blame for wasting the people's money in this way, and the people should find out who is at fault and retire him to private life." A grand jury visit met with public skepticism when it claimed that the land was poor, but the houses were fixed up well and the residents were all right.[30] One local Minnesota paper helpfully suggested that county officials clear the land themselves and sell the firewood. In Ramsey County, Minnesota, officials took part in a merry-go-round of land selling and buying until the matter was settled: at one point the county owned three farms simultaneously while trying to figure out which one to use.[31] Olmsted County, Minnesota, officials did the same, buying a farm in 1868, trading it for a new one in 1874, and doing so again in 1896.[32]

Location was a primary factor affecting the overall costs of an institution. Some officials thought it cheaper to buy land in a remote part of the county but this strategy ended up being exceptionally inconvenient for county officials responsible for inspections, for doctors' visits, and for moving farm products and supplies. One of the only benefits to isolating poor farms was to keep residents from going into town where they sometimes got access to alcohol. Remote land might be thrifty but buying convenient or strategic pieces of land was usually more effective. St. Joseph County, Indiana, and Ottawa County, Michigan, officials situated theirs between the two most populated towns/townships to keep transportation costs down.

The location of poor farms was an important decision for local officials. This c. 1915 image from Jefferson County, Indiana, shows the poor farm situated near the Ohio River along a road known as "Devil's Backbone." Hard-to-reach poor farms discouraged transients but made it difficult for doctors and other officials to visit regularly. Photo courtesy of the Indiana Historical Society, P0062.

Poor farms also moved locations over the course of their existence; officials sometimes found it necessary to move the poor farm in order to serve more people, improve the land, or get out of the way of a growing city. Franklin County, Ohio, officials faced all three issues. The poor farm building was being propped up by beams, and increasing land values near Columbus made it cost effective to find a better farm and larger institution site elsewhere. The original poor farm was sold for a profit and officials selected a new location. The final site featured 223 acres, creating a large farm that the growing city again eventually surrounded.[33] After a fire destroyed the main building of the Uxbridge, Massachusetts, institution, town officials created a short list of six available farms that had better land, timber stands, existing structures, and were located away from the railroad line. They suspected that the previous location led to a substantial number of transients from other towns being dumped on their doorstep via train. Likewise, Mississippi counties worried about poor people arriving via ship, in both coastal and river areas of the state.[34] Hennepin County, Minnesota, set a specific goal of finding land between four and eight miles from Minneapolis, so that "the farm will not be in the immediate vicinity of Minneapolis. Thus the temporary rush of idle vagabonds during the winter months will in measure be obviated."[35]

There was no standard choice for where to situate a poor farm; like so much else about the institutions, the best option was highly localized. In 1884, H. H Giles, a member of the Wisconsin State Board of Charities, dictated slightly contradictory advice to attendees at the National Conference for Charities and Corrections, claiming that "a poor farm should be located near the principal town of the county . . . [but] it should not be [too] near a town, as it might become the resort of idle loafers; and the paupers will be more liable to leave the farm to loaf in town. From one and one-half to three miles we should advise as the proper distance." Proximity to town and transportation also meant that as a benefit, "the prying eyes of the people will be upon and into them," meaning that both residents and management would be supervised by citizens. Giles also recommended that focusing on location and soil quality was a better idea than buying the buildings that might come with the purchase. He wanted buildings specific to their purpose to be constructed, without ornamentation or decoration.[36] Alexander Johnson reinforced some of these same ideas in 1911, when he discussed the benefits of easy transportation to the institutions alongside the recommendation that they be located on farms. It is noteworthy that while separated by almost thirty years, the two men made similar suggestions regarding the importance of a farm to go with the institution.

Despite the efforts by some counties not to make their poor farms *too* easy to access, many were located in convenient places, on or near major road intersections. Although Uxbridge supervisors did not appreciate the intrusion of the railroad on to their farm, county crossroads just outside a town or the county seat were popular options. Joanne Cross of Murphysboro, Illinois, remembered the Jackson County farm near an intersection where her family had a farm. "I remember going to visit the nice folks there," she said. "There was a big porch across the front and the ladies would be sitting on it, shelling peas or darning socks. The men would be working in the gardens or throwing washers." That was her perspective as a child, but she noted that "later I learned how difficult it must have been for the people who lived there, back then people were as independent as a hog on ice. You did not want to be a burden to anybody or be beholden to anybody. It was a prideful thing: no one wanted to admit things were so dire you couldn't take care of yourself." Situating the poor farm in a reasonably convenient location helped keep residents connected with the community, allowed people to visit, and made for easier access by county officials, doctors, and employees.[37] In the 1870s Sangamon County, Illinois, officials discussed moving their farm because it was too far away from Springfield, where a majority of the residents came from. The physician worried a move would place people too far from medical care. The issue of placement was no less important fifty years later, when counties in North Carolina went on a building binge. During the 1910s and 1920s more than $1 million worth of structures were built in new locations with better transportation access. These improvements were not universal, however, with one visitor reporting that he found it impossible even in dry weather to get to one poor farm, and after a day of rain he was "advised not to attempt to reach the new county home in Burke County."[38] Although Joanne Cross liked visiting, some locals preferred a bit of separation from poor farm residents. Martin County, Minnesota, moved its poor farm to a new property in 1915, and the local paper noted that neighbors were pleased since they had been "more or less annoyed by the presence of some of the county charges on the streets and at public gatherings."[39]

Location and land quality were considered as part of the strategy of a farm as an investment. Despite urgings to not overinvest in land, county officials did not always listen to men like General R. Brinkerhoff of Ohio, who claimed, "a large farm is unnecessary . . . all that is needed is a large garden to supply vegetables, an orchard for fruit, and pasture land for cows . . . fifty acres is none too little where the inmates do not number more than 100."[40] Minnesota official Hastings Hart, who noted that a "large poor farm is undesirable," may have had Goodhue County officials in mind, who considered purchasing a farm of 621 acres before settling on a more reasonable 200 acres approximately three miles north of Red Wing.[41] It was not just newly settled counties that bought big properties. In West Virginia, one county eventually owned 484 acres that did not result in comfort for residents. The institution itself was apparently in poor condition, and people lived in what locals called "the shacks" until a better facility was constructed during the Great Depression.[42]

The land was only one part of the startup costs for poor farms: counties needed a building. There were a variety of options, but all experts advised for separation between the superintendent, the women, and the men, which was easier said than done if a wood-frame farmhouse had been converted for the purpose of institutional living. Improvements or new buildings were constructed across the lifecycle of the institution: what began as a log cabin or basic farm-house might eventually become a multistory brick structure or a building with multiple additions. Particularly in places where the original institution was from the antebellum period, counties found themselves in need of bigger, more modern facilities by the 1880s and 1890s. Several New York counties were reno-vating or constructing new stone or brick institutions with larger capacities in the 1870s as states farther west invested in their first poor farms.[43] Newer insti-tutions often had wings or were laid out like an I, E, C, or L. Having no more than two floors helped with what today would be called accessibility, but at the time multistory structures were common. In the 1870s, the Hancock County, Ohio, Infirmary was criticized by a visiting superintendent, who believed that a building of four stories was much too high for the "class of persons occupying it." He did, however, have many compliments for the farm.[44] With no elevators, a four-story building would not only make the top floors prohibitive for residents who were arthritic, immobile, or bedridden, but also make evacuating in the event of a fire challenging.

County budgets dictated details of construction and design. A special build-ing for vagrants and very specific plumbing were among the items on experts' wish lists. William Letchworth, president of the National Conference of Charities

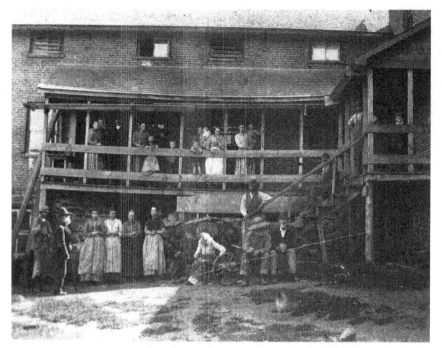

After the Civil War, counties often replaced poor farm structures built from wood frame in the 1840s and 1850s to meet the demands of larger populations as well as the expectations of improved standards of care. Photo courtesy of the Sheldon, VT Historical Society.

and Corrections (NCCC) in 1884, recommended the type of hay for bedding, furnishings, and a note about landscaping because he preferred "broad spaces of green lawn, with here and there a stately tree."[45] Alexander Johnson also provided specifications in his 1911 book to try and combat the habit of making spaces allocated for the men and women the same size, when more men tended to inhabit poor farms. He recommended bedroom space to be about four feet to every one foot of day-room space, and separate housing arrangements for elderly married couples, of which poor farms had few.[46] Although such specific details were rarely all followed, the architecture of some poor farms was strikingly similar as the use of more standardized plans became commonplace around 1900.

Although many buildings were basic and unsophisticated, counties sometimes spent tens of thousands of dollars on new poor farm buildings with intricate or ornate architectural details, constructing impressive, almost fanciful structures to represent civic pride and humane intentions: they were meant to be visible and were showcased in county histories and on postcards. An article in 1908 about the steady and incremental growth of the DeKalb County, Indiana, farm

County Home, near Vinton, Iowa.

Chickasaw County Home, NEW HAMPTON, IOWA

Although there was no standardized requirement for poor farm buildings, counties sometimes ended up with strikingly similar structures thanks to shared architects, state advisory boards, and planning visits between officials. Benton and Chickasaw County, Iowa, constructed similar buildings, and both regularly housed a steady population of about twenty people annually during the 1910s. Photos from the collection of the author.

noted that the county was prepared to build a new $30,000 addition on its 320-acre farm. Twentieth-century modifications made some institutions impressive. Nancy Swinford was mesmerized by the scale of the poor farm that employed her family in Michigan. "The whole place was beautiful," she said, "especially in the summertime, with its big maple trees. And the house was grand. The brick building had all terrazzo and marble flooring and stairs, and everything was as clean as it could be." Imogene McClanahan called the farm where her husband worked in 1968 "a showplace. It was beautiful." One of the residents broke a law every winter—"just a little something"—then requested, and was granted, a sentence of labor at the poor farm.[47]

While there was purposeful architecture in some counties, there was no nationwide or statewide consistency. D. L. Edson of Missouri's State Board of Charities and Corrections complained in 1918 that his state had ninety-seven poor farms and "a striking lack of uniformity." Edson claimed, "It is possible for 97 different policies to be employed," with "institutions elaborate and expensive, imposing and beautiful, or lodge them in old shacks, log build, chinked and dobbed with mud, reeking with vile filth and alive with vermin." States may have granted permission to build, but they did not dictate amounts for construction budgets and rarely indicated what the minimum standards were to be for habitation.[48]

Other startup costs related to farming and equipping an institution. Outfitting a farm could be "surprisingly expensive," with tools and livestock adding large costs on top of land and housing that included plows, hoes, and household items such as mattresses, chairs, stoves, and more. Joan Marshall noted that Warren County, Indiana, commissioners "had to borrow because of the unexpected expense."[49] In 1868, Fillmore County, Minnesota, bought 400 acres of good land, then spent $3,000 on stock and building a three-story house. The farm was valued at $15,000 once finished.[50] Any notion that poor farm residents provided a meaningful source of labor was dispelled quickly, so labor expenses also had to be factored in. As early as 1830 Indiana counties were authorized by the state to hire laborers for their poor farms.[51] In 1883, charity expert Franklin Sanborn made a telling comment about who actually labored on poor farms when he assessed some of the better institutions of Massachusetts by saying, "it seldom happens that these large farms can be cultivated by the labor of the pauper inmates, who are generally aged or infirm men, unless they are insane or epileptic."[52]

After their construction, poor farms transferred county spending from private households, as was common under leasing and boarding out, to businesses. Poor farms were not self-sufficient, so items were constantly purchased. Local businesses and service providers wanted that business to be distributed fairly. Expenses ranged dramatically, but normal annual spending could be in the thousands of dollars and included drugs, groceries, burials, doctors' visits, transportation, hardware, telephone service, oil, clothing and shoes, feed, lumber, dry goods, and labor. In 1889 Ohio counties reported spending $725,000 to care for 13,500 residents in more than seventy poor farms. For those counties less inclined to spread their business, it meant a valuable customer to a few vendors, but new merchants and individuals regularly appeared in invoices.[53] Poor farm officials also joined in the rural trend of using a purchasing agent to buy wholesale to get better prices. Michigan counties and superintendents reported that it saved time and money, with one superintendent remarking that he "had to trade with all the town" and haggled with some local merchants who claimed that "they paid taxes to keep up that home just as much as anybody else, and they didn't owe the superintendents of the poor anything."[54] Their unwillingness to bargain was a gain for wholesale houses.

Multiuse Properties

Having invested considerable sums in land, counties sometimes tried to make a poor farm serve multiple purposes. The most common combinations were that of poor farm and asylum (which will be discussed in chapter 5) and poor farm and jail, but occasionally a children's home and poor farm were also paired. As Cybelle Fox points out, the relationship of jail and poor farm was not rare in the South: eighteen of the sixty Georgia poor farms had prison wardens for superintendents.[55] Multiple Mississippi counties kept the poor on convict farms. While primarily a southern practice, combining jails and poor farms happened sporadically across the country. The Windham, Connecticut, Town Farm had a workhouse on-site with the poor farm. The poor farm in Dodge County, Nebraska, was used when the jail was overfull, and two "cell" rooms were added at the poor farm for nonviolent criminals so those people could labor on the farm. Prisoners were locked in the cells at night, a dangerous practice when so many poor farms suffered from fires.[56]

　　Poor farms also occasionally housed nonviolent offenders sent to work off their sentences on the farms and around the institutions.[57] Experts like Alexander Johnson advocated strongly against having any prisoners at a poor farm, so that the stigma of criminality did not taint the residents.[58] Counties, however, did it anyway; the practice persisted in to the twentieth century. In 1927, Amy Dawson, "the first full blooded squaw to be arrested in Muskingum County," ran away from an Ohio infirmary, "as far away as a fleet-footed red-skinned maiden can make in two days and two nights travel." Dawson had been jailed for robbery but was taken to the infirmary because she exhibited signs of mental illness. The newspaper sensationalized her stay at the jail by saying that "she went on the warpath with a vengeance while in the institution not more than a week ago and after shattering furniture, smashing windows in the women's corridor and terrorizing the other prisoners, she calmed down only long enough to attempt suicide."[59] After another robbery, she was recaptured and sentenced to ten years in prison. Cases like Dawson's, which combined both the issue of possible mental illness and lawbreaking, did little to situate poor farms as sites of care as opposed to spaces of contested containment.

The combination uses of institutional property came down to costs and expenses. Reporting on the 87 percent of asylum residents who could contribute labor to the farm, one Wisconsin superintendent wrote, "stock is nearly entirely cared and provided for by insane. Much of the work done was on a rented farm a mile away from home, much of which consisted of grubbing and chopping wood. Also an occasional job of contract work (not that I am an advocate of prison labor which might by some be so construed, but because I feel justified in using any honorable means by which proper employment can be obtained that will prove a healing balm to these wounded and disturbed brains)."[60] Making distinctions between the labor of the residents classified as insane and that of the incarcerated was easier said than done. In 1893, an Austin, Texas, grand jury foreman suggested "that some plan be adopted by which county convicts can be utilized as laborers on the county farm."[61]

Doing so reduced the cost of hired labor, but mingling the poor and sick with the detained and convicted was neither secure for the prisoners nor complimentary to the poor. Henderson County, Illinois, received special permission from the state to use the poor farm basement, which flooded regularly, as the jail. From 1855 until 1927—when there was a disastrous fire—the two remained combined, so much so that the 1876 hanging of riverboat brothel owner and convicted murderer Bill Lee took place in the front yard. The county doubled the guards at the poor farm and turned his execution into a well-attended event: 5,000 people along with beer and food vendors came. The notoriousness of this poor farm/jail combination continued in 1880 when two prisoners, aided by one or more of the dozen or so poor farm residents who gave them table knives, broke out after sawing off door hinges. Officers had to go to Nebraska to get the men, one of whom eventually reformed himself, married, and stayed in the county. State officials disliked this arrangement, with charities official Annie Henrichsen writing that "the combinating [sic] of the jail and almshouse is very far from being a humane procedure . . . the sheriff of this county should not be expected to be sheriff almshouse super farm manager and jailer." By 1907 the state said the buildings were "dilapidated" and "unfit for occupancy" although the food and clothing were good. Despite these complaints, officials bought more land instead of improving the buildings.[62]

Unfortunately, any connection between criminals and poor farm residents created a stigma for the poor that worried experts and formed lasting associations of poor farms as jail-like. Calling poor farm residents inmates did not help; moreover, the aims of prisons—reform, punishment, work, and rehabilitation—were not the aims of poor farms.[63] Despite the association of poor farm and prison, the distinctions are significant. Poor farm residents, while known to contribute labor depending on their condition, did not labor for private profit, or disrupt local labor markets in the same way that convict-leasing did by providing massive pools of captive labor. Records do not suggest that poor farms institutionalized people of color to control their behavior or manipulate their labor and reinforce white supremacy. It is significant to note, however, that in the South, where the use of convict labor drove demand for more convicts, people who might have otherwise been in a poor farm were sent to prison or jail instead. David Oshinsky and Mary Ellen Curtin both document cases of the sick, those with mental illnesses, and those with disabilities being sent to prison, which, when done in large numbers, would have reduced the need for poor farms. The fact that African Americans in the South were the targets of vagrancy and tramping laws also meant that they were sent to prison for something that landed white people in other parts of the country on the poor farm.[64] In his antebellum study, Timothy Lockley notes that "poor relief was whitest in those states with the highest proportion of enslaved persons." White, rural poor people "always had the safety net of public relief beneath them," a trend that continued after the war.[65] White supremacy was enforced through poor farms' refusal to admit African Americans who needed relief.

Even when poor farms allowed the admission of people of color, they often adjusted the architecture during the construction phase to ensure segregation, featuring multiple cottages instead of congregate buildings or putting Black residents in basements, barns, or attics. The distinction of race was significant even among the poor. North Carolina drafted plans for a single building, divided into white and Black sections. Cottages, most common in the South, helped keep things like cooking and eating entirely separate. When counties failed to segregate it drew the ire of southern visitors. Writing about Virginia, Frank Hoffer complained, "one can find instances where Negroes of both sexes mingle with white men and women. . . . In another almshouse were found three very old colored women, one colored girl, an epileptic who had a child . . . and a blind man . . . all sleeping in the same room." Hoffer's concern was not that these arrangements were substandard for all residents, or that these people needed better care: his concern was that three Black women were sharing space with three white people.[66]

Administering Poor Farms

When it came to regulating their operation, states offered poor farm officials little in the way of guidance. Iowa law claimed that no one could be admitted to the county poor farm without the written permission of a trustee, and Ohio tried to codify denial of relief to anyone who had been ordered to work but

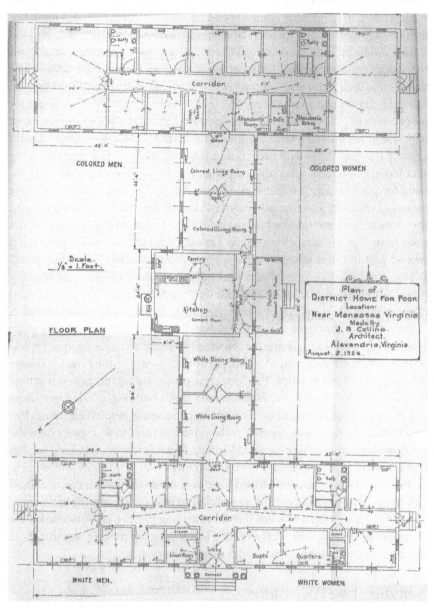

Harry Evans and other eugenicists advocated for regional poor farm buildings, segregated by race and gender. Virginia officials hoped regional poor farms like the one proposed here could be constructed for approximately $30,000 to serve six or more counties, but the concept did not catch on. Source: Arthur James, *The Disappearance of the County Almshouse in Virginia*, 1926.

refused to do so.[67] These statutes, while sounding authoritative, were similar to poor farm rules: existing in written form but not always followed in practice. At first glance they gave the appearance that states dictated how counties operated their institutions, but in reality, the power over poor farms resided with local officials who held the purse strings and the power. These county or township officials were sometimes referred to as overseers of the poor, directors of the poor farm, or supervisors of the poor, but who could also be county commissioners, judges, or township trustees. In Texas and Tennessee, county courts presided over poor farms. No matter the form county oversight took, these men made critical and individualized decisions about the administration of aid.

The practice of having a body of local men in charge of the poor dates back to the colonial period.[68] It was recommended that their supervision "be that of a kind father, with a fatherly love for poor, unfortunate human beings with whom he may come in contact. . . . [He] should be a man of pleasing personality, and one to spread encouragement and good cheer to the unfortunate by a pleasing word. . . . His heart might overflow with pity for distressed humanity, still his sense of justice and right should be so well under control as not to let his sympathies over rule his judgement." More often than not, voters wanted these men to be thrifty with tax dollars and keep their expenditures honest. Even during the Progressive Era when women became politically active in social welfare efforts, there do not appear to have been any women selected as poor farm directors, although they were eventually appointed as county visitors.[69]

While each state organized county governance slightly differently, the overseers of the poor reported to county supervisors, township trustees, or commissioners, and were usually required to file public reports and visit any institutions under county control. Indiana officials noted that "as a rule where the county officials have manifested the most interest in the poor asylums we find the better buildings and improvements and the best administration." Taking an interest in the job ensured better results.[70] Failing to do so generated criticism, as in 1873 when a local paper in Illinois editorialized that "it is hardly probable that there is one Supervisor in this county . . . who has a proper knowledge of how matters are managed at the county farm—whether the farming operations are managed intelligently and with economy . . . what is the sanitary condition of the buildings; whether the poor are properly cared for. . . . It is the business of the Supervisors to know all these things." Public critiques like this one could generate improvements; Rock Island County formed a board to oversee the poor farm shortly after that editorial.[71] Because their responsibilities involved the spending of local tax dollars, board business frequently ended up in the newspaper. In 1887, editors vented frustration that the board of supervisors stopped budgeting funds to publish their proceedings in the paper because the paper critiqued their billing practices.[72]

Men were elected or appointed directors of the poor farm in part because of their successful farming careers, business leadership, or other respectable community roles. In Wood County, Ohio, "prominent agriculturalist" Joseph Mitchell was a poor farm director, and the first to install drain tiles on his farm. Joining him were Allen Ferguson, a farmer known for his business abilities and sound judgment, John Isch who owned a "model farm"; and F. J. Schriber, an implements dealer. Other farmers also appeared on the directors list during the 1880s and 1890s. These men were selected for the job not for their interest in the poor but because they could help manage a successful farm for the county.[73] In 1934, St. Louis County, Minnesota, renamed its poor farm for long-time director A. P. Cook, who retired after forty years of service as the clerk of the Board of Poor Commissioners. An article commemorating his retirement described the position he held as requiring "patience, understanding, fairness, and both soft-ness and hardness at times of depression, unemployment and epidemics. Terrific pressure is brought to bear on the Clerk of the County Poor Commission and

Local elected officials who oversaw poor farms were expected to visit regularly to check on the farm, the staff, and residents. Those meetings allowed county officials to make suggestions and comments, examine financial reports, and often enjoy a meal. Longtime superintendent Edwin Farmer and his wife, Charlotte, are on the far right-hand side of the image. Photo courtesy of Wood County, Ohio, Historical Society.

it is no job for a weakling."[74] The job, when done well, required a fair amount of travel and routine involvement in the lives of distressed residents.

Most pressing was the financial accounting that included the farm, the household expenses, and the needs of residents. Although the farm income hardly ever exceeded the expenses, economic thrift was expected of all poor farm directors.[75] Sometimes that meant making specific decisions about individuals. In a single meeting, Wood County, Ohio, directors ordered a man to the soldiers' home, returned another to Erie County, and sent someone else to the Louisville Lunatic Asylum.[76] During the depression of the 1890s, they ordered the dismissal of five men they believed could fend for themselves and became embroiled in a multicounty legal argument over the legal residence of people at the farm. Transfers of people and money between counties was not new or unique but suing other municipalities was an indication of the ways in which the depression affected budgets.[77] County officials wanted to ensure they were not paying for the care of people who might have residency elsewhere, and wanted to bill the appropriate county for the costs. North Dakota officials did not simply move poor farm residents between counties, they paid passages for people to go to Sweden, Norway, and Washington state.[78]

In other cases, overseers of the poor decided between direct aid or authorizing admissions to the poor farm. If admitting, they either brought people directly to the farm or arranged for their transport with a note or permission form. Few of these forms survive, but those that do stated where the person came from, what their condition was, and whether they had legal settlement in the county. The issue of who admitted a person was sometimes recorded in the ledger to determine which townships sent the most people. This was particularly important during periods when each township, as opposed to the county, paid for its own poor. Versions from the 1910s demonstrate the influence of concerns about exploitation of aid and hereditary poverty, asking whether the person had received previous aid and if they had relatives who previously were public charges.[79] Counties did limit the options for those considered unworthy of direct aid, such as intemperate men, and occasionally followed through on the threat to withhold all but poor farm residency. Ottawa County, Ohio, officials told a man who requested relief to go to the poor farm, but when he refused, they extended no aid.

Hiring staff for and supplying goods to the poor farm was another financial responsibility of county officials. Some boards took sealed bids for positions, including superintendent, doctor, and suppliers. While they sometimes selected the lowest bid, officials occasionally paid slightly more to secure someone reliable. Dade County, Missouri, took the lower bid for county physician but decided to keep their superintendent, Madison Foncannon, even though one of the four bids was $40 lower than his. In exchange, he had to post a bond of $1,500 to ensure the county did not lose property and to cover any potential damages.[80] The posting of a surety bond was not limited to Foncannon. Ohio required one as an assurance of "faithfully and impartially" performing the duties associated with the position, but requiring such a deposit also deterred men without means from applying, potentially discouraging those who wanted to skim off farm resources.[81] Once hired, poor farm directors also managed the superintendent or steward of the farm who in turn managed his wife, the hired workers, and the residents. In rare circumstances, as in Searcy County, Arkansas, the poor farm was lightly managed by a farmer who did not live on-site. Local officials noted that things were in decent condition and that the residents did the "greater portion of the housework." They recommended that someone on-site actually supervise the residents for "fear of fire, or other accidents that might happen."[82] The poor farm superintendent also had the authority to admit those who presented themselves at the farm.

Some of the more detailed, personalized responsibilities of poor farm officials involved transferring residents to other institutions and finding new homes for children. Counties economized by moving residents to other institutions where their cost might be paid for by the state. Niagara County, New York, sent people to a dozen different institutions annually, among them children's homes, asylums for the insane, a firemen's home, and other county homes.[83] Each of the more than 100 people sent elsewhere represented a savings of more than $1 per week to the county. Counties also took back residents from overcrowded state institutions when states offered reimbursements. Officials were occasionally charged with finding homes for children living at the poor farm. Children there with a parent were less likely, but not entirely safe from, being placed out. Children considered orphaned were placed out more often. Unfortunately, the quality of the homes found for them varied widely and not all county officials were vigilant about investigations. In 1905, poor farm officials in Wood County, Ohio, placed the Lonergan children in an indenture with the Mervins, who were childless. In 1910, they were still there, aged thirteen and eleven, listed as foster son and daughter. Both were literate and had attended school. They did not have an occupation listed, and the Mervins employed a hired man on their farm, which reduced the amount of work expected from the children.[84] Ada Taylor, a thirteen-year-old African American girl placed out in the 1880s, was not so lucky. Officials put her with a local white farmer named James Pinninger (or Pinniger). He was in his thirties and had four young children at home. That the poor farm directors later "ordered James Pinniger to return Ada Taylor" is a clear indication something went wrong and that they were paying attention to her wellbeing. Among the common problems for placed-out children were sexual and physical abuse and refusal to send them to school. Ada was quickly re-placed in a different county, which suggests at the very least she was not pregnant.[85]

Funding the Farm

Each state had its own rules concerning funding sources for the operations and routine expenses for poor farms, and poor farm directors worked within those limits to budget for their institutions. Using property taxes and sin taxes were two common methods. Ohio's Dow Tax on alcohol, for example, helped fund relief until Ohio counties were swept up in the prohibition movement, causing those revenues to decline.[86] Taxes typically generated more income than the farm itself. In a handful of surveyed Virginia institutions, tax revenue accounted for 64 percent of institutional support compared to 29 percent from the earnings of the farm.[87] In 1890, Fulton County, Ohio, recorded income of $1,624 from the poor fund levy and $666 from farm sales. Wisconsin also used taxes from alcohol, but in the 1870s Dane County officials made an interesting argument, claiming that their relief numbers were higher because of drinking: "the number, we believe, is made much larger than it would be if no intoxicating liquors were sold in our midst. And yet while this traffic is allowed, increasing pauperism and enhancing yearly our county expenses, the money derived from licenses is diverted to purposes other than the support of its paupers." Seeing a direct correlation between drinking and relief, they asked voters to elect politicians who would support all the saloon license money going toward the poor fund.[88]

By the late nineteenth century local municipalities collected "over half of the tax revenues collected by all governments," which they used in part to fund relief.[89] States including Georgia and North Carolina used property taxes as a means to fund poor farms, if counties chose to build them.[90] The taxation rates for counties in North Carolina varied widely—from $0.002 to $0.083 per $100 of property—but most levied less than $0.40.[91] The diversifying uses of property taxes at the local level caused some rates to increase considerably. Between 1900 and 1925 Pennsylvania saw a more than 60 percent increase in poor taxes, although the population only increased 22 percent during that time. The state collected $12 million in 1925, a quarter of which went to almshouse expenses.[92] Across the Midwest, tax assessments on farmland followed the valuation of that land, doubling and tripling after 1900. From an average rate in 1900 of 26 cents per acre in places such as Illinois and Wisconsin, rates increased to more than $1.10 by 1920.

Whether the expenses of poor farm residents were to be absorbed by the county or township was another funding battle. In counties where there was a city that sent a disproportionately large number of poor farm residents to the county institution, officials sometimes preferred to force townships to pay a daily fee per resident. In counties where townships sent people to the farm in approximately equal numbers, counties frequently used general revenue. In states such as Michigan where both systems existed simultaneously, some townships provided direct aid as an incentive to keep people out of the county home, seeing it as a cost-saving measure; this contradicted prevailing beliefs that poor farms saved money on direct aid costs.[93] It was not uncommon for counties to continue to spend as much—or more—on direct aid as they did the poor farm. In 1900, for example, Illinois counties spent $1.6 million on poor farms and $7.6 million on direct aid.[94]

Officials could also try to force family members to pay for care, but rarely did they receive full reimbursements.[95] Idaho, for example, passed legislation mandating that family members take care of indigent relatives and kept trying to enforce it through the 1890s. Nevada, Illinois, and Mississippi all claimed counties would charge immediate family members for expenses too, but the counties do not appear to have recouped much money.[96] Family and friends did sometimes send money, but amounts varied widely. Edward Waters, who died in 1904 at his local poor farm, had been rendered "disabled and almost helpless as a result of rheumatism." The local paper reported that he had no wife or children, but relatives had paid for his stay at the poor farm.[97] Niagara, New York, reportedly made almost $1,000 a year in the early 1900s from family members sending money, almost as much as the institution made from selling farm products.[98] Occasionally the possessions of new intakes were seized to help pay for their care, but it is not clear what the stipulations were for this step. In 1909, an Ohio newspaper advertised the public auction of the "household goods of Ivy Ramsey and Mrs. Dorothy Swartz." Ivy Ramsey arrived at the poor farm earlier that summer with her husband, who had injured himself falling from his wagon. Dorothy Swartz had been a housekeeper, was eighty years old, and had been a widow since at least 1880; she did not appear to have any living children.[99]

State Involvement

In 1871, more than twenty years after Dorothea Dix rattled the foundations of institutional care by testifying to legislatures about dismal poor farm conditions, scion of society Louisa Schuyler visited a New York poor farm with almost 400 residents. She found many illegitimate children, poorly cared for residents with disabilities, and no separation of men and women. Instead of complaining to the county, she went straight to the state; New York responded to her complaints with a State Charities Aid Association, a new type of committee established to monitor conditions in public institutions.[100] New York was not alone—by 1881 nine states—a majority of them in the Midwest—had formed boards to inspect and advise institutions.[101] Because poor farms increased in number at the same time that institutions such as asylums, hospitals, and orphanages also proliferated, attempts by state officials to administer quality control, a fraught and mostly unsuccessful effort, became more common.

When state legislatures authorized counties to open institutions for the poor, they provided no funding and therefore wielded little power. The members of state boards typically began with the inspection and improvement of state-run institutions: the insane asylums, prisons, veterans' homes, and feebleminded homes administered by the states. Once formed, board members connected with counterparts in other states for discussions about the care of the institutionalized. The NCCC was the early result of those efforts, with meetings beginning in 1873. Even southern states sent representatives to the annual event, with Louisville hosting the first southern meeting in 1883; only Arkansas and Texas failed to send representatives that year. Few professional social reformers lacked an opinion about poverty, pauperism, illegitimacy, immigration, and relief—all issues that involved poor farms—but county-operated facilities were initially not the priority for state boards, nor were county officials anxious for such oversight. But by the 1890s, board members wanted to inspect all public institutions, including poor farms, where they faced challenges because they were encroaching on local control.[102]

The NCCC gave state boards increased legitimacy, and some set out to position themselves as experts in institutional matters. In 1883, nationally renowned reformer Hastings Hart made his first attempt at visiting all of Minnesota's public institutions, studying the populations, offering suggestions, and uncovering myriad problems. He set up annual reporting about demographics and met with county officials. His details from the Itasca County Poor Farm said that the men were "a hard lot with habits characteristic of their type," but that they did get taken to town to vote.[103] One of the most renowned boards was that of Ohio. Initially led by the Reverend A. G. Byers, the board caused such an uproar in state politics that, for a short time, it was disbanded by the legislature. During the 1870s and 1880s county officials expressed an equally low regard for the board and Byers personally, in part because he broke one of the precedents established by the New York board, which was to limit the "public exposure of errors in the management of county institutions" and use the press only "when all else has failed to effect reform."[104] The Ohio board had no such compunctions about saving the political futures of local officials or sustaining political patronage, and took their role as advocates for the institutionalized seriously. Stark County officials publicly dismissed Byers because of a disagreement about the approval of new building plans. The local paper reprinted an article from nearby Zanesville that highlighted Byers's "hobbies" of demanding certain types of construction and accommodation in jails and poor farms alike. In 1878, the paper took him to task for his criticism of Muskingum County's poor farm, which he noted in his report had "been allowed to run into shameful neglect." According to the newspaper, "If Mr. Byers's powers of observation and inquiry had been properly used, he might have learned that the 'inexplicable' cause of the present condition of the infirmary buildings is the length of time they have been in constant occupation, and their constant wear and tear, by hundreds and thousands of unfortunate fellow-beings of all sorts, sane and insane, including many vicious and destructive beings." The paper noted that the structures, initially built in the 1840s but enlarged in 1860, were suffering from leaks and plaster cracks, but that "the infirmary directors and the county commissioners have been far better acquainted with the dilapidated condition of the infirmary buildings than Mr. Byers." The county planned a replacement as soon as the funds could be raised.[105] In 1880, they did just that, constructing a massive, three-story brick building complete with steeples. It was a design used in other Ohio counties including Washington and Mahoning.

At the national level, these state boards became de facto spokespeople for poor farms even though they did not actually administer any. Ohio sent a report to the national charities conference in 1888 claiming that conditions statewide were improving and that quality management in some places set a good example for others.[106] Sometimes the most effective method state boards had to encourage local improvement was guilt, as used by Byers, applied liberally via newspaper stories or publicity. The Indiana board used its 1922 annual message to the governor and legislature to shame Crawford and Martin county officials, reporting that the buildings in those two counties could "not be too severely condemned. These buildings are old frame structures, dilapidated, decaying, insanitary. . . . They are wholly unfit for human habitation. . . . The continued use of them is a disgrace to the communities in which they are located and to the state." A handful of other counties joined the list for having fire hazards and bad sanitation. Despite reiterating the same calls for improvements each year, the state board noted that some counties were still not following laws regarding hiring practices and "no asylum has a record of all products produced on the farm and garden. There is no means of telling how productive the institution has been. This is not good business." Shame got boards only so far when it came to requests for modernization and improvements.[107]

One of the most significant findings by state boards was the discrepancy in expenditures, an unsurprising circumstance given the variance of funding methods. Among twenty-four of Minnesota's poor farms, for example, expenses per person per day varied from 58.3 cents to an astonishingly low 3.0 cents. One of the benefits of state boards was their ability to make county-to-county and state-by-state comparisons. These comparisons tended to provoke action and change, lest any one county be an outlier among peers. Typically, Hastings Hart and others believed that simply circulating information like the expenses per day could help level the playing field and create consistency. Hart used this tactic when he said, "It is a disgrace to Fillmore County to herd her paupers together in the poor house like cattle in a stable, while the expenses of the poor house with an average of 14 inmates, are but $439 for a year. It is equally discreditable to Houston County to hire an overseer at $150 a year and keep her paupers in a dangerous fire trap, partly unplastered, while the entire pauper expenses of the county are but 8.2 cents per inhabitant." He went on to criticize two more counties.[108]

State boards helped bring county-level relief methods into a national dialogue about welfare, charity, responsibility, and the use of public aid. Members went to national meetings and sent reports about the status of their institutions, providing information and points of comparison. In the same way that counties were compared to one another, states also lobbed accusations at one another about poor farm conditions. A 1910 exposé by James Oppenheim opened with a missive about the hypocrisy of those in Missouri and Pennsylvania criticizing New York, when all three states had been accused of abusing and mistreating institutionalized residents. Having castigated other states for bad behavior, Oppenheim gave his own appraisal, calling the people he encountered on his poor farm visits "unspeakable creatures." He specified he meant not the old and poor but the "babbling idiots," "jerky epileptics," "hardened, vicious criminals," and "consumptives."[109]

Eventually, state boards relied less on volunteers, hiring case workers or trained visitors in an effort to inspect all public institutions because the workload was too arduous for board members alone. In 1908, Minnesota's first state inspector, Louis Foley, visited 208 "lockups," 41 jails, 25 poor farms, and 132 hospitals.[110] In 1874, an early effort at organized visiting in New York demonstrated the arduousness of the tasks when the state board, aided by Frederick Law Olmsted, assembled a series of more than fifty questions to be asked during the site visit. He and his fellow board members viewed visiting as an opportunity to set a good example for poor farm residents. He remarked that "every life with which the visitors will come in contact at the poorhouse is necessarily a broken one, probably a wasted and hopeless one, made so by the fault, by the sin of the sufferers themselves, or by that of those with whom they are connected, and it is the highest office of the visitors to show to these poor forlorn fellow beings that their life, even in a poorhouse, may have its use and its beauty." Olmsted's suggestions noted that "however unsuitable the buildings may be, the committee should, by shrewd, patient and resolute efforts, seek to stimulate a disposition to make the best of them while their use continues." In other words, their suggestions might fall more gently on the ears of local officials if they could use what was already there in some efficient way.[111] Recommended questions to ask included inquiring about provisions for the sick, the size and operation of the farm, and the age of the building. Others bordered on minutia including: "How often are the ceilings lime washed?" "What is the cubic air space in each single bedroom?" "Is vinegar on the table daily?" "Are there trees close to the building, if so what kind, evergreen or deciduous?"[112] These visits, while numerous, were just the first step in a process of professionalization that sometimes ended without effect, as states retained no ability to mandate corrections to problems visitors found.

This lack of state power over local institutions became an important characteristic of poor farm administration. Improvements that state boards suggested, building plans they recommended, and expertise they extended could only be implemented through the participation of local elected officials. Many of the recommendations cost money, such as improving ventilation, water sources, building layouts, and health care. State boards could not compel counties to spend money, nor were they successful in shaping legislation that specified what conditions or expenditures were required. Instead, they encouraged local boards of county visitors to be formed. Ohio had them as early as the 1890s with between four and six members, both men and women, serving multiyear terms. Their formation seemed to indicate a lack of trust in elected officials to do a conscientious job and a recognition that county outsiders did not wield much influence. Locals did effect change; Edna Gladney of Sherman, Texas, publicly protested the conditions at her local poor farm; when she met with resistance she marched on the facility with other women, cleaning, whitewashing, replacing mattresses, and sending children to a local orphanage.[113]

The Debate about Direct Aid

One of the most unsuccessful attempts by state boards to use ideas gleaned from national conversations came during the 1890s, when a nationwide depression strained all relief budgets. At the time, private charities and cities were trying to eliminate direct aid, but away from urban centers, county officials demonstrated the necessity of the dual system of indoor and outdoor relief because the crisis increased the number of younger men, women, and families in need. This habit of blending relief types did not sit well with the burgeoning group of reformers calling for rationalization in aid and decrying the dependency of direct aid recipients. In 1890, the National Conference on Charities and Corrections established a committee for outdoor relief. Worried that giving people direct aid would make them lazy and encourage dependence, the NCCC tried to measure how much aid of this type was distributed. County officials ignored their requests for data. Committee member Franklin Sanborn claimed that while cash might be easily tallied, other support options—such as paying for a burial—were not always included. Sanborn, unlike some of his colleagues, did not disagree with direct aid entirely, emphasizing that providing certain types of people with direct aid provided a far better bargain than indoor relief, which could break up families.[114]

Early social work expert Amos Warner tried to use statistics from six states to measure direct aid. Shortly before the depression of the 1890s, Pennsylvania, New York, Ohio, Michigan, Wisconsin, and California all spent more than $2 million annually to help hundreds of thousands of people. Although noting that it was less common in the South to provide direct aid, Warner agreed that the practice was more economical for families, and that institutions could not handle the needs of everyone in distress. However, he worried about its creating more recipients and fueling corruption in government. In his opinion the intimacy of relief in rural places changed its administration, noting, "those who favored outdoor relief . . . draw their facts from rural communities where the problems are comparatively simple, and where abuses are readily checked." With few options for charity, that perceived intimacy was indicative of more than just simple problems; it also spoke to the limitations.[115] Warner was right, county officials sometimes knew who they were helping and why. Those personal connections and familiarity helped make decisions. Although Warner and other professionals discouraged this emphasis on rural communities as the blueprint for aid, at the time most Americans still lived in rural communities, making their tactics significant to the overall picture.

The 1890s pushed all forms of relief to their breaking points, exacerbating issues of insolvency and creating new ones. Farm income reached its decade low between 1895 and 1896.[116] During the same period, Indiana reported an increase of 22 percent in the number of poor farm residents in the state.[117] Tippecanoe County, Indiana, records show that 30 percent of 1896 institution entrants were homeless.[118] Counties in Ohio reported helping hundreds more people than normal with groceries and other direct aid during the decade, and that the new recipients were not the typical requestors of aid.[119] In Fayette County, Ohio, almost one-third of the requests during the decade came from African American residents. Whether or not they had fewer alternative resources such as family, church, or charity, or simply struggled more because of limited opportunities and discriminatory pay, they were overrepresented in the records based on population. They may also have been unwelcome at the county poor farm.[120]

During 1896–97, Indiana provided direct aid to one out of every thirty-one residents, costing approximately $500,000. The relief effort was so large that some townships were put back in charge of their own relief, with county officials finding it too cumbersome to handle so many cases.[121] Similar issues arose in Ohio, where at least one county complained about this exchange of duties, claiming that some townships refused the task and continued to beg money from the county while other townships followed the new rules.[122] President William McKinley's 1897 inaugural address noted the hardships in rural areas when he mentioned that the depression "has fallen with especial severity upon the great body of toilers of the country, and upon none more than the holders of small farms. Agriculture has languished and labor suffered."[123] The depression of the 1890s made it clear that poor farms alone could not provide the amount of assistance needed, and that not all who needed aid were well served by institutionalization; there continued to be a need for outdoor relief without means testing or a loss of autonomy.

The continued use of direct aid by counties contradicts assertions by some historians that indoor relief "dominated the public response to poverty."[124] Across the country, reformers talked a great deal about the perceived evils of direct aid and the desire to discourage it by putting relief-receiving people in institutions built specifically for such a purpose, but theory and practice were two different things. Private charities might have rationalized direct aid use or restricted it altogether, but public county-based aid was another matter. Expenditures for direct aid outpaced spending for poor farms. In not uncommon accounting, the state of Kansas reported that for 1899, the poor farms cost counties approximately $135,000 while direct aid totaled $209,000.[125] Forcing people to be institutionalized in order to receive relief sounded like a good way to discourage the idle, but it made no sense to overseers of the poor to put everyone in the poor farm when it was much easier and more neighborly to extend some of them store credit, provide coal, or pay a doctor's bill. Local officials knew who lived at their poor farm, and they knew that it was not the best place for healthy people, young people, or those who could be cared for at home with assistance. They hesitated to separate older married people; they avoided moving whole families or women with jobs; they paid to allow some people to convalesce and even die in the comfort of their own homes.[126]

Homer Folks theorized that the elimination of direct aid and mandatory poor farm residency for relief recipients would mean that poor farms and almshouses could be made nicer, because only deserving old people would reside there. If the intakes were done correctly, "only those who are actually unable to earn a livelihood and whose immediate relatives are actually unable to maintain them, and who are unable to do any regular and ordinary work, are allowed to enter . . . the danger of its becoming 'attractive' is minimized."[127] While poor farms did eventually evolve into institutions primarily serving the elderly, the idyllic version Folks suggested never existed. Although the idea dominated national discussions about poverty, eliminating direct aid did not become a common public policy at the county level.[128]

It was not just economic variables that kept direct aid alive. As institution expert Alexander Johnson noted, when "the institution is known to be so bare of comfort, so severe in its discipline, or so badly managed, that public opinion will not sanction a decent old person's being forced in to it, then outdoor relief inevitably increases in amount."[129] Public opinion did not demand institutional aid for acute emergencies either. In the 1890s Nebraska provided direct loans to farm families, and within six months 40 percent were repaid. One official noted, "This proves they were not paupers. It also appears that no one was pauperized by the aid given."[130] Elizabeth Brown Gaspar, a chronicler of early Wisconsin relief, noted that "the supplementary and temporary nature of outside relief must have afforded an additional stimulus for its recipients, wherever possible, to do their best to make a go of it for themselves. Even for those who could manage only by the intermittent acceptance of this relief, the knowledge that they had been able to avoid the Poor Farm must have done much to contribute to their own self-respect." In other words, she believed that direct aid success-fully helped people get back on their feet. That perspective is vastly different from those who believed that direct aid encouraged idleness.[131] Direct aid and poor farms created a complementary system of local welfare, with each serving specific populations.

Reporting to the State

When state officials tried to interfere with local control of poor farms, conflicts erupted. This tension is instructive because it sets the stage for the more sub-stantial changes in jurisdiction of the institutionalized that occurred during the mid-twentieth century. State board members were considerably more influenced by national trends in social welfare than local officials were. An example of this took place in 1906, when an Ohio state visitor attended the board meeting of the Wood County poor commissioners and "gave them a talk saying they had no right to pay out single [direct] relief and that they had better quit it."[132] Telling local officials what to do with their tax dollars might have been a message more easily delivered than it was enforced: Wood County moved its direct aid to the townships instead. State agents could also be seemingly nitpicky. A 1925 report from California complained that the "county hospital was found to be in very poor condition partly due to the hot weather and the fact that painters were engaged in renovating the building and the equipment was piled on the porches." This two-sentence report filed by Mary Crogen did not offer any constructive criticism for improving the weather or hurrying the cosmetic improvements. It was not her first visit to the facility, and it was not the superintendent's first encounter with state visitors. Six months earlier Crogen reported in greater detail the lack of lighting in the operating room, but she noted that things seemed clean and residents well cared for. State agents visiting in earlier years made substantial recommendations for better housekeeping, a trained nurse, and, ironically, paint. A 1919 visit noted a serious lack of sanitation: dirty kitchen conditions, fumigation by burning charcoal, smelly toilets, and bed bugs, but the superintendent pointed out that the institution was struggling to recover from the flu epidemic, which had caused an overflow of sick residents and patients.[133] Prior visits had noted that the general conditions were good but that the buildings needed replacing.

Among the changes that state boards were more successful in implementing was better record keeping at the institutional level. In Illinois, for example, counties were asked to use a standardized Almshouse Register "designed to secure uniformity and accuracy in the record of relief in this county." Compiled by the Board of Public Charities and published in Chicago, the volume came with specific directions for use, which would "greatly facilitate the methodical study of pauperism, its causes, and its cure." What was inside the volume was another matter. State boards requested county information in a composite report, on a standardized form, filed once a year from data copied over from the institutional register that included farm production, the number of people admitted, dismissed, and present on a stable date, and their condition. Among the other information sometimes collected were resident demographics, education, health, habits, property, authority for admission, and supposed cause of pauperism. Morgan County, Illinois, noted trades of residents, which included farmers, laborers, tailors, basket makers, students, wagon makers, and a watchman. Reasons for arrival included insanity, drunkenness, idiocy, being crippled, epilepsy, laziness, old age, chronic diarrhea, and kidney disease.[134]

Staff often struggled to keep such detailed records, especially as the same people came in and out of the institution and entire families, transients passing through, and critical patients arrived without notice, to say nothing of the literacy of the superintendent.[135] Haphazard spellings, receiving inaccurate information, and residents simply not knowing some of the requested information all made for gaps in the record. The Ohio State Board of Charities complained about this problem in 1899, noting that no standard for record keeping existed.[136] Kansas was still trying to enforce record keeping as late as the 1930s. Unlike other states, which received compiled reports from counties on an annual basis, Kansas poor farms apparently did not, as part of a routine, even keep intake records. State officials complained that some people should not have been given admission and that the reasons for admission were unclear because they had not been categorized. They clearly doubted the efficacy and legitimacy of locally made decisions.[137]

The administration and construction of poor farms was pitched as a way to save money on direct aid expenses, but in reality local officials used various types of aid, determining what they thought was best for their residents.

Depending on population, expense, and voter approval, they bought land and opened a poor farm, relied on boarding out and direct aid, or did all of these things. Few counties did nothing to support their poor, and some were proud of their provisions. When institutions opened, they were profoundly inconsistent in design, funding, and quality, and there was little state-level control over the process. As different types of institutions proliferated after the Civil War, states sought a tenuous grasp on oversight of local poor farms with mixed results. Local officials held the power, determining everything from admissions, to relief amounts, to farm practices. Despite criticism from supposed experts, counties did not eliminate direct aid in conjunction with poor farms, but instead opted for a hybridized relief system. This created a massive patchwork that included poor farms as the institutional foundation, each with its own particular character. That distinctiveness affected who lived at poor farms, and their experiences as residents.

2 Populations and Conditions

"Is there anything more pathetic than the lives of men and women who have been failures?"

—*Springfield [IL] Evening News*, November 11, 1905

Transient farm laborer Willie White was a typical poor farm resident. A seasonal laborer, he stayed at a poor farm during the winter of 1922, and each winter from 1929 to 1932, arriving in December and leaving in the spring. When not housed by his seasonal employer on a farm, he had nowhere to go.[1] Like others who left poor farms, he did so on his own accord.[2] The circumstances of men like Willie White were so common that Robert Frost wrote a poem entitled "Death of the Hired Man" that reads: "Home is the place where, when you have to go there, they have to take you in." The title character is Silas, who returns to a farm where he had previously worked. The farmer's wife takes pity on him; he is tired, homeless, and delusional. Her husband, however, believes the man had no right to return because he left their farm for better wages elsewhere. But men like Silas and Willie had to strike while opportunity lasted, lest they be without money for the off-season. Most poor farm residents were unmarried men, lacking full-time employment and a family to care for them in a time of need. Sick and delirious, Silas went to the place where he felt at home, where he died sitting in front of the fire. Home did not have to take you in; for some the poor farm was as close to a home as they had.[3]

The relationship of farmers to hired hands has been described as a "customary intimacy." For laborers, the "customary intimacy" was supposed to protect them from unemployment and provide them room and board. But as mechanization and specialization in agriculture increased, farmers no longer wanted year-round hands and farm labor no longer assured protection or familiarity. The intimacy required between hired hands and the families who employed them was viewed as beneficial only to the laborer. As Kenyon Butterfield phrased it, "In some farm communities the presence of hired laborers in the family circle has been distinctly deleterious to good social customs."[4] In a job that no longer provided year-round wages, men like Willie White turned to the poor farm to bridge the gap. Nationwide, unskilled and farm laborers accounted for the majority of poor farm residents.

The changing nature of wage labor in the late nineteenth century meant a higher incidence of job loss and more time spent unemployed.[5] In Michigan, farm laborers reported spending approximately one-fifth of the year unemployed and 73 percent reported at least some unemployment. Nonfarm laborers faced similar challenges but made 50 percent more than farm laborers.[6] The labor shortages that sometimes plagued farmers drove wages up one season, and then filled counties with too many hands the next, driving wages back down.[7] Other industries also used seasonal employees who could not cover year-round expenses. Poor farm populations increased during the winter as a result. In 1909 Ross County, Ohio, officials tried to stop the practice of wintertime use by announcing they would attempt to refuse admission to those men who left in the spring only to return in the fall, calling it "a trick upon the present management."[8] According to Ann Ellis, whose father Otis ran the Franklin County, Ohio, Infirmary, some of the residents were "victims of low paying occupations, who, once their physical ability to earn a daily wage was reduced, automatically became candidates for the county home. Some of these trades where workers were farm hands, ditch diggers, teamsters, painters, laborers etc. . . ."[9] The older they were the less likely they were to be hired full-time, and those who went to the poor farm seasonally stayed where they hoped jobs would turn up in the spring.[10] Landless laborers, including those in rural extractive industries such as mining and timber, were particularly vulnerable to economic or environmental catastrophe, having "little in the way of livestock, poultry, or even gardens . . . no accrued savings or capital assets."[11]

Causes of poverty and distress were myriad, but unemployment and homelessness remained chief among poor farm admissions. Transient men like Willie White were among the least worthy at poor farms: they were thought to degrade worthy residents and make conditions inside poor farms worse with their presence. Katz believed that "no clear line existed between the 'respectable poor from the paupers,'" and poor farms consistently combined the two groups. Reformers blamed poor farms for "herding together" such people, bringing everyone in the institution down to the level of paupers.[12] Conditions inside poor farms were frequently criticized for either being too nice for the undeserving or too mean for the worthy. That most people came and went in a matter of days or weeks is not a reflection on the quality of food or accommodations, but instead evidence of a range of needs. That others spent years of their lives in poor farms was neither an endorsement of their benefits nor a confirmation of their prisonlike reputation; it was a result of being unable to live independently.

Personalizing poverty is no small task. Historian M. A. Crowther cautioned against writing about the poor as an "abstraction" or "stripping them of their humanity."[13] Historically, distinctions were made between those experiencing the "unavoidable evil" of poverty while others were blamed for "the consequence of willful error, of shameful indolence, of vicious habit."[14] Poor farms did have their share of residents with bad habits, but ingredients of poverty drove people to poor farms: sickness, domestic distress, unemployment, and old age. Once they arrived, people had to accept whatever counties provided. Optimistically they would be fed, sheltered, cared for by a doctor, and find solace in other residents for company. Realistically, they may have discovered that a lack of upkeep on the buildings made things dirty and drafty, that some residents were unpleasant to be around, and there was little privacy. Decisions about how much sympathy the institutionalized poor deserved affected the quality of the institutions provided for them.

The number of urban poor people and the scale of their need often drew attention away from the realities of being poor in rural areas. The "myths of abundance," as Katz calls them, assumed that people on farms could, at minimum, feed themselves.[15] Although federal reports claimed that "the public at large has not been aware of the poverty that has constantly existed among farm people . . . merely living on a farm is no proof of economic security," county officials had long been aware.[16] Private charities in cities dealt with large numbers of people whose ingredients of survival needed to be purchased with cash. In the late nineteenth century cities had Charity Organization Societies (COS) that tried to rationalize aid by determining who received what from which charity and why. But poor farms were often out of reach both geographically and administratively for these city-based groups. Rural areas had few privately funded charities. Neighbors stepped in to provide nursing, supplement bare cupboards, and help bury the dead.[17] People became sick, accidents maimed wage-earners, spouses died, crops failed, rents increased—counties provided public relief because of a steady stream of need.

At the same time poor farms reached their most numerous, rural poverty became nationally prominent. Founded in 1908, the Country Life Commission examined rural conditions and blamed a lack of social life, subpar schools, and isolation for the decline of rural America. But irregular wages, the increasing cost of land and tenancy, dangerous and physically hard labor, a lack of medical care, a shortage of year-round healthy food, and underemployment were the real factors facing people in rural areas. Between 1900 and 1920 land prices in Iowa almost doubled, making it difficult to move into the owner class; land valuations increased across neighboring states as well.[18] Connections were made between the mental health of people and the challenges of farming: "isolated farm life has its own perils as is shown in the frequency of insanity, crime, and suicide." Any one of those three travails could send remaining family members to the poor farm.[19] While rural is often identified with agriculture, many rural

households were not on farms. Smaller communities supported artisans, laborers, craftsmen, tradesmen, and others. Personalizing the poor farm requires
knowing who lived there and why, and what conditions they experienced.[20]

Reasons for Admission

One of the clear trends in poor farm populations nationwide after the Civil
War was the increasing number of male residents. The poor farm was where
men with no kinship network went when they were sick or worn down from
a lifetime of hard but low-paying labor. In different parts of the country, work
conditions affected gender ratios greatly, and men labored in whatever industry
was specific to the area. In the upper Midwest this included railroad jobs, lumber, iron mining, and of course agriculture; as a result the Ontonagon County
Poor Farm in Michigan was established specifically for indigent miners and
lumberjacks. Historian Tobias Higbie referred to these men as "indispensable
outcasts."[21] Most were unmarried and like poor farm residents, their average age
increased between 1874 and 1930. Depending on the location, men over the age
of forty accounted for as much as half the homeless population.[22] The poor farm
in Yavapai County, Arizona, a mining area, admitted thirty-three men before
a woman was listed in the admission records. In 1897 Mary Bell was a widow
with three children when she arrived at the farm. Another fifteen men, some
of them miners, but also a cook, a painter, and laborers, came before another
woman arrived. That pattern continued into the next year.[23]

Men who were migratory and employed intermittently had diminished opportunities to start families.[24] Without a household to belong in, men lacked
what historian Alice Kessler-Harris called "the central provider of life-sustaining
goods and services." In times of distress, those without "life-sustaining" household membership relied on charity, and institutional records demonstrate that
poor farm residents often lacked a nuclear family.[25] For some people, the poor
farm was a survival strategy—but not one they took lightly. Homer Folks noted
that, "Everywhere men have instinctively spoken of going to the poor house
as the last and bitterest of earthly misfortunes."[26] Bitter as it might have been,
not going could mean death, as was the case for occasional poor farm resident
Lester W. Hays who instead preferred to stay in a little log hut. Despite cash
aid from the county and help from neighbors, he was found frozen to death on
Christmas Day after a minus 33-degree night.[27]

Among those men without a stable family life was sixty-year-old John White,
who arrived at the Morgan County, Illinois, Poor Farm in the winter of 1925.
White listed himself as a cook by profession, and during the month he stayed he
helped do the cooking for the superintendent's family. His skill at this position
inspired the superintendent to underline *good cook* in the ledger. White had a

unique connection to the institution because he lived there as a child. In 1870, his family consisted of both parents and five siblings; his father listed no profession. As early as 1880, White was living at the poor farm where he attended school and was listed as an orphan with a lame leg. But he was not technically an orphan; his family lived in a nearby county. White stayed at the farm until the summer of 1883 when he disappeared from the records. As a teenager old enough to work it may simply have been time for him to strike out on his own, or he may have gone to find his relatives. When he needed help as an older man, the facility may have had a comforting familiarity since it had provided him with a childhood home.[28]

Although almost every county had rules about admissions and residency, they were not always enforced for short-term stays or emergencies. If people simply showed up on the doorstep they were usually allowed inside. In summer a poor farm might be partially empty, leaving only the unemployable; come winter, the population grew, leading to a description of the poor farm as a "hospital and rest stop for tramps."[29] Even those who demonstrated clear signs of unworthiness, including alcoholism and venereal disease, were admitted. Betty Groth Syverson remembers men at the Emmet County, Iowa, farm dealing with the effects of drinking, and in Grayson County, Texas, one man's 1886 admission was publicly attributed to "the harlot, her touch is worse than the leper's." He later went blind, suggesting he had contracted syphilis.[30] Rules for staying, if enforced, could be behavior hampering: no alcohol, no smoking or tobacco inside, a curfew, or limits placed on travel were common, but they were not unlike rules that farmers put on their hired men and threshing crews, that timber companies placed on camps, or bonanza farms placed in the bunkhouses. In other words, there were a variety of circumstances where people surrendered certain liberties in order to be provided room and board.[31]

Poor farms served a seasonal need, filling with more people—especially men—during the winter. Historian Bruce Smith documented this trend during the 1870s and 1880s, when the St. Joseph County, Indiana, Poor Farm took in more people during January, March, and May, but also saw smaller increases in July, October, and December. Smith attributed the other peaks as traveling months for people getting in position for future work because South Bend was on a major transportation corridor.[32] Transients were a vital component of the rural economy in the spring and fall, providing affordable labor to farmers and their families; locals preferred that laborers stay at the poor farm rather than beg from house to house or sleep uninvited in sheds and barns.[33] It kept them nearby as a reliable labor source for the spring, but refusing to hire people year-round did make farmers vulnerable to shortages. In 1907, the *Annals of Iowa* argued that labor shortages contributed to mechanization, saying, "The situation [labor shortage] has existed for several years and has been a factor in an evolution of agricultural and domestic processes. Devices and methods which have been exploited as 'labor saving' have in fact been of necessity labor substitutes."[34]

When poor farms admitted transients and tramps, they not only added to the number of mouths to feed, but also to other farm expenses like medical care.[35] Lawrence O'Neil came to a poor farm sick with typhoid in 1888. He lived for three weeks and then died. The superintendent recorded that "he said he had no friends, and we buried him on the farm."[36] Historian David Schob notes that sometimes the illnesses and injuries sustained from farm work seriously impeded future labor, from which some never recovered enough to gain financial stability. Farm accidents leading to infection, amputations, and lingering disabilities, injuries from riding the rails, and a variety of industrial hazards could leave a man vulnerable and in need of care.[37]

In Indiana, officials reported that they tried to have a room set aside for tramps to be lodged temporarily, so they could have a place to get a meal and a night's sleep without being integrated into the regular life of the institution. Michigan's largest poor farm did the same, forcing transient men to bathe and hand over their clothes for washing when they arrived. Apparently, this sharply reduced the number of "strawstack" tramps who came calling for dinner, breakfast, and a warm bed.[38] Some institutions tried to require labor from tramps, but one superintendent claimed, "It would cost us a dollar to get twenty-five cents work out of them." Most poor farms did not have a wood or stone yard where nightly residents had to work in exchange for their bed, but where they did, numbers declined. As soon as Massachusetts mandated labor in exchange for tramp quarters and meals, the number of men seeking shelter in almshouses decreased dramatically. In 1905, 23,341 people in the state checked into the tramp rooms kept by most almshouses to separate them from the normal residents, but by 1907 the number was down to 3,127.[39] Tramps were not the only temporary residents, however. People stayed for short times if family were coming to get them or if they had been injured and needed to recuperate. Such leniency toward transients did not hold true in the South, especially for African Americans, who faced extended jail sentences and forced labor. South Carolina and parts of Mississippi had reputations, even for white men, for being hostile to tramps. Generally, the notion of freedom of movement and untethered laborers ran counter to the entrenched race-based control of labor in the region.[40]

Worthiness

Not all poor farm residents were entirely blameless for their plight. A New York State report from the 1870s used a small sample size to deduce that intemperance was an issue for an astonishing 80 percent of men and 40 percent of women in poor farms, but those estimates are not borne out in other records.[41] J. S.

Meyers, a superintendent in Wisconsin, recorded in his journal that he had a few male residents seeking access to alcohol. After one resident went "on a spree," Meyers launched a multiday effort to "entrap a pauper whom I suspicioned for going after liquor." One suspected drinker got "a severe lecture" and another a sentence "in the calaboose but he preferred to go away from the place entirely rather than be shut up."[42] This was not the last time alcohol was a problem in Dane County. The coincidentally named Edward Beers arrived at the farm in 1891 suffering the results of "hard drink." Beers had been widowed twice and all three of his children preceded him in death. He died almost immediately after his admission. A Connecticut newspaper also reported an issue where farm residents "blacklisted" from town bars sent friends to town to buy bottles.[43]

Despite these examples, records from poor farms challenge the assertions made by temperance advocates that drinking was the predominant cause of poverty. When the causes of poverty were ranked in 1890, intemperance was sixth, and 59 percent of the cases came from the North Atlantic region. This did not stop temperance advocates from linking poverty to drinking. In Ohio, home of the Anti-Saloon League, a local paper made a poor farm–related pitch for the ASL, claiming that the local poor farm was full of "old gray-haired feeble men and women. Just 265 of them at present. And strong drink is responsible for the condition of most of them. . . . No stronger temperance sermon could be preached than is told to the infirmary visitor." While alcohol abuse did send people to the poor farm, the description hints that old age and exhaustion were also factors. Leah Jones, who followed in her mother's footsteps as a matron, remembered that a 1915 county campaign for temperance encouraged people to "Vote Dry and then Burn the Poor House Down." Whether intentional or not, that same year a fire started in the attic of the institution that torched all three floors.[44]

Rules banning strong drink did not stop male residents from wandering to town and returning drunk; generally poor farm superintendents and commissioners were unsympathetic but still allowed admission. As Elaine Frantz Parsons points out, the late nineteenth century saw a conflict between the concepts of individuals having little control over their impulses, and societal problems like poverty and a loss of manliness. To be poor as a woman did not necessarily denigrate femininity because women were not expected to self-support; to be poor as a man at any stage of life or failing to support one's dependents was a different matter. Poor farms forced a certain amount of submission: men who could not earn a living wage or who drank to excess surrendered their power to the poor farm superintendent, who managed the household and set rules and regulations that sometimes punished intemperance.[45] Drinking at the farm was one of the only behaviors that appears to have been punished with any regularity. Some states, such as Texas, required those living in poor farms to surrender not only any personal property of value, but also to take a pauper's oath, which forfeited their rights as citizens and declared publicly that they were dependent.[46]

Intake records for poor farms indicate a variety of problems not limited to alcohol. A single page in an Ohio ledger lists the following issues: "shot gun shell exploded in hand and tore it off, sore eyes and rheumatism, husband is a drunkard and wont [sic] provide, epileptic, nearly blind and got the rheumatism very hard, consumption, destitute and badly crippled, paralysis with kidney and bladder trouble, mother died, spinal trouble, rheumatism and stomach trouble, pregnant and no friends to care for her." This list could be reproduced at poor farms across the country.[47] Reformers and experts recognized the multipurpose use of the poor farm even when they were criticizing the users, or listing synonyms for the institution:

> The refuge of the hopeless, the death-house of the pauper sick, the winter home of the diseased vagrant, the last refuge of the broke down prostitute, the asylum for the insane, the lying-in hospital both for the feebleminded woman whom society failed to protect from its vicious and often feebleminded members and also for the poor unfortunate girl, the victim partly of ignorance and partly of lust, and perhaps saddest of all, the home of some independent, high-spirited person whom misfortune or filial irreverence in his declining days left with only such a place in which to close his eyes in the last long sleep.[48]

Those who were blameless for their situation sometimes elicited sympathy. One superintendent recorded: "this man brought here in a terrible condition"; "broken down with old age and no friends to care for her." He need not have been so detailed, but in his job some sympathy made for kinder treatment.[49] This type of goodwill was not uncommon. The Rev. A. G. Byers, from the Ohio State Board of Charities, pointed out that poverty was not a crime, and instead should be considered a misfortune. His colleague in Indiana noted the appropriateness of providing good care for those unfortunate people in need.[50] A year later, C. W. Chancellor of Maryland encouraged improved almshouse conditions because the poor deserved better, acknowledging that even hardworking people could, and did, end up at the poorhouse. Chancellor went further, encouraging counties to provide activities like books for those sick and unable to contribute. The debate about whether it was better to give good treatment to all the poor, regardless of worthiness, or potentially punish all to discourage the laziness of a few had no clear winner.

Progressives tried in vain to pinpoint the causes of poverty in order to vanquish the problem. After one such attempt Amos Warner concluded that it was nearly impossible to reach a conclusion because he could not isolate the effects of accidents, drink, bad luck, or employment conditions. Warner's recognition that a combination of problems pushed vulnerable people into poor farms aligned with similar assessments by the secretary of the New York State Board of Charities, Charles Hoyt, who decided that while he could estimate the immediate causes of dependence, the long-term issues were seemingly unknowable.[51] A four-state study years later also failed to determine the causes of poverty, and declined to try and classify them.[52] Another study tried to suggest a connection between poor farm residents and criminality, but showed only a negligible amount of overlap.[53] Others indicated that larger national problems were to blame. In the South, slavery was blamed for degrading the opportunities of whites while emancipation was blamed for presenting the formerly enslaved with responsibilities they could not handle. Yet another conclusion was reached by a farmer who explained: "Many of our farmers have recently been forced off their lands by the relentless suction of the devouring mortgage and are now part of the poorly paid and exploited working class."[54]

Wages repeatedly came up in these studies as contributing factors. Nationally, the average weekly wage of farm laborers in the 1890s was $4.39 compared to $12.07 for factory workers.[55] In the South, farm hands could expect $8–$9 a month if they got room and board compared to $17 in the Midwest and West and closer to $20 in the Northeast. Domestic servants could expect $2 a week without board. As historian Crandall Shifflett noted for Virginia, in order to meet basic necessities a family of five needed $175 a year, a wage that could only be made by a breadwinner who worked virtually every day of the year: a rare circumstance. Shifflett claimed that in Louisa County, Virginia, 41 percent of whites and 56 percent of Blacks had to survive at wages rates that "seem impossible to sustain life" and that another untold number scratched out a living on bad land. The phrase "juleps for the few and pellagra for the crew" was coined to describe the disparities in the "New South."[56]

In the North the burgeoning greed of industrial capitalists was blamed, but the problem also involved agricultural issues. As Michigan State Board of Charities member Dr. Hal Wyman noted, farm mortgages combined with hard times precipitated institutionalization for some in Michigan: "The high rate of interest common in some parts of the state often imposes debts which the diminished earning power of age is unable to pay . . . the added principal and interest increasing in greater ratio than the value of the farm."[57] This discrepancy, fueled in part by the declining value of farm products, only worsened leading up to World War I. Many people and families sat precariously close to ruin and poverty as it was difficult to save wages for emergencies, old age, or to move into the landowning class of farmers.[58] While studies of tenant farming are not comprehensive, Earl D. Ross estimated the national average in 1880 to be slightly more than 25 percent. Between 1890 and 1910 the rate increased to 38 percent, which Ross attributed to increased land cost and capital startup needs.[59] The

USDA estimated similar numbers and noted that tenancy was less likely to be a step toward ownership than it had been in the nineteenth century: tenant farmers were older in 1930 than they had been in 1890, a sign that they were not moving into the owner class. In a smaller sample of farm transfer behavior, Mark Friedberger notes that approximately one-third of his Iowa sample died without owning land.[60] For farm laborers who were "a rung or two below the tenant farmer on the agricultural ladder," it was even harder to acquire land.[61]

Despite clear evidence that economic circumstances were altering the ability of people to support a family, or have stable income, late nineteenth-century reformers disagreed about whether economics or heredity and degeneracy were the more likely drivers of poverty. These were the parameters when Progressives picked up where Warner and others left off. One estimate from 1894 claimed that 25 percent of poverty stemmed from personal misconduct. Another gauged that it was closer to 12 percent. Yet another found that 12 percent of poor households were headed by a man with a disability or mental illness, 30 percent by a widow or a man with a permanent disability, and 6 percent by old people. All such people could be found in poor farms, but their residents were not "devoid of all ennobling traits of character." According to one superintendent, people who believed that were "very much mistaken."[62] Among those most sympathetic tended to be poor farm superintendents themselves, who saw firsthand the combinations of issues facing residents. County officials dealing with the problem of dependency treated it not as a puzzle to be solved, but one to be coped with as best they could.[63] Visiting reporters writing about poor farm residents also tended toward circumspection, with one describing poor farm residents as "men who have worked and toiled and tried to live well; women who have mothered their babies and seen them die or go out in to the world, and then who, by reason of sickness, or incapability or the irony of fate—who knows what—have lost and utterly given up hope in the struggle for further existence."[64]

The way people considered causes of poverty mattered in the treatment of poor farm residents. Some of the opinions about what type of provisions the poor deserved came from men like A. O. Wright from the Wisconsin State Board of Charities, who believed they should all be classified as paupers because they delighted in "dirt, disorder, and idleness." Wright also supported a labor test for poor farm intakes, estimating that while a quarter of them could do little work, winter residents were just lazy. He urged clean facilities, and giving residents the opportunity to complete little tasks about the institution as a way to redeem their pride.[65] Alexander Johnson, like Wright, thought that small jobs did wonders for even the most downtrodden poor farm resident.[66] Poor farm records indicate that some people did try to find employment rather than staying at the institution, but the efforts were not always successful, as was the case for one man who returned "worse looking if possible than ever. Lousy and dirty and watch and clothing gone. Oh such a wreck."[67] It was harder to leave and find a job as farmers became less charitable about who they hired, which increasingly excluded those with disabilities; a blind fifty-three-year-old in poor health found himself unemployed after the family with whom he had been living and working let him go. In 1893 he spent a year at a poor farm.[68] The Rorie brothers, both blind, faced similar difficulties. They operated a successful door-to-door broom-selling business before ending up at the Searcy County, Arkansas, Poor Farm, and eventually a state hospital.[69]

Critics charged that the mere existence of a poor farm would encourage its use, in the same way reformers believed an orphanage encouraged parents to dump children. This complaint focused heavily on a perceived lack of a work ethic by institutional residents. One writer noted that, "The squalor does not disturb men and women who have known nothing else; the immorality is a temptation; and even in the worst kept houses there is usually plenty to eat and little to do; in any case, they have not the heavy and irksome task of thinking for themselves."[70] Howard Good, a Van Wert, Ohio, resident, shared a local anecdote about "shiftless Tommy" who, while being taken to the poor farm by a neighbor, was offered a bag of corn so he need not leave home. When Tommy found out that the corn had to be shelled, he said "drive on."[71] Dr. Hal Wyman from Michigan told fellow charities meeting attendees that the city poor with whom he was most familiar all suffered from drunkenness, while the rural poor represented perverse shiftlessness. Hereditary illnesses, bad grocery-shopping habits, and too much food were all blamed for poverty and poor health. From what was probably a secure perch, Dr. Wyman asserted against readily available evidence that "no one is allowed to die of starvation or exposure." Poor farms were meant to be a guard against this, but people died of hunger and malnutrition-related diseases across the country. In 1895, an Ohio newspaper told of a baby who died "from neglect and want of proper nourishment." The report indicated that "the baby had wasted away until almost nothing but skin and bones remained." The child's mother, who lacked proper food herself, had struggled with illness while being homeless. She had recently moved, and as a result may not have been eligible for relief. Had she been admitted to an institution her child might have died anyway, but starvation would have been avoided.[72]

Even the Populists, known for their desire to level the playing field between the rich and the laboring classes, tried to assign culpability for dependency, saying, "If any will not work, neither will he eat." But that was easier said than done, because the people who were considered unworthy were not excluded from poor farms. Usually they did eat something, even if they did not work.[73] Wyman helpfully suggested that states should use poor farm residents as soldiers, saying "they would not make first-class soldiers . . . but such are not required in times of peace. They would prove useful as guards for the property of the state and, in times of threatened disaster by flood or fire, could be used to protect private property. Even in time of war, they would be better than nothing." No responses to Wyman's unique ideas were recorded in the meeting minutes. He would have been disappointed by the army fielded; "a composite of nearly every kind and degree of physical and mental disability, of social maladjustments and moral shortcomings, and a scattered few of the element which in popular phrase has 'seen better days.'"[74] Poor farm residents were not considered able to staff a farm, let alone fight a war.

Demographics

Even among the more charitable voices about poverty, racism and nativism were apparent. Amos Warner noted, "Those who know the colored people only casually or by hearsay may be surprised to find the misconduct cases running so low . . . while sickness as a cause is of greater relative importance. . . . The colored people are weak physically, become sick easily . . . at the same time they have a dread of being assisted, especially when they think an institution will be recommended." He went on to say, "There are many associations among them for mutual help, and the criminal and semi-criminal men have a brutal way of making their women support them." The central theme of Warner's asser- tion, that African American people preferred to handle their own struggle and that the men were shiftless and inclined to laziness, contributed to a damaging stereotype. Given the nature of segregated facilities for African Americans, it is unsurprising that people avoided indoor relief. Some of Warner's own sta- tistics indicated that 30 percent of the poverty among Black Americans related to employment, more so than for whites, while they were last in drinking and shiftlessness, which accounted for only 13 percent of applicants.[75]

White people were overwhelmingly more likely to be poor farm residents: in 1890 66,000 poor farm residents were white while 6,400 were classified as "non-white," a ratio that remained stable through 1910.[76] During the Pro- gressive Era, attention was paid to whether or not the white residents were native born. That metric depended largely on location, with cities having more immigrants in their institutions than rural areas. County demographics also mattered: counties on major waterways, with mining or timbering, or with rail lines frequently had larger numbers of immigrants; counties settled by people predominately from one country had more people in their poor farm from that location. Studying the West, Thomas Krainz found that local variables including religion, environment, kinship ties, settlement patterns, and economics affected poor farm demographics. For example, one Colorado county that had a Hispanic and Catholic population majority had charity *penitente* groups instead of a poor farm, showing a clear preference to care for their sick and poor at home.[77]

The Census Bureau noted the demographic variances between regions related to poor farms, stating, "The older southern states can hardly be brought into comparison. Racial conditions, climate, the preponderance of a rural population, the generally scanty almshouse facilities, and other peculiarities make it necessary to judge their pauper ratios by themselves."[78] Remarking on the smaller numbers of people in southern poor farms, John Koren, the special agent in charge of the 1903 census report of poor farms, made some judgments of his own. "It is not so much the absence of dependents," he said, "as the lack of proper conveniences for their support which explains in part the singularly favorable percentages exhibited . . . of perhaps even greater importance is the fact of the homogeneity and general stability of the white population in the Southern states. Nowhere else are family ties so strong and aid in time of need so abundant. It is rather exceptional that others than the 'poor whites' seek the almshouses. The pressure of negroes for admittance would undoubtedly be greater but for their ability to subsist on a pittance."[79] While Koren attributed the general absence of African Americans in poor farms to this supposed talent of surviving on next to nothing, local policies played a commanding role: South Carolina, Georgia, Tennessee, and Louisiana had few Black almshouse residents while other southern states had close to 50 percent Black almshouse residents.[80]

Anecdotally, the evidence for poor farm diversity is variable. Will County, Illinois, for example, had African Americans, Germans, Irish, Scots, Swedes, and French at the poor farm during the 1880s. In Travis and Van Zandt, Texas, a few African Americans at a time stayed in the poor farms, and while they may have been segregated inside it is not apparent that separate buildings existed for their care.[81] In 1884, Grayson County, Texas, supported seven white women, four children, five white men, one Indian, two Black men, and two Black women.[82] In Georgia in 1880 there were 385 white and 165 Black poor farm residents; when the numbers of people receiving direct aid were added in, another 400 or so Black people and 1,000 whites were recipients of aid across the state.[83] In 1929, Colusa County, California, housed three Indians, three "negroes," ten Mexicans, five Italians, two Germans, and forty-seven Americans: 50 percent more white native-born people than all others combined. Several Chinese men lived at the Talent County, California, poor farm during the early 1900s.[84] Nationally, in 1903, approximately half of poor farm residents were native born; of the immigrant population, almost half were Irish, and 96 percent had been in the country for more than a decade.[85]

African Americans were not always welcomed at poor farms, as residents or as employees. This man appears to have been either a worker, or a well-regarded resident capable of helping on the farm and with the animals. The man and the mule worked on at least one road-grading project nearby. Photo courtesy of Ross County Historical Society, Chillicothe, Ohio.

Conditions Inside

The debate about worthiness and populations factored into discussions about what type of treatment and care people deserved. As an 1881 *Atlantic Monthly* story phrased it, "To tempt the poor into pauperism is a bad business; but it is the business of every State which is unwisely lavish with its poor-fund." Having warned people of spoiling the poor, the magazine went on to provide a sensationalized description of a poorhouse that described chains, beatings, "underground dungeons, cold and damp, with mouldy straw for furniture and rats for company," and constant isolation.[86] Generally, the most offensive reports made for the best copy. An 1882 investigation into management malfeasance at one Ohio farm provided commentary about the conditions, which ranged from subpar in terms of household cleanliness and food to dysfunction on the farm, with broken fences, dead hogs, and poor harvests. After one resident gave his testimony in the matter, the newspaper noted that "it might be well to state that not much importance is attached to Mr. Towsley's testimony, as he is not noted for having a Websterian intellect." Despite the dismissal of his intelligence, Towsley had lived there on and off for years, and so had a retrospective take on the situation.[87] Reports on dismal poor farm conditions dated to their earliest years, but institution visits became more commonplace in the late nineteenth century, which spurred change.

Improvements and entirely new buildings being constructed during the 1890s led one reformer to optimistically remark, "The typical poor house of twenty years ago, dilapidated and awkward in its architecture and wasteful and neglectful, and therefore cruel in its management, still exists in out of the way places, but it is fast disappearing." Large, congregate-style institutions made of brick, with multiple stories, various outbuildings, and porches or verandas attached became popular. Some were substantial, with space for more than one hundred residents, while others were smaller with accommodations for around forty people. Residents frequently shared rooms with at least one other person or slept in dormitory-style quarters, ate as a group at set times, sometimes in gender-specific dining rooms, and spent much of their days with little to keep them occupied. An alternative design option featured separate cottages meant to segregate residents based on race, family group, or gender. Creating an institution that suited all stakeholders to their satisfaction was no easy task. Reformer Alexander Johnson reasonably suggested that more comfortable conditions came from buildings made specifically for their purposes. As he phrased it, "institutional life cannot be made homelike, yet the more plain and simple the arrangements, the nearer is the approach to homelikeness. 'Palaces for paupers' as some great almshouses have been called, are not a source of happiness to their inmates. The common people prefer to live with their feet near the ground," but he offered no evidence for this assertion.[88]

While improvements were a noted part of Progressive Era reforms, it was also true that substandard institutions only got worse as they aged and not all counties invested money in repairs. Some were well maintained with fresh coats of paint and functional kitchens but one visitor noted, "as to the condition of many poor houses, the less said about that the better" because buildings also were found with peeling plaster, mold and bugs, and no convenient water source.[89] What was true was that no two were identical, even when they used the same architectural designs. Michigan poor farms were once referred to as "an aggregation of misery."[90] Coles County, Illinois, received annual rebukes in the 1910s for treating its twenty or so residents shamefully. The local paper echoed state inspectors, saying "the committee found the same old building, the same vermin infected walls, the same rough floors, the same small windows, the same impossibility of proper ventilation, the flies swarmed everywhere and were especially noticeable on the poor food prepared for dinner." Elderly and sick residents did the laundry and cooking, and no one was apparently on-site to supervise. The newspaper took a position sympathetic to the residents, noting that they were deserving of better: "Most of them have lived honorable lives. Many have always been a little below the average in intelligence, and in their old age find themselves friendless and dependent. Some have worked hard and intelligently enough but could accumulate little, that little has been swept away by sickness and other misfortunes." The paper called on citizens to amend the cruel treatment of residents and the disgraceful institution, noting that the jail was plenty nice.[91] In Georgia, the state described its poor farms as "tumble-down shacks often vermin ridden" lacking "proper toilet facilities, bathing facilities, nor any other minimum requirements for sanitation and health." The segregated cottages forced residents to do their own cooking and lacked the general living space provided in congregate buildings.

Reports did sometimes find better circumstances. Around the same time that the *Atlantic Monthly* published its 1881 description, a reporter in the small county of Coshocton, Ohio, visited his local poor farm. He noted that "the management of the house was in the hands of persons who understood their business and who recognized the trite saying that 'cleanliness is next to Godliness.'" He went on to describe the gleaming surfaces throughout. As for the residents, they too seemed in good condition: "All that were able were engaged in some kind of light work. Some cooking, washing, ironing, scrubbing, and the many other things that are to be done around a house. The old people and those who are crippled and thus unable to perform such duties have nothing to do, but sit around and content themselves as best they can." He closed by saying, "Some of them have been under his [the superintendent's] care for so long a time that they have come to view him as a father." John Richeson and his wife were long-time employees, beginning in 1871 and continuing until 1884.[92]

Improvements came about as people began to consider the poor farm a substitute home for those without one to call their own and to emphasize the need for specialization in institutions. The language of domesticity used by Johnson and his contemporaries reflected other Progressive ideas including social housekeeping and the Social Gospel.[93] One way to fix conditions was to build a new institution. When counties prepared to construct a new building, they sometimes sent visitors to other places to bring back ideas. Muskegon County, Michigan, commissioners did this twice: once when they built a new building in 1901 and again in 1904 when that one burned down. The county went with a standard building shape in 1904, a two-story structure with two wings at right angles, a C-shape made of red brick. Locked doors separated the men's and women's sections. The superintendent's apartment also contained the medical supply storage. Each side had a sitting room and dining room served by the main kitchen, in addition to sleeping quarters. County official Willard Gordon said that it was "the pride of our people and the consummation of the hopes and ideals of our board."[94] County investments like this acknowledged a community duty to the poor and the ways in which poor farm conditions were considered a reflection of the values of local residents.

The 1920s delivered a fresh series of investigations, some of which were based on the eugenics studies completed in partnership between the Committee on Mental Hygiene and an association of fraternal groups. What was called "a surprise investigation by women and a reporter" uncovered heinous conditions in Cape Girardeau, Missouri, in 1923. A local man named James Cotner, who had chronic diarrhea, was kept in the basement of a new but unoccupied building on the property. His only care came from two African American residents. Cotner had family in the area so there is no clear explanation as to why he had been left at the farm and why his care was so abominable, but his health problem was probably a factor. The superintendent was fired as a result, and further investigation noted that the low farm output was complicated by the fact that county officials were privately purchasing goods from the farm for sharply reduced prices, suggesting mismanagement from all sides.[95]

Ohio farms also came under media attack during the 1920s. A Cleveland paper published a series accusing at least one county of running "chambers of horror." Officials tried to handle the fallout by hosting a visit and releasing this statement: "We want the public in this county to know that statements made by a Cleveland writer regarding conditions at the Sandusky county infirmary were grossly exaggerated, highly colored and unjust to the superintendent and his wife and to the people of the county." In the article, the institution was described as having "loathsome holes" in which it dumped people and was categorized as "exhibit A of man's inhumanity to man that exists in the state of Ohio." What visitors found a month or so later seem to have been sad cases, but not the torture and neglect outlined in the original story. One blind and paralyzed man was bedridden and totally helpless, but county officials said there were no other facilities in the state to take such a patient. One resident remarked that conditions were better at that time than they had been under past administrations. The local reporter remarked that the furnishings and conditions inside closely resembled many of the homes in Sandusky. The story concluded with a familiar laying of blame on taxpayers and voters: "It is a sad commentary on life to record the fact that conditions exist which make it necessary to have homes of this character in the midst of the life which we see around us daily, but until some better system can be devised, they will remain, and all that can be asked is that taxpayers do not begrudge the little that is required for the operation of this and similar homes." Showing contempt by not supporting the poor was an unacceptable failing of moral virtue.[96] Visitors saw an institution treated with indifference by locals, maladies among the residents that had no easy solutions, and a staff with few financial resources. Clinton County, on the other hand, was criticized in the original story and by state visitor S. C. Griffin. He told a local paper that the county infirmary was "one of the most deplorable in the state," a notion that the Cleveland paper also supported. At issue was the stability of the building itself, and Griffin worried the old brick structure was in danger of collapse and needed to be vacated immediately.[97]

Tactics for inciting change focused on visitors making comparisons across county and state lines. In 1912 Buchanan County, Iowa, was shamed for "the distinction of being one of the oldest and one of the worst [poor farms] in the state." The county was still using its 1865-built institution, and the vote to build a new structure passed by a narrow margin.[98] A study in Connecticut indicated that some of the smaller rural institutions were in the best shape, but Pennsylvania reports completed in 1922 claimed that the poorhouses run by small municipalities—the townships and boroughs—were in the worst condition. Problems of sanitation, management, building safety, medical care, and even food were reported. At least a handful of these small institutions were still housed in wood-frame buildings, more akin to cottage conditions in the South than congregate-style institutions. Visitors singled out the terrible treatment of an African American man for special censure. He was bedridden, isolated in a corner room, and his nails were "equal in length to those of a polar bear." The racist steward openly refused to care for "that kind of a case" so other residents provided him with some attention and help.[99] Responding to the criticism, a local paper claimed that "farmers who live in comfortable homes do not want to care for the poor. . . . We have been utterly indifferent to the needs of our poor, and now we are shocked and humiliated at the revelations of the results of our negligence."[100] Feelings of disgust mingled with pity were common in poor farm descriptions. Scholar William Miller explains, "Disgust is a feeling *about* something and in response to something, not just raw unattached feeling . . . part of disgust is the very awareness of being disgusted . . . disgust must be accompanied by ideas of a particular kind of danger, the danger inherent in pollution and contamination, the danger of defilement."[101] Community responsibility often collided with a desire to avoid the physicality of people who were poor, sick, or disabled.

The tangible experiences of poor farms frequently shocked visitors. Alexander Johnson wrote about "Institution Odor" where he detailed the issues, related to cold weather and closed windows, that came from "the bodies, breath, and clothing of the inmates, and emanations from the floors." Johnson wanted undergarments changed weekly and other garments "washed at moderate intervals" to help. In most places, basic, nondescript clothing was provided but residents did not typically wear uniforms and sometimes helped with the sewing and laundry. Johnson noted the presence of bed bugs and lice too, and the battle against these vermin appears to have been a constant struggle.[102] Johnson was not alone in noting the smell or in barely masking his disgust of the sensory issues surrounding poor farms. Ann Ellis, who grew up at an Ohio infirmary, remembered a "peculiar odor" and Michigan visitors complained that "in every institution there was a peculiar odor, an odor peculiar to almshouses . . . it seemed to be an admixture of cooking cabbage, onions, tubers, tobacco smoke, and laundry steam."[103]

Simply providing facilities for bathing was easier said than done because of the water, fuel, and labor resources needed. Following the advice of a state visitor who recommended weekly baths, a new superintendent and a hired man accosted "a big fat tramp" and told him he had to bathe. The man refused, saying he had not done so since childhood, but the superintendent wanted to follow the visitor's suggestions about hygiene. The man had on "two pairs of pants, and a pair of overalls, three shirts, two vests and a wamuss [sic] and between them all he had old newspapers and chaff that filled a bushel basket. When we got him stripped we found he was not as big as I am [the superintendent weighed about 125 pounds]." They burned all his clothes because they were swarming with bugs: "oh, but he was dirty; but we scrubbed him well in lots of hot water and soap," and gave him new flannel suiting to wear and an old overcoat. The superintendent claimed, "He couldn't seem to get warm; he just shivered and shook; so we put him to bed and sent for the doctor, who said he had pneumonia, and he died in three days. . . . The inspector thereafter was cautious in giving advice about bathing, usually qualifying it with the recommendation that in extreme cases it is always well to make improvements gradually."[104] This strange cautionary tale featured both pity and disgust to drive home many of the issues facing those trying to maintain cleanliness in poor farms.

Architecture had the potential to make residents content or miserable. Remodeled farmhouses were common for institutions that housed fewer than thirty people. Wallingford, Connecticut, used a "big rambling farm house," which visitors described as "homelike in all its aspects." That feeling may have come less from the structure and more from a thirty-three-year tenure by the superintendent and his wife, who had grown up on the property when her father served as superintendent for twenty-six years.[105] Wings added on to existing houses typically did not age well and they were hard to modify to institutional needs. In Stafford, Connecticut, the remodeled double-house that served as a poor farm had one bathroom on the second floor, but most residents lived on the first floor. There were not enough common spaces for both the men and the women so the ladies used the kitchen for dining and sitting.[106] New Jersey institutions struggled to remodel buildings more than one hundred years old. Sussex County added electric lights, bathrooms, and new flooring and heating.[107] Facilities constructed for the express purpose of being poor farms fared better because they tended to be newer, and came with features including running

Poor farms with congregate buildings used secondary, smaller buildings for infirmary or hospital space, and as a place to segregate those residents considered insane from the general population. Photo courtesy of the Indiana Historical Society, P0468.

water, more modern heating systems, laundry, and kitchens. They also had sitting rooms for the residents and safety features such as fire escapes.

Well-kept buildings were equipped with things found in a normal farmhouse but in greater numbers. A 1910 inventory for an institution of fifty-eight residents included bedding, tableware, 143 chairs, mirrors, nightdresses, underwear, and pillows. There were also farm tools and animals: horses, hogs, cows, plows, two cultivators, a corn sheller, root cutter, three farm wagons, a carriage, 163 acres of land, and a variety of harvested crops. The superintendent donated a bookcase with books and photos of himself and his dead wife. The inventory indicates a well-equipped farm, home, and generally decent furnishings for the residents.[108] As far as some taxpayers were concerned, it was possible to make poor farms *too* nice. After a fire destroyed the Floyd County, Iowa, Poor Farm in the 1920s, a new building was constructed with indoor plumbing, which locals complained was an amenity few of them had at home. That expression of resentment or contempt, while rare, did sometimes emerge in local newspapers and commentaries.[109]

There were affordable ways to make poor farms more comfortable. To combat the monotony, Johnson suggested there be books, entertainments, even cards and dominoes. He also recommended that people be invited to sing, bring a gramophone, donate magazines, and observe holidays. His recommendations were acted on at some institutions. In 1923, the new superintendent of a large California poor farm reported some of the changes made for the benefits of residents. He wanted as few rules as possible, varied menus, recreation and religious services, and other benefits that would create an "esprit de corps." In addition to requiring weekly baths and handing out fresh clothes each week, a library was added, the dining room improved, a new dormitory built, and manufacturing shops constructed. Men could help in the mattress shop, the carpenter shop, the paint shop, the shoe shop, the tailor shop, or the store. All of these made or dispensed items for the institution.[110] The benefits were clear. One resident, a seventy-nine-year-old man, could not find employment as a painter because of his age, but at the poor farm he excelled at refinishing furniture, painting fences, and related tasks. The superintendent remarked, "He more than earned his maintenance . . . after his death, the painters' union, of which he was formerly a member, buried his remains. A floral piece made up from flowers raised here was sent by the hospital. His whole relation to the institution was profitable and pleasant." Like many poor farm residents, this man was considered an undesirable worker outside the institution but contributed beneficial labor suited to his capabilities while there.[111] It was not always necessary to keep residents constantly occupied to create a good atmosphere. In Amador County, California, the forty-five or so residents pitched in for small tasks like gardening or making window screens, and inspectors noted that "the food is good, beds are clean and the spirit of the place seems kindly. The old men have the freedom of the place and were sitting in groups out in the sun talking."[112]

Poor Farm Characters

Local newspapers could spur improvements through their reporting, but they also used poor farm residents as subjects of feature stories—and not always kindly. An 1887 Texas newspaper referred to "General" Bayliss Massey, a regular escapee of the poor farm, as "a long headed old coon" who came to town to drink and discuss his close personal relationship with President Grover Cleveland. The writer played up his delusion and said it would "take some watching to keep him upon the poor farm."[113] In describing another unscheduled departure from the poor farm, an Ohio paper called Charles Slaughter "quite a character and although weak mentally, is rugged physically and a hard worker on the infirmary farm." Born in the county and known for a habit of always wearing mittens, even during warm weather, Slaughter sometimes wandered away from the infirmary. In 1911 he ended up thirty miles away, where authorities took him into custody because his habit of summer mitten-wearing was viewed as "strange." The story noted that "he started on a longer trip although he was unable to give his destination." He "is perfectly harmless and quietly submitted . . . later telling the authorities who is he and from whence he came." Charles and his mittens were taken back to the infirmary, where he died a few years later helping in the fields during a heat wave.[114] He complained of feeling ill, and headed to the barn; when he did not show up for supper, a search located his body. He was thirty-five years old.[115] The focus on these men and their mental health was meant to entertain readers at the expense of the residents.

Because of tight budgets and the fact that they were not designed to punish or contain residents, close supervision, even for those who needed it, was not a poor farm priority; unfortunately this led to injuries and deaths eagerly reported by papers. Georgia McFerrin was only around twenty-five years old when she accidentally drowned in Cannon County, Tennessee. McFerrin previously lived with an elderly relative who had recently died, leaving her homeless. Residents who wandered at night risked getting lost or hit by a car. In 1959 a Pendleton, West Virginia, Poor Farm resident's charred body was found a mile away, where there had been a fire of unknown origin in the woods.[116] William Templin had paid his own board of $60 a month to stay at the Iroquois County, Illinois, Poor Farm because of his failing health. He went missing and his body was located two miles away. He was a widower with two children, a stepson, six grandchildren, a half-brother, and four great grandchildren.[117] In 1913, the body of Evan Stricker was found in a cornfield. He had run away from the poor farm a week earlier. The inquest regarding his death ruled death from natural causes.[118] R. M. Melton was found in a gully near the Searcy County, Arkansas, poor farm, and died shortly thereafter. Melton was blind and deaf, and officials theorized that he became disoriented after going to visit some relatives and may have stumbled down the side of the gully.[119]

Poor farm accidents also drew attention to the various dangers of outdated buildings. In Williamson County, Illinois, a headline pronounced, "AGED WOMAN WAS BURNED TO DEATH." Seventy-one-year-old widow Mahala Boles died after her dress passed too close to a fireplace, and she was enveloped in flames. Her funeral services and burial occurred at the farm.[120] Buildings still relying on fireplaces instead of furnaces caused hazards. A similar fate befell an Ohio farm resident in 1929 as he tended the fireplace in his room. He ran outside where fellow residents extinguished him.[121] Another long-time poor farm resident was killed sitting outside when a heavy wooden shade weighing 500 pounds fell on him. The man had lived at the farm on and off for thirty years.[122]

Firsthand Account

Edward Sweeney wrote perhaps the only published autobiographical account by a poor farm resident. He was a single man, unable to successfully support himself because of an accident that left him physically disabled; he lived in a poor farm for extended periods of time. He had various part-time jobs and had family members living nearby, but they were unable to support him. His 1927 book was prefaced by Theodore Dreiser who critiqued Sweeney not only for his writing, but also for his ungrateful and haughty stance: "one sees him . . . soon limping back to the poorhouse . . . but still protesting, quarreling, being put upon, as he felt, by all with whom he came in contact. Yet coming back. And himself really no better. Seeking his share of the best to be had, and yet vilifying, criticizing, quarreling with others, because they were doing likewise."[123] The issues of dependence and the lack of status and power that Sweeney emphasized no doubt bothered many residents. His account and illustrations show a man generally dissatisfied with the management, the other residents, the food, and the governance. Sweeney made clear that he believed himself to be superior to residents and management alike. In explaining their habits of observation, Sweeney noted "I get more pleasure out of keeping these envious yokles [*sic*] guessing." He called some residents "nuts" and weighed in on what he saw as personal slights. He outlasted two sets of superintendents and matrons, and a variety of hired hands and household staff.[124]

Sweeney's first complaint was about the admissions process. Although a county official saw him on the streets and told him to request admission, it took weeks to approve him. Like many poor farm residents, he was not able to support himself through his own labor outside the institution but that did not mean he was incapable of any work, so at various times his chores included baking bread in the kitchen, helping in the dining room, cutting hair in the barbershop, and staffing the laundry. As he detailed the minutiae of each day, he noted, "everyone that is able has a little stunt to do daily. Their [*sic*] has been three old men at different times did the cooking. They have a girl hired to do it but the older a man gets the greater his ego, especially among small minded people." He observed that residents fought fiercely over privileges because the stakes were so small, a habit he himself developed.[125] He saw slights from all sides: someone criticizing his bread baking, the matron not wanting him to switch bedrooms, unacceptable posturing and power struggles between the superintendent and the residents, and a litany of similarly minor grievances.

What becomes clear from *Poorhouse Sweeney* is that while some people fell easily into an institutional routine, others chafed under such a system. Boredom, an obvious but unspecified companion in his account, meant that any new person, new behavior, or interesting activity received exaggerated attention. He believed the other residents were watching him out of a specific interest, but it seems clear that there was little to keep most of them entertained and items including a radio and a piano went to the superintendent's apartments. Eventually his protestations, complaints, and letter-writing campaigns to various officials about how his work went unappreciated and uncompensated resulted in his temporary departure. He was lucky to be able to circulate those letters, because sometimes superintendents and matrons read the mail before it was sent.[126] The comradery he described among residents, while seemingly genuine during card games and moments when they provided care for one another, did not overshadow the loss of control he felt at being an institutional resident. Doing these jobs may have helped with some of the dissatisfaction but laboring without being paid came with its own set of complaints. Sweeney was aggrieved at being treated like a poor person, even though that is what he was and how people viewed him.

Sweeney was forty-eight years old when the book came out and described as having gray hair and being "slender almost to boyishness." He stayed intermittently at the farm between the 1910s and 1940s, including stays after the publication of his book. He told the local paper that he wrote the book in secret over a six-month period, and after being turned down by publishers in Columbus, sent the manuscript to the Russell Sage Foundation where a social worker helped him get it published. The reporter noted that much like in the book, "his conversation is often filled with bitter reminiscences and allusions to sordid details of life." Regarding his writing style, Sweeney noted that he only had an eighth-grade education, but that he hoped to keep writing.[127] Newspapers reviewed the book, with the *Detroit Free Press* concluding that "Sweeney himself seems of so little worth that the whole matter becomes unimportant."[128] Another reviewer called it the "oddest chronicle of the season." Sweeney's account was not fictional; he is listed on the Coshocton County Poor Farm census and intake records, but the details he provided are impossible to substantiate. Shortly before the publication of the book Coshocton County made a management change, hiring a couple who stayed for more than fifteen years.[129]

Visiting

Sweeney alludes to the idea that he had been forgotten, and the book was part of his effort to have his life mean something more. As a partially employed, single man with a disability he was vulnerable to many problems, anonymity being one. To ensure that the institutionalized poor were included in their communities, experts suggested locals should visit their poor farm and charged ladies' aid groups with making poor farm residents feel remembered.[130] People were urged to inspect their county facilities, ensuring good conditions were kept.[131] Visiting was surprisingly common at some poor farms. Some Ohio counties kept a register of visitors, who left remarks about the conditions or the cause for their visit. Victor Greenwald went to the Fairfield County, Ohio, farm in 1886, and noted, "I think that these unfortunate people are properly cared for and kindly treated." This 145-page register of visitors had approximately thirty-five names on each page.[132] Local people as well as those visiting from out of the area came to poor farms, particularly those they knew were well run. As Janet Miron's scholarship about institutional visiting explains, institutions were sites that "fostered popular understandings of and insight into criminal behavior and mental illness," but it also encouraged sympathy for poor farm residents. Although true institutional tourism sometimes cost a fee, visiting a poor farm was part of a "web of regulation" to guard against corruption and abuse, and evidenced "a new social interest toward institutional care." Miron notes a decline in tourism visiting during the early twentieth century as people became uncomfortable with "gawking," and while visitors' registers at poor farms also show this trend, officials needed public support, encouraged civil participation, and wanted to "allay social fears of corruption and abuse."[133]

As part of a spirit of volunteerism, visiting poor farms made middle-class people feel good about helping the less fortunate. They put on programs, dropped off food baskets, made gifts, and attended events such as picnics that were hosted annually at poor farms. One man wrote that the poor farm was in "better shape than I ever expected." A comment on the farm noted it was in "splendid condition." Another person who clearly enjoyed himself said he was "well pleased lots of fun and plenty to eat at all hours." The residents did not get to eat at all hours, so it is curious to imagine what that visitor was up to in the kitchen. In Williams County, Ohio, between 1876 and 1899 it appears as though hundreds of people came through and many of them were "well pleased," including the superintendent and matron of a neighboring county. Williams County may have been more accommodating than most. In addition to the kitchen raider, one guest who stayed the night in 1891 wrote, "slept like a log, will come again" and another person in 1896 noted that he too had spent the night. Guest quarters are not well defined on blueprints of institutions, so they may have stayed in the superintendent's apartments or a vacant room on the residents' side. With this much visiting taking place, superintendents, matrons, and employees had the added burden of keeping the institutional facilities as clean and tidy as possible all the time.[134]

Visits from the family of staff and relatives of residents probably did more to boost the morale of residents than those of strangers. Hazel and Ruth Messerly regularly visited their grandparents, who ran the Fairfield County Infirmary in the 1880s and 1890s. The Messerlys' mother was dying so the girls came for the companionship of their family, but also the residents with whom they spent time. Lee Williams's children visited their father regularly and were grateful for the care he received at a county infirmary during the mid-twentieth century because his alcoholism was dangerous and had gotten him into legal trouble. They fondly remembered his roommate, who helped with the farm animals and loved the dogs living at the nearby animal shelter. The Williamses recalled that

Community gatherings like this picnic in Sangamon County, Illinois, brought entertainment and socialization for residents and situated poor farms as a part of their community by providing an opportunity for visiting in a celebratory setting. Photo courtesy of Sangamon Valley Collection, Lincoln Library.

when the new nursing facility was built, the dogs and other animals could not come, so their dad's roommate saved enough money for a tombstone before hanging himself in the barn.[135] Alexander Johnson recommended visiting to improve morale and conditions, for "friends and family of residents, whom should be allowed during visiting hours, local people who want to see the institution and official visitors there in a public capacity." To Johnson, the visiting had the added benefit of bringing attention to potential problems and helping to clean up any issues at the farm.[136]

Poor farms hosted community events such as farmer's picnics, homecomings, and holiday events. One 1898 Christmas Eve program featured singing, music, and readings. Residents got candy, popcorn, and oranges from "old Santa" and "all who witnessed the interesting proceedings will not soon forget the delight and pleasure the occasion afforded."[137] On holidays poor farm residents in Blount County, Tennessee, received visits from local ladies' groups that gave small gifts and snacks. Matron Stella Marsh rounded out the celebrations with "large pans of biscuits and skillets of fresh sausage along with homemade pickles, canned peaches, and dried apple stack cake." The Marsh children decorated with popcorn and cranberry strands.[138] Across the country counties printed postcards with the image of the poor farm on the front. In Wisconsin, where county insane asylums and poor farms regularly shared grounds, visiting hit remarkably high numbers. Sauk County had 620 people visit in 1907, and by 1912 more than 1,600 people had visited, in part because the institution hosted the local farmer's picnic.[139] These community events helped connect residents and community members and showcase poor farm facilities. Clergy visited, but not as regularly as perhaps the Social Gospel movement's good works philosophy would suggest. Most poor farms lacked regular religious services. The county supervisors in Rock Island, Illinois, voted against authorizing a "neighboring pastor to hold religious services once a month," not wanting to show a preference for one pastor over another or concerned about the messaging.[140] C. J. Johnston remembered "the preachers who yelled at these older, poor, and sometimes ill people, 'you are sinners' with threats and predictions of a flaming hell. It was information this captive audience did not need."[141]

Residents spent the most time with employees and their families. Children and grandchildren of superintendents and employees fondly remembered many of those relationships. Ann Ellis was fond of Freddie, a resident who built his own lectern to hold funerals for farm cats. Bonnie Gross, whose grandparents George and Mertie Conley ran the same poor farm where Ed Sweeney lived, was walked to the bus stop by a trustworthy resident, and they played games and pranks with another. One of her favorites was dropping mice into the older women's rooms. Residents showed their affection for her by pooling their money to buy her a Christmas gift and another gave her a cedar chest. Gross also re-members the farm as a fairly hectic space, and she recalled residents helping to care for the child of a narcoleptic woman when she fell asleep, and a rare evening when the northern lights were visible, which frightened some of the residents: "those poor souls were kneeling, crying, praying—sure it was the end of the world. I don't know how my grandparents ever got them calmed down." She concluded that "those years for me were very happy times and educational. The people who had to live there seemed to be an extended family, and they were happy. . . . They accepted everyone as he or she was. They were tolerant of one another, watched out for each other and helpful to each other." Her grand-parents stayed from 1928 until 1945, providing a period of stability and a safe home for the residents.[142] While children no doubt had a different experience than residents, they kept each other company on many farms.

Poor farms housed a diverse array of people, but they were typically men unable to support themselves and facing changing economic circumstances. As the market for farm labor changed and it became increasingly difficult to earn year-round wages or move from laborer to landowner, fewer men were able to support a family and create a network for care later in life, resulting in more poor farm use. While not all residents met the definitions of the worthy poor, poor farms usually admitted everyone, even if only for short stays. Nationally, discussions about causes of poverty did not alter the day-to-day efforts on the local level to house and feed poor farm residents. Counties got recommendations for design, changes, and improvements from experts, visitors, and the local press, but conditions varied dramatically—not only based on deservedness but also on the generosity of taxpayers and how they wanted the poor farm to reflect their values. Their architecture, location, furnishings, management, and even diets were dependent on the county officials, finances, and employees. For every rundown cottage or old farm home, there were multistory brick buildings with plumbing and modern heating. Some residents enjoyed the amenities they were given, and others found regulations restricting and insulting. The management of each institution could be the difference between a decent home and a miserable experience.

3 Farming for the County

"Selection on the basis of success as a farmer hardly qualifies a
person to take care of and promote the general welfare of the
present day type of almshouse inmates."
—Frank Hoffer, *Counties in Transition*, 75

On May 12, 1881, J. S. Meyers recorded that his day had been full of frustration:
"I was at home except going up to the Baird farm which I did *principally* to
capture a mischievous letter written by Sprowl. . . . I fixed pasture fence this
morning after which I felt very bad and was unable for the balance of the day to
do anything, old kidney trouble again." Poor farm superintendents like Meyers
balanced the needs of the farm with those of the residents. In this circumstance,
he believed a resident was mailing out complaints to local officials and sought
to stop the correspondence, lest it undermine his authority.[1] Superintendents
of poor farms worked in challenging environments: they were farmers and
tenants, managers and subordinates, and patriarchs of strange "households."[2]
Living on-site meant little separation between labor and leisure.

The awkward hierarchy created a system ripe for conflict. Charles Sprowl had
found a vulnerability because despite his patriarchal role, charges of corruption,
mismanagement, and abuse against Meyers had to be investigated by county
officials. Adjacent to this dynamic, the superintendent typically brought his own
family to the job, needing his wife and children to help staff the institution. They,
too, supplemented their family roles with poor farm responsibilities. Almost
none of them were truly in charge of their domain because it was owned and
operated by the county. Men in Meyers's position answered to more than one
person, and while being a good farmer did not necessarily qualify someone to
care for poor farm residents, it was the skill that most county officials wanted
in a poor farm superintendent.

The diversity of skills required for the position included the ability to serve
as a responsible patriarch. An 1890 advertisement soliciting a new superintendent requested a "person of good morals and character. . . . They are to do all
the work on the farm; also all the matrons work in and about the building."
The language used by officials reflects the notions of poor farms as households,

going so far as to refer to them as "a happy comfortable home," "instead of the dreaded poor house."[3] For this to succeed, superintendents needed to serve as the head of household and were praised when they did so kindly, as was the case for one man who "seems to feel and act toward the unfortunate paupers as a wise and tender father feels and acts toward his family."[4] This fatherliness had to compliment "a practical farmer and one who farms with brains, and not merely follows a routine of old custom. He must have fair business ability, strict integrity, good habits, even temper, a kind heart, and a good reputation among his neighbors."[5] Counties able to find such a paragon for a poor farm superintendent provided stability for the residents and productivity on the farm.

The sheer volume of responsibilities for superintendents could be staggering, including "farmer, lawyer, executive, merchant, diplomat, purchasing agent, sociologist, baker, laundryman, dietician, judge, minister, mechanic, doctor, and nurse." The employees or residents handled some of those tasks, but the general notion that a successful superintendent wore many hats—only one of which was farmer—was true across the country.[6] Rarely did a poor farm have two separate people to oversee the residents and the farm, although the state of Iowa considered codifying the qualifications for stewards, as they were known there, to ensure that at least one employee was a farmer in the event the steward did not have such experience.[7] Given all their responsibilities, one study concluded that "it is surprising to what extent, for all this haphazard selection, superintendents and matrons really have the essential qualifications for the work they undertake."[8] Clyde McKinniss was a rare superintendent who operated a massive institution for Pittsburgh that separately employed a farmer for its productive land. McKinniss assessed his job as a balance of business acumen because of the "capital invested," and understanding the needs of residents beyond that of "food clothing, housing and medical care" to discovering the root cause of their dependency.[9] Ann Ellis described her father's job running "an extensive farm together with the care of a large public house, and the management control and discipline of a multitudinous and ever changing household of all ages, and all shades of mental, moral, and physical degeneracy is not an inviting field of labor."[10] Despite not seeming like the most enticing of professions, many who chose it did it well and for long durations.

Those interested in poor farm care acknowledged that superintendents were burdened with substantial responsibilities.[11] It is easy to overlook the fact that men like Meyers and McKinniss did their jobs well, because those who did the job poorly or abusively made more headlines. It served the best financial interests of counties to appoint a competent and honest man to the position of superintendent, and it was in the best interests of residents to have someone compassionate and steady. After all, life at the poor farm was "what the superintendent and matron make it."[12]

Hiring a Superintendent

Superintendents of institutions with more than 100 residents had bigger administrative roles because of the sheer size of their institutions, but in most
scenarios the institution was small and the work constant and physically challenging. While they were often experienced farmers, men had varying levels
of proficiency for the job. Hugh Gamble may have been hired because his wife
came with infirmary experience: Lucinda "Ellen" Gamble previously worked
at the Stark County, Ohio, Infirmary and came recommended by the former
superintendent of that institution. Sometimes advertisements were placed in
local papers, or county officials solicited applications from men already known
to them. Otis Ellis, who ran the large Franklin County, Ohio, Infirmary during
the early 1900s, had been employed at the coroner's office where he earned a
reputation for being organized and responsible, which helped secure him the
position. The job of superintendent was not always a respected one. Reformer
Estelle Stewart claimed that "the superintendent belongs to a class only slightly
superior to the majority of the inmates." She critiqued them as generally poor
farmers, since they did not own their own farms.[13] Farm renters were commonly
chosen as they typically had a higher social standing than laborers, who made
up so much of the poor farm population. That was the case for Edward Mortimore and his family, who took up residence at the Umatilla, Oregon, County
Hospital, where he managed the poor farm located on the grounds. Mortimore
had attempted to farm in various locations, worked on road grading crews, and
appeared to be a good poor farm superintendent. The income and housing for
fifty-year-old Edward probably came as a comfort.[14] His previous farm failures
as an owner did not make him any less likely to succeed at the job.

Generally, employment contracts for superintendents lasted one year and
outlined key details about responsibilities. Glen Leaders agreed to a 1913 contract that included "all the work and labor necessary to properly carry on and
cultivate the infirmary farm . . . see to it that food is furnished to the inmates . . .
to keep their clothing in proper repair . . . to look after the board and lodging
of hired help." To manage these tasks and more took both husband and wife,
and the Leaders received a total of $900 annually, which placed their earnings
as a couple on par with teachers, ministers, and skilled laborers of the time,
but since the Leaders received room and board with the job it equaled an even
higher sum.[15] This salary, while competitive, required constant labor since they
lived on-site. The issue of superintendent salary—and the type of person such
salaries attracted—was a concern to reformers. Hastings Hart complained about
the low pay for superintendents, half joking about one superintendent that "the
county evidently intends to keep him, for at a salary of $150 he will inevitably
become a permanent inmate."[16] At least one Kansas County did just that, paying
a man who oversaw their resident-free farm $104 annually, "which is done to

keep him off the township trustee's orders, as he is poor, and the county would have to keep him outside."[17] With no people to care for, the minuscule wages paid for the farm caretaker in this scenario acted more like direct aid than a salary, although very meager. Hart worried about the quality of person who could be hired at such low wages; on one of his visits to an institution he found the superintendent drunk with a dead body in the poor farm wagon. Overall, however, he was pleasantly surprised to find most superintendents to be good, industrious people.[18]

Hart's concerns about low salaries were justified. In West Virginia, contracts from the 1890s offered between $165 and $225 annually, wages comparable to the lowest bracket of wage-earners that included servants. At $225, the salary covered the work of the superintendent's family as well.[19] Small salaries may have encouraged the skimming of resources: one man was caught housing a distant relative at the poor farm and taking care of his horse with county supplies. The scale of salaries varied by county in the same way conditions at the institutions did. In 1900 the average superintendent working in Kansas made $540 and stayed in the position three and a half years.[20] For some, it was a good job. Olive Brammer Boley recalled that her parents made $700 a year running a poor farm and only spent about $100 a year on expenses. She claimed they saved roughly $2,000 while at the poor farm.[21] One Texas poor farm matron said that the salary her husband earned was a "bonanza in our small financial world."[22] Madison Foncannon, who tended the Dade County, Missouri, Poor Farm, won his position by bidding around $300 a year in salary during the economically depressed 1890s. Despite wages akin to a farm laborer, he worked diligently: more livestock were acquired, the barn areas were cleaned, repairs were made, fields were plowed in a timely manner, and the yields of fodder, foodstuffs, and meat increased. His first year on the job earned him a commendation from county officials who wrote lavishly about the farm while devoting only a single sentence to the residents, indicating that their health was good, and they had enough clothing. Foncannon occasionally increased his income by leasing his farm equipment to the county.[23]

While records indicate that some counties struggled to find a conscientious person for the wages offered, others had competing bids. The superintendent in St. Joseph County, Indiana, found himself out of a job in the early 1890s because another candidate undercut his salary price by $50. The state visitor indicated that he had done a fine job, making only $500 annually to run a 240-acre farm and a house with seventy-five residents.[24] Wages of that level, excluding room and board, while welcomed by many, put poor farm superintendents squarely in a bracket just above those they supervised. In lieu of salaries, a few counties opted to pay superintendents on a per diem for each resident, a system more commonly found in jails. Kansas Bureau of Labor investigators expressed concern over this wage arrangement because it encouraged superintendents to pare down all spending on the residents to maximize their own income. In Alabama, a state whose facilities were constantly criticized, poor farm managers were frequently paid in this way, and they kept whatever was not spent. It did not encourage good treatment of the residents.[25]

Since appointments were made by county officials, that meant political patronage also played a role in hiring. Kentucky charity reformers noted in 1888 that their poor farms were "subject to selfishness of county politics" and that residents suffered as a result. State officials in Kansas considered twenty superintendents to be political appointments, and fifty-two hired on merit. Kansas also allowed counties to lease farms to a superintendent for independent operations, but it was not a popular option because county ownership ensured that directors could give "instructions . . . to the superintendent how the farming was to be done for the season."[26] Most reformers identified political appointments as a problem, assessing that politics had a negative effect on institutional integrity.[27] These criticisms came at a time when corrupt political patronage at all levels was scrutinized by reformers; poor-farm hiring based on merit was in line with other efforts at political reform.

Issues between political factions placed poor farms in the crosshairs, and some superintendents found their performance maligned as a result. In 1868, a Coshocton County, Ohio, newspaper began complaining about the cost and record keeping of their farm. One of the headlines, "Copperhead Economy," accused officials of cooking the books regarding livestock inventories.[28] As Reconstruction tensions continued, the paper covered the drama between political factions of the county commissioners and appointments at the farm. In another heated 1880s squabble, the paper supported long-time superintendent John Richeson, crediting him with turning a badly situated farm into a productive source of food for residents. Likewise, the paper lauded the cleanliness with which the house was kept and the happiness of the residents. Despite this public display of confidence, Richeson was replaced later that same year when local elections changed the balance of the county board.

The issues of political appointments and superintendent corruption were so common that they featured in a Horatio Alger storyline. In his book *Jed: The Poorhouse Boy*, the title character is tormented by the Fogsons, a couple who use poor farm resources for their own gains, share kickbacks with a corrupt overseer of the poor, and rely on Jed's labor to offset their own. In positioning the Fogsons as inept and corrupt, Alger articulated real problems. The Muskingum County Ohio Board of Visitors claimed that "the constant changing of superintendents of the house and farm is detrimental to the efficient and economical management of the institution." They continued, "salaries are paid to initiate new men into new duties, which are scarcely more than understood, when they are displaced to give way to others." The visitors articulated the problems with partisan elections changing the party affiliation of the county board, which then used the position of poor farm superintendent as patronage for supporters. What best served counties and residents alike was explained in a 1920s study of Connecticut poor farms, which claimed that smaller institutions were less affected by political patronage because of the lowered financial stakes. They found one superintendent who had served in his post for thirty-three years, and many men newer to the job had replaced long-serving superintendents, some of whom died on the job. Short-term superintendents could pass off responsibility for problems and delay repairs.[29] Annual turnover was hard on institutional residents as well and took up valuable time and resources on the part of county officials.

The concept of a hired patriarch to create a homelike atmosphere for residents clashed with the use of poor farms as political tools or profit-making enterprises. Some of the trouble came from the need to run a successful farm for the county, as opposed to prioritizing the home. A Kansas report criticized superintendent record keeping, which "clearly point[s] to the fact that the cultivation and improvement of their farms and stock occupies more of their time and attention than do the problems surrounding the inmates." The superintendent of Dickenson County drove that point home by listing his official title as "Superintendent County Farm, Breeder of Poland-China Hogs, Shorthorn Cattle, and Standard-Bred Poultry." His narrative report spoke only of the farm operation and contained no mention of residents.[30]

Farming

What happened in the fields and barns had the potential to drastically affect not only the budget but the quality of life inside the institution, so it is not surprising that a county would hire someone who specialized in agriculture. Few people in the United States had experience managing institutions, let alone those with such diverse residents. Requiring someone to have such familiarity would have left counties without superintendents: finding someone with farming experience was much easier. The intention of having a farm with an institution was to provide food for the residents. Some institutions were more successful at this than others. Institutional farms provided milk, meat, eggs, and vegetables to poor farm tables. The poor farm located outside of Denver had excellent irrigation and land, and produced bountiful amounts of food including tomatoes, berries, peas, corn, honey, butter, milk, and meat. Visitors reported that "the quality and quantity of food served to the inmates would do credit to any hotel."[31] Visitors to New Jersey farms were pleasantly surprised by what they found, with a wide variety of dishes and a surprising lack of monotony. New York counties reported selling surplus grain, hay, and cream regularly and many

Poor farms were not always hidden or anonymous, as the painted logo on this barn
in Montana advertises. Residents here frequently sat out on the large porch in nice
weather. Photo courtesy of Lewistown Public Library.

of their farms supplied products to more than one institution.[32] Good farmers
yielded good food and profits on surplus.

Likewise, badly run farms did the opposite. Butte County, California, had
eighty acres, but only sixteen cultivated. During the 1910s the county spent nearly
$9,000 a year for food at an institution that only housed up to 100 people.[33]
During the 1920s, North Carolina officials admonished the state's poor farms,
and by proxy their management, claiming, "as a rule the county home farms
are poorly equipped with farm machinery and livestock. It is hardly necessary
to add that they are poorly farmed." The report noted that "thirty-six counties
with farms ranging from a few acres to three hundred acres report no farm
machinery. . . . It is most unusual to find any livestock belonging to the county
except hogs."[34] Additionally, most of the land belonging to county farms was
underutilized—little more than 4,000 of 16,000 acres was cultivated. The resulting yields per acre were unimpressive, with most making around $10-$15
per acre annually. In contrast, Pennsylvania poor farms reported in 1923 that
of their 17,000 acres, around 60 percent were cultivated. Farm yields provided
approximately 50 percent of institutional food need, although there was little
farm profit to offset expenses.[35] In complaining about the poor farms, North

Carolina officials placed the blame on low salaries attracting substandard superintendents who did sloppy work. They noted that almost no records were
available from which to draw their conclusions, saying, "there are not one half of
a baker's dozen of the county home superintendents in the state who could keep
the simplest set of books."[36] That criticism targeted both the education level and
social class of the superintendents, but it would be hard to expect better when
twenty counties still let the job out to the lowest bidder, nineteen paid less than
$600 a year, and only twenty paid their matrons. As Estelle Stewart predicted,
"A large number of these superintendents are practically illiterate . . . most were
farmers before they came to the county homes . . . thirty of these were tenant
farmers."[37] Stewart and her reform-minded peers clearly believed that the status
of the superintendents affected the quality of their work, but with low salaries
and ill-equipped farms counties could hardly expect to recruit better men.

Because many county officials were farmers themselves and were elected to
those posts because of that knowledge, when they wanted a more productively
run farm, they went searching for a new superintendent. During visits in 1877,
Wood County, Ohio, officials noted things on their farm were "generally not in
good order" and it went on that way for three months. Potato bugs destroyed
an entire crop, residents did not contribute, there were no hired men, the cattle
did not have enough shelter, and grain was missing. Inside the house itself they
found no governance. The resulting action was the hiring of a new superintendent and matron, who were ordered to start almost immediately. A month
into his new job, Edwin Farmer had things back on track. Officials reported
the animals were well fed and cleaned and the house was functional again.[38] In
the year that followed, the farm had more than 100 acres under cultivation that
produced wheat, oats, corn, clover, timothy grass, and potatoes. The hired help
labored steadily from March until August. The aptly named Farmer remained
in his position for more than twenty years, bringing Wood County profitability
and stability.[39] The same sequence took place in Dade County, Missouri, where
the county report about farm conditions said that things looked rundown and
in disrepair: "considerable manure about the barn and yards, should have been
hauled to the fields. No fall plowing has been done. The cultivator, double shovel
and some smaller tools out of repair." If the farm was in such disarray, one can
only imagine what the house looked like. Officials hired Madison Foncannon,
who had his hands full, but luckily only thirteen residents to take care of.[40]

Managing the farming investment of a county was a significant task because
unlike farming for one's own gain, superintendents oversaw a county investment, the value of which could be considerable. In 1887, Iowa poor farms with
1,700 residents possessed 16,373 acres valued at $901,498.[41] Kansas's eighty poor
farms with 1,600 residents were valued at $558,454.[42] With that much money
and acreage on the line, it is no wonder that smart county officials appreciated

a good superintendent when they found him. County officials in Minnesota praised their superintendent by saying, "everything had been found to be in order. Good crops had been raised, 'much better, we think than the County will average.'" These included 217 bushels of wheat, 700 bushels of oats, 410 bushels of corn, 500 bushels of potatoes, and a large quantity of vegetables. The committee summarized that "a brief inspection of the premises indicate good husbandry and frugality in every department." The twenty-five residents were "well cared for and apparently as happy as their circumstances will permit." As in other places these men worried about the farm first and the residents of the farm second, because the land was an investment while the people were expenses.[43]

Good management contributed to a productive farm, but counties had to spend money to keep the farms apace with modern agriculture. Those that did not risked higher food costs and less production. Early improvements included things like drainage tiles, which increased the value of the land at the Franklin County, Iowa, Poor Farm three times over. In the 1870s, county officials in Ohio authorized ditching to bring swampy land into production.[44] Superintendents were typically responsible for completing these tasks or helping to hire those who did. Tiling, ditches, drains, and cultivators were all expenses covered by the county to improve the viability of the farming operations, not necessarily the viability of the residents themselves. The early 1900s ushered in new types of modernizations that county officials embraced if they wanted to stay up to date. Sauk County, Wisconsin, upgraded its property during the early 1910s, which ultimately had two barns, two corncribs, a cowshed, a sheep barn, a milk house, a smokehouse, a henhouse, a brooder house, a machine shed, a hog house, a windmill, and an old greenhouse. Annually, the grain and produce from this farm were worth $5,327, almost all of which was consumed by the institution's residents.[45] Licking County, Ohio, officials also approved substantial investments at their farm, including the addition of a silo, feed grinder, and cream separator, repairs to boilers and the water tank, and a change in cow breed in favor of higher butterfat content. They even improved the house, building a new porch and remodeling the kitchen and dining room. This 226-acre farm provided over $3,000 worth of food products to residents and cleared an additional $240 when other products went to market.[46]

New breeds of livestock were a popular upgrade: Monroe County, Michigan's farm was known for its Clydesdale horses, Fulton County, Ohio, got a registered herd of Holsteins, and the massive 900-plus-acre farm operation in Wayne County, Michigan, went with Holstein-Friesians, which were thought to give an additional pound of milk at each milking. The farmer noted that the cows were set up for production success thanks to quality animal care that ensured sunlight, pure air, and nice stables.[47] Such changes could make substantial differences to profits and mealtimes. The expenditures for improvements on poor farms mirrored that of many family farms of the era: most of the money at the poor farm was spent on improvements to the farm, with the house getting what remained.

Delaying improvements could be detrimental to residents and employees alike, but spending money on improvements had to be justifiable. In 1910, the Johnston family suffered a tragedy in Allen County, Indiana, when one of their children and two employees died after using river ice contaminated with typhoid. The county added a refrigeration system on the property as a result.[48] In 1902 Kaufman County, Texas, added a telephone while Summit County, Ohio, invested in a refrigerator, some wallpaper, a world atlas, and a car.[49] These may have been more than taxpayers had in their own homes. At a 1919 Michigan meeting for poor farm officials, a superintendent of the poor bragged that his county spent $100,000 to replace the poor farm house, and that county was not alone in its upgrades.[50] Alabama's largest poor farm in Jefferson County constructed a brand-new institution, spending almost $250,000 for space to house more than 300 residents. Officials in one Ohio county opted for steam heat that was $500 more than other options because it was thought to be more comfortable and efficient.[51] The consistency with which counties made similar improvements demonstrates an effort to keep up with innovations in farming, but also reflects aging infrastructure at institutions built or last updated in the 1870s and 1880s.

With Edwin Farmer at the helm, the Wood County Infirmary provided an example of a well-run farm whose products were used at the institution. Raising 1,800 pounds of beef, 6,000 pounds of pork, 300 pounds of poultry, and hundreds of pounds of cabbages, potatoes, turnips, and beans meant that the county only spent $1,000 annually on groceries. With 30 tons of hay coming off the farm, the stock had plenty of fodder without more needing to be purchased.[52] When the "farm is a good one" and "cows, sheep and swine are raised on the farm, generally sufficient to supply all wants," it meant that money only need be spent on "a little flour and the usual plain groceries."[53] As was the case on many farms, profits from agriculture during World War I allowed county officials to expand farms. Wood County officials authorized the purchase of additional acreage, adding another 40 to the 160 already owned. With 200 acres total and 170 in production, the farm sold $2,700 worth of surplus products three years later. That was a marked increase from the 1890s, but expenses rose alongside the profits. The farm proved profitable again during World War II.[54] While most produce and meat from the farms was consumed by institution residents, some counties did put money back into their treasuries. In the early 1890s, one Ohio farm paid the county $666 from the sale of products including wheat, corn, oats, and beef while using more than $2,000 worth of farm products for residents. This amount equaled half the entire revenue from the local poor fund tax.[55] In 1915, the Summit County Infirmary began selling wheat from its new farm to the Quaker Oats company. The initial sale of winter wheat made close to $200, with the next sale netting over $350.[56] Farm profits could contribute in a substantial way to all the facets of aid: doctor visits, fuel, and food. With good farm management, the livestock, equipment, and buildings would maintain their value.

Publicly drawing attention to how successful the local poor farm not only helped superintendents keep their jobs, but also validated the purchase and made county officials look good. The Boulder County, Colorado, poor farm won more than a dozen awards at the county fair. Clyde McKinniss in Pittsburgh hoped to make the institutional farm a place "where the farm agent can get together the farmers and give practical demonstrations of the various problems of farming and stock husbandry."[57] The Travis County, Texas, superintendent bragged that "the corn grows so fast out at the farm that I can not sleep at night for the crackling of the ground and the bursting of the ears. We will grow seventy-five bushels to the acre, for we have three to five ears to a stalk."[58] Bullitt County, Kentucky, superintendent W. A. Cook told his local newspaper in 1922 that they grew some of the finest wheat of the year. A local dairy expert in El Paso, Texas, went to see the poor farm cows in person and "found them to be much better than I expected. One cow in particular, I think worth $500 in gold to anyone." Another local farmer said that he "would be very glad to purchase all the cows on the county farm" since he believed the region would "become a great dairy center." The same paper noted that the land itself was increasing in value, and local real estate experts believed the county made a wise investment. Nothing in these stories relates to the welfare of the residents; taxpayers needed constant reassurance that their money was being put to good use on a farm. That the newspaper chose to focus on those attributes as opposed to resident comfort is reflective of the priorities of the institution.[59] The El Paso County farm also got a small mention in 1921 for "Some Punkin," a delightfully symmetrical pumpkin that was given to the local chamber of commerce to showcase local produce.[60]

Farm improvements were designed to increase output, but it was difficult to keep food and farm expenses on a steady budget from year to year, and purchases for supplies were always necessary. Bad weather, an outbreak of rot or insects, or illness among livestock could devastate the food budget as it did for farm families everywhere. No farm was truly self-sufficient; counties purchased things including coffee, sugar, and other items to supplement the kitchen. As a result, poor farms purchased substantial amounts of food and supplies from local merchants. Less productive farms spent more on groceries or residents went without. In 1901, the swampy 200-acre Summit County, Ohio, Infirmary bought flour, meat, and vegetables for approximately 100 residents, some of

HERE'S ANSWER TO QUESTION: DOES FARMING PAY IN ST.
LOUIS COUNTY? POOR FARM MORE THAN SELF-SUPPORTING

1. Group of purebred Holsteins now on test at the St. Louis county poor farm. 2. Miss Julia Segis, one of the nobility of the bovine family; 1,00 pounds of butter in a year and has given more than 100 pounds of milk in a day. 3. His Majesty Sir Mercedes Ormsby Forbes, 2nd, undoub' edly one of the greatest bulls in the state. 4. Aggie Ondine De Kol Dolde, 118 pounds of milk a day is her highest.

The Holsteins from the St. Louis County, Minnesota, Poor Farm won a variety of awards at the state and national level for milk production. Many poor farms during the 1910s and 1920s improved their livestock herds to increase profits, joining a larger trend of farmers who focused on market needs to help pay for improvements. This herd was auctioned off in 1956.

which should have been provided by the farm.[61] Items that most institutions raised themselves, like potatoes, were being sporadically purchased during the early 1900s. Cherries and peaches were also bought, although fruit was a standard item produced on many farms. Among the many farm-related expenses were fertilizer, equipment, animals, and $115 for "shrubbery." The farm struggled to produce the hoped-for yields, and in the early twentieth century county officials relocated the entire institution to better land farther from the city of Akron that they hoped would be more fertile. They sold the old property to a developer.[62] With so much business surrounding a poor farm, there was plenty of room for graft and corruption. Thomas Krainz noted that in Montezuma County, Colorado, a local paper not only blasted the bad investment made in purchasing a poor farm, but also complained that the farm was an excuse to funnel county money into a county official's store.[63]

As discussed in chapter 1, the job of buying for the poor farm was a fraught one, with superintendents usually having the responsibility but needing to have expenses approved by county officials. Reformers, including Alexander Johnson, encouraged oversight in purchasing. He was so impressed with one superintendent's judicious quarterly purchase order that he reprinted it in his own book.[64]

Calico	100 yard	Bed spreads	6
Brown Crash	50 yards	Linoleum	17 yards
Apron Gingham	50 yards	Mosquito bar	4 bolts
Bleached muslin	50 yards	Thread	6 doz spools
Cotton blankets	1 dozen	Silkoline	10 yards
Window shades, linen	14	Large bath towels	6
Large toilet towels	6	Carpet chain	25 pounds
White swiss curtains	4 pair	Nottingham lace curtains	4 pair
Granulated sugar	400 lbs	Roasted coffee	100 lbs
Tea	10 lbs	Rice	50 lbs
Babbitts soap	4 boxes	Ivory soap	25 bars
Lye	1 case	Baking powder	4 lbs
Pepper	5 lbs	Starch	50 lbs
Yeast foam	¼ box	American ball blue	¼ gross
Brooms	1 doz	Scrubbing brushes	6
Cotton mops	6	Coal oil	100 gallons
Soda "Arm and Hammer"	5 lbs	Wooden buckets	6
Lamp chimneys	24	Morgan sapolio	1 dozen bars
Salt	25 lbs	Navy beans	3 bushels
Oats	1 case	NY cream cheese	5 lbs
Ground cinnamon	1 lbs	Ground cloves	1 lbs
Ground allspice	1 lbs	Ginger	1 lbs
Elastic starch	6 boxes	Moss rose syrup	30 gallons
Michigan butter crackers	1 barrel	Mekin ware dishes	1 set (100)
Good prunes	25 lbs	Dried peaches	25 lbs
Canned corn	1 case	Canned tomatoes	1 case
Seed potatoes	10 bushels	Carbolic acid	2 gallons
Camphor	1 qt	Turpentine	1 qt
Sulphur	5 lbs	Copperas	5 lbs
Rochelle salts	2 lbs	Castor oil	1 qt
Chloride of lime	5 lbs	Arnica	1 qt
Ammonia	1 qt	Jamaica ginger	1 lbs
Glycerine	1 qt	Borax	1 lbs
Alcohol	1 qt	Neat foot oil	1 gallon
Quinine	1 oz	Paregoric	1 qt
Tangle foot fly ppr	1 case	White wash brushes	6
Mixed paint	1 gallon	Cotton socks	24 pair
Suspenders	6 doz pair	Bandanna handkerchiefs	12
Heavy work shirts	24	Wool suits	4
Working jackets	6	Straw hats	12
Light weight underwear	6	Overalls	6
Cotton pants	6	Heavy shoes	10 pair
Medium shoes (women)	12 pair	Old ladies shoes	6 pair
Fresh beef	300 lbs	Plug tobacco	24 lbs
Smoking tobacco	15 lbs		

The list makes clear this farm did not supply all the foodstuffs used by the institution, and that attention was paid to providing some considerations to the residents for tobacco, clothing, and seasonings. Franklin County, Ohio, Superintendent Otis Ellis claimed that it was not uncommon to be "held up by the corner groceryman" for business and that issuing fair contracts to the lowest bidder allowed superintendents to "look the coal man and the meat man square in the eye, you can discontinue your old-time dodging tactics." No under-the-table negotiations were needed.[65]

Cruelty and Mismanagement

Typically when there was a problem at the poor farm, the superintendent was responsible. County officials may have spent most of their time worrying about the farm, but that came with risks: neglect and abuse by employees appear to have been more likely at institutions where county officials took a hands-off approach and rarely visited. In order to complain of abuse, residents had to be able to contact someone. If no officials visited, then they were left alone with their tormentors. Accusing a farm superintendent or his wife of malfeasance usually prompted a local investigation, either by grand jury, county officials, or both. Records indicate more mismanagement cases than cases of physical violence, but the latter are the more horrifying. This sort of problem, while seemingly rare or underreported, left poor farms with dismal reputations. In Marion County, Indiana, an 1881 investigation turned up allegations against Superintendent Peter Wright. He allegedly used a cowhide to beat an inmate, refused to provide needed medication, and served bad food. A lack of blankets, separating a young child from its mother, and collusion with an abusive physician were also reported.[66] A troubling scandal in 1870 shocked a Rhode Island community when an anonymous accusation was made that the town farm manager hastened the death of an inmate, impregnated a teenager, and allowed residents to starve. The claim sparked an investigation, which uncovered little evidence but led to the closure of the farm.[67]

A variety of claims of abuse and mistreatment sporadically appeared across the country. In 1901, Superintendent George Zinkon and his wife Sadie were accused by Ohio poor farm residents and local political opponents of torturing a man who had stomach cancer, beating another with a piece of iron, and assaulting a crippled man. Phoebe Kleinknicht, a ten-year resident of the farm who did the cooking, accused Sadie Zinkon of slapping her in the face and confining her to a cell. The local newspaper reported these charges with relish; of course it made a good story, but the paper's editorial board also objected to the political appointment of George Zinkon. His only advocate was the one remaining county official who shared his political affiliation. It is difficult to know what transpired at the institution because of the partisan nature of the charges. It appeared that Zinkon billed the county for a variety of personal expenses like oysters and surrey washes, but while that demonstrates suspect ethics, it does not definitively prove abuse. The Zinkon case—and the newspaper's praise of his successor—highlights how politics affected poor farm management. Many of those who celebrated Zinkon's removal, however, were long-time residents, which may indicate their treatment was as bad as reported.[68]

Neglect and mistreatment took place, as did financial misdeeds that could result in diminished supplies for residents. In Ohio, county officials scrutinizing the bills caught the superintendent charging them for fixing a buggy and setting ten horseshoes in a single day, but the county did not have a buggy and owned only two horses. He also billed them for a silk dress, finery poor farm residents did not wear.[69] Across the state, one of the country's only female superintendents was accused of a variety of faults, including using county supplies for her daughter's family, stealing possessions from residents, not turning over profits, and abuse. Her case will be detailed in chapter 4, but Julia Glines did not stand accused alone—the board of directors faced charges that they mismanaged farm operations, used funds incorrectly for travel and cigars, and employed their own relatives. In the end, the most serious charges were invalidated, and the erroneous expenditures explained as a misinterpretation of poor farm fund use. Glines was cleared of charges by state officials but resigned shortly thereafter.[70]

Glines's employer, Summit County, did not remediate their issues. Five years later they were again under investigation by the state board of charities for mistreating residents, misappropriation of funds, and a general laxity of management. In the public debriefing that followed, the investigating commission found that the superintendent, Millard Hamlin, and his wife, Nancy, were overburdened by responsibility, lacking enough hired help for the more than 100 residents at the farm. Investigators scolded that, "in the employment of help there has been a false economy. To make a good showing for the farm, even at the neglect of the infirmary inmates, has been the policy. This is wrong. The farm is of very minor importance. The care of the inmates is the first consideration." However, five years earlier, it was decided that the ramshackle condition of the farm was a reason to accept the resignation of Julia Glines.[71]

County officials were sometimes found to be more at fault than their employees. Seth and Catherine Mills managed the Henry County, Indiana, Poor Farm for $1,000 a year during the 1910s and 1920s, having previously rented a farm with their two sons. When the Millses were hired the institution was not in good condition, but they were given a reprieve from criticism when a grand jury inquiry investigated conditions at the farm shortly after their hiring. The jurors specifically commended Mills and his wife for their care of the forty-five residents. However, the problems they found were many: a shortage of clothing and bedding, no plumbing and fire equipment, inadequate heating systems, an unsafe boiler, and washing facilities that were "dark, damp, and in general poor repair." The foundation of these problems was subpar county oversight—not the superintendent's laxity. The grand jury noted that instead of using the recently allotted $10,000 for recommended repairs, the county should build an entirely new institution. In closing the grand jury said, "We believe that Henry County is rich enough and prosperous enough to afford a proper and sanitary home for its aged and infirm unfortunates and we feel it our duty both as grand jurors and as citizens of Henry County to call these matters to the attention of the court."[72] Their report expressed not only embarrassment that their institution did not reflect well on the county, but also the acceptance of community responsibility to do better. Three years later, progress had been made but not as much as expected. A generator had been purchased but not installed, and the barn and other buildings still lacked electricity. Visitors wanted this fixed because of who did the milking in that barn, saying, "carrying lanterns is not only unwise, but it is really dangerous as there are seven men who can help feed and milk, yet are not mentally able to be trusted."[73]

Managing the Employees

One of the ways to ensure better conditions for residents was to have a fully staffed institution. More employees meant cleaner laundry and facilities, well-prepared food, and extra conversation and attention for residents. Not all superintendents managed a staff, but generally the larger the farm operation, the more employees needed, and more residents created more household chores. Unlike family farms, which reduced the need for full-time hired hands with modernizations and family labor, poor farms hired staff because there was more work than could be covered with upgrades to equipment. Employees were a routine part of the poor farm structure. Hired hands were more common than household help because their salaries were more likely to be paid by the county to benefit the farm. The Franklin County Infirmary housed hundreds of people and employed nurses, attendants, a cook, a dining room girl, an engineer, a watchman, and a hall attendant for the residence as well as a dairyman, and between six and seven hired hands to deal with the 100 acres of crops, herds of pigs and cows, a vegetable garden, and a substantial orchard.[74] The farm operation was productive enough that it provided extra food to the county hospital and children's home.

Labor appears to have been a considerable expense on most poor farms, and examples abound of its wide-ranging costs. Specialized labor was sometimes hired for reaping, mowing, painting, masonry, repairs, and ditching. Between 1872 and 1884 Cedar County, Iowa, spent between $0 and $470 on labor, with

Poor farm employees, like those seated here, helped with chores including farming, nursing, and domestic duties. The larger the institution the more likely it was to be a substantial employer in the community. Photo courtesy of Ross County Historical Society, Chillicothe, Ohio.

an average of $250 annually.[75] In some years the household chores were done by the superintendent's sister and mother-in-law, which saved the county money. In the 1870s, Dane County, Wisconsin, routinely spent hundreds of dollars a year on hired help. The farm required the most labor, costing between $350 and $500, but the household staff was not small and cost around $300 a year.[76] That did not include additional costs for special jobs such as blacksmithing, wood chopping, and carpentry. Those costs totaled another $325. By the early 1900s labor costs had increased in many places to more than $1,000 a year.

The typical poor farm employee was an unmarried man or woman who stayed a short period of time. German immigrant Christopher Krassow is a good example. In 1900 he briefly worked at an Ohio poor farm, making $20 a month, before moving on to the oil fields. Wages for farm labor at that time ranged from $23 to $37 a month.[77] Unlike other hired hand jobs that were seasonal, year-round employment on the poor farm provided steady, if not great, wages. James Day and Robert Frantz worked from at least September 1899 through the census enumeration of June 1900 at the Putnam County, Ohio, Infirmary. Day made $45 a month, and Frantz $25.50, a difference probably accounted for by the demands of their assigned tasks or room and board. Krassow's lower wages might reflect his recent naturalization or the tasks expected of him. Hired men did not just work the farm; some also helped with the residents, supervising their labor, repairing things around the institution, and even taking charge of the men's bathing. Some employees lived on-site and had room and board factored into their wages.[78] In Allen County, Indiana, as many as twenty-eight employees lived in rooms on the second floor of the main building. Locals who might be in danger of being dependent on the county were also hired because the wages and board would keep them off aid, but healthy, strong people were preferred.

Hiring family members was a useful way to staff an institution. W. P. and Estella Frantz operated a poor farm and employed their children, Dwight and Mildred, ages twenty and twenty-two. Mildred was listed as a servant in 1930, and Dwight as a laborer, but also hired were Samuel Billingsley and Esther Buckingham, both twenty-one years old. She cooked while he worked on the farm.[79] For young people trying to save their wages, a poor farm job that came with housing and food provided financial benefits. For the Frantzes, having four young people on staff no doubt came as a substantial help. Joyce Marti, whose father and grandfather ran the same poor farm for a combined forty-four years, remembered that the employees made her life better: "I lived like a little rich girl. We had our meals cooked by the staff, cleaning done, and very nice private living quarters—it all came with my parents and grandparents being employed at the County Farm."[80] The efforts of the staff allowed her father time to invent a manual patient lift to help people out of bathtubs. Emily Williams Smith's sister married one of the hired hands at the poor farm her father managed. So did Lottie, one of Edwin Farmer's daughters. She and her husband Frank Brandeberry ran the poor farm after her father's death. C. J. Johnston's mother cooked for $10 a month when her father was the superintendent. He refused to recommend that her salary be raised because of concern about the appearance of favoritism.[81] Women working at poor farms made less than their male counterparts but played an important role, especially when the superintendent and matron had no family help; this will be discussed at length in the next chapter. Superintendents had more direct supervision of those hired for the farm and matrons generally supervised the domestic help.

Poor farms hired not only full-time employees but seasonal or task employees as well; in the tradition of communal agricultural work, barter, and labor-sharing arrangements, neighbors often filled these jobs.[82] Seamus Shultz was hired by Dane County in 1879 to cultivate corn in the spring and again in the fall for $17 a month. Will County, Illinois, hired Thomas Langdon to butcher and plow, and other neighbors for planting, blacksmithing, and privy maintenance.[83] For years, Fred Sheets threshed grain for Summit County, making between $30 and $60 each fall. Hiring neighbors with implements increased labor costs but

The more physically challenging farm jobs were usually left to hired hands and the superintendent to complete. These employees at the Ramsey County, Minnesota, Poor Farm were storing hay in the hayloft. Photo courtesy of the Minnesota Historical Society.

saved counties from buying their own equipment. Picking up seasonal work at the poor farm helped neighbors like Hiram Ridenour in Putnam County, who supplemented his own income as a farm renter. Hiram and his wife had eight children under the age of seventeen, and based on census records, he wavered between unemployment, farm renting, and eventually worked at a sawmill. His poor farm wages would have considerably supplemented the family income.[84] Ridenour was someone whose family might have been kept off direct aid thanks to his occasional employment by the county.

The employees who lived on-site interacted the most with residents and occasionally undermined the hierarchy and rules. At the height of spring planting, J. S. Meyers faced a crisis after he fired three of his workers for violating curfew and fraternizing, behaviors that challenged his authority and set bad examples for residents. The two men had been there more than a year, and Julia Perrot was a resident hired to staff the kitchen. Meyers called it "one of the hardest of poor farm days." Perrot and George Schroeder, one of the fired men, later married. Meyers and the residents had grown close to these people; Schroeder had been particularly trusted, having bathed male residents and managed their work, handling hard physical tasks like rock hauling, and even building a coffin for a beloved resident.[85] Meyers had to add hiring replacements to his already loaded job responsibilities. In 1948, poor farm housekeeper Grace Bible was dismissed on charges of misconduct. She had been "meeting an inmate of the home in the spring-house after she had been warned against trysts in the cellar of the institution." The report noted that her husband lived about a mile away and that the superintendent was tipped off by an intercepted love letter.[86]

Like getting a matron with a superintendent, hiring couples was another way to try and ensure a steady workforce. Sauk County, Wisconsin, found hiring couples so important it renovated the old poor farm building in 1918 to use as housing for married employees. The institution doctor remarked on the staffing in his annual report: "I have been rendered valuable assistance by the superintendent and matron . . . both of whom manifest an intense interest in their charges. As attendants, Mr. and Mrs. Weller, Mr. and Mrs. Arnt and others have aided much."[87] The superintendent, Christian Christenson, was an immigrant from Denmark who began working there in 1908. Ten years into his tenure, he thanked county officials for "the deep interest that you have always taken in trying problems that are constantly confronting us," and acknowledged the "faithful service" of employees including Hugh and Clara Weller and John and May Hooseman.[88] The following year, having these couples on-site saved the lives of an untold number of residents when a fire broke out. Christenson's account of the fire is not only harrowing, but a testament to the importance of good employees and neighbors:

> The farm hand who retired was awakened by smoke penetrating his room and he gave the alarm at 10:15 PM. . . . We soon concluded that the building could not be saved. The fire having made such progress that the building was doomed. The wind being from the southwest, the poor farm was in imminent danger. The people in this building were therefore removed to the general dining room where they would be out of danger; many were transferred on their beds, being unable to walk. After a time as the fire traveled toward the south, the men's dormitory was gravely endangered, due to the close proximity of the two buildings. This building housed one hundred patients . . . at least 50 of the men [residents] did valiant service in doing what could be done to save life and property. With heroic labor of the patients, neighbors, and the staff, we were fortunate to save the other buildings. There was no loss of life, no one was injured. I desire to publicly express my gratitude to the many neighbors who worked so valiantly and fearlessly, also the work of the patients and employees will never be forgotten.

Christenson immediately noted that the fire created a serious shortage of employee housing needed to recruit and keep good help.[89]

Managing the Residents

While county officials and superintendents might have come to their jobs with farm experience, almost none of them had familiarity dealing with the residents. Much of the advice dispensed about this aspect of the job came from those who claimed expertise without experience. In a discussion of poor farm discipline, for example, a presenter at the National Conference of Charities and Corrections cryptically suggested, "Let your hand be steel, but cover it with the proverbial velvet glove." Other ideas including not having too many rules, giving people basic tasks, separating the genders, and consistent discipline were given freely.[90] Superintendent S. I. Meseraull noted that there were challenges and aggravations to his job, but classified it as paternal by saying that "all the inmates are a lot of children, grown out of the noontime of life, calmly waiting for the golden sunset. Rule them, but kindly."[91] New superintendents might have appreciated a few more specifics and elderly residents may not have appreciated the condescension.

Speaking about issues of discipline, Ernest Bicknell from the Indiana State Board of Charities encouraged a "humane spirit" combined with executive capabilities and moral soundness. He used an example of what not to do as a superintendent: "When I visit a poor asylum, and hear the inmates address the superintendent as 'John' or 'Bill' I know without further investigation that discipline in that institution is not what it should be." He encouraged the firing of one man and his wife who were referred to by their first names. The casual act of calling a man by his first name indicated an informality that was unbecoming a patriarchal structure, and Bicknell expected an elevation of superintendent over resident. When it came to rules, Bicknell believed that too many and there would be exceptions, too few and things were lax.[92]

While some institution rules specified that all who were able had to work, this was unevenly enforced and often entailed very light chores.[93] There are few indicators that the long lists of recommended rules and policies that came from experts were strictly followed or enforced in any meaningful way.[94] Examples typically included a schedule for meals, behavioral codes such as no swearing, no leaving without permission, no drinking, and meal privileges attached to labor. But it remains unclear how many of these were implemented: meals were usually on a schedule, but lots of people, especially men, came and went without authorization. Buchanan County, Iowa, officials annually griped about imposing discipline, expecting to see "temperate firmness be enforced with all paupers regarding the rules of the house." One of those rules was not leaving without permission. That this issue came up annually indicates it was easier decreed than done. Kansas reported that they had at least one poor farm where "no punishment is administered in any form, though the inmates are sometimes unruly," and another where troublesome residents were expelled until they agreed to follow orders.[95] Michigan superintendents agreed that they had some rules for residents, but when asked about punishments for breaking the rules, one responded, "There is no punishment . . . it is stated in the rule that they are liable to be removed from the house. That is the only punishment we have," but admitted that no one had been subjected to such a fate, and that people were permitted to return.[96] Limits to punishments for residents were codified. Erie County, Ohio, for example, banned corporal punishment unless the superintendent was attacked by a resident.[97] The notion that white adults would strike one another as a disciplinary action was not acceptable; class distinctions were not marked with physical punishment.

Like forcing people to labor, it took perhaps more time than it was worth to impose certain non-essential rules. Lewis Peck may have been the nation's longest running poor farm superintendent, holding the position from 1909 until 1950, but even he ran into conflicts with rules. In the 1920s, Peck tried to eliminate smoking because he rightfully worried about the fire hazard. The community, when hearing of the rule change, responded with pity for the residents whose pastime and coping mechanism was removed. As one said, "Only God the almighty can take away that desire to smoke." County supervisors stepped up to support Peck and the smoking ban, but in a twist of bad luck, lightning hit the barn shortly thereafter, burning it to the ground.[98] The dangers of having lax rules were made plain in 1879 in Clayton County, Iowa, during the "poor farm murder" in which a longstanding quarrel between residents, "neither of whom were mental giants," resulted in a death. In an indication of how relaxed the rules were, the shooter, a fifty-five-year-old German immigrant and blacksmith, had possession of a hunting rifle, which he used to fire off a celebratory Fourth of July shot, and then, apparently seeing an opportunity, went in and killed thirty-four-year-old Charles Schultz. He was convicted and sentenced to twenty years in prison.[99] Indiana state official A. W. Butler made a shocking discovery in 1902 while visiting the Adams County Infirmary. Buried under a pile of "rubbish" in long-time resident Charles Echerman's room were considerable amounts of dynamite, two bombs, and a fuse. Echerman had recently been reprimanded, which made him "sulky," and apparently bent on revenge; he ran away after the discovery.[100]

Violence was reported in poor farms across the country, some involving staff and residents. An Indiana matron was pinned to the ground by a resident; a different institution had a resident rip his toilet from the floor and use it to batter down the wall, after which he escaped while wrapped in sheets. Basil Worth of Saline County, Kansas, was the first resident of his county's poor farm, opened in 1873. His various physical and mental ailments kept him from living with his wife and children: they requested the county discontinue his visits to their nearby farm. In addition to bouts of violence, his feet had been frozen and then rotted off so that he walked on the ends of his legs. He had been sent to the state asylum but returned as incurable. A county official remembered him as having "a very strong constitution, a powerful body, and a very disagreeable disposition, greatly tormenting the superintendent." After Worth tried to stab

Superintendent George Hawley and beat him with a club, he was labeled a "dangerous character" but was not removed. In 1880, a conflict related to a tobacco allowance escalated to a physical confrontation in which Worth wielded clubs and failed to respond to a warning shot. It ended when Superintendent Hawley shot him in the chest and neck, killing him. A grand jury did not indict Hawley for the shooting.[101] Walt McDaniel, another Kansas superintendent, was sliced in the stomach by a "knife-wielding" resident who apparently did not like a piece of meat he was served.[102] Superintendent Otis Ellis had his hands full with Harry, who knocked him down, fell out of a tree, and threw an ax. The position of superintendent was not one for the faint-hearted.

Even with rules in place, enforcement could cause conflict. J. S. Meyers noted he had "trouble again in camp tonight relative to too great intimacy between paupers." In addition to policing illicit sex, Meyers also had several physical altercations with residents, some of whom had knives and were jailed as a result. The most persistent discipline problem Meyers faced was with Dennis McCarty, or as he phrased it: "dirty scrapes to settle with the Irish (Dennis McCarty and McMullen) who had a fall out about their bed. Resulted in McCarty leaving the poor house this morning." The two men did not share a bed, but apparently argued about the positioning of the beds in their shared room. After this incident, Meyers and seventy-two-year-old McCarty began a months' long cycle in which McCarty left, sometimes with a train ticket paid for by the county, but came back only to be kicked out again for not following the rules. His other punishments included a stay in the "crazy house," being housed at the jail, and bread and water rations. Some of their conflicts were physical, and Meyers reportedly "had to handle Old McCarty rougher than was agreeable." When McCarty was housed at the jail the sheriff wanted him removed, so back to the farm he went. Apparently, McCarty was not a good occupant no matter the surroundings. Meyers also reported having a physical "tussle" with a man named Andrew Drogswold, a thirty-five-year-old immigrant with a wife and large family. Reports suggest he may have had a drinking problem and removing him to the poor farm was the way his Norwegian neighbors policed his behavior. Other residents used abusive language or attempted to fight. These sorts of events were not easily prevented by posting rules on the wall. County officials who put residents like McCarty back in the poor farm made the job of the superintendent more difficult.[103]

Experts viewed poor farm resident labor, as was requested of McCarty, as one way to keep behavior issues under control. Superintendents, however, had different opinions. In 1899, when Kansas asked superintendents to value their resident labor, most ignored the question. Those who answered provided an assortment of data that did little to clarify matters. Many remarked that they had no data, had to hire supervision for the resident labor, had residents "too old and lazy to work," those who did "only light chores," and some who "did not earn their board."[104] An Ohio superintendent ranked the value of the "pauper labor" at $30 for the entire year, or equal to approximately one month's salary for a hired man. In another year this superintendent listed it as "not of any value."[105] Edwin Farmer told state officials in his 1894 annual report, "you cannot put any value on pauper labor as it is more work to see after them than to do the work."[106] Normally Farmer left that prompt blank on his form, so perhaps some recent frustration made him honestly account for the absence of a number and the dismissal of the question. Later, when his son-in-law took over, he made one note on the line, "does not pay for supervision," which summed up decades of Farmer family experience at the institution.[107]

While reformers came to understand that there were physical limitations on some residents that hindered their ability to labor, there was a fundamental misunderstanding about the amount of time and effort it took superintendents to manage a farm, institution, and assign specialized tasks to residents based on abilities. Those interested in scientific charity believed that some form of work would not only be beneficial but should also be required by anyone accepting aid. The reality, however, was that getting troublesome residents to do so was enormously time-consuming and those who wanted to work did so without much prodding. When J. S. Meyers tried to get McCarty to help feed the pigs he had to attach threat of punishment; it was not feasible to do such a thing with dozens of people and a small staff. There was a substantial difference in tasking people with small chores, such as helping with sewing, picking vegetables, or setting the table, and the heavier jobs required to run a farm and a household like maintenance, plowing, fence repair, and laundry. Residents frequently helped, but not with labor enough to operate a farm. Even Hastings Hart admitted that "the popular idea that pauper labor ought to be utilized would find little useful material."[108]

One example of the ways strategies for resident management changed over time came from Alameda County, California, which hired a new superintendent in 1923. Reasoning that residents had an interest in the wellbeing of the institution, he crafted a new set of rules focusing on accountability and spent a few months on gradual implementation. He reported that cleanliness had improved as a result of steps such as recording weekly baths. This type of management for more than 100 men took considerable effort, but it resulted in approximately half of the male residents participating in some type of work as a way to remove "the stigma of the almshouse and poor farm" to "better and more economically meet the needs of this group of men."[109] There were manufacturing shops on-site for shoes, mattresses for all other county institutions, and laundry. Similar efforts in Pennsylvania seemed to yield decent results. One superintendent indicated that he found useful labor for 58 percent of the residents based on their physical capabilities. These chores included helping on the farm and dairy, in the greenhouse, weaving carpets, sewing, and making mattresses. His methods aligned with recommendations from the American Occupational Therapy Association that sick or injured people, and those with disabilities, benefited from ways to exercise mind and body as part of their treatment. By the 1920s the state department of welfare partnered with occupational therapists to make their services available in poor farms across Pennsylvania.[110]

The seasonality of farming tasks created other challenges for requiring resident labor. During the spring, summer, and fall, people able to work left institutions, so superintendents relied on their own family members, residents with disabilities, and hired hands. When the need for labor was greatest, farmers offered wages that helped bring men out of the poor farms and into the fields. During the winter when paying jobs were scarce and poor farms were more crowded, there was little to keep residents busy.[111] Certain farms provided more year-round work than others. A dairy, for example, needed to be staffed constantly. Household improvements cost money, so while they might have been a likely wintertime occupation, counties did not typically allot money for them to be completed. Husking corn and other light chores aligned with resident capabilities, but participation was another matter.[112] In Texas, one group of poor farm residents unsuccessfully went on strike in 1888, refusing to work unless they were paid wages. This may have been a response to the arrival of a new superintendent, or about reports that conditions at the institution were bad. It worked no better for them than it did later for Ed Sweeney.[113] Only a few poor farms reported paying residents to labor and in some cases, like that of Wayne County, Michigan, those being paid were the psychiatric patients. At institutions where the insane asylum shared property with the poor farm, inmate labor could be valued at as much as $3,000 a year. People at the asylum helped out as part of their treatment and did up to a full day's worth of work.[114] Those who suggested that poor farm residents were fit for farm labor because "many of them came from the country, and know more about agricultural work than any other form of industry" did not understand that such work physically broke people down, sending them to the poor farm in the first place.[115]

Institutional records indicate that the most common type of labor arrangement for residents was allowing them to pick their own tasks. "Auntie" Rook, an Allen County, Indiana, farm resident, helped in the kitchen and C. J. Johnston remembered that while she had some type of cognition issue causing her to misremember employees as her children, and "her lips moved constantly," she liked the socialization that came with being in the kitchen alongside as many as eight other residents helping there as well. Amos Warner would have been pleased that these women were taking on chores, because he believed it easier to find small tasks for women since there were so few of them in poor farms and so much domestic work to be done.[116] It was not just women, however. John Mackey came as a resident and ended up a hired hand. Johnston remembered him as always cheerful, despite having an open sore on his heel and a homemade peg leg to shift his weight from his heel to his knee while he worked. Some superintendents rewarded residents for helping. J. S. Meyers took "several paupers to see the fair, who had been faithful helps and paid to Shoemaker $1.00 for faithful services in feeding hogs and who preferred to remain at home."[117]

A study in Virginia recorded that "most inmates are of very little value to the almshouse. No thorough medical examination is made at the time of admission, with the result that no one knows whether some of the inmates can work or not." Having doctors on-site to inspect people was expensive, and a superintendent worth a fraction of his salary could determine whether a person was fit to work and how much effort it would take on his part to get the person to contribute.[118] Dealing with the poor farm population was an on-the-fly task, and superintendents found it hard enough to manage the farm operation without having to invent jobs for the residents and then supervise them in the tasks.[119] People regularly showed up on the doorstep of the institutions and were allowed in, given a meal, and the details were sorted out later.

The Superintendent's Perspective

Despite the hazards and challenges of the job, a seemingly large number of skilled and ethical men served as superintendents. Starting in the early 1870s, E. P. Titus began a nine-year stint running the Dane County Poor Farm. He wrote daily in a journal about work, residents, and weather updates, including one of the most severe El Niño cycles in history. Writing his annual summation on New Year's Eve 1878, he claimed the weather had complicated his job because the wet warm season "has been the most remarkable month on record since this country was settled . . . roads have been impassable for drawing full loads the past three months."[120] His 1877–78 diary is littered with strange weather events that challenged the farm and the residents, including a May hailstorm that dropped two-pound, ten-inch hailstones, "the hardest and the largest hail stone I ever saw," that broke 140 panes of glass on the property.[121] In September the mercury reached 103 degrees, so residents stayed in the shade as much as possible. By early November there were full days of snow followed by cripplingly cold temperatures that prevented residents from husking corn. On December 20, he recorded a temperature of 64 degrees. Luckily, the hog butchering had already been finished.

Titus used the journal as a business record as well. He noted the terms of contracts and the struggle to find employees: every couple of weeks during 1877–78 hired women came and went. One day his only entry said, "I was away looking for a hired girl." Titus's wife Viola is not mentioned in his journal, but during part of the time she was pregnant with and caring for their daughter, increasing the need for domestic help. He was one of the rare superintendents who had the opportunity to participate in national discussions of institutional care thanks in part to the reliability of his hired hands. When he went to Buffalo, New York, to attend the Conference of Charities and Corrections for two weeks, he entrusted the institution to the employees. It was probably good that Titus had valued staff because in March 1879, new handwriting appeared in the journal. The first entry in two weeks was made by Jesse (J. S.) Meyers, the new superintendent. He dutifully picked up where Titus left off, both at the institution and in the journal. E. P. Titus died after what was apparently a head injury related to a farming accident. In one of his first entries, Meyers recorded that the hired men were helping Viola Titus move. In contrast to her absence in her husband's notes, she appears in Meyers's entries frequently. He occasionally drove her to the farm from Madison for visiting and appointments. He helped her with some type of claim on her husband's estate, then later assisted with tax paying. E. P. Titus had been dead for almost three years when Meyers reported he went to Madison and returned with Viola Titus, who stayed a few days. She may have been there to help Adelaide Meyers, but payments to her were not noted.

Meyers quickly became disenchanted with the labor contributed by the residents. He made notes such as "what the paupers done today was done in the garden" and "paupers did not do anything to amount to anything." One man left because "I told him to go and help shell corn." Like Titus, he faced challenges staffing the institution, often going to neighboring homes looking for hired girls. He managed to secure a husband and wife to cook, but they only stayed six months, leaving "in consequence of fault with me in not allowing time when away and not willing under existing circumstances to raise wages." Julia Perrot and Amelia Antelman, both single mothers and poor farm residents, were hired as replacements. Meyers used the journal more personally than his predecessor. Six months into the job he noted he "had a hard day of it with the paupers." As it turns out, what seemed a trying time to Meyers was routine. He hurt his hand trying to get Mary Isley under control after she made a bedsheet rope and escaped out a window. After the New Year, he recorded that "nearly all the [hired] girls are sick. Patience very sick [she died shortly thereafter] Alice and Betty quite sick. Wife very sick next day." He also got sidetracked by visitors on a regular basis. In May he "was much perplexed today at numerous poor house visitors who came just before dinner hour." Later that week he wrote, "Most of *my* time was occupied this pm with showing visitors about premises." One day after traveling to Madison (a twenty-mile round trip) he spent the day at home tending to the sick, repairing a vault on the women's privy, entertaining people

Most superintendents believed that residents were not capable of full-time work, but that did not mean that they did not help around the farm and house with tasks appropriate for their abilities like gardening and kitchen chores. Photo courtesy of the Minnesota Historical Society.

who came to see the poor farm, then dealing with the county supervisors, who showed up with twenty or so people.[122]

Meyers struggled with illnesses, both his own and those of residents and staff. In addition, the county began accepting incurable residents back from the state insane asylums, bringing nine in a single day. Meyers opened one entry with, "This was a day to try an overseer's soul." The day was productive until county officials arrived with an elderly woman who Meyers described as "a pauper that is about dead with diabetes." Then another exceptionally sick person arrived, with notice of two more for the next day. Meyers had no choice but to deal with the new residents deposited by his bosses. Staff members started to get ill later in the day. As he closed, he noted, "all in all, had our hands full."[123]

As a result of the return of so many from state asylums, in 1882, Meyers and his employees embarked on constructing a new building to house them. After its completion in 1883 his job became more complex, as he oversaw both institutions. Once the county asylum opened, each institution housed approximately seventy-five people. This was not more people than other superintendents cared for, but the separate staffs and buildings complicated the job. Meyers expanded farming operations to compensate for the increased population.[124] The efforts succeeded, and in 1887 the board of supervisors described the institutions and farm as "very nearly or quite self-supporting."[125] Despite the challenges of the job, Meyers remained in the position for more than a decade, succeeded by Lewis P. Edwin. Edwin and his wife enjoyed an even longer tenure, leaving in 1912. Dane County had a series of long-running superintendents, with the Edwin's successor lasting until 1923. This remarkably good streak of leadership provided stability and productivity to the institution.

Good superintendents could bring about positive change at county farms. In Gage County, Nebraska, Samuel McKinney relied on experience and empathy; he had been a Colorado jail attendant and building supervisor. Comparing his employment at the jail and poor farm, he noted that many conveniences given to prisoners were not given to the poor. Farming 160 acres and caring for approximately fifteen people, McKinney asked, "Why should the public not be willing to make comfortable the unfortunate ones who, not by choice, but often from circumstances not of their own making, are obliged to be inmates of the almshouse?"[126] His progressive stance on the treatment and care of residents may be attributable to his work in other institutional settings, but few of his peers had such experience to draw on. Although some states like Michigan provided meetings for superintendents, most labored in isolation, not getting to participate in wider discussions of institutional practices. Otis Ellis believed that the people in his care deserved comfort, happiness, good food, and even some entertainments. His attitude about what residents merited indicates that he kept up with larger ideas about reform and the role of the institution in providing care. After he left the county infirmary in 1917, he was hired at the county children's home before eventually ending his long career for the county at the tuberculosis hospital in 1944.[127]

The number of long-serving superintendents, matrons, and interfamily poor farm employees is impressive, and refutes some of the claims that poor farm superintendents were simply political appointees or tyrannical brutes. Frank Shumaker and his wife Susan worked at a poor farm for approximately twenty years before retiring to their own farm.[128] The Richesons stayed in Coshocton County, Ohio, from 1871 until 1884, and at their departure residents "expressed their grief in violent and affecting manner."[129] Summit County improved its poor farm by hiring Sherman and Della Stotler, who were there for twenty-five years.[130] Will County, Illinois, also kept superintendents for long tenures. Philip Smith did the job from 1884 until 1892, and Charles Rost stayed from 1893 until 1910. Rost left a lasting mark on his county, campaigning for a new hospital and better treatment of those considered insane. Rost's collaborators at the county level also stayed in office a long time. Judge Solomon Simmons and Charles Cropsey served as county officials or "poor farm keepers" for decades.[131] It was not only in the Midwest: a study done of four New England states found numerous superintendents serving terms of longer than a decade, among them a third-generation superintendent, and a Paterson, New Jersey, man in his thirty-seventh year.[132]

Long-term superintendents also passed the job down to the next generation. In 1925, Henry Reier was hired at the Washington County, Minnesota, Poor Farm. In 1941, Reier's daughter and her husband were managing the facility. They stayed until 1975, lasting even through the transition to a nursing home.[133] The Wood County, Ohio, Infirmary was managed by members of the Farmer family for decades. When Edwin Farmer died his daughter Lottie and her husband, former hired hand Frank Brandeberry, took over. They stayed from 1904 until they retired in 1949. Lottie Farmer Brandeberry spent almost her entire life on the poor farm. The frequency of multiple-generation and long-term management is, however, matched by the frequency of men who stayed a year before moving on. One created generally positive outcomes for residents while the other created uncertainty.

When J. S. Meyers resigned after eleven years the board of supervisors praised his efforts as receiving the "unqualified approval of all who have been acquainted with it."[134] Before leaving he reflected on the job:

> While much still remains to be done, which I contemplated doing before closing my work with the institution, I feel that not a misspent opportunity was let go where we were not fully engaged in doing what we could for the good of the institution. Now, as we leave our work, we wish again to thank you for the many kindly words of encouragement and sympathy in a work that cannot be any other than a tremendous weight upon the mind of any conscientious person. We have fully realized our responsibilities, have felt our weakness, and have endeavored to do our work to the best of our ability.[135]

Having taken over from E. P. Titus after his fatal accident, Meyers constructed the new asylum, managed both institutions simultaneously, broke new farmland, and handled the care of more than 100 residents. Despite the frustrations, their comfort and care were his top priority, a mission reflected in his daily diary entries and his annual messages to county officials whom he encouraged to provide good food, good health care, clean spaces, and fresh air. He lost a child at the institution and faced tribulations with employees. Although he claimed to have left some things unfinished, Meyers may have been worn out by the never-ending challenges inherent in a superintendent's job. For many superintendents, the labor of women was a critical component of their success.

4 Poor Farm Women

"Women were too proud to go out there."
—Emily Williams Smith, Interview, Montana Historical Society
   Research Center

In 1885, Johanna Antleman was sixty-six years old. Having raised two children, she lived with her husband on a farm, but the marriage was an unhappy one. She fled to the Dane County Poor Farm because of domestic abuse; her intake listed the reason for admission as "old age with husband too brutish to live with."[1] Violence in the family was not new, nor was using the poor farm as a resource. The year before, Johanna's brother-in-law Charles Antleman, a man described by neighbors as "an eccentric, violent-tempered farmer" shot his wife twice in the head before killing himself. She survived the assault, but the newspaper reported Charles "had long been regarded as a miserable, dangerous fellow, and his death caused the people of the neighborhood to breathe a sigh of relief." Johanna was not among those relieved by these events, living as she did with someone the press called "crazy Antleman." Johanna had stayed overnight at the farm previously, visiting her unmarried daughter Amelia who lived there with her infant daughter. Perhaps worried she would end up like her sister-in-law, Johanna went to the poor farm as a refuge from an abusive marriage.[2]

There are two histories of women at poor farms—those like Johanna and Amelia who needed a resource during different parts of their lifecycle, and women who utilized the institutions as opportunities for wage work.[3] The two are not mutually exclusive; residents like Amelia also sometimes worked for wages during their stay. The poor farm reveals the limited resources for rural women both in terms of paid employment and charity or relief.[4] With no maternity facilities, women went there to give birth. Young, unmarried women and laborers' wives whose families needed the income could earn wages cleaning, sewing, and cooking. With no shelters for abused women, they fled there to get away from dangerous spouses. Older women trying to piece together a living wage and widows could live and work on-site. When older women lacked a kinship network, they relied on poor farms to house them when they could no longer be self-sufficient.

In the growing literature about women and the social welfare system, women tend to be either recipients or arbiters of aid. Much of the maternalist welfare state situated relief in a middle-class, patriarchal notion of household organization where families were governed by a male head. Poor farms, never part of a welfare state per se, were outliers in this framework. Through their assistance of women county officials and superintendents circumvented traditional household governance by creating a different type of patriarchy. Despite the assertion that women did not go to poor farms, it was not necessarily pride that kept women away in large numbers: women had different resources. During the late nineteenth century, fewer women utilized poor farms than men, for a wide variety of reasons. Kinship networks were more likely to assist women than men, and other types of relief policies accommodated women. In their employment of women poor farms provided wage-earning jobs in rural areas at a time when those were sorely lacking.

Unlike many other types of relief during the Progressive Era, poor farms were not designed with women's input, aimed at women specifically, nor were they usually administered by women. Unlike examples such as the Indian Service, female employees were not necessarily tasked with teaching or modeling specific behaviors to residents; poor farms shared at least one similarity with the Indian Service in that they employed large numbers of women in government jobs, but at the local level. However, the amount and type of work they did—food preparation, gardening, nursing, laundry—placed them well outside the bounds of middle-class behavior and most closely resembled the labor of farm wives or boardinghouse operators.[5]

Poor Farm Matrons

Leading the female staff and tending to the residents was the job of the matron, the most visible female employee. Farm men may have worked from sunup to sundown, but women's work did not begin or end with the light of day. One study estimated that farm women averaged 100 hours of work a week no matter the season. Matrons did not run a normal farm household but instead practiced a form of professionalized housewifery. No facility could long function without one. Generally, county officials assumed that a woman hired with her husband came with a certain set of abilities from her time as a housewife. That assumption was not always a safe one, but hiring a farm wife was one way to virtually assure the matron had domestic skills.[6] If the institution was to be homelike, it was up to the matron to make it so. When they succeeded, they were praised for being "industrious and large-hearted," and for taking good care of an "exceedingly troublesome family."[7] While the role of household patriarch was filled by the superintendent, any emphasis placed on domesticity frequently fell to matrons.

Counties were advised to choose their matron carefully. Although one critic called matrons "a public official by marriage," some were considered as part of hiring decisions for their husbands. Reformer Mary Vida Clark reinforced this idea, saying, "The matron, while usually appointed for no other reason than that she is the wife of the keeper, frequently brings to her work a thorough knowledge of housekeeping, a conscientious devotion to her work, and an abundance of sympathy and tact."[8] Inclined county officials could interview both husband and wife for the positions, and many matrons made a wage specified in the contract.[9] H. W. Giles suggested that, "Having found a man who is all right, before a bargain is closed the proper officers or committee should visit his house and look upon his wife. If she 'stretcheth out her hand to the poor,' if 'she openeth her mouth with wisdom, and in her tongue is the law of kindness,' if 'she looketh well to the ways of her household, and eateth not the bread of idleness,' if 'her children rise up and call her blessed, her husband also, and he praiseth her,' let the bargain be closed with a fair salary." Like the complicated expectations for superintendents, counties asked a lot of matrons.[10]

In their capacity as public employees, women were subjected to some of the same oversight as their husbands. The matron at the Sandusky County, Ohio, Infirmary received praise in an otherwise blistering exposé published in a Cleveland newspaper. A reporter doing a follow-up claimed that "the work of Mrs. Stine as matron of the home should be given in any article in which the institution is mentioned." She took on the unenviable task of stocking the cellars, which were apparently empty when she and her husband arrived. During 1926, she put up 3,000 quarts of produce and 1,000 pints of jams and jellies.[11] Likewise, women perceived as failing in gendered expectations of caregiving were called to task. Nancy Hamlin, who served as a matron for five years, was cited for her lack of compassion: "There seems to be a lack of motherly kindness and humanity in her methods. She governs her household as though it was a reformatory rather than a home retreat for the unfortunate beings under her charge; governs by fear rather than by kindness and sympathy. She is a good governor but not a tender nurse." There may have been few more critical assessments of a poor farm matron published.[12]

The difficult tasks facing matrons did not go unnoticed, and county officials acknowledged the role they played, calling Wisconsin's Viola Titus "untiring" even though her husband failed to mention her in his own records, and Indiana's twenty-seven-year-old Ida Scott "excellent" while running the "[best-] conducted institution of the kind to be found in Indiana." Scott had at least two young children to raise during her time at the farm, in addition to tending the house and its residents.[13] Will County, Illinois, officials lauded Margaret Rost, commending the "splendid services of Mrs. Rost in the conduct of the business of the County Farm, and endors[ing] the able manner in which she has assisted Captain Rost in the management of his duties as Superintendent. Her services have been invaluable."[14] For a short time, the Williams County, Ohio, Infirmary featured a section in its annual report called "Matrons Report," which explained how much food was produced and used from the farm. In 1895, during a serious national depression, the report included thousands of pounds of meat, hundreds of loaves of bread, 318 pounds of butter, and 121 dozen eggs, all going toward feeding staff, residents, and visitors. Garments made included shirts, skirts, pantaloons, and pillowcases.[15]

Matrons faced daunting daily tasks of cooking, cleaning, laundry, nursing, and outdoor jobs including gardening. Although many poor farms were improved between the late nineteenth and early twentieth centuries, cleaning chores were constant, and sometimes blamed on the "characteristics and habits of the class of people who become almshouse inmates [that] make immaculateness impossible."[16] While no other job for women in the nineteenth century quite mimicked this type of effort, women who ran boardinghouses may have been able to commiserate. Matrons had the added burden of caring for residents with a wide range of needs and abilities.[17] Occasionally women performed the job of a matron without the title. Eliza Plummer was listed in the 1870 census as keeping house, but the house she was keeping was the county poor farm, and inside were thirty-nine residents, four of whom were listed as insane, three of whom were blind, and one listed as idiotic. No hired staff were living on the property, and both of her sons attended school. Plummer undoubtedly did the job whether she had the title or not.[18]

Inventories at poor farms typically highlight the importance of the farm and indicate far fewer items were in the home to simplify the matron's job.[19] Two inventories from 1897 and 1905 have more than fifty items listed before a household tool appears. The house of twenty-five residents managed by matron Susan Shumaker had a refrigerator, hand-washer, thirty flat irons, fifty chamber pots, a butter churn, a sewing machine, and a gas stove. It is a list that summarizes a matron's responsibilities.[20] Between 1885 and 1892 during Ella Gamble's tenure as a matron, her institution had no running water and no plumbing, which she pointed out when she visited the farm again fifty years later as a guest. At the time she began as matron, she was newly married and only around twenty years old. Her husband was thirty-seven. She had two children while there, making her experience undoubtedly challenging. Among the changes she and her husband helped implement were a water supply and sewer disposal, after the spring was contaminated and caused an outbreak of typhoid.[21]

Alexander Johnson spent only two pages of his almost 300-page manual of poor farm suggestions on matrons, whom he tellingly called "house-mother[s]."

He recommended not hiring couples with children like the Gambles to run the poor farm because "a young mother with a group of little children of her own to care for, will have neither the time nor strength for these duties." Many women proved him wrong on that count. Johnson pointed out that while a successful farmer's wife would be most likely to excel in the position, managing the labor of others was also part of the job, which was a skill more likely possessed by a woman used to having household help.[22] Other characteristics of the job separated poor farm matrons from their peers. In 1933, an Auburn, Indiana, newspaper reported the death of local matron Nelia Morr, who had a heart attack while churning butter in the basement. She was fifty-four years old, and her husband told the paper that she must have only recently started churning, based on the appearance of the milk in the churn.[23] While all farm work was physically demanding and farm homes fell behind modernizing standards, matrons were not balancing time between the fields and the house: they were doing wage labor that their husbands depended on as a condition of employment. There were instances where the matron was not married to the superintendent: a Michigan superintendent noted that he "never meddled with the ladies" because the matron, "a fair-sized Dutch lady," did such work.[24]

Although Johnson objected to hiring couples with young children, counties did so anyway. Matrons Julia Glines, Viola Titus, and Adelaide Meyers all gave birth during their time as matrons. Two of the women lost those children in infancy. For poor farm matrons, raising children in a poor farm meant additional challenges. When Charlotte Farmer and her husband Edwin started their twenty-year careers, in 1878, their three children were nine, seven, and two years old—probably giving more worry than help—but as the children grew they provided additional labor. In 1900, their youngest daughter, Lottie, was a "servant" on the farm, and their other daughter and her husband were also employees. Charlotte's wages as matron increased from $100 to $500 over their tenure. While this appears to be a considerable sum of money for a woman to earn during this time period—one study noted that 77 percent of working women made less than $8 per week—the wages earned by Charlotte Farmer included the labor of her daughters as well.[25]

Charles and Amy Reed also brought children to their jobs at the Sangamon County Poor Farm. When they began, their youngest daughter was ten and there were seven older siblings. Relatives recall visiting them on weekends, playing with wheelchairs on the staircase, and enjoying meals. Amy Reed was noted for her care of the older women at the institution. Having older children aided in running the large institution, which frequently had more than 100 residents. Reed and her daughters had a tall task: previously the institution had been regularly and publicly criticized by no less prominent a group than the Russell Sage Foundation for being dirty and not providing good care. The

Reeds improved the institution and held their positions for twelve years, until Charles died in 1927.[26]

County officials were well aware of the benefits the superintendent's family could bring: in 1894, nineteen-year-old Cora Foncannon, the daughter of the Dade County, Missouri, superintendent, became sick. County officials noted that they were "very sorry to report the superintendent's daughter sick and has been very bad for three weeks, consequently it makes it very hard on them, it leaves the burden of the housework on Mrs. Foncannon, which is very heavy. There are several of the inmates that are helpless and they require a great deal of waiting on." Cora recovered, but her illness had increased her mother's responsibilities, which officials recognized as being typically shared between the two women.[27] The family labor used on poor farms was noted by reporters as well. Although highly critical of the institution she visited, Octave Thanet from *Atlantic Monthly* had nothing but compliments for the women helping to run it: "The keeper's wife and daughters . . . were neatly dressed and gave every token of being of a kindly disposition. I believe that they tried hard to make their charges comfortable and that whatever abuses were apparent were caused in the main by the construction of the house."[28] These children helping their mother made a good impression, but Nancy Hamlin's sons were more liability than asset. Their negligent and crude behavior was used against Hamlin and her husband when both boys were accused of mistreating dead bodies and harassing the residents.

Helen Hammett, whose parents ran the Pleasants County, West Virginia, Poor Farm in the 1930s, remembered helping her mother, who did the cleaning, cooking, and laundry for the ten or so residents. Helen recalled, "I bet I made ten million buckwheat pancakes." They got a gas-powered washing machine to help with laundry that Helen described as "never ending." Hammett's father died on the job in 1940, but the rest of the family stayed and Hammett's mother and brother remained until 1950.[29] Margaret Marsh also remembered her mother, Stella, doing all the cleaning, cooking, and laundry for between fifteen and twenty residents at the Blount County, Tennessee, Poor Farm. She had one hired woman who helped supply the kitchen with wild greens, while her husband had two hired men.[30] In addition to kitchen and domestic tasks, some women handled the clerical aspects of poor farm management. Maud Ellis, wife of Otis Ellis, served as the poor farm clerk, for which she earned $25 per month. The institution hired other women to care for residents and cook.

Cora Williams in Yellowstone County, Montana, also did all the bookkeeping and record keeping required by the county and state, in addition to much of the domestic work, for $50 monthly. The institution had a nurse for the sick ward when necessary, but Williams handled details including delousing new residents and keeping up with a bed bug problem. She worried about her daughters being near men who might have syphilis. Emily Williams Smith re-membered being slightly afraid of some of the men, but also helping with chores such as ironing and scrubbing floors.[31] Her mother was not alone in worrying about the contact her children had with certain residents. Some relationships were remembered fondly, like those the three Ogard boys made in Nebraska with Sarah, a blind former enslaved woman who sometimes wandered into their room in the middle of the night thinking it was daytime, and Old Joe, a lifelong resident who helped with chores. But there could be stigma attached to working at the poor farm because they lived alongside "the disabled, the deformed, the mentally ill, the grotesquely ugly" and the sick. The Ogards, who managed a poor farm from 1922 until 1933, reported that people occasionally drove by the farm and threw things while shouting obscenities, and someone shot the children's two dogs from the road.[32] The constant presence of sick residents also made living at the farm dangerous for matrons' families. Along with the acutely sick were those with long-term illnesses such as tuberculosis and syphilis, and the medical care provided is the subject of chapter 7. These incurable residents joined those with debilitating and sometimes dangerous mental illness. States urged counties to remove indigent children from the poor farm environment for these reasons, but the children of poor farm employees were not included in these calls.[33]

When poor farm residents required nursing not every county provided one, so the matron performed those duties, even when it was difficult or dangerous.[34] A skin cancer patient in Allen County, Indiana, suffered as the disease destroyed parts of his face and received much of his routine care from the matron. C. J. Johnston remembered his grandmother caring for that patient. "Grandma was gentle," he said. "She was the one who brushed his open face with Kloria. He said she was an angel of mercy." Charlotte Farmer helped rehabilitate the legs of an orphan named Amy Carter who lived at the farm from the time she was thirteen. Amy was not a good candidate for home placement, so she did tasks around the institution and was taken under Farmer's wing. She eventually worked for wages on the farm and married one of the Farmer's sons.[35] The role of the poor farm as a hospital, hospice, and clinic meant that matrons were intimately involved with health care, which sometimes placed their labor well outside the bounds of what would be expected from either farm wives or middle-class women.

Given the wide range of tasks associated with the poor farm that were gen-dered, it is somewhat surprising that there were women who oversaw the entire operation. It was most common in cases where the husband died on the job as superintendent. Antebellum records from Ohio and Massachusetts show women serving in that circumstance, as did Indiana's Clarissa Shaw, who had two grown sons to help "clean up the property and build fence" at a time when male labor was scarce during the Civil War.[36] Historian Heli Meltsner noted that following the war, institutions in Massachusetts hired women to serve as superintendents but typically at facilities without farms, suggesting that officials there demarcated the tasks of management between care of residents inside the institution and the external needs of a farm operation.[37] Some women did, however, manage institutions with farms. In 1899 Elk County, Kansas, kept on their widowed matron who had been at the farm since it opened in 1887.[38]

Widow Edna White worked for Colusa County, California, for more than fifteen years as both superintendent and matron. Before her husband's death she served as the assistant superintendent while raising two young children. After he died she took over his position, raising her children, managing the care for between twenty-five and forty-five residents, and supervising a staff that included a steward, a farmer, a washer man, nurses, and a Chinese cook. White sometimes drew the ire of state visitors because her institution needed updating, with one writing that he was "not satisfied with place" and that it "needs some careful and continuous visiting to determine real conditions." Since many of the complaints were about structural problems out of her control, she improved what she could, including cleanliness, diet, and the isolation of tubercular patients. Everyone bathed weekly and got their own towels and fresh linens, and the thirty-nine-acre farm produced corn, potatoes, fruit, pork, and chicken.[39] During the 1910s White made $75 a month, which increased during the 1920s to $100. She worked at the facility as matron until at least 1930, and in that census the enumerator assumed that the farmer, a man named Herman Bowers, was the head of the property. He was listed first in the enumeration as "head" and White, while listed as the matron, is the last entry, where it is unclear if she is a resident or a staff member. White's daughter served as the bookkeeper. North Carolina also had female superintendents, at least one of whom served for thirty-seven years under less than desirable circumstances, as her employer refused to pay for running water and sewage service. Despite this, they reportedly had a decent institution of cottages. According to visitors, "Mrs. Williams has made the Craven County home one of the most homelike and attractive in the state."[40]

Julia Glines managed the Summit County Infirmary for multiple years without her husband. When she and her husband were hired, she was pregnant and had a young daughter. Glines suffered the loss of that baby, and her husband, a farmer and Civil War veteran, died in 1878.[41] She served as the superintendent for four years without him. Toward the end of her tenure at the institution, the county and state board of charities launched an investigation about fraud, theft, and mistreatment of the residents. Employees, residents, and a few neighbors testified that among other things, Glines gave county property to her daughter and son-in-law, that she abused certain residents, and that supplies purchased with county money were missing. Glines publicly responded to the accusations:

This trouble has originated with my enemies. The good people of Summit County have made no complaints, you notice. There have been none from any respectable lady or gentleman out of the hundreds who have visited the institution. Chaplain Byers, of Columbus, in a printed report has ranked our infirmary among the first in the state. He made annual visits and has often said, 'I can't help noticing how this institution has been improved.' I deny that we had three dead babies at once; but four babies in all have died in 14 years. I deny, too, that I ran away to escape investigation. I attended an infirmary conference in Holmes County, and having then severed my connection here I paid my own expenses. I have been so filled with disgust at the charges made that I haven't read them myself—my children have read them to me.

One of the complaints against Glines had to do with the condition of the farm. Since county directors hired a man to manage the farm, he answered directly to them. Glines admitted to not knowing much about the farm operations but did acknowledge it was in bad condition. County officials, for their part, stood up for her, agreeing that certain farm-related issues were not her fault and that they had "no reason to doubt the correctness of her reports—not in the least; nor her honesty, nor integrity in the management of the institution." But, her gender and the presence of a farm to run clearly played a role in her departure: "We [the directors] talked the matter over and came to the conclusion that it would be best to make a change, because we thought that a woman who had had to depend on a hired man [the farm manager] could not run it satisfactorily."[42] Her opponents also cited her gender as a problem, with a former superintendent remarking that "he didn't think a woman was a fit person to run a farm," and accusing her of embezzlement. It was later revealed that one of his relatives applied for her job. At least one of the directors believed that this former superintendent was responsible for leading the attack on her character and reputation. A. G. Byers from the state board of charities claimed he received a letter questioning the "legality of employing a woman as Superintendent of a County Infirmary." Byers indicated that there was no law to prevent it, and he "congratulated the Directors upon securing her for Superintendent." In the end, the investigation found that some of the expenses were questionable, and potentially in violation of the law, but that the directors themselves were most at fault for this problem. Glines was cleared of accusations of cruelty, theft, and corruption but lost her job anyway.[43]

Despite these issues, Julia Glines was not the last female superintendent in Summit County. Sherman and Della Stotler managed the institution together for twenty-five years until his death in 1912. They were paid a total of $1,500 annually for at least the last five years of their work, and the farm and home appear to be well managed and the residents happy. The county decided to hire Della to serve out the rest of the contract. They noted she was "fully capable of filling the position." That fall, farm business proceeded normally, and Della Stotler appears to have maintained the status quo until a new superintendent was hired the following year.[44] The example of the Stotlers' custodianship indicates that not only were women an integral part of a successful poor farm management scheme, but that county officials were capable of separating the needs of the residents from that of the farm in order to keep good employees. Having lived her life on a farm, Della knew enough to keep the institution afloat.

Female Employees

Faced with considerable responsibilities, matrons benefitted from having female employees. By hiring everyone from teenagers to aging widows, poor farms served as economic engines, paying wages for sewing, cleaning, cooking, and nursing. The need for wage-earners in a cash-strapped farm economy played a crucial role in family finances. Likewise, saving money in anticipation of a wedding was a desirable and sometimes necessary preparation for young women to set up their households. But finding domestic help on farms, let alone on poor farms, was not always easy. Cities and towns were a strong draw for younger farm women seeking work. An 1894 State of Wisconsin report asked more than 500 farmers about wage laborers, and more than 70 percent said they had increased wages for women because "many girls think it degrading to be [a] hired girl. . . . Too high toned to work on a farm. . . . Farm work too hard." That type of labor was magnified at poor farms.[45]

Ed Sweeney, who documented his time as a resident of a poor farm, discussed the female employees, who typically labored in the kitchen. He claimed at least one matron selected women who were incompetent at their tasks to make herself look better. Whether or not that was the case, bringing in young women to cook for dozens of people was no doubt a trial-and-error scenario. Sweeney, who thought highly of himself and less so of his fellow residents, claimed that the employees did their share of flirting with the men, including him, which gave residents something to gossip about and boosted his spirits. The interaction with residents no doubt gave the hired staff something to break the monotony of cooking, baking, washing, ironing, and sweeping. Where Sweeney lived, hired women split their time between chores for the residents and chores for the superintendent and his family, which may indicate that the superintendent paid the household staff out of his own pocket, a not uncommon occurrence when counties refused to pay for household staff but were more inclined to pay for hired hands.[46]

Being a domestic at a poor farm came with different experiences from serving for a family: more employees to socialize with, more activity, and in all likelihood, less oversight as busy matrons and superintendents did other tasks. However, female staff did not stay with any consistency. Superintendents Titus and Meyers in Wisconsin made visits to local farmers in order to try and hire their daughters. The Gordon family received visits on multiple occasions because they had daughters of working age. Twenty-year-old Jane agreed to work at the poor farm and stayed at least eight months. Her family had three other adult children at home to do chores.[47] In 1906, Josie Offerdahl cooked at the poor farm the year before her marriage and move to Madison. She was twenty-two and the oldest of eight children. She had been previously employed as a dressmaker. Like many women her age, she may have been trying to establish a nest egg for her new life as a married woman.[48] Some women already working as domestics or servants also took a turn working at poor farms. Emma Edseth did so in 1908 before moving on to domestic labor in Madison and eventual self-employment as a dressmaker.

The wages paid to women at poor farms varied, just like those of men. In the early 1900s Ina Cherry, Nettie Harris, Eva Frantz, and Daisy Sanders were on an Ohio poor farm payroll making $26 a month. This wage placed them well above the mean earnings of other servants who made on average $144 a year without board.[49] Twenty years later Etta and Pearl Basinger, two of eleven children, worked at their local poor farm for a substantial $40 to $50 a month.[50] Like many poor farm employees, they stayed a few months, made what money they wanted or needed, and then left for other opportunities. People like the Basinger sisters could make life at the poor farm much easier for the superintendent and his wife. In Michigan, the superintendent of a seventy-resident poor farm noted that he and his wife employed two "girls" to help with cleaning and cooking. In 1909, they paid between $4.50 and $5 per week but struggled to retain staff because of "the attractions of factory work in the city." One of his peers claimed a similar problem, causing him to hire a husband and wife to split the farm and house tasks for $35 a month, which included room and board.[51] Married women typically appeared in payroll statements for situational tasks such as sewing.[52]

Widows and single women were the most common hires at poor farms. Cooking was steady employment for both Gertie Stuckey, a thirty-three-year-old single woman, and Elizabeth Patterson, a forty-two-year-old widow. After her only son married, fifty-one-year-old widow Mary Winkleman served as a poor farm nurse until she remarried. One of her coworkers was sixty-five-year-old widow Francis Cole, a seamstress. At the time Cole and Winkleman were employed, eight other servants, including three women from the Kiehl family, worked at the Summit County Infirmary, which had 150 residents. The Kiehls lived on a farm in a neighboring county.[53] In 1900, while thirty-year-old Ida Ritchie and her husband served as assistant matron and assistant superintendent, her twin sister Ada was the cook. Ada later worked a seamstress while boarding in the home of her former poor farm colleague Lyda Acker, an arrangement that

Finding a job at the poor farm was a good way for local women to earn wages and work in a more social setting than in a private house as a domestic. Doing the wash for an entire institution was time-consuming work. Photo courtesy of Steven Mizer.

suggests some comradery among female employees.[54] Poor farms competed for domestic help with local farmers, and in the 1910s between half and a quarter of midwestern farmers reported hiring female labor.[55] Serving in a home did not carry the burdens of washing, sewing, cleaning, and cooking for a crowd, nor would it have the stigma of working at the poor farm. However, complaints of overwork, low pay, boredom, and no privacy or entertainment, all made domestic labor in the country undesirable.[56]

Poor farms also employed single mothers, a demographic that struggled to find jobs that allowed them to keep their children. Dane County, Wisconsin, had at least two residents-turned-employees, who were both unmarried and gave birth at the poor farm. In early 1880, Amelia Antleman arrived at the poor farm pregnant and involved in a bastardy case. Antleman and Julia Parrott, another single mother, were both living at the farm when they were hired after some of the staff quit. Parrott's son died during a scarlet fever outbreak and she was fired alongside her future husband for insubordination. Antleman stayed with her daughter for more than a year until she married a local widower. There is no evidence that the county garnished their wages for their stays, which suggests the earnings were viewed as a path toward leaving the institution.[57]

Older women also benefitted from earning wages while they lived at the poor farm, although they were less likely to have the opportunity because they were considered unlikely to live independently again. After a life of physical labor, Summit County Infirmary resident "Aunt" Phyllis Burney did the cooking until she became too ill to do so. When she had to stop, the quality of the meals apparently declined considerably, and residents complained that they missed her cooking. An employee testified that "when the old colored woman was sick the food was not properly cooked," and Burney was quoted as saying, "there is plenty to cook but when I ain't about the rest don't know how to cook. . . . I used to make rice soup, and make drop dumplings, doughnuts, and all such things that the girls don't know how to make." She noted that the hired girls did not know how to cook for such a large group of people.[58] Burney told reporters and investigators that she came to Ohio around the time of John Brown's execution and that she purchased freedom for herself and a son. Three of her sons were still missing, and she used the interview opportunity to publicize her desire to find them.[59] It is unclear if they reunited, and Burney died of exhaustion in 1894, still at the infirmary, at the age of ninety-five.[60]

Women Living at the Farm

Assertions that women were the primary residents of poor farms apply most accurately to the antebellum period and to urban almshouses. Nationwide, ratios of women to men declined after the Civil War (see appendix), and eventually men outnumbered women in poor farms, sometimes by as many as three to one.[61] After the Civil War, women ceased to make up 50 percent of poor farm residents in any of the aggregate census data. Officials noted the skewed ratio of men to women, and tried to understand the reasons.[62] In 1905, the secretary of the California State Board of Charities, W. A. Gates, noted that of the 2,899 "paupers," only around 10 percent were women. He accounted for it by saying that "almost all of the males in the hospital are old bachelors, so that you see the women of California have been able to maintain themselves, and keep out of the county poorhouses, and those of them who have gotten married have been able to keep their husbands out. The conclusion is evident to the unmarried man."[63] Gates was right: more men who lacked immediate family went to poor farms than women.

The only study specific to women in almshouses was completed in the early 1890s by sociologist Mary Roberts Smith on behalf of Stanford University. She studied the 228 women living at the San Francisco Almshouse, but did so with a nativist attitude. For example, while analyzing nationality, Roberts Smith commented: "If to the characteristics of Celtic temperament in the mass be added the emotional instability of women, it is easy to see that the Irish women of the immigrant class could scarcely fail to exhibit the results of so fatal a combination in an overwhelming preponderance in the almshouse." She concluded that working-class women were less likely to be rendered wholly dependent by widowhood, the result of middle-class women lacking marketable skills. As she phrased it, "if the common woman were intelligently trained for self-support as well as the duties of marriage, the spectacle of the disruption and dependence of families because of woman's incapacity would be comparatively rare."[64] This issue of women depending on men—and the dangers inherent in it—have been discussed not only by historians such as Kathy Peiss and Mimi Abramovitz, but also in nineteenth-century literature, as in Edith Wharton's *The House of Mirth*. Women not trained to earn wages because of their class status were economically vulnerable because they lacked employment experience.[65]

Most of the women Roberts Smith interviewed previously worked as domestics and had at least one child; it was more likely for poor farm women to be mothers than the men to be fathers. When trying to establish why these children were not taking care of their mothers (whose average age was sixty-three), Roberts Smith reached an interesting conclusion: "A crotchety, quarrelsome, sensitive old woman, who can do very little work and who thinks much should be done for her, is a serious burden in any poor family, and a source of family trouble anywhere. The majority of women in the almshouse are difficult of temper." The same could be said of men with children as well, but that it deserved highlighting in this study of women is instructive of the passivity and gratitude expected of women when at the mercy of their children. Occasionally, a poor farm account echoed Roberts Smith's opinion. Connecticut's Betsy Babcock was recorded as "so unpleasant to get along with no one would care for her although she has money." Brown County, Illinois, had a sixty-year-old woman whose entry said, "cranky—has 80 acres of land."[66] Typically property enticed someone to step in and provide care, but her temperament may have also hinted at larger health issues such as pain or a form of dementia.

Overall, women were more welcomed inside other people's households than men, which in turn kept them out of poor farms. The "efficacy of strong kinship networks" especially for groups marginalized from public resources such as American Indians, African Americans, and Mexican Americans is often assumed by scholars, but poor farm records suggest that those connections kept more women of all races and ethnicities out of poor farms. The emphasis on the nuclear family was a middle-class concept, and lower-income households were more likely to contain extended family. As poor farms made clear, there was a growing reliance on nonfamilial sources to handle the care obligations previously assigned to relatives.[67] Children may have felt they owed their mothers care, and even sick women might help with small tasks. Although they had less opportunity to make enough money to self-support, women could offset their expense with domestic labor.[68] Men whose bodies were worn out, on the other hand, sometimes upset the patriarchal role of the husband, contributed almost nothing to another person's household because of their unlikelihood to contribute to domestic tasks, and as a result were more likely to find themselves at the poor farm if they were unattached to an immediate family.[69]

Women during the late nineteenth and early twentieth centuries were expected to be part of a family unit, so living at a poor farm signaled some type of dysfunction. Single women were not supposed to have children, disobey parents, or leave home before marriage; women with adult children were supposed to rely on them for care; married women were to live with husbands who were supposed to provide for their families. Officials allowed single women to keep their children and take them when they left; poor farms allowed children to leave their mothers in the care of strangers; they allowed women escaping abuse to utilize the institutions as a form of "moral economy" of the community, even though doing so broke up households. This interventionism relates to what Elizabeth Pleck outlined as the "consistent barrier to reform against domestic violence," the "family ideal . . . family privacy, conjugal and parental rights, and *family stability* [emphasis mine]."[70] The lack of stability within homes because of poverty or abandonment gave county officials an opening to offer women shelter. Women using poor farms as refuges from abuse was not new; records indicate that the Philadelphia Almshouse, one of the country's oldest, regularly accepted women who complained of being beaten and abused by men. Local poor farms provided an outlet for women close to home that they could use for the same purpose.[71] When familial norms broke down, for whatever reason, women joined the atypical family structure of poor farms.[72]

Pregnancy, Birth, and Bringing Children to the Farm

No group of poor farm women was given more national attention than those who had children at the poor farm. Although county officials intervened by placing some children out, they were less interventionist than charitable aid groups. This laxity did not go unnoticed. In 1879, when Josephine Shaw Lowell took the stage at the National Conference of Charities and Corrections, she recounted anecdotes of dozens of women living inside New York county poorhouses who, because of their "degradation" and ability to move in and out of the institution freely, had given birth to numerous illegitimate children. They ran the gamut of young, old, widowed, and affected with intellectual disability, but their shared traits included multiple stays of long duration at the poorhouse and "depraved" behavior. Her examples included a thirty-five-year-old woman from Otsego County first married at age thirteen. She had since married two more times and had seven living children. She had spent twelve years in poorhouses. Many of the women had a family history of poverty.[73] Lowell claimed: "The community itself is responsible for the existence of such miserable, wrecked specimens of humanity. These mothers are women who began life as their own children have begun it, inheriting strong passions and weak wills, born and bred in a poorhouse, taught to be wicked before they could speak plain, all the strong evil in their nature strengthened by their surroundings and the weak good crushed and trampled out of life." Lowell recommended punishments for "moral insanity" in reformatories with long sentences, so women's behavior and sexuality could be more stridently policed: "Such training would be no child's play, since the very character of the women must be changed," but she made no suggestions for the incarceration of the men who impregnated them.[74]

This type of language eventually found a home in the eugenics movement, where it fueled state legislation for mandatory sterilizations and institutionalization for women of childbearing age classified as feebleminded. Few poor farm ledgers, however, specifically singled out the sexual promiscuity of women as their reason for admission. There were, of course, women listed as pregnant and those who arrived alone with children. Sometimes they were simply noted as "bad girls."[75] One woman referred to as "a noted character" was taken by the chief of police to her local poor farm. Reputed to be a "dope fiend of the most depraved order," a reporter recalled her "twenty-five years ago, when she commenced going to the bad, as a very pretty young woman" who had since been living in squalor and filth.[76] A Michigan woman, "not considered very virtuous," had her shanty pulled down by officials, so she and her children spent the winter at the poor farm before leaving together.[77] These classifications in poor farm records and the intervention by local officials were the exception and not the norm. More intakes were women like Sarah Vogt, who gave birth at her local poor farm in 1881, and Ellen McMeans who gave birth in 1884. Both were in their twenties and had no husband listed. Prior to going to the farm, Vogt had lived with her sister and brother-in-law and their two children. Both of her parents were dead. Visiting county officials noted that a week after the birth Sarah was "very poorly." She appears to have survived, got married, and remained in the county her entire life. Her daughter Nellie, born at the poor farm, lived with her mother and stepfather and took his surname.[78] McMeans stayed for three years with her child, but ten days after he died, she left. In Vogt's case and that of other unmarried women, using the poor farm provided a path to normalcy.

Although the poor farm helped Vogt keep her child, it was just such behavior that spurred critics such as A. O. Wright of Wisconsin to suggest punishment with poor farm residency for single mothers.[79] He wanted them to stay and work off the cost of their care as punishment for immorality. But poor farms assisted women victims of assault as well. Bonnie Gross, whose grandfather helped a victim of incest, provided one documented case of a rape victim using a poor farm as a resource, but there were undoubtedly many more. The 1943 case required that the victim testify at her father's trial for incest. She was physically and emotionally supported by the superintendent and matron, who sat alongside her as she testified.[80] Typical attitudes of the nineteenth century were closer to that of Wright, and reflected by the New York Charities Aid Association, which recommended that no more than three pregnant women be allowed in the same ward or room, to "be as carefully isolated as the most infectious."[81] Alexander Johnson believed that being able to use the poor farm as a maternity hospital was "certainly more of an encouragement to immorality than a deterring influence," and there were county officials who agreed. In 1895 Ross County, Ohio, officials placed the blame for an increase in unwed mothers at their infirmary squarely on the shoulders of township trustees who were accused of "trying to fill up the county infirmary with enceinte women." Like Wright, Johnson thought that forcing women to remain and nurse the child should be required, laboring as she was able. He did say, however, that "the mother and her babe must be carefully and kindly treated and well nursed."[82] Writer Octave Thanet claimed to observe the following conversation about maternity on her tour of poor farms:

> "Seven of 'em has been born in this house since I come," said the matron. "I thank God they was all born dead but this one and one other, and I pray God this one may die, too." Then she spoke of a proposed law to take the children out of the almshouses. The [pregnant] girl interrupted her with an eager inquiry: "Will they take my baby away?" "You wouldn't want him brought up here, yourself, would you?" She looked up, with a sharp change of expression. "God knows I wouldn't! Anywhere else!"[83]

While a poor farm was not an ideal place to be born, the harsh position of the matron hints at the type of care pregnant women might have received at this institution. The proposed law that worried the young, pregnant woman did not pass.

Suggestions on how to solve the problems of women using poor farms to give birth varied widely. One involved severing parental rights for women who stayed longer than three years. Another was a mandatory prison sentence for anyone who engaged in sex with a female pauper under the age of forty-five. This was based on the idea that poor women reproducing magnified the problem of poverty and expense for the county.[84] Despite these ideas, women who gave birth at the farms do not appear to have faced any special punishment from officials. J. S. Meyers repeatedly took Amelia Antleman to Madison for a bastardy case involving her newborn daughter and gave her a job. Most had two choices: they could either stay long enough to gain their bearings and leave with their child, like Antleman, or they could have county officials place the child with another institution or a different family.

County officials did place out children, but thousands of them lived in poor farms because they were there with their mothers, and severing that tie was not done lightly. During the 1870s and 1880s, reformers demanded that children be removed from environments believed to cause long-term dependency. Ohio, for example, encouraged counties to open children's homes, often on the grounds of the poor farm. Michigan and Wisconsin opened state children's homes, and other places contracted with private charities. All had the immediate goal of getting children out of poor farms. Estimates indicate that during the campaign to remove children from poor farms, between one-third and one-quarter of the children there were under two years old, which strongly suggests that they were there with their mothers, and considered too young to be separated.[85] The removal of children came down to cost. County officials found it more affordable to care for the children inside the poor farms until local indentures could be arranged, and officials hesitated to take children from parents if the family had the potential to be reconstituted outside the institution.[86] Universal removal was an unmet goal; during the 1920s North Carolina reported seventy-nine children living in poor farms, forty-two born there and a few placed there as a sentence for delinquency. This was not uncommon; poor farms continued to serve as a stopgap measure for children despite reformers' efforts.[87] In 1934, Kansas reported with a fair amount of distress that there were sixty-two children who stayed at poor farms during the year, but failed to indicate how many of those children had a parent at the institution or how the Depression factored into their need for care.[88]

The poor farm typically represented the best chance parents had to keep their family together in a time of crisis. Significantly, Black women in the South lacked even the poor farm as an option. After the Civil War it became common to remand African American children to the guardianship of a white person, for whom that child would labor in a long-term indenture. Poor farms would have been on the front lines of such a policy had women arrived with their children. It is highly likely that this reason contributed to the smaller numbers of Black women entering institutions with their children. When they did, they struggled to keep their families intact. In 1881, widow Emma Watson left two of her sons at the Hardin County, Ohio, Infirmary for a month before reclaiming them. But she returned six months later with three children. Their time at the poor farm was again brief, and Watson took her family out three months later, but it was temporary. Early the next year Emma, with a baby on the way, returned. The infant died, and she and two children left again for good shortly after. It appears the Watsons had recently moved to the county, which may be why they lacked friends or connections to help them stay out of the farm. Watson may have already placed some of her children with friends and family, because in 1880 she had seven children under the age of fifteen in her home.[89]

Like Emma Watson, pregnant women used the poor farm because it was hard to find paying work. Of the nine babies born at one New York almshouse, all were still with their mothers when visitors saw them, and two of those women had been deserted by husbands.[90] Being pregnant at the poor farm was not at all uncommon: there were almost no resources for pregnant women in rural areas, and maternity homes were not widely available for single women until the early twentieth century.[91] Unlike religious institutions or Crittenton Homes, poor farms did not have the moral obligation of redeeming unwed women. There was no evangelism in their efforts, only utilitarianism, and occasionally employment. Maternity homes could selectively admit certain types of women, rejecting those with more than one child, women of color, and women who might be a bad influence on others.[92] Not only did poor farms admit pregnant women freely, some almshouses, like the one in Richmond, Virginia, appeared to have had a better reputation than the unwed mothers' homes nearby.[93] For some women, poor farms were their only recourse. Some single, pregnant women like Amelia Antleman were kicked out of their homes by family and left with no economic resources. Employers regularly fired women after learning of their pregnancies. The demographics of who gave birth in poor farms differ based on location. In urban poor farms like that of Bangor, Maine, more than two-thirds of the women who gave birth were immigrants.[94] Historian Regina Kunzel notes that women came to towns and cities to use the services of unwed mothers' homes for the anonymity and because there were few resources in rural areas other than the poor farms.[95]

At poor farms women who gave birth were not pampered, but they would not have had much to do beyond caring for their child and possibly doing small chores.[96] If they were lucky, other residents might provide company. Most poor farms did not have maternity wards. The prevalence of communicable diseases, the noise, and in some cases the filth, did not always make for good surroundings.[97] Lizzie Drum went to her local Illinois poor farm in 1888 and gave birth to a child who lived only twelve hours, and she was not alone: numerous records indicate that women giving birth at poor farms suffered the death of their infant.[98] Infant mortality at institutions was not good, but babies stood a better chance staying with their mothers. Giving birth at a poor farm provided access to health care that some women would have lacked had they delivered at home. Having a baby in bad conditions was not something confined to poor farm residents, however. Overcrowded, unventilated housing plagued cities in the United States, and farm homes could be little better. Historian Molly Ladd-Taylor documented the realities of farm women who labored up to the hour of delivery in fields and homes. Women reported not getting any rest and being back at work immediately after the birth, even when doing so was an obvious detriment to their health.[99]

It was rare for children to be abandoned at poor farms since they offered shelter to mother and child. The Dane County Poor Farm did have an infant left with a note pinned to her blankets which listed her birthday, said that her mother, a Catholic, was dead, and begged poor farm officials to take good care of her. The author of the note asked the finder of the child to "never forsake it."[100] Even though residents sometimes took children under their wings and treated them as pets, infants and toddlers without a mother to take care of them had the highest risk for death inside any institution.[101] The poor farm officials found a placement for this abandoned baby. Dane County also became embroiled in an infanticide investigation. Charles Gary and Mary Taylor were apparently unmarried but living together. When the couple realized that Mary was pregnant, Charles took her to the poor farm to give birth. Residents reported that Mary refused to nurse the baby and wished it dead, which speaks to the lack of privacy at poor farms even after delivering a baby. Shortly thereafter, Charles arrived and retrieved Mary and the child. The couple apparently tried to drop the child off at the farm, but officials forced them to take the baby. Tragically, the baby then went missing, prompting infanticide charges. The couple claimed that the baby died a natural death, but they were tried and convicted. Superintendent E. P. Titus testified about the birth and the involvement of the poor farm.[102] The county was also involved in Amelia Antleman's bastardy case, which disappeared from court records, but may have been prompted by officials seeking payment for her care. The matter may have been dropped when she married a local widower who informally adopted her daughter. In 1891, Ohio officials asked their county prosecutor to charge local Civil War veteran Julius Richards with bastardy so he could help pay for his child being supported by county funds.[103]

Married women with children who stayed at poor farms were a less controversial population. In 1870, the Henderson County, Illinois, Poor Farm enumeration showed five women with children staying at the institution. Of the twenty-two people there at that time, thirteen were members of family groups. None of their husbands were listed but their absence was often noted in the register with notes about abuse, "husband not working," "non-support," abandonment, "husband in jail," and divorce.[104] One Illinois woman whose husband was no longer providing for her arrived with three of her ten surviving children in 1903 when she needed temporary housing. The superintendent noted in the register that her children were "good kids." In the 1890s Ella Hallock used the poor farm twice, bringing her children with her because of problems with her husband, but both times they eventually returned home. By 1910, Ella had made some type of change. Although the census recorded her as married, she and the now adult children had moved to Minnesota from Illinois. She was the head of household and four of her children and one son-in-law were all employed and living with her.[105]

Women who brought their children to a poor farm risked losing custody, especially if the mother was not expected to recover her finances or health in order to resume raising the children. Sophrona Miner Harris grew up the second of eight children of a farm laborer in Illinois. She married in her early teens and she and her farm laborer husband moved frequently. They had at least seven children. During the 1880s, Harris and her children were admitted to the Henderson County, Illinois, poor farm. The children appear in the records repeatedly under the notes "parental neglect" and "destitute conditions." Obviously, things were dire. The children went through a cycle of multiple placements. When those failed the children ended up back at the poor farm. Nancy, the oldest daughter, ran away at age sixteen, but approximately ten years later she was living in the Hamilton County Poor Farm. One of the other girls, Rettie, married young but also continued to use the poor farm for temporary stays, including at least one when she was pregnant. When she left with the infant there was no destination listed. Female members of this family repeatedly relied on poor farms for help.[106] Their multigenerational poor farm use was not rare and would become one of the oft-repeated criticisms of the institutions: that they provided the means through which families continued to propagate poverty. For the Harris girls, growing up poor with parents trying to raise a large family on a laborer's salary and then marrying early were probably more telling predictors of poverty than using the local poor farm.

Sometimes the help provided by poor farms came too late, as was the case for Emma Rathburn, a German immigrant living in Illinois who died at a poor farm from starvation and exposure, having been "ill-treated and neglected by a husband who refused to support her." She was only twenty-seven years old and had three children under the age of five, living in a "tumble-down house."[107] Margaret Butler used the poor farm after the death of her husband in 1910 but could not keep her family together. She had her five youngest children with her; they ranged in age from sixteen to eight. Three months after they arrived, the youngest daughter was "adopted in Springfield." A month later a son was sent to the Illinois Asylum for Feebleminded Children. Six months after they arrived, two other children were sent to an orphan's home. Margaret left a week later with only her oldest daughter.[108]

Thirty-six-year-old Emma Beard Price arrived at the Dane County Poor Farm in 1881. Emma's family was likely in crisis around the time of her admission. She had recently been abandoned by her husband of three years, had a two-year-old, was pregnant, and had an older daughter from an unknown father. In 1880, Emma's mother and three adult brothers were struggling to find work and raise another grandchild; her father was in prison. The year Emma went to the farm, two of her brothers married and moved away. The family support was dissolving, and she had nowhere to go. Her older daughter disappeared from the records, but it is likely she was sent to the Wisconsin State School for Dependent Children. Eventually both her remaining children were placed out, the last in 1886, leaving her at the poor farm alone. With her family scattered and her children taken away, Emma stayed at the farm until 1906, when she was recorded as being "a great sufferer for several months previous to death."[109]

Because of the risks of family separation, women who came were often desperate. Emma Saxton was a twenty-five-year-old widow in 1895. At the height of a nationwide depression, she had six children under ten to care for. The oldest child, ten-year-old Cora, was a good candidate for placing out because she was old enough to work. She was taken by county officials and placed shortly after the family arrived. Charles, age eight, was placed next. Then two of the younger boys were sent to the Soldiers' and Sailors' Orphans' Home, indicating Emma's husband was a veteran. Things must have been severe for so many children to have been removed from her care, but it did not stop her from trying to earn a living. Emma left the farm in August with the two girls who were too young to be good candidates for placement or institutionalization. A year after they first arrived, Emma and the girls returned to the poor farm. Trying to find employment in a depression with two young children in tow had not been successful. For the next six months poor farm records reflected a family in turmoil. Emma took one of the placed-out children back, but the youngest were taken from her and placed, and the baby became sick. Emma did not leave again until November of 1897, but she did so without any of her children. No further records for any of the children remain, and Emma appears to have moved from a women's prison in 1900 to a domestic job in 1910.[110] In this circumstance the poor farm did not provide a path for a woman to keep her family together.

The help of family or the return of a spouse allowed some women to leave with their children. Gertrud Mills arrived at a poor farm in 1919 with her toddler. The register listed his parentage as "father unknown negro." Since Crawford County, Indiana, was considered a sundown county, this must have been a serious issue for Gertrud and a potentially deadly one for her partner. She was also recorded as having epilepsy. A year later she was back in her father's home, where she stayed through 1920 with her son. Sarah Bobbitt and her six children stayed in a poor farm for two weeks before her husband arrived to remove them all. With no accounting of her reason for admission, it is impossible to know why she and the children came to the farm.[111] Cases like these were increasingly rare by the 1920s, thanks to growing efforts at providing direct aid to women capable of managing their own household.

The increasing diversity of direct aid funds meant fewer women with children were admitted to poor farms during the early twentieth century. The effect of

veterans' pensions for widows and orphans is unclear, but the increasing emphasis placed on mother's aid and direct aid more generally helped keep women and
children in their own homes. As Susan Gooden points out, in some places the
recipients of mother's aid were separated from "the mass of paupers," and viewed
instead as "the epitome of motherhood." By keeping them out of the poor farm
that separation was physical as well as theoretical. A woman acknowledged as
having "divided her body by creating other lives for the good of the state" was
worthy of provisions better than the poor farm.[112] Ladd-Taylor notes that the
sentimental concept of (white) motherhood as a service to the state placed the
blame for the economic vulnerability of women with children on men.[113]

Using county funds, local officials subjectively awarded aid as they saw fit,
but mother's aid emphasized worthiness.[114] Mother's aid was not a windfall for
women, nor did it result in an overhaul of existing direct aid. Women without a
home were hard-pressed to use mother's aid because it supplemented household
expenses but did not cover the total. Discrimination against women of color and
single women was rife; they were excluded or received lower amounts of aid.
Places instituted residency requirements, prohibited aid for property owners,
denied divorced and abandoned women, and required social worker visits.[115] By
1919, a seemingly impressive thirty-nine states had mother's aid, but only sixteen
included deserted mothers, six allowed divorced mothers, and three specifically
permitted unmarried women to apply.[116] Unsurprisingly, studies like that done
by Kay Walters Ofman suggest that rural counties were consistently more likely
to offer aid benefits to single mothers than their urban counterparts. This tactic
consistently applied decades' worth of experience with direct aid. Mother's aid
added funds to the preexisting pattern of direct aid for women with children.
With different streams of potential direct aid and an increase in the number
of children's institutions including those where board could be paid to retain
guardianship of one's children, fewer women with children used poor farms by
the early 1900s.[117]

From One Patriarchy to Another

Poor farms were sites of substantial intervention when they took in women
fleeing family violence. Records suggest that they served in this role almost as
soon as they opened. Morgan County, Ohio, housed Katherine Ludlow and
her children briefly in the 1850s while her husband was in jail. They provided
her funds to return home to Pennsylvania, using local assistance to physically
sever the Ludlows' marriage. The county official told the superintendent she was
"sent to you because of cruel treatment by husband."[118] Fifty years later, tactics
to help women in abusive marriages were surprisingly similar. In 1901, directors
in Williams County, Ohio, called a special meeting to handle the case of the

Austin family. Mary Austin and her children went to the poor farm because her husband, Bud, was sentenced to six months in the workhouse for "cruelty to his wife and family." Lacking support, they went to the poor farm where officials confiscated their remaining property to pay for care. The Austins lost their land, fifteen hogs, two horses, a variety of tools, and the corn already harvested. The punishments intended for Bud fell hard on his victims. Bud and Mary had been married since 1887, and their children were all under five. The year before his arrest the family lived in a neighboring county on a rented farm. After their time at the poor farm, none of the Austins appear again in records.[119] In their case, the loss of an abusive breadwinner created a domino effect of harm. Even when jailed husbands were not abusive, their absence sent women to poor farms. At least two women with children stayed at the Butte County Hospital in the 1920s when their husbands were arrested for bootlegging.

While urban charity associations were beginning case work and home visits documenting abuse against women and children, county officials admitting women to poor farms did not always provide details. Maria Funston arrived at her local poor farm in 1880, sick and with her child. Her entry note said "ill health and disagreement with husband." That husband, John, was fifty years old, and between their marriage when she was fifteen and her entry to the farm, she had had at least seven children. Shortly after arriving, Maria's child died, and she followed shortly after from a "brain inflammation." Her husband claimed her body. Whether her illness sparked some disagreement, or he was unwilling/unable to take care of her and a sick child is unknown. In 1929, Butte County, California, records noted the admission of several women receiving medical treatment, "with broken bones." While they could have been injuries related to accident or illness, these are also injuries common to abuse victims.[120]

Women abandoned by husbands faced uncertain futures.[121] Pregnant Kate Mc-Clellon and her five children were left by her "drunkard" husband for months at their local poor farm before he returned and claimed his family. Their departure notation said, "*Bad Crowd.*"[122] Morgan Holmes of Iowa demanded county officials release his wife and four children. Mrs. Holmes claimed she was "helpless and homeless and in no way able to support herself and family. Being abandoned by her husband." While the county prepared to place the children out, Holmes "enticed his children from the poor farm" and his wife then left without permission. The county, angry at the imposition of being involved in a case that was perhaps not as clear as they believed, kept the Holmes's possessions until an attorney told them they had to return them to the family. The problems resulting from the dissolution of marriages and the stress of bad marriages was evident in women's institutional use.[123]

Measuring desertion or disruption of marriages is difficult because they sometimes ended informally or even temporarily. States had unique laws related to justifications for divorce but between 1867 and 1906, a period of rapidly increasing divorce rates, women received 66 percent of all divorces granted. The most common reasons for divorce in the late nineteenth century were desertion, adultery, cruelty, drunkenness, and neglect to provide. However, states frequently dictated a multiyear duration for these conditions before a divorce would be granted, which meant that married women who were abandoned, for example, might use a poor farm in a period when they were still legally married but ineligible for court-ordered support. Poverty alone was not typically a justification for divorce, and the rate of divorces decreased during the depression of the 1890s, which supports assertions that during periods of economic distress people were less likely to marry and more likely to informally dissolve a marriage without a divorce. Desertion or abandonment, a "poor man's divorce," was more commonly used by economically insecure couples.[124]

Because poor farm officials did not do much investigating of circumstances, women did sometimes claim to be widowed when they either dissolved a marriage or were abandoned: it made getting support easier and allowed them to remarry quickly. Small-scale studies suggest that this was historically more common among couples married a shorter amount of time, in part because it was harder for couples to simply separate if there were children, community, and property involved.[125] Minnie Rupert briefly stayed in her local poor farm in 1899 before being dismissed to go live with her parents. A newspaper report from 1900 claimed that Minnie was "after her husband." He had been convicted of grand larceny in November of 1898, shortly before she went to the poor farm. He then spent a year in jail. After his release, the paper claimed that he refused to support her and that she was compelled to earn her own living.[126] The census taker recorded her as having been married for eight years and having had two children, with one surviving, but there is no record of what happened to the child.[127] She remarried the following year, listing herself as a widow, despite the fact that her first husband appeared to be very much alive and that her divorce case was listed in an Indiana newspaper in 1902.[128]

It was rare for healthy, young, unmarried women to use poor farms since their labor was highly sought, but they appear sporadically in records. In 1891, twenty-year-old Zilpha Wilson arrived at her local poor farm for reasons unknown. She stayed during the summer and early fall before leaving. Almost nothing is recorded about her stay. Her records in the census suggest that her previous home life was not orderly. In 1870, when she was a year old, she lived with a domestic servant named Elizabeth Wilson. By 1880, Elizabeth did not have custody of Zilpha and her whereabouts are unknown, but to be at the poor farm as a young woman suggests she did not have family to rely on for help or housing. After leaving the poor farm, Zilpha married a local laborer and started a family; the poor farm had provided her a temporary shelter.[129]

Although poor farms served more men than women in the period from 1870 to 1930, they were still significant spaces for women. Female poor farm employees faced challenging circumstances but usually did their jobs well, caring for strangers and making needed wages. Their labor could make the institutions cleaner, better places for residents. Matrons frequently acted as both farm wife and wage laborer, even occasionally serving as superintendents themselves. Whether as residents or employees, women used poor farms as resources and an alternative to their reliance on unstable or financially unsuccessful patriarchs. The intervention into domestic life that poor farms provided did not save everyone: Johanna Antleman's fate is unclear, but her daughter Amelia managed to earn money, leave with her child, marry, and enjoy a normal life. Poor farms allowed some women like Amelia to bounce back—recovering their health, keeping their families together, or making wages to begin a new life. Others needed the farm for shelter and lost their children as a result. Women dealing with mental illness or cognitive disabilities were the most controversial residents and relying on poor farms to substitute for asylum care resulted in negative publicity and intense scrutiny.

5 The Poor Farm and Mental Health Care

Rob, the Pauper, is loose again,
Through the fields and woods he races . . .
Rob, the Pauper, is wild of eye,
Wild of speech, and wild of thinking . . .
Rob, the Pauper, is crazed of brain;
He hath broke loose from his poor-house cell;
He hath dragged him clear from rope and fetter,
They might have thought; for they knew full well
They could keep a half-caged panther better.
—Will Carlton, "Rob, the Pauper," *Farm Ballads*, 40.

Will Carleton's poem recounts the tale of a man whose marriage dissolved and who ends up being killed by local people because of his escape from the poorhouse. Violence, as noted by superintendents, was a troubling problem at poor farms, but most residents dealing with psychiatric issues were like the Franklin County, Ohio, resident who spent her days sitting on the steps of the back porch, "clad in a stout blue frock, for she has a prejudice against clothes and frequently destroys them. She is bareheaded and seems to enjoy a sun bath. . . . She is intensely filthy, and her habits are decidedly more animally natural than humanly decent, and none of the other inmates will associate with her." She spent much of her time alone and without specialized care because she was considered incurable.[1]

As detailed by Dorothea Dix on her tours of institutions during the 1840s, poor farms had long been sites of care for people considered insane. As part of her advocacy for the institutionalized, she found plenty of people like fictional Rob, restrained and dirty. At her stop in Muskingum County, Ohio, she shamed the county for keeping a woman "in a state of complete nudity" and another "idiotic from continual fits is equally incapable of possessing any forms of decency, yet in these small, close cells they must be kept."[2] In Massachusetts almshouses she found people naked, cold, alone, and chained.[3] Across the country she uncovered much the same problem: people with mental health issues or disabilities were being neglected at poor farms. Partially as a result of her well-publicized advocacy, poor farms became known for housing the "defective and disabled," "deaf, dumb, and blind," and "insane," all of whom typically stayed for long durations.

Their languishing in poor farms helped encourage state institution-building, not just of insane asylums, but of feebleminded schools, facilities for deaf and blind people, and epileptic colonies. Reformers like Samuel Gridley Howe, famous for helping both Laura Bridgman and Helen Keller, frequently touted the almshouse-to-school stories of students like Keller's teacher Annie Sullivan.[4] But institutions built for these specialized purposes were plagued by constant shortages of space, so poor farms continued to house those whose families and states could not. Increasingly during the late nineteenth and early twentieth centuries, "the link between disability and dependency became a problem," in part because the opportunities for the independent employment of disabled people—especially farm work—became more part-time, making it hard for them to self-support and less likely that their income would contribute enough to other households where they might live. As a result, they became more reliant on the poor farm where they could, and did, contribute to the work of the farm and the home.[5]

While the substandard care of the mentally ill and people with disabilities elicited criticism, at poor farms their presence could be financially advantageous. They tended to be more physically capable of work than other residents, and some states compensated counties for their care. Matron Johanna Dohrmann claimed, "The insane are 100 percent better to take care of than the poor. They are just tickled to death over what you can do for them. They won't step out of the yard when they shouldn't and if you're good to them that's all they ask."[6] Dohrmann was not alone in recognizing the strange dynamics of an institution that served both the poor and those with a diverse range of disabilities. This range was problematic, for poor farms and other institutions, as staff tried to determine who would do well with some tasks and whose condition took considerable time to manage. Experts believed that agricultural and domestic labor were best suited to their abilities, making farms a popular component of many types of institutions.[7]

Obviously, the terminology and categorizations people used in the past are no longer appropriate, but insane and feebleminded are the two most commonly found in poor farm ledgers.[8] Historian Catharine Coleborne cataloged a variety of historic "indications of insanity." They included: "talkative/raving, peculiar/eccentric, unfounded fears, wild expressions of face, anxious/depressed, fits of temper, forgetful, listless, mind unhinged, craving for drink, dirty in habits, eating like an animal, goes naked, no appetite, tears hair, unexplained laughter, wrings hands." Another system broke down the "educational classification" of the "feebleminded" this way: "Idiots" who could not be improved or who were "apathetic and excitable" should be given asylum care; "Moral Imbeciles" who were mentally and morally deficient but potentially trainable were suitable for custodial care or care under a guardian; "Imbeciles" who were mentally deficient but trainable were suited for "long apprenticeship and colony life under protection"; the "backward or mentally feeble" had normal mental processes but were slow and required special training, and suffered from overstimulation but could be "trained for a place in the world."[9] People classified in all these ways lived in poor farms across the country.

Conditions and Criticisms

There was no shortage of terrible stories regarding the treatment of the people with psychiatric disabilities in almshouses. Some read like a catalog of horrors: people being horsewhipped, tied to the bed with straps, chained to a stump in the yard, or hosed down with water. Like Dix, observers found one resident in a cage where he had been left "without a bath or a change of clothing for more than three years. His hair and beard were one huge mat, his nails like birds' claws." This man was moved to a state institution, and when next seen, "he was sitting on a cobbler's bench, mending shoes for his fellow patients."[10] Often space was provided in an attic, basement, a barn, or a converted outbuilding. Sometimes a separate building existed, but rarely a separate staff.[11] Wood County, Ohio, constructed an outbuilding in 1885 to isolate residents and ensure that they did not start a fire in the main building. It was a legitimate concern. The population at the Washington County, Iowa, Poor Farm increased when the overflowing state asylum returned patients and a terrible fire at the poor farm followed, resulting in the "cremation of five female inmates" who had been locked up. The entire main building was destroyed after a woman "got a broom and then stuck it in the stove outside her cell. The four women in her cell could not be got out because there were no keys readily available, so they all burned to death in the cell." A local jury cleared the superintendent and matron of any wrongdoing, especially because he apparently tried to rescue the trapped women.[12] A visitor to a rural Illinois poor farm noticed a variety of chained patients outside enjoying nice weather. The reporter said that, "Mingling with these men were others without chains, men and women some of whom were painfully deformed." These were some of the ninety-seven residents, including thirty-seven of whom were considered insane, along with nine children.[13] This combination meant that "people slightly demented and raving maniacs were in the same rooms, while there were also those utter wrecks which sat in heaps on the floor, mumbling and muttering unintelligible words." It was this sort of environment that reformers deemed inappropriate for all involved.

Chaining and restraining poor farm residents could be dangerous and it remained a serious criticism of the type of care provided, but a different set of

The threat of fire was omnipresent for poor farms. After a 1912 fire destroyed the Henry County, Illinois, building, residents were temporarily sent to other counties' poor farms. A similar replacement was built that featured beautiful flower gardens. Photo from the collection of the author.

concerns centered around their behaviors making the living conditions more miserable for other residents. The Franklin County, Ohio, Infirmary housed a former circus performer with a head injury who yelled so loud neighbors could hear him, and a woman who went to the backyard and cursed her husband at the top of her voice.[14] It was not just the noise: the physical descriptions of people are telling as well, with an observer complaining that "the poor but sane are compelled to daily associate with the deformed and grinning idiots and forced to look upon these horrible scenes."[15] Another commenter complained that the poor had as their daily companions "the driveling, drooling idiots, the sight of whom is most repulsive and to inflict one with their presence is surely punishment fitting a greater crime than poverty." One critic singled out the inappropriateness of such scenes for women in particular: "A more horrible existence than a modest woman must endure at very many of our almshouses it is impossible to imagine. She lives amid unclean disorder and constant bickering; she is always hearing oaths and vile talk, the ravings of madmen and the uncouth gibberings of idiots; she is always seeing scarred and blotched faces and distorted limbs,—hideous shapes such as one encounters in the narrow streets of Italian towns, but which, here, we hide in our almshouses. She is exposed to a hundred petty wrongs."[16] These evaluations positioned disabled people as dreadful for their behavior and appearance, and the connection of physical and behavioral characteristics was intended to foment pity for the worthy poor and not for those whose bodies were being described.[17]

Women, more likely to be categorized as insane, were also more likely to be in poor farms with that designation. In Elizabeth Gaspar Brown's study of Wisconsin, she found it at least "possible that the six individually received women listed as 'insane' whose ages at reception fell between 41 and 50 years well may have been suffering from menopause," and suggested that the older a woman was the more likely she was to be deemed insane. Likewise, women with what would today be labeled as postpartum depression or posttraumatic stress syndrome would have also been considered "insane."[18] One Franklin County woman was hosed down with cold water for two hours until she settled down from hysterics, a diagnosis almost always associated with women.[19] Issues related to childbirth or children were frequently reported. Illinois poor farm resident Nancy Meyers was only thirty-eight when she was reported to have "unmistakable signs of dementia." The poor farm superintendent called county officials who in turn called two doctors. They believed her to be insane and theorized it could be complications from an attack of typhoid in her childhood, or "an attack of puerperal fever, or an umbilical hernia caused from a kick by her husband later in life." They described her symptoms as profane language and a "mania largely directed toward repelling with a broom imaginary attacks of spirits, which she insists are bothering her." She was transferred to a nearby state asylum.[20] The Ellis children in Ohio believed that resident Mary Bakes was insane because her husband had stolen her children. Dr. Thomas Salmon in Texas gave a cautionary tale to men to take care of their wives, claiming, "If the young wife by your side has a baby, and during her confinement the delicate mechanism of her brain is injured and she becomes insane, we will have her charged with insanity, send the sheriff to arrest her, and we will lock her up in jail. If there is no room for her at a state hospital we will, after her conviction, put her in an iron cage in the county poor farm and if no vacancy occurs in the state institution we will keep her there, without care or nursing."[21] This account reflects both the process in Texas through which people were declared insane, and the relationship between poor farms and state institutions.

Investigations about mistreatment at poor farms frequently centered around psychiatric patients. In 1879 an Ohio newspaper that generally lauded the conditions inside its local poor farm noted that the "crazy house . . . is not suitable for a pig pen." All the residents of the structure were women who wandered the property during the day. The superintendent reported that "when he took charge this building was the filthiest place he had ever seen, a den for rats and mice, and bed bugs and other vermin reigned supreme. The walls of the building were literally red with blood where the poor demented wretches had killed the vermin."[22] In 1882, Julia Glines in Summit County faced accusations of financial mismanagement and mistreatment of residents, who claimed that she slapped and denied clothing to certain individuals. Her defense did not do much for her credibility, as she admitted, "I slapped Ollie Spencer's ears, but I never whipped her. She was an ungovernable girl and shutting her up didn't do her any good. She was an imbecile, 22 or 23 years old but knew enough to be awful mean. I had to resort to means to make her afraid of me. I never treated her cruelly." That trying to inspire fear did not rank as cruel in her eyes is telling. She also claimed that she "locked Lizzie Pontius up many times. It was necessary, and it may be that I have locked her up with a harmless lunatic." Another woman who had jumped from a third-story window was placed in the "crazy-house" because they could not contain her, and she had epileptic fits. Visitors and employees also complained about conditions inside the "crazy house," which lacked fresh air, smelled awful, had bed bugs, and lacked heating. Glines deflected that criticism at the county officials who controlled the budget for improvements, but even as they tried to repair the problem with a new building, they kept the residents in a space that partially lacked a roof.[23]

Sexual abuse of women with disabilities of childbearing age was a driving reason to keep them contained. Despite frantic pleas to keep them institutionalized, women with intellectual disabilities arrived at poor farms pregnant and got pregnant while there. Although the commonality of the latter seemed exaggerated by eugenicists for effect, the 1880s case of Nellie Towner in Ohio generated statewide attention. A resident at the Summit County Infirmary for six years, Nellie had not been abandoned: her mother tried to care for her for the first two years of her illness and remained nearby to visit on occasion. Nellie had been institutionalized because of violent outbursts and was isolated in the insane ward because she struck a woman in the head with a cleaver and bit one her caretakers. During this confinement she became pregnant, and employees scrambled to come up with an explanation to exonerate themselves. As testimony began in hearings held by the state board of charities, a local paper indicated that early evidence was damning: "This is a case that comes home to every decent family in the county, for no matter how cruelly hardened one may be as to those compelled by poverty to take refuge in the public poor house, the possibility of imbecility and insanity is not absent from even the most favored home circle, with the change that their most helpless members may be at the mercy of an infirmary management lacking either tenderness or decency." George Keck, a long-time employee of the farm, was initially arrested for her rape, but as evidence came to light it was clear that many men had the access and opportunity to assault Nellie.[24]

The investigation into her rape revealed just how vulnerable Nellie and women like her were. In addition to the numerous keys to the ward floating around, a resident had been "locked up several times for feeling around the girls" and had coaxed one into his room who later gave birth to a child. Nellie had been bathed by Keck on a number of occasions, a drastic violation of social norms, even for

This Summit County, Ohio, Infirmary received updates and improvements as a result of investigations and problems in the 1880s, which uncovered bad treatment for residents with disabilities, including the assault of Nellie Towner. This 1910 image shows employees in front of the main building shortly before the institution was relocated to better farmland. Photo courtesy of the Summit County Historical Society of Akron, Ohio; housed at Akron-Summit County Public Library.

poor farms. The superintendent, Millard Hamlin, indicated that he heard rumors about Keck taking "improper liberties with some of the inmates" but was apparently less concerned because the rumor did not involve the psychiatric patients. Hamlin was also forced to defend one of his own sons, who was accused of being overly familiar with female residents and taking his friends to the ward where they taunted residents in cells and cajoled "Irish Ellen" to dance.[25] A. G. Byers from the state charities association said of those cells, "I would not put my cow in. . . . They are not fit for even a brute. And this is so in many places in Ohio." Despite what seemed like blatant evidence of mistreatment, doctors testified that they had visited and thought conditions as good as to be expected given the staff resources.[26] Dr. Alvin Fouser, who examined Nellie and testified to the favor of the Hamlins, was later charged with body snatching from the infirmary cemetery.[27] Fouser claimed that Nellie "manifested maternal feeling for the baby for a few minutes, and then became indifferent."[28] Keck took the stand to defend himself, reiterating how many people had keys to Nellie's cell.

No one was found guilty of the crime, in part because Nellie could not testify, and in a damning admission of poor farm mismanagement, too many people were found to have had the opportunity. The Reverend Byers, who led the investigation, made it clear that the vulnerability of women was not limited to one county: "This infamy does not alone belong to the infirmary here. Why, over here in the Guernsey County Infirmary a woman, totally insane, gave birth to twins, without the brute instincts left to know that she had been delivered of her young. And in the Vinton County Infirmary a woman, not only crazy, but deformed and most horrible repulsive gave birth to a child, a perfect monstrosity, not having an upper part of its head . . . as long as the present system of caging and mixing these unfortunate ones is kept up so long such infamous and disgraceful acts will happen."[29] The state board interviewed more than one hundred witnesses and toured the facility in the course of their investigation.

Other accusations of mistreatment and neglect were leveled against Superintendent Hamlin at the Towner hearings, related to residents whom he categorized as "more or less violent." He also used the "crazy house" as a punishment for residents. Hobbles were used on violent people and on those who regularly ran away. They also used the hose on those who would not settle down. A man whose father lived there testified that, "I found my aged father locked in a cell in the crazy house. He was burning with thirst and loathsome with excrement. My father had become insane. Three days before he was stricken with paralysis and that's why he was taken to that cell. Food and drink were laid out before him but he was helpless and couldn't reach it and nobody had given it to him. He had many [bowel movements] in his clothes." This man witnessed Nellie in labor and noted that at first no one helped her.[30] The county fired the Hamlins and Fouser, and the new matron was taking care of Nellie's baby who was reported to be "bright, fat, handsome and healthy, and is as observing as any child of its age."[31] Nellie remained institutionalized for the rest of her life. She stayed in the infirmary until at least 1900, and that census enumeration noted that she had given birth to a still-living child. By 1910 she had moved to the State Hospital built nearby where she died four years later from epileptic convulsions and secondary dementia.[32]

In other circumstances even when no intentional harm was meant, the lax supervision and lack of specialized care caused residents to be left to their own devices, sometimes to the entertainment of locals but also to the detriment of their wellbeing or happiness. An Illinois newspaper shamed local boys for "having such great sport with George," a "poor simple minded fellow from the county house" and warned they might find themselves in his position someday. It is unclear if this bullying was physical, emotional, or both.[33] Locals in Dodge

County, Nebraska, remembered many residents who were unemployable except at the farm but appreciated at the institution, and those whose antics made for interesting anecdotes, including an elderly man who believed "the revenue" was after him, causing him to hide in the hayloft. In Nebraska, some sparsely populated counties had poor farms, which meant they had space at the county level when the state institution did not.[34] C. J. Johnston recalled a man in Allen County, Indiana, who "scraped the ground smooth and drew architectural images." Then he studied them and talked about it so quietly no one knew what he said.[35]

Texas continued to house residents with mental illness and disabilities in their poor farms even after state asylums opened to alleviate some of the backlog of cases.[36] In 1917, Dr. Thomas Salmon said of the care provided at a Texas farm, it is "a tomb, but not for the quiet dead." Psychiatric residents were kept in a dark, single-story brick building with iron cages. He noted that men and women, Black and white, were all thrown into the building with no privacy but complete isolation from the rest of the residents, not because they were necessarily dangerous, but because they tended to wander off.[37] Instead of containing residents in such a cruel way, other poor farm superintendents allowed them freedom to move about, leading some to become well known in the community. Such was the case of Columbus Wilson, known as "Pigeon," an African American poor farm resident in Illinois who claimed to have been enslaved. He told one reporter he owned the poor farm: "With true pride of ownership of what to him is a palace, 'Pigeon' took me about, showing me into all the rooms and explaining them to me. He was particularly solicitous that I see where he sleeps in a huge room on the basement level with a door opening out to the south." Black poor farm residents were often the focus of teasing or demeaning newspaper stories, especially when they were considered harmlessly insane. Wilson appears to have been sleeping in the basement as a form of segregation. Locals knew him because he tried to cash large checks at banks, like the one he gave a reporter for $75,000. In 1944, before the closing of the poor farm, a reporter remarked, "When I parted from him, I could not help feeling that, after all, mental aberration is not wholly a misfortune. It must be something to live continuously in a world of pleasant fantasies." In a follow-up story, locals guessed about Wilson's age (he was in his eighties) and how long he had lived there. One person claimed that he used to do odd jobs for farmers and saved his money, but his fiancée stole it and left him, triggering his condition.[38]

There were real dangers for poor farm residents who posed no threat to others but who harmed themselves. An Ohio man believed he was working for his meals, so when he got sick and had to stop working, he also stopped eating. Once his fellow residents coaxed him back to the breakfast table, he ate a hearty meal, went to the top floor of the building, took off his coat, hat, and boots, and jumped to his death.[39] Suicides were not uncommon at poor farms. A woman under the care of J. S. Meyers took bed bug poison as part of a suicide attempt and in the 1890s Will County, Illinois, had two men cut their own throats only months apart.[40] One superintendent's daughter recalled that a formerly wealthy man, who had repeatedly asked her father to kill him, went outside and slit his own throat.[41] Ann Ellis also remembered a woman who killed herself by hanging from a stocking, and in Montana Emily Williams Smith recalled a "dope fiend" admitted by a local doctor for a detox who tried unsuccessfully to hang herself during the process.[42] Hazel Broadwater's parents were infirmary employees during the 1920s; her father interceded with a resident who threatened to jump from a window. While trying to coax him down, her father finally said, "If you are going to jump, jump, I ain't got all night, I got haying to do." The man asked if he could help with the haying if he got down, so her father agreed and off the man went to help on the farm.[43]

Asylums

Accounts like these became powerful evidence urging states to fund new institutions and expand existing facilities, where such residents could hypothetically receive more humane care. One Michigan critic said, "There is no chapter in the history of our charitable institutions so fraught with painful and revolting interest, as that which relates to the treatment of the idiotic in our poorhouses." This debate was so heated that the State Board of Corrections and Charities was almost abolished because of its vigorous campaigning for a feebleminded school, which was seen as money "for the education of fools." It took until the 1890s to pass the legislation, fueled in part by concern about the reproduction of women with intellectual disabilities "constantly exposed to the design of evil men."[44] These building ventures added to the long and complex relationship between state policing of institutionalized women's sexuality as an element of social wellbeing. Advocate Mary Vida of Kansas reported that there was no class of dependents "for whom almshouse care is more generally considered improper than for the insane . . . lacking skilled medical attention, trained nursing, attractive environment and intelligent direction of work and play which are essential." She believed institutions caused unnecessary suffering for all poor farm residents and that the combination of people in poor farms meant that proper care could never truly be provided, nor could it be done economically. It would, Vida said, "require in the superintendent a combination of special qualifications which no one human being could possibly possess, and an amount of money which no almshouse ever received."[45]

At their founding, most state asylums were intended to help remove people from poor farms because as David Rothman put it, "better the asylum than the almshouse." Dr. James Woods Babcock, a leader in southern mental health care, followed his peers in recommending state asylum treatment for curable patients instead of simply custodial care at poor farms.[46] States intended asylums specifically for people considered fixable, and across the country at least seventy-five had opened by 1880.[47] While this helped remove some cases from county care, asylums filled with chronic cases anyway, making it more difficult to transfer people from poor farms to the state.[48] Amos Warner documented that even though California had 6,000 spaces for psychiatric patients in its asylums, these institutions could not always take people from almshouses because they were so overcrowded, leading to the refrain, "he is better left in the almshouse."[49] In Massachusetts, Dr. C. A. Walker of the Boston Lunatic Asylum urged farms be acquired for state asylums specifically to accommodate more patients "languishing in poorhouses."[50]

Although some counties tried to do well by all their poor farm residents, the inability to individualize their care resulted in situations like that found in Grayson County, Texas, which had long-term child residents with disabilities. One was kept in arm restraints for most of the day to prevent undressing, while another crawled about the place. An epileptic boy was kept in a cell and managed to avoid slamming his head against the cement by "holding the bars when he could." Judges from other parts of the state submitted their own examples, describing poor farm residents as "simple minded." One admitted that his county kept all the poor, intellectually disabled people at the farm, some since infancy. At the Bexar County Farm a "low grade imbecile" photographed by C. S. Yoakum spent his days climbing trees, getting onto small branches that broke, bringing him crashing to the ground. "All of his energy," Yoakum noted, "almost that of a full-grown man, is expended in this useless fashion."[51] With no treatment and no tasks to do, poor farms made some people's conditions worse. Cases like these helped publicize the need for not just asylums, but state facilities for custodial patients as well.

Poor farms remained part of the care landscape because of state asylum overcrowding and pressure to demonstrate successful treatments on patients. In the 1870s New York estimated that 30 percent of poor farm residents were insane, and the demand for state asylum space never kept pace.[52] Those not cured or without financial support from family were frequently sent back to county institutions. So common was this that newspapers like the *Rock Island Argus* noted the arrival of three men "pronounced incurable" who returned to the local poor farm in 1877. In Ohio, one critic claimed the state "is responsible for the wrongs visited upon the insane at our infirmaries. . . . The incurable insane have, therefore, been thrown back upon their respective counties, which are without the proper buildings, appliances and experienced attendants for them." States could better deal with the costs associated with large congregate-style asylums, leading many to agree that, "on the score of economy, to say nothing of humanity, every effort ought to be made to get the state to care for all its insane."[53] It was a lofty but unmet aspiration. States differed in their willingness to pay; some counties had to pay the bill for custodial cases, prompting officials to recall long-term cases or incurables. If the "poor, old, and decrepit, its 'freaks of nature' (human) and mentally weak" were dependent and in the county, the county had to provide some means of care.[54]

This practice of shifting responsibilities resulted in people like Nettie Carson spending her lifetime in county care. A 1927 newspaper exposé revealed Nettie tied to a staircase at the poor farm where she had lived since the 1880s. Nettie, who was nonverbal, was not a candidate for state care because she could not be cured. When reporters saw her, she was staring out a window but, "She looked up," a reporter claimed, "the dull blue in her eyes seemingly scanning the faces of the visitors for something that she has never known. Spoken to, she merely growled." Nettie refused to keep shoes or stockings on her feet, and unlike other residents, she slept on an old-fashioned straw tick "for it is necessary to continually change it." She appeared clean on the day of the visit, and officials acknowledged that Nettie deserved a place where she could receive constant supervision.[55] Despite knowing that the poor farm was not a good place for her, officials had nowhere else to send her; the best the staff could do was keep her physically safe.

Counties also had the option of giving family members financial support to care for people at home. Historian of mental health Gerald Grob believes that many of those categorized as psychiatric patients in almshouses were probably older people either without family, or whose families could no longer provide care for their senility or dementia because they lacked the means. However, even those able to contribute some labor to their families were left to the county when family members died, became ill, or faced financial crises.[56] It would not have been an easy task, even with financial aid. Doctors and asylum administrators acknowledged the role they could play in helping, with William Fish of Illinois inquiring, "How much of misfortune and suffering do these figures represent? How many saddened homes? How many worn and weary mothers? How many fathers, struggling to keep their families from want, weighted down by this burden of misfortune?"[57] The number Fish sought was in the thousands, judging by census data about in-home care. Poet Robert Frost dealt with the topic in a "A Servant to Servants":

> My father's brother wasn't right. They kept him
> Locked up for years back there at the old farm.
> I've been away once—yes, I've been away.
> The State Asylum. I was prejudiced;
> I wouldn't have sent anyone of mine there;

You know the old idea—the only asylum
Was the poorhouse, and those who could afford,
Rather than send their folks to such a place,
Kept them at home; and it does seem more human.

Although much attention was paid to the interactions of poor farms and state asylums, county officials actually had a more pressing problem—many of their cognitively disabled people were in jails instead of poor farms. People classified as insane and jailed received priority admission to state asylums because their housing was considered even worse than those at poor farms.[58] Texas reported in 1912 that its counties frequently shuffled residents with disabilities or mental illness between poor farm and jail: one man who refused to keep his clothing on at the poor farm was moved to the jail where his nakedness would not be offensive.[59] Yoakum called the keeping of the mentally ill in jails the "shame of Texas." That was a damning indictment, considering that the state's few poor farms were considered dirty, ill-equipped, or as one employee described his worksite, a "bat cage."[60]

Local institutions retained residents eligible for state care if counties had to pay for that care. In Vermont, for example, the opening and expansion of asylums between 1890 and 1910 reduced the number of psychiatric patients in poor farms from 1,000 to 34 because the state paid. But overcrowding at state asylums encouraged doctors, including James Babcock, to campaign for the development of a poor farm system that could handle the chronic cases. He worried that the shortage of places to house incurable but poor patients was turning his institution into "a large state almshouse" instead of a legitimate medical facility.[61] Unlike poor farms which generally accepted most people, Babcock and other asylum superintendents had the ability to selectively admit. In the selection of patients for state asylums, certain groups, such as African Americans, were intentionally excluded. Paying patients took priority.[62] Pressing demand, a preference for private pay patients, budget constraints, and priority given to the jailed helps explain why states never had enough space in asylums, and why poor farms continued to house the overflow.[63]

Similar problems existed when states opened other types of institutions, which dotted the landscape by the end of the nineteenth century. None of them removed all epileptics or people with disabilities from poor farms, but they did help. Between 1880 and 1923 there was a noteworthy reduction in older people with disabilities living in poor farms, declining from 24 percent to 6 percent.[64] Feebleminded institutions, for example, initially accepted children before expanding to older residents. They became massive, overcrowded facilities, with Ohio's housing more than 1,000 residents by 1900.[65] Adults considered intellectually disabled, primarily men, were released back to county care as a result. Returning home to family was an option for some, but not all, especially if their families lacked financial resources. Women were held as custodial cases to ensure they did not have children.[66]

Because they never stopped housing people with disabilities or those labeled insane, counties took them into account when building or rebuilding poor farms. Blackhawk County, Iowa, built a "magnificent" structure for the "reception of the insane." In 1885, Jefferson County, Alabama, claimed that 8 percent of its poor farm residents were insane and took the opportunity to transfer many to the asylum at Tuscaloosa. However, by 1912 the county built a new psychiatric ward on its property because there were no state facilities with vacancies.[67] Other counties built special wings or new, separate buildings. New York encouraged poorhouses to build separate sections for these residents and Kansas decided it was cheaper for the state to pay counties fifty cents per day to house their own "incurable, and harmlessly insane," but then failed to reimburse promptly.[68] Kansas commenter Albert Paine said that "the few pennies we save in taxation are saved at the price of blood. Our luxuries are filched from a beggar's pocket, our tea is salted with blind man's tears." [69] He vigorously opposed the conditions this expenditure created in poor farms, with people living behind barred windows, eating worse than prisoners, and sleeping in smelly, cold conditions.

The Wisconsin System

Around the same time Kansas was implementing a county reimbursement system badly, Wisconsin officials made the bold but expensive choice to respond to their asylum overcrowding in a similar way. In 1881, the Wisconsin legislature voted to reimburse counties on a per diem rate of more than a dollar a day to take back their nonviolent residents in state custody. The Wisconsin Plan used the generous per diem to encourage counties to build not simply an insane ward in their poor farm, but rather their own asylums. Counties that participated typically used their existing poor farm property for the asylum so the two could share a farm. In the years prior to this decision, Dane County claimed that as many as half of the poor farm's 100 residents could be classified as insane.

These properties were not simply a convenient choice for an asylum: doctors and reformers believed that farms and clean air could improve the health of patients. Experts deemed the rural environment calming and healthy, and farming gave residents purpose and routine. Far from being viewed as exploitative, it was considered a therapeutic treatment. Some of the characteristics that were thought to be isolating for the poor were beneficial for the asylum residents.[70] Counties stood to benefit as well: people classified with certain types of disabilities could do farm chores, as could the "insane but harmless." Michigan reported that among its poor farm residents were many on the "dividing line between insanity and pauperism" who looked on the institution as their home and contributed in some ways to its upkeep.[71] While the most severe cases might need constant care, others were good candidates for farm and house labor.[72] By adding these people and their per diem to their county properties, Wisconsin poor farms/asylums increased in acreage and productivity.

Shortly after the state incentivized counties to take back residents, Dane County began construction of a new building on the grounds of the poor farm. Other counties followed suit, and by 1915, thirty-five of seventy-two counties were taking care of 5,320 patients.[73] In Dane County, poor farm employees and Superintendent Meyers did some of the construction in addition to their regular tasks.[74] When the new building was finished Meyers managed both. He earned two separate salaries: $500 for managing the poor farm and approximately $500 for the asylum. In 1885, the county added his wife's salary of $300. In 1890, the asylum expanded, at which time the staff between the two institutions separated, although they shared the same farm and grounds.

The new institution came at a good time in Dane County; prior to its construction county officials brought incurable cases back from state custody because it saved money, but it complicated the jobs of the superintendent and staff in immeasurable ways. Meyers wrote that he was "having a serious time with insane." One man repeatedly ran away, once despite wearing a ball and chain, which he removed and flung in the privy. Staff found him sleeping in the carpentry house. Other Wisconsin superintendents reported similar struggles with the large number of psychiatric residents in the poor farms, noting they had "a large amount of care and labor" to cope with as a result. Waukesha County officials reported that almost half its poor farm residents were considered "insane or idiotic" and several did not leave their cells.[75]

These tactics of cells and leg irons were precisely why reformers did not want these patients in poor farms to begin with. A lack of proper supervision, a common problem at poor farms, could be dangerous, just not always in the way reformers worried. Helen Bovers was sent back to the county in 1881 and then escaped in the dead of winter. Her body was not found until April when Meyers wrote, "I found the long lost Helen Bovers corpse this morning." John Swenson ran away three times before he "finally hung himself at a farmer's barn in Christiana."[76] These were good anecdotal examples for why poor farms were not safe places for those with mental illness. There was no staff to constantly monitor residents. Reformer Alexander Johnson suggested that "mental defectives" needed protection from "rough or vicious inmates" and in turn needed to avoid annoying the elderly residents. He hoped their skills could be put to good use in smaller places where they could have tasks tailored to their abilities. The Wisconsin system provided both space and tasks. Johnson cited successful examples, including a man who took care of and talked to the cattle and horses but refused to talk to people and one "profane in speech but perfectly kind in action," who did housework and laundry. He worried about overwork, noting that "their errors of judgement in such things as loading a wheelbarrow, or taking too heavy a load on their shoulders, must be guarded against." It was the job of the superintendent to protect them and be watchful.[77] There was at least one case which demonstrated the danger, from 1914, when an asylum resident in Sauk County, Wisconsin, died after being gored by a poor farm bull.

The Dane County Asylum filled up fast, while decreasing the population in the poor farm because of transfers. Meyers reported that not all the "insane" residents wanted to move from the poor farm to the asylum, telling officials that there were "three who preferred to occupy their old quarters and whom on account of their peculiarities we permitted to remain giving them such fare and treatment as those receive who were removed to new quarters."[78] Employees like Meyers could consider the feelings of residents he knew personally. In 1883, the first year both institutions operated together, there were a total of 107 people cared for at the asylum with a steady population of 75. A matron had been hired to help oversee the asylum, while Meyers's wife stayed on at the poor farm. In a noted departure from poor farm life, Meyers estimated that around 75 percent of the asylum residents were doing between one-third and half a day's work in the wards, laundry, sewing room, kitchen, yards, garden, fields, and woods. The advantages of a separate asylum on the poor farm grounds became immediately apparent, as Meyers noted, "the products of the farm and garden mentioned in my report for poor-house has been largely the result of insane labor." While there were more mouths to feed, they were contributing more substantially to their own care. He also claimed that since the residents were closer to home, "we received numerous visits from friends of patients during the year for which we were pleased."[79] Similar advantages were seen elsewhere. Wayne County, Michigan, doctor E. O. Bennett emptied many of the cells holding patients and unchained others, putting them out on the farm to work, where "they ceased to be such fearful creatures."[80]

As the Wisconsin system demonstrated, poor farms and asylums could be successfully paired to the benefit of residents and counties, with asylum residents doing some labor for the good of the whole. Dodge County Asylum residents built furniture, dug a basement, and helped on the 150-acre farm that provided food for both institutions.[81] Drastically increasing the number of county institutions in the state also came with financial cautionary tales, as state funding did not necessarily offset all the county expense. Sauk County was proud of its asylum, claiming that "we believe it to be in the foremost rank, and justifies the interest displayed by the taxpayers of our county." It still needed improvements, however. In 1913 there was a heating issue during the winter and the needed new laundry equipment had not been installed. The request had been made because "we believe it is unjust to ask insane men and women to wash and iron the clothes of over 200 people [in the poor farm and asylum] in this building under existing conditions."[82] Addressing the issue of cost in 1896, James Heg, a member of the Wisconsin State Board of Control, spoke to the National Conference of Charities and Corrections. He indicated that the state now paid a per diem of $1.75 per person to counties, which provided better care and food. He also emphasized the role of the farm, claiming that, "In these farms lies the secret of the beneficial results that are manifested in the county asylums. Occupation is found, if possible. For every inmate not entirely bed-ridden, with the result that the demented are roused from their stupor, the violent become calm and quiet, the filthy become cleanly, and the physical condition of a large proportion is decidedly improved."[83]

The Wisconsin estimates of the contributions of asylum labor were markedly different from that of poor farm residents. Amos Warner generously estimated that perhaps only 20 percent of poor farm expenses could be defrayed by resident labor. However, he noted that "certain classes of the insane are the most efficient workers, and their presence in the almshouse contributes much towards making it self-supporting."[84] The asylum labor further supports the idea that people with disabilities living in poor farms made considerable contributions at those institutions. Massachusetts superintendents complained they would have to hire workers when the state took those labeled insane into centralized care, and a 1930s report from Kansas suggested that the poor farm superintendents wanted patients capable of labor transferred from state to local care because counties "cannot afford to employ sufficient help for the operation of the poor farm and these patients are physically able to do the work of regular employees."[85] Those residents most likely to be laboring on poor farms were those with mental illness or intellectual disabilities.

Eugenics

Although sometimes considered desirable poor farm residents for their abilities to work, housing those considered feebleminded in poor farms was wholly unacceptable to reformers. No concern drove more commentary, investigation, and panic than the worry about poor farm residents who were thought to have abnormal sex drives and a lack of inhibition, engaging in intercourse and reproduction. Alexander Johnson, more explicitly than Dorothea Dix before him, articulated the dangers to the individual and to the state: "It would be easy to give hundreds of instances of abuse, usually sexual, of feebleminded persons in almshouses. . . . It is the common understanding that few or none of the women of child bearing age escape maternity . . . the feebleminded woman of child bearing age is not in her proper place in an almshouse, . . . the superintendent and matron, and the governing board too, are under the strongest obligation to protect her against abuse and the state against her possible progeny."[86] They were taken advantage of because they did not always understand sexual activity and its consequences, and like Nellie Towner, could not always speak on their own behalf.

In 1919, a conversation among Michigan county officials discussed keeping these men and women separated inside poor farms. While most superintendents and matrons claimed this was not an issue, at least one indicated that he locked a man up at night to keep him away from a woman, claiming that "the first thing you know you will see a pair of rubber boots sticking out of the girl's window, and you go there and pull and haul while he rears around." Both were labeled as "feebleminded." In an indication of how attitudes about poor farm care changed over time, discussants expressed concerns about the legality of locking someone up at their institution. Many noted a clear difference in the practice of restraining someone overnight for safety, as opposed to containing a person in a jail-like setting. State officials recommended all such poor farm residents be remanded to the Michigan Home for the Feebleminded and Epileptic, but superintendents were quick to point out that the wait time for that facility was more than six months. One county official said, "The only thing we can do is to do the best we can. . . . If it is necessary to lock one of these people up to keep him and the girls apart . . . we are going to stand behind the keeper [superintendent]."[87]

Arguments in favor of custodial care for developmentally or cognitively disabled women of reproductive age typically centered on controlling their sexuality as opposed to protecting them from predation. In New York, for example, a shortage of space for children with intellectual disabilities—not yet or almost to reproductive age—resulted in an institutional swap of sorts, with counties sending young women/teens to the state in exchange for the return of disabled adult women "who have passed child bearing age." Senile dementia and "harmless insane cases" were also sent back to counties to make space for new, younger commitments in state facilities. State officials reportedly complained that poor farm staff sent female residents they found burdensome instead of the "feebleminded."[88] The concerns about women considered developmentally or cognitively disabled living in poor farms did not diminish over time, even as the number of younger women, pregnancies, and births recorded at those institutions declined. They were blamed for undermining the social order and causing prostitution, vagrancy, and pauperism, which lead directly to the institutionalization of more people.

When these women were assaulted or taken advantage of, sometimes the poor farm served as their only option for care. Goldie was twenty years old, unmarried, and had an intellectual disability when she entered the farm, pregnant, in the 1930s. The county took guardianship of her daughter and placed her with a family. Goldie spent the rest of her life at the poor farm, staying so long she made the transition to a county nursing home. Upon her death in 1992, a nursing home attendant familiar with her story wrote this in the old poor farm ledger next to her intake record: "Goldie was brought here due to her pregnancy. The child was adopted out and later, many years later, Goldie's daughter found her. The daughter passed away several years ago. Unfortunately, in those days, no social agency existed to help Goldie find housing and employment, so she remained here for 62 years. She worked in the laundry and kitchen."[89] While the circumstances surrounding her pregnancy are not known, it is clear she arrived at the institution already pregnant and it is not known whether she was capable of consenting to sex. No legal action was taken on her behalf.

The inability or unwillingness of poor farms to act as penitentiaries vexed eugenicists. As historian Matt Wray pointed out, most of the research done by eugenicists focused not on urban immigrants but on poor rural whites, which in turn made poor farms popular sites for their investigations.[90] Studies between the 1870s and the 1920s tried to trace the links between families labeled "feeble-minded" and poor farms. Reformer Josephine Shaw Lowell made such connections when she talked about the inappropriate presence of vagrant women and prostitutes in poor farms because it exposed them to weak-minded men.[91] The consistency with which eugenicists located such connections is considerable. In the "Dack Family," researchers tracked down "Mike," who had been admitted to the poor farm for "lack of ambition" but left when the superintendent would not "let him carry firearms nor manage the place . . . activities he felt were necessary for his happiness." He went to live in a shack in the woods while others in his family tree spent time in poor farms after stints in the state asylum. Charles Hoyt tried in his 1877 report on New York to determine how many dependent people had been produced by families in the almshouses of that state.[92] Like many of his peers, Ernest Bicknell of Indiana believed women more likely to carry the hereditary problem of intellectual disability, while failing to consider the effects of generational poverty, a lack of education, and a lack of health care. As an early eugenicist, Bicknell provided a case study from a poor farm in southern Indiana where one family had been represented in the institution for thirty-five years. Much like the notorious Jukes, Kallikaks, and other families written about in social welfare circles, he traced the members of this family to no fewer than four marriages between people he labeled "feebleminded" and classified most of the children and grandchildren of these unions that way too. It is a wonder so many such people found each other in rural Indiana, the likelihood of which Bicknell did not address. He summarized it by saying, "The history of this family is not closed. In truth, its productive power for evil is probably greater today than at any time in its history."[93] Three decades later, Harry Evans would heartily disagree, believing the threat to have magnified.

Other lesser-known studies added fuel to the fire. Author Frank Blackmar recommended the "Smoky Pilgrims" of Kansas be sent to the poor farm to labor while admitting that the farm administrators did not force anyone to work, and the "Happy Hickories," who were a rural Ohio family with sixteen intellectually disabled members connected to poor farm residency.[94] Author Mina Sessions described them this way: "Two were low grade idiots unable to do the slightest thing for themselves. The others, seven men and three women, were of such low mentality that they could perform only the most simple tasks and could under no circumstances earn their own livings. The remaining twenty, twelve men and eight women, were able to do manual labor if some one remained near to direct the work." Sessions was of course most interested in those who were young enough to bear children, labeling one "a common prostitute" and accusing another of making "trouble because of her attempts to approach the male inmates." Sessions labeled five women a "decided menace to the community . . . yet there was nothing beyond the influence of the superintendent and matron to prevent them from leaving."[95] In addition to these women, the study determined that certain family names appeared in the records over the decades, referring to them as "feebleminded strains." Since many of the studies indicated that this disability was not randomly scattered through the population but instead concentrated in families and regions, poor farms provided sites to study this supposed density.[96] At the National Committee for Social Work, members of the Committee for Mental Hygiene accused poor farms of housing "incestuous relations between brother and sister" and Mississippi poor farms of being one-third full of the "feebleminded."[97] The focus on poor, rural populations as a source for degeneracy focused on isolation, monotony, a lack of economic opportunity, and "irregular workers of vile nature," which appears to refer to hired hands.[98]

These studies culminated in 1926's oft-quoted eugenics pamphlet *The American Poorfarm and Its Inmates*, a partnership between the Committee for Mental Hygiene, Harry Evans, and various fraternal organizations, which dramatically connected fertility, poor farms, and mental illness. One of the opening salvos of Evans's thesis claimed, "Paupers come and go to poor farms at their own sweet will. . . . Thousands of them were mildly insane or feebleminded—turned loose to marry and inter-marry and procreate their kind. . . . Society is not warned of their coming. Decent, healthy men, women, and children have no chance to protect themselves against this dangerous army."[99] Much of what Evans and his colleagues asserted is not substantiated by historical records. For example, his suggestion that half of poor farm residents had syphilis and that as many as 70 percent were intellectually disabled bears no correlation to actual documentation. It was modeled after the earlier reports that emphasized rural incest, inbreeding, venereal disease, and sexual immorality.[100] Evans was particularly vitriolic about supposed miscegenation in poor farms, where he claimed the "birth of half breeds was common." In Delaware he accused an "imbecile" woman of having seven children by seven men and another of having "two illegitimate colored children."[101] Throughout, it is unclear by what standards Evans and his colleagues judge the cognitive abilities of their subjects. In Missouri visitors "discovered" four women who had given birth to seventeen illegitimate, intellectually disabled children in a single county. St. Genevieve County claimed to have a forty-seven-year-old "feebleminded deaf and dumb" woman married to a Black man with whom she had a son.[102] In the hundreds of poor farm records I examined, I found no women who gave birth to anywhere near this many children while being a poor farm resident, and few interracial births.

Evans intended to boost the profile of eugenicist arguments about the propagation of the unfit, and to outrage taxpayers by suggesting that their money was going toward institutions that supported illicit relationships. He stressed the inefficiencies of poor farms and was irate about the amount of land owned by counties for their institutions. He used a single year's population to gauge the investment of land per person, even though that land had been owned for decades and had provided care for a great many more people. Evans wanted poor farms to resemble state or regionally operated penal institutions or feebleminded institutions where sexuality could be tightly controlled, and sterilizations were more easily accomplished. In at least one county, this vision was put into a practice of sorts. Lapeer County, Michigan, located a "state home" on their poor farm property. These paired institutions were, after a lawsuit and various pieces of revised legislation, the site of more than two thousand sterilizations. Ironically, Evans did not visit many poor farms with large populations and surveyed no state-run congregate institutions, but he explicitly connected poor farms and eugenics in ways meant to support sterilization laws that would stop, as writer Ira Caldwell phrased it, "poverty and ignorance bred through generations."[103]

Evans's opinions about the supposed degradation of Europe provide some context for reconsidering his writings. Evans criticized France for having a "deficient generation . . . of sick and senile fathers. Like begets like." He then connected this to the United States in a conclusion recognizable as a component of white supremacy: "The pilgrim fathers were a hardy, clean, pure-blooded group of people. They and their forebears gave an example of hundreds of years of right living. They were not subject to prostitution and drunkenness, to sources of mental trouble. While they suffered from economic poverty, they escaped biological poverty. Notwithstanding the physical hardships they endured, they furnished us more national leaders than any other group of similar numbers." Having made that remarkably ahistorical judgment, he then turned to Australia, claiming that their convict immigrants' "opportunity for developing a high standard of civilization was as good as the pilgrim fathers. What they actually established was the largest slum community in the world, populated by paupers, thieves and prostitutes. Like begets like." These concepts of nationalism and white supremacy were comfortably situated in the 1920s and the eugenics movement. With this mindset, he and his affiliates studied poor farms, regularly deploying phrases like "hereditary taint" and "human derelicts" to describe what they found.[104]

It makes sense that eugenicists would target poor farms looking for evidence of the failures of social welfare, but their obsession with the propagation of defective classes was misplaced: there were not a lot of babies being born at poor farms by the 1910s and 1920s, and certainly not a lot of young women staying there and having multiple children. The time for poor farms as maternity homes had passed, but distinguishing poor farm residents as inimical to white middle-class values helped push eugenicist ideas like sterilization forward.[105] It would be easy to classify Evans's work as a product of its time, published in the midst of a nativist, Klan-dominated decade when states passed sterilization laws, but using it as an accurate picture of poor farms in the 1920s belies the fact that a majority of residents by that time were men, and most were over fifty years old.[106]

Sociologists were not the only people using poor farms as laboratories: medical professionals shared their curiosity about heredity and dependency. Dr. T. O. Hardesty of Morgan County, Illinois, made an interesting turn toward eugenics by studying particular conditions in his patients. He kept detailed patient records, sometimes including photographs, with family histories. In so doing he joined a wider array of physicians that included Henry Goddard and other eugenics leaders, some of whom believed there were physical "stigmata" associated with intellectual disability and who used their institutionalized patients as subjects of inquiry.[107] Goddard explained that "those who are familiar by long acquaintance with the feebleminded are able to recognize them almost at a glance."[108] The connection between disability and dependency grew stronger during the early decades of the twentieth century, as scientists and reformers tried to find a medical answer for why, despite efforts at improvements, people continued to be poor, have disabilities, or suffer from health issues that rendered them unable to self-support.

Most of the forms that survive in Morgan County appear to be those of patients considered by Hardesty to be "feebleminded." In categorizing his patients in this way, he was making determinations about fit and unfit bodies, and measuring these people against his own concept of normalcy. His classifications were powerful: as the medical expert on-site, he was defining the institutional standards of able-bodied and disabled.[109] W. was labeled "feebleminded simple" with a health history including appendicitis and pleurisy. His picture shows a man squinting at the camera and wearing a watch chain in his front pocket. When he died in 1915 after struggling with stomach ailments, his brothers came to claim his body. P., who arrived on the farm in 1906, was listed as "idiotic" and had no family history because he came from a New York City orphan's home on one of the orphan trains. He had been placed with a local man but ended up at the poor farm. In 1914, Dr. Hardesty treated him for a burn after the lid came off a syrup pot and scalded his face and arms. He died in 1930 at the state hospital. Other residents like K., who had lived at the poor farm for decades, had a family history that hinted at why. Her father had frozen to death, she had no history about her mother, her two siblings died in early adulthood, and her surviving child was institutionalized. In her photo, she wore a variety of necklaces and trinkets around her neck. E. was "deaf, dumb, blind," and a "dwarf." Hardesty measured her at around four feet tall. She had no health history, but he included a slightly blurred photo of her all the same. Her size was relevant because at the time, "the idiot, commonly dwarfed and under-sized, exhibits those signs of physical weakness which at once betray mental degeneration."[110]

Since dependency, insanity, alcoholism, and intellectual disabilities were associated with a lower class of "unfitness," and some poor farm residents could be classified by one or more of those descriptors, it is not surprising that physicians interested in eugenics would turn to them for study.[111] Recommendations at the time for using photos to study this population suggested angles for the photos: straight on—or "frontality"—and to look for the "vacant expressionless stare of imbecility." Hardesty took photos in this style.[112] By attaching photos to their records, he was following the suggestions of more prominent researchers, who supported their use as part of the diagnostic process. However, the practice as used by amateur photographers has been classified as debasing since "every surgeon and physician could do his own button-pressing" and it is unclear whether the residents gave or were asked for their consent. One image of a patient walking away from the camera suggested not everyone was interested in being studied.[113]

Not all of Hardesty's photos demonstrated clear "symptoms" as outlined by his peers, but many did. E.'s photo shows a posture with her hand folded against her chest and blurred motion. Her eyes are closed. This is described under "Posture" with curved hands and "Blurring" that reinforce the notion that the intellectually disabled "lack self-control."[114] The use of "Props" was also suggested as noteworthy in eugenics photos, but only one person, a man with paralysis, has a prop (which appears to be a hoe). K. wore a variety of necklaces that seem to be a part of her outfit and not something she was given as part of a pose. The physicians who followed Hardesty kept medical records of their own, marking similar diagnoses although without images.

The problems associated with poor farms as sites of care for people with mental illness or disabilities never abated, nor were they ever resolved. Poor farms continued to be places where work was encouraged for those deemed capable and continued to be places where those with disabilities could be segregated from the community. There was no permanent solution to the dependency caused by these conditions. Employment opportunities were rare, state institutions remained full, funds for specialized care ebbed and flowed, and the blame for why this continued passed from entity to entity. Poor farms were not the dens of inequity presented by the eugenics movement, although they did not provide particularly compassionate care for the variety of issues that brought people to their doors. The difficulties of running a farm and an institution with no specialized training or staff gave little to those who might have benefitted from attention. The medicalization of studying these populations increased in part thanks to the growing emphasis on poor farms as sites of health care, especially as the populations inside them grew older and required more long-term custodial care. Dr. Hardesty unintentionally recorded a developing change in poor farm populations: in the early decades of the twentieth century, younger, healthy, and temporary poor farm residents decreased in number while older, sicker, and disabled people remained.

6 Old Age and Poor Farm Residency

Over the hill to the poor-house I'm trudgin' my weary way—
I, a woman of seventy, and only a trifle gray—
I, who am smart an' chipper, for all the years I've told,
As many another woman that's only half as old.

—Will Carleton, "Over the Hill," *Farm Ballads*, 51

For the elderly, being sent to the poorhouse was a common fear—and occasionally a threat. Author Nathaniel Hawthorne articulated the fear of aging alone by describing characters as "coming finally to the alms house, as the natural home of their old age."[1] For most nineteenth-century Americans, however, the "natural home of their old age" was either their own home or that of their children. But for those who lacked those options, like Luise Baun, who spent her final years at the Erie County Infirmary in Ohio, being alone and elderly was an unpleasant reality. Baun came to the United States from Germany in 1891, never married, and worked as a maid for the same family for decades. As they aged, so did she, and by the 1950s most of the members of the family with whom she had lived and labored were dead. She was unable to continue working and had an unknown illness. This combination of issues caused her to spend the end of her life at the poor farm.[2]

After Will Carleton published his 1871 poem about a woman abandoned by her children, poor farm superintendents reported an increase in adult children reclaiming their parents from institutions, having been shamed by the popular verses in which the woman emphasizes her usefulness.[3] Despite this brief uptick in reclamations, the average age of poor farm residents increased with each passing decade. In 1880 older people made up 25 percent of poor farm residents, but by 1923 that statistic increased to 53 percent.[4] Such demographic change gives credence to the idea that poverty among the elderly was an early twentieth-century phenomenon. As part of this "discovery" of the aged poor, Homer Folks proclaimed that "proper respect for and care of the aged, who are rightly charged upon us, is a measure of civilization."[5] Objections to housing the elderly at poor farms focused on the lack of modern health care and the often-depressing conditions, but few people outright rejected the notion that they deserved care. Despite a general agreement that older people in need of charity merited respect and sympathy, the poor farm was the best that could be offered. With no universal pension system or comprehensive care for the elderly, the growing population of older Americans had nowhere else to go if they lacked family resources. They brought new challenges to poor farms, not the least of which was structural: they needed buildings that were easily navigated and care for chronic conditions.

Carleton's verses tugged at the heartstrings because they exposed deeply held fears about being abandoned in old age and dying alone. Selfish children could be blamed in some cases, but many elderly poor farm residents were like Luise Baun and lacked immediate family. Economics also played a role, as Mary Roberts Smith noted about the San Francisco residents: "very many of the old are poor, but old age is not responsible for their poverty. They were in most cases poor before they were old." Those who struggled during the prime of life were most likely to struggle at the end of their lives as well. Property could entice family members to provide care, but families on the verge of poverty were ill-equipped to add an extra member to their household. Fears of propertied people being dumped on public charity, while not entirely without example, were not representative of the population at poor farms.[6]

There was shame associated with the loss of physical capabilities, and fear in needing to rely on the help of strangers. Spending life's final years at the poor farm "symbolized the callous treatment awarded the elderly in an industrialized society," and "violated the longstanding belief that the elderly deserved respectful treatment." The poor farm was thought to "include the composite horrors of poverty, disgrace, loneliness, humiliation, abandonment, and degradation." These concerns expressed larger fears about aging: bodies quit and children moved away. Such total dependence frightened those used to self-sufficiency, and many people hoped their family would support them in their time of need because, "a well-conducted family life was 'the chief safeguard against poverty and dependency in old age.'" But there remained some people who reached old age with no family, or family not "well-conducted."[7] Of course, most older people did not live alone or die at a poor farm, even as fertility rates declined and fewer children existed to take care of parents.[8] Multigenerational households were common, with older relatives living alongside younger couples.[9] The poor farm was an intervention for those without other options, highlighting the long-term consequences of a labor market that did not provide wages enough to sustain a family.[10]

Scholars of old age debate whether respect for the elderly in the United States declined, and if so when. The increase in the elderly population in institutional care suggests that it did. But various factors played a role: most poor farm residents lacked property, which then offered little incentive for family to provide care. The late nineteenth-century emphasis on dedicating resources to immediate family members earmarked more for children and less for extended family. Farm tenancy for people older than sixty-five increased more than tenancy for the general population, jumping 10 percent in the early 1900s.[11] If this was a cause, then finances—not respect—had held together a tenuous care plan for the old. Most people with property to pass on did not end up at the poor farm, and sometimes those who did saw that property turned over to county officials for reimbursement of care, providing further encouragement for family members who stood to inherit to step up.[12] Guilt, however powerful, did not induce everyone to house an aging relative. Florence Nolan, the last matron of a Vermont poor farm, remembered the final resident as "one old guy . . . was up in his nineties and he was the father of 16 girls . . . they all lived around Sheldon but only one ever came to see him . . . he died there."[13] The private dynamics of family life frequently played a role in deciding whether older relatives were given care or spent their last years in an institution.

The increase in the elderly poor in poor farms during the late nineteenth and early twentieth centuries did not result from a massive generational change; the proportion of those over sixty only increased about 2 percent. However, since the general population got much bigger during this time, there were in fact a great many older people—just as there were a great many younger people. The 1890 census defined old age as sixty-five, as opposed to a designation given based on health or capability. Between 1850 and 1890, the age at which men and women married and had their last child changed little—the marriage age was around 25 and the last child was born for men at 37 and women 33.5. But the average age at death increased: for men it went from 62 to 66 and women from 61 to 71. This meant that on average, couples had more time on their own without anyone in the household to help.[14]

The average age of poor farm residents—which hovered around fifty years old by the early 1900s (half of all poor farm users in 1903 were fifty-five and over)—had multiple causes. Beginning in the late nineteenth century, campaigns to remove children from poor farms succeeded in placing most into other institutions or homes, and direct aid programs tended to help younger families.[15] The development of maternity homes in towns and cities caused many women of childbearing age to use those resources as opposed to giving birth at poor farms. The multiplication of state asylums and institutions also tended to remove younger people from poor farms, while cases of chronic senility more common among the elderly were returned. The modernization and industrialization of the country appeared to make the struggle of growing old while poor more severe.[16] By 1910, 25 percent of older Americans were in dependent poverty, and that increased to almost 30 percent at the start of the Depression.[17] Almost no new resources were spent with an aim of removing older people from poor farms; only the elderly were left without specialized care facilities.[18]

By the twentieth century older men were the most common poor farm residents. Having residents complete manageable chores and tasks around the institution helped keep them engaged and active but did not eliminate the need for paid employees. Photo courtesy of the McLean County Museum of History, Bloomington, Illinois.

The practicalities of having so many older residents caused dilemmas for institutions: the elderly tended to be chronically sick and have long-term debilitations. They were far less likely to pitch in with labor around the institution. Bedridden people needed constant care, which in turn required more staff. The results could be tragic: Putnam County, New York, had no real staff for its poor farm resulting in four old, bedridden women receiving care provided by other residents, all of whom were described as elderly, infirm, or senile.[19] Conditions did not have to be that sad to be noticeable. Leah and Jack Jones worked at a poor farm until their retirement in 1952. Jack said, "People don't come in as good physical condition now as they did in the early days. They stay out of the infirmary now until they're older and less able to work."[20] The old and infirm had a harder time navigating the stairs found in multistory poor farms, causing them to spend more time in one room.

Making poor farms nicer did not necessarily remove the stigma. Rural sociologist Benson Landis noted that while poor farm conditions may have improved, "it is still a disgrace to live there."[21] In describing the judgments placed on the institutionalized elderly, one reformer remarked, "The almshouse in our state would hence forth be a home for those who have made a failure of life and who are stranded in their old age without friends or means."[22] Howard Good grew up on a farm in Van Wert County, Ohio, and recalled that while many farmers occasionally found themselves indebted, "In the eyes of most people we knew, nothing so distinctly marked one a failure as arriving at old age penniless, due allowance of course being made for circumstances. Contemplating their own sunset years, they felt that nothing, when those years came, could be quite so dreadful, so humiliating, or so shameful as to find themselves at last homeless, bankrupt, and dependent, going to the poorhouse for shelter and a place to die."[23]

Surrendering Independence

Twenty-first-century research about institutionalizing the elderly highlights the dehumanizing and depersonalizing characteristics found in nursing home facilities. They are places where people go to "live out their allotted lives and die."[24] Communal living does not equal a community; there can be a minimum amount of privacy, limited social experiences, and the environment is routinized, noncreative, and deprives residents of familial relationships. People can become apathetic and their personal habits deteriorate. Some studies suggest that older people living in institutions are psychologically worse off, withdrawn, and likely to die sooner.[25] These problems echo those of poor farms, which were criticized for robbing people of their autonomy, making the elderly bored and isolated, surrounding them with unpleasantness, and not giving them any meaningful activities. Essentially, critiques about modern nursing homes mirror some of those levied at poor farms.

Transitioning to the institutional environment of a poor farm presented challenges for adults who had lived independently for decades. While male residents could claim no power over their domain, women could not manage a home, a kitchen, or fulfill many of the domestic duties to which they were accustomed. Unlike staying with relatives where their opinions might matter, critics charged that poor farm governance infantilized residents, particularly the elderly. Told when to wake, when to eat, and what to do helped make the poor farm a terrifying destination for many, as did its seeming permanence for older residents; they were the least likely to leave. They could do small tasks around the farm and home if able, but those who were incapacitated faced countless hours of monotony and boredom. The surrender of autonomy and the relatively new phenomenon of relying on strangers added trauma to an already challenging circumstance. Acknowledging poverty or loneliness was one aspect of the distress, but so too was the loss of identity that came with the lack of self-guided work, privacy, and agency. Poor farm residency also severed community connections such as church attendance and neighborhood functions. When they were included in community events, it was cause for special comment, as noted by one newspaper writer who appealed for a holiday party for "seventy six old, gray haired men and women out over the hill, who sit by the fire and rock, recalling the days of the Huskin' Bee, the Quilting Party and the Spelling Schools they attended in the time of the Civil War. These people were the very 'salt of the Earth,' the sturdy pioneer stock, who settled Fairfield's wilderness. . . . To these grand old burden bearers, the splendid people of the county owe a debt of gratitude." Residents of both the infirmary and the children's home received a holiday celebration as a result of the article, but this consideration did not resolve the regular monotony the party was intended to temporarily alleviate.[26]

Some suggestions for improvements were offered by men like Alexander Johnson, who thought the cottage plans in Virginia extended slightly more independence for the elderly because it allowed them to bring furnishings from home, provided they had any. But those same cottages did not fare well in visitor inspections because they were not well maintained, nor did they encourage group activities or socialization.[27] Generally, Johnson believed that grouping the "better grade of inmates" together and extending them such courtesies as were possible was the best response. He was referring to the perceived indignities of the elderly spending their final years surrounded by the insane, the sick, transients, and alcoholics.[28]

Among the ideas of Homer Folks and others were improvements for elderly institutional care, or as he phrased it, "a considerable reconstruction of our ideas of the proper care of the destitute aged is necessary and proper." These included buildings constructed with private rooms as opposed to dormitory-style sleeping quarters, varied menus so that meals were not reminiscent of prison food, decent and seasonally appropriate clothing, and small tasks that would be "beneficial upon the moral well-being of the inmates," especially outside chores. In Montana, superintendent F. C. Hallyer agreed, saying that his eleven residents (nine men, two women) were "all comfortable and in a contented frame of mind," and that they were quite helpful around the farm. A reporter described them as "all old people not capable of doing a day's work, yet some of the men were out in the garden hoeing and others were mowing the lawn."[29] Folks wanted county officials to "contemplate a life for the aged and infirm, which will not be simply waiting for the end . . . but a life which shall round out the closing years in a more natural way," free from stigma and discomfort.[30] No one objected to the idea but funds were not readily forthcoming. G. W. Evans, who inspected the Dade County, Missouri, Poor Farm, requested "the purchase of three rocking chairs for the old ladies at the poor farm, for they have none, and they need

Buildings were not constructed with the mobility limitations of the residents in mind. Residents who used wheelchairs needed first-floor accommodations or elevators, which modern nursing homes were more adept at providing. This c. 1910 photo shows an Ohio woman enjoying time outside with an employee. Photo courtesy of Steven Mizer.

them very bad, the chairs they have are of the poorest quality and they have never had any rockers." Simply getting better seating required a public, formal requisition.[31]

When Family Fails

Why some older people ended up at the poor farm when most others lived out their days with family is a complicated and individualized issue. Living in an extended household of non-immediate family members made older people vulnerable, and the poorest of older people were most likely to live in that situation because they lacked the finances to maintain their own household.[32] In 1880, 35 percent of people over sixty-five lived with extended family or in extended households, as compared to 7 percent of the entire population.[33] Being without immediate family increased the likelihood of poor farm residency, as did being divorced and widowed. By 1923, more than half of the men and more than a third of the women in poor farms were unmarried, widowed, or divorced.[34] Gender was a significant variable: widowed men were more likely than women, in their older age, to live as boarders in the houses of nonrelatives, and childless widows "were the losers in the great gamble, marriage, of a conjugal family system" because they were left without the income of either a male breadwinner or children to provide care.[35] Children were more likely to take care of mothers because it was a "most disgraceful thing for relatives or children to allow an old woman to go to the almshouse." As one report noted, children "will make greater sacrifices in order to keep an aged mother at home and prevent her going to a poorhouse, than they would for an aged father or other male relative."[36] In contrast, men were viewed as more personally responsible for their fate: "men are supposed to have had their chance to lay up money, and if they have not done so they must take the consequences."[37] This did not mean, however, that older women in poor farms escaped judgment. A study done by a women's association concluded that elderly poor farm women possessed particular traits that made them undesirable to care for, including "mental incompetence, moral obloquy, or chronic disease."[38]

Additionally, more women survived to be taken care of. Between 1880 and 1910, the percentage of people aged forty to forty-four with living mothers was twice as high as those with fathers.[39] Over the course of the nineteenth and twentieth centuries, life expectancy for women doubled, from forty to almost eighty, while the average number of children they had decreased. By the early 1900s there were more older women with fewer children to provide care.[40] A report from Ohio indicated that some women struggled to earn an independent wage after their husbands died, an assertion supported by studies from San Francisco and the state of California.[41] Mathilda Waterman died in 1901 after a short stay at a poor farm. Local reports noted that she had lived in the county since 1847, and that her husband had been presumed dead since around 1849, when he left for the gold rush and never returned. Only one of her three children survived to adulthood and she never remarried.[42] When elderly women lived alone it was more affordable for counties to house them in the poor farm than to provide them with the amount of direct aid needed to keep them independent.

Children could not always be counted on for care or incentivized to help, but county officials sometimes tried. Wilson Bunch, who was seventy-four in the early 1920s, had the following intake entry: "bad health, no home, widower, [county] helped a few times, his son agreed to keep him but didn't want to go to county home."[43] Bunch had received aid but was now homeless, so the county enticed his son to take him through aid payments. Children were sought after by officials, with one county using the sheriff to track down the adult children of some elderly men, with the intention of making them pay for the care of their fathers or taking them into their homes. Such a plan only succeeded when there were children who could be located and who could afford to help; it did counties no good to drive an entire family into poverty for the care of an individual. One study estimated that 90 percent of children with parents in a poor farm were not financially able to provide care.[44] Former farmer and poor farm resident Charles Martin told a reporter for the local paper, "When a man loses his wife he is wrecked. . . . I have been here 18 months; rheumatism knocked me out." He had not heard from his three adult children since being admitted to the farm.[45] Joseph Clark of Ohio was a farmer and day laborer. He and his wife had at least seven children between the 1840s and 1850s, but by 1880 the seventy-three-year-old man needed care and came to live at the local poor farm. He did so despite having a son, his namesake in fact, living nearby on a farm with his own family. The elderly sometimes had ailments too challenging for their children or grandchildren to handle. Clark, for example, was listed as maimed, or "crippled."[46] Older men like Clark lacked both the familial participation and economic benefit that incentivized adult children to keep them.[47] Without land to pass on in exchange for care, it may have simply been too much strain on the finances of his son's household.

Between 1880 and 1910, there appears to have been little demographic difference in the number of households made up of immediate family, extended family, or no family at all. For certain communities, such as some of those studied in Colorado by Thomas Krainz, there were cultural expectations for elder care. Steven Ruggles also makes a convincing case for the nineteenth century being a time period when an unmarried child was more likely to stay behind to take care of an elderly parent, as opposed to elderly parents moving in with children, but this was most applicable to parents with property to pass on. The more economically prosperous the parents, the more likely a child was to remain at home: inheritance was a powerful motivator to provide care.[48] It makes the lines from "Out from the Poorhouse" all the more charged, as an old man explains that his children took the farm and sent him to the poorhouse: "Why did I give them the farm clear from debt / and all my savings for years, too? But yet—/ it is better so now as I soon shall be above, / out from the Poorhouse, where dwells peace and love."[49]

While poems and songs made going to the poor farm sound like a one-way trip, children did claim their parents from the institutions. Elizabeth Bailey, who was an eighty-four-year-old widow, was retrieved by her daughter two years after admission; Charles Dunbrack, age seventy-one, stayed for six months before being claimed by a daughter.[50] Nan Stone was in her sixties when she lived in the Searcy County, Arkansas, poor farm after her husband died. Eventually her son came and removed her.[51] It took Martha Watson's daughter three months to claim her, and Joseph Mathers's relatives took him home after a similar stay.[52] The varying lengths of time it took for these reclamations hint at the potential complications an elderly parent caused for children. By the early twentieth century, social workers intervened in some cases to encourage retrieval of parents. In 1918, Clyde McKinniss, the head of the Pittsburgh City Home, voiced confidence that abandoning parents at poor farms was a relic of the past; instead "our modern investigator or social worker" intervened. But, at the same event where McKinniss made this assertion, other speakers decried the lack of social workers in rural areas.[53] Will Carleton's last stanza about the older woman bound for the poorhouse carefully negotiates her feelings of disappointment that her children "shirked and slighted me," with her love for them:

> Over the hill to the poor-house-my chil'rn dear, good-by!
> Many a night I've watched you when only God was nigh;
> And God 'll judge between us; but I will al'ays pray
> That you shall never suffer the half I do to-day.

But eventually the character has a happy ending in a sequel, when one of her sons returns after hearing about his mother's plight. He buys her old home and moves in with her.[54]

Adult children faced financial challenges in caring for an ageing parent, but there were also occasional complaints about the emotional difficulties of dealing with the elderly. A Ross County, Ohio, man found himself in an infirmary across the state after moving in with his daughter and son-in-law. The paper reporting his trip noted that he was "not angelically disposed" and had "attempted to assume guardianship of the household." The younger couple offered to pay his lodging elsewhere but he refused, instead being transported back home by county officials.[55] Dr. Edward T. Devine noted that "the feeble old men and women . . . querulous and crotchety though they may be, outliving their usefulness, surviving their children and grandchildren, cherishing in their infirmities the memory of their active years, are yet entitled because of their need to sympathy." In 1900, reformer Mary Vida Clark claimed, "The ordinary almshouse 'old lady' is a person of little tolerance or sympathy and extraordinary sensitiveness to fine distinctions in the social position of herself and her fellow inmates."[56] The attitude described might speak to the fear and humiliation older women felt. One recommendation was for poor farms to provide "little luxuries or comforts" to make for fewer complaints.[57] Betty Groth Syverson lived at a poor farm in Iowa during the 1930s, and she recalled that most of the older residents brought her and her siblings joy, and vice versa. However, an older woman who lived in one of the boxcars converted for married couples gave the children pause. She hated hearing them play and placed razor blades in the grass to warn them off. It is unclear how she came to have those blades, but Syverson said her father moved the woman's boxcar farther away from the main building.[58]

Older people were, both with caregivers and at the poor farm, vulnerable to neglect and abuse. At least one former poor farm matron returned to the site of her previous employment as a resident because her son neglected her in his own home. A 1921 report charged that Mary Palmer's son and daughter-in-law left her upstairs in unclean clothing and linens. Neighbors called the Humane Society, who removed the eighty-year-old, who was described by her son as "unbalanced" and "bitter." He claimed she had "not a dollar" left, although she had deeded him all her property.[59] C. J. Johnston recalled a widow who came with gold coins sewn to the inside of her dress. She stayed at the farm for eight years and had $10 left when she died. Her funeral was on-site because she wanted it to be among friends. Then, her twelve children came and fought over a violin she kept. Matron Johnston broke it and told them to divvy it up that way, as punishment for their selfishness and unwillingness to care for her in her old age. The sewing of the coins might have protected the funds from her family or other residents. Taylor McVey's family did not come get him either: he was sixty-eight years old in 1920, with a wife a third his age and four young children.[60]

In rarer cases, family members had more complicated decisions to make about the care of a parent, especially when they were taking care of a disabled adult child. When her husband died, Rebecca Sheckells could not take care of both herself and her son John, who had a disability, so they moved to the poor farm. She had seven other children, but it took more than two years before relatives came to remove Rebecca and John from the farm, after which time they both disappear from records.[61] Harriett Meek was in similar straits as an eighty-year-old widow who did not own her home or have a trade. She was responsible for her fifty-six-year-old daughter Minnie who had lived with her parents her entire life. When Harriett's husband died, it the two women lost their breadwinner and no family members stepped forward to help.[62]

Wage Work and Old Age

By the early twentieth century, the most likely resident at a poor farm was a man over the age of forty-five who had no family and who worked as a general laborer. Saving for old age proved difficult for men who struggled with irregular and underemployment during their best earning years. People who barely maintained solvency when they were younger fell further behind as they aged, became sick, and slowed down. The farmer in Frost's poem "Death of the Hired Man" highlights the issue of older workers when he says of Silas, "What good is he? Who else will harbor him / At his age for the little he can do?"[63] Historian Sarah Rose described laborers on a "spectrum of productivity" during their lives, which can be seen in the decreasing median earnings of laborers after the age of forty. Between 1889 and 1918 those earnings hit an all-time low after age fifty, closely aligning with the average age of male poor farm residents during the same period.[64] A Pennsylvania study completed in 1919 indicated that out of almshouse residents in that state, 75 percent of whom were fifty and older, more than half categorized themselves as unskilled laborers or domestics. A similar story played out in Massachusetts, where 70 percent of the older almshouse residents had never owned any debt-free property and earned $10 a week or less before coming to the institution.[65]

A fast-paced, industrializing nation was a difficult place to grow old with no financial security. But industry was only part of the problem. The belief that in rural areas, "there is always work . . . and rent is negligible" was far more applicable to younger, able-bodied men.[66] As sociologist Barbara Brents notes, old age and a slower pace seemed an obstacle of sorts for the technology and increased productivity associated with industrialization and progress, which is why pensions would have met the needs of both the elderly and industry.[67] One state legislative committee noted in 1929 that "the advent of labor saving devices and machinery, duplicating nearly all formerly purely manual operations, has taken away employment from thousands of aged people, and left practically no jobs for the old man or woman."[68] In ways similar to the exclusion of people with disabilities, fewer employment opportunities for older people left them more reliant on aid.

Programs designed to help wage-earners did not benefit older working adults. The growing number of state workers' compensation acts in the early twentieth century made it less likely that older people, especially men, would be considered for jobs, since they were the most likely to be injured on the job and were blamed for causing additional on-site accidents. Compensation payments varied across state and frequently did not cover expenses or lost wages. The new laws also excluded domestic and agricultural workers, which in 1910 accounted for more than half of wage-earning women and four-fifths of wage-earning African Americans.[69] At the same time, NCSW president John Lapp reported that "the mechanization of industry . . . has taken away the chance for the older and less supple. It is a bitter irony that life has been lengthened for the aged and the means of living have been lessened." Farm labor, too, was physically harder for older people, and many children went to cities for other opportunities. Steven Ruggles described the change this way: "all a family needed for a secure old age or to ride out a period of depression was a quarter section of good land and a couple of sons to help farm it . . . old people simply lived on the farm until they died, [but] by the time people got old, the children had already left and gone to the city. There was no one to take care of them." The belief that a national transition from farm to industry increased the burden of aging by dissolving the extended family as a unit of help directed a considerable amount of policy.[70]

The changing nature of labor for the aging made things even more difficult for those with a disability. Martin Hoag was not a stranger to the poor farm. Labeled as having "mania" in 1880, he was locked away at night, and multiple stays at the Morgan County Poor Farm during his adult life demonstrate that he used it as a way station of sorts as he struggled to earn a living with his illness and disability. On at least one occasion the superintendent removed him after he refused to cut corn. He was labeled a "crank" and "lame." It was clearly difficult for him to keep a job; in June of 1900, he returned for a couple of weeks. He listed his profession as laborer. Then he left, only to come back again in October 1901 and March of 1902.[71] He was around sixty-five years old by this time with limited options. The poor farm at least gave him the opportunity to come and go as he was able. Harvey Case was also around sixty years old when the Wood County Board of Directors tried to remove him from the poor farm because they were overwhelmed by expenses. He had been widowed twice and worked as a laborer. His removal was short term: by 1900 he was back living at the farm, and in apparently poor health. He died there in 1901.[72] Being elderly, unemployed, and reliant on the poor farm proved too much for some. Between 1888 and 1897, during the heart of the depression of the 1890s, Fritz, a seventy-year-old laborer, found himself in and out of the Dane County Poor Farm five times. Saying he was leaving to find work, the superintendent recorded that instead he killed himself in a nearby village.[73]

Although poor farms were associated with robbing the elderly of autonomy, a few examples suggest some leniency. When older people did not want to live at the poor farm, officials did not force the issue, nor did they prevent men like Hoag and Fritz from leaving to look for work.[74] Sometimes officials went so far as to provide small amounts of direct aid to men who refused to use the poor farm. Perhaps not wanting to rob them of their independence or opportunities to pick up wages, officials in Pennsylvania supported three men who lived in shanties and a hut described as "not fit for human habitation." The men refused to come to the poor farm for care and got various small sums for groceries.[75] There were also older people who essentially checked themselves into the poor farm, like lifelong farmer Albert Stout, who went to his local poor farm in April 1932 because he was old and could no longer care for himself. The census of 1930 recorded him living with a nephew and his family on their farm, but that arrangement did not last although it is not clear what, if any, factor the financial upheaval of the decade played in his departure. Upon admission, and anxious to not be buried at the poor farm, he told the superintendent he had prepaid for a lot and marker in a cemetery nearby. He was seventy-five, a widower, and had two brothers and one sister still living. Ohio's Samuel Trethewa also apparently arrived at the poor farm willingly, having given most of his savings away to friends and acquaintances. When he died in 1878, the local paper claimed that there were "several farmers in this section who owe their property to the liberality of Mr. Trethewa" and expressed dismay that none of them had taken him in.[76]

Pensions

Advocates of a pension program for the elderly firmly believed it would help keep older people out of poor farms. Everyone from Thomas Paine, Civil War veterans, fraternal groups such as the Order of Eagles, the 1912 Progressive Party platform, and advocates of Social Security used the fear, shame, and embarrassment older people might feel about the poor farm to lobby for pension programs.[77] Early twentieth-century efforts to help the elderly poor included a California law that allotted $100 annually for every indigent person over sixty. By 1935, twenty-eight states had some type of old-age assistance, which varied widely in terms of eligibility and funds.[78] These joined existing military pension programs, which helped keep many elderly veterans out of county poor farms. They also had specific care institutions to use, to both honor their service and save counties money.

For those who were not veterans the options were far fewer, which made pensions seem all the more necessary if the goal was to save the elderly poor from the almshouse. Old-age homes, most of them private, often had long waiting lists and required considerable entrance fees or specific qualifications, like the rest home for Minnesota farm women founded by a doctor and lauded by a 1915 *Ladies' Home Journal* story.[79] Various religious denominations and fraternal organizations founded facilities for the aged in recognition of members' fears of the almshouse. Sometimes these efforts were couched in the premise that certain classes of old people deserved better conditions. One request for admission to a private home noted that the recipient was a "refined aged woman" who would "die of a broken heart if she were compelled to go to the county farm."[80] The trauma associated with loss of status and security affected people differently, but issues of abandonment and loneliness crossed class boundaries.[81] Without veteran status or a pension-qualifying profession, older men did not have much chance of leaving the poor farm without family intervention.

The benefits provided by veterans' pensions have been referred to as "one of the world's largest singularly targeted welfare plans." Their development, alongside institutions specifically for veterans, was intended to keep veterans out of poor farms, whether they resided there as a result of injury, illness, or some other problem.[82] The Iowa Grand Army of the Republic took up the cause of veterans in poor farms, claiming that more than 300 penniless veterans were being supported by that state's poorhouses; newspapers sympathetic to the construction of a state soldiers' home reported a "large per cent" of its residents would come "from parties now in the alms houses of the State, and for those dependent upon the various charitable societies to which they belong for their subsistence."[83] These efforts were similar to those advocating for state asylums to remove people labeled insane from jails and poor farms, and they filled just as fast. The Illinois Soldiers' Home at Quincy (ILSH) was so overwhelmed with dependent veterans that they prioritized "only those old soldiers and sailors who are now inmates of poor houses or infirmaries." The scale of this problem meant the hoped-for commitment to wives and widows never fully developed, and some of them remained in poor farms without their husbands. The Indiana Soldiers' Home (INSH), which admitted both men and women from its opening in 1896, was flooded with letters from local officials trying to send veterans' widows. Trying to argue for a widow's admission to the INSH, a county official wrote, "She is alone without money friends or anything else in the way of comfort and the trustee is talking of sending her to the poorhouse. She has promised me if I would assist her to get back to the Home she would stay I don't think she will stay very long as she is so feeble. . . . Please let me know at once as she is in hard luck and in a rough part of the town."[84] One elderly Illinois woman filled her time at the poor farm by mailing letters to her husband. After a lifetime of labor, an injury followed by an illness had separated the couple when he gained admission to the Soldier's Home and she did not.[85]

Assistance for veterans helped alleviate the need for institutionalization at poor farms for a significant number, but never cleared poor farms of veterans entirely. One estimate suggested that in Massachusetts the charity rolls would have grown by a third without military pensions; in 1889 Ohio's infirmaries were estimated to contain at least 600 veterans. Delegates to New York's state constitutional convention estimated that "between six and seven hundred disabled soldiers" were still housed in their state's poorhouses. Iowa veteran Henry Clinton Parkhurst complained about living alongside "the utter scum of civil and military life—the ignorant refuse of jails, almshouses, insane asylums, and penitentiaries."[86] Despite those strong opinions, officials believed that veterans and counties benefitted from their removal. Sometimes help arrived too late, as was the case for a man found unconscious on the streets of Uniondale, Indiana, "on the pan handle." County officials delivered the comatose man to the poor farm, where his only form of identification noted his veteran status. The superintendent then transferred him to the soldier's home where he died having never awakened.[87]

Special Circumstances

One of the problems with veterans' homes was that they broke up married couples, but in poor farms there was at least the possibility of remaining together.

Married couples made up an exceptionally small percentage of poor farm residents; one study of nearly 14,000 people counted only thirty-six married couples. The death of a spouse was commonly the event that caused institutionalization. While some poor farms separated couples upon admission because of the division of men and women, a few places offered an option of a shared room, individual cottage housing, or, in at least one case, converted train cars for older couples.[88] Some of the southern cottage-style arrangements allowed for cohabitation, as did Cooley Farms outside of Cleveland, which served as the poor farm, workhouse, and old folk's home combined on a large campus. Because admitting couples was rare, allotting such space was not seen as a particularly efficient use of resources.[89] With a grim outlook on lifelong partnership, Alexander Johnson said such rooms "should not be obligatory; it is frequently the case that old couples prefer to separate."[90]

Records do provide some evidence of couples arriving together and help explain the circumstances that contributed to such a decision. In the 1930s Bill and Emma Pillow were long-term residents at the Grayson County, Texas, Poor Farm, staying for at least a decade before his death. She remained in county care, eventually transitioning to the public nursing home until her death in 1968.[91] Joshua and Charlotte Wheeler were in their eighties when admitted to the poor farm. He died eight months later, and she left three days after his death to live with a daughter, suggesting that caring for a mother was more feasible than for two parents at once. The Wheelers had at least three grown children living nearby, but for reasons that could have had to do with Joshua's illness, they waited until he died to intervene.[92] Christina and John Robertson were both listed as sick and feeble in 1913 when they were admitted. John died only a month after arriving and she left six months later, with no destination listed. The Robertsons were childless, so perhaps Christina had extended family willing to help her, but not him. Julia Hendricks came with her sick husband to a poor farm in February 1907 to nurse and comfort him. The day after his death she left the institution and was hired as a housekeeper for a widower. She died two years later. Julia was capable of work but presumably could not maintain a job and care for her husband simultaneously.[93]

For people with disabilities, it was not uncommon to grow old at a poor farm. Johnson believed that "in the small rural communities, much of the population will be constant for many years" and should be kindly treated because for them, the institution truly served as a home. The Henry County, Ohio, Infirmary had a substantial number of residents who lived for decades at the institution. Clearance Strong, who entered in 1886 at the age of thirty, spent his whole life there, dying in 1939.[94] As historian Kim Nielsen notes, people with disabilities are more likely to live in poverty because of structural components of society that "hinder their social advancement" and because not all families were financially able to provide care.[95] Poor farms' long-term residents included those with conditions such as Down Syndrome, cerebral palsy, and intellectual disabilities. Some municipalities also passed "ugly laws" that banned any "crippled, maimed, or deformed person" from begging in public or exposing any part of a "diseased, mutilated, or deformed" body part. Those laws barred people from trying to support themselves, and the poor farm was a place to hide those "deviant bodies" and potentially find them suitable and useful tasks to do.[96] Many helped with livestock, in the gardens, or around the house—not as forced labor but as contributors.

In much the same way they liked anecdotes about residents with disabilities, local press also focused on elderly poor farm residents of long duration. In 1929, an Auburn, Indiana, paper reported on five residents at the Dekalb County Farm, all of whom had lived there for fifty years or more. Among them were seventy-six-year-old Silas Casebeer who worked a big team of horses because "someone got him interested." He also took the horses for their shoes and received a nickel for a cigar while in town.[97] In 1925, reporters from the Williamson County, Illinois, paper did a running series about life at the poor farm. They found about twenty people, mostly elderly, who struggled with various ailments. In the winter they had little to keep them occupied, but one woman quilted while another man weaved willow rods together to make decorations. A chief complaint documented in the articles was the comparisons of treatment between the poor farm and the jail, which was particularly offensive for the elderly. One resident said, "We are fed well and treated well, but if we are as good as your criminals, give us as good a home as they have; if we are not as good, let us live here." The reporter added:

> The men sleep on army cots and on an average there are four cots in a room. The rooms are heated by open fireplaces. Some improvements have been made since Mr. Cummins became superintendent of the farm. There are now electric lights in the room although at present the lighting plant has broken down so that the rooms are lighted only by the glow from the fireplaces, which until two years ago was all the light afforded at any time. Since then a water system has been installed, providing bath and toilet, these things may be regarded as bare necessities. There is nothing about the place to hint as comfort for these old people who are unfortunate. All but three of the folks living on the county farm are over fifty years of age.

Comparing the elderly poor to criminals proved to be one of the longest running concerns about old people living at poor farms. They had done nothing to deserve such stigma. Among the types of comforts that could be provided to older poor farm residents were a library, radios, movie nights, pool tables, and visits from local entertainment groups.[98] In Ohio in 1941, community outrage about the confiscation of poor farm pets subsided after a local person read the newspaper story about their seizure and volunteered to pay for dog licenses.[99]

When counties built new institutions, they sometimes planned for larger capacities than needed. The Ross County Infirmary rarely filled this building meant for hundreds of residents. Multistory buildings like this one did not lend themselves to long-term care facilities for the elderly. Photo courtesy of Ross County Historical Society, Chillicothe, Ohio.

Dying at the Poor Farm

In 1910, 17,000 of the more than 100,000 people who stayed at poor farms during the year died. In comparison, more than 40,000 people left of their own accord, and 14,000 left having been claimed by family. The death rate typically exceeded that of the general population because the institutions concentrated the sick and old.[100] In 1909 when the term "geriatrics" was coined, no medical school offered classes on aging and no one specialized in diseases or decline specifically related to growing old. Aging was simply seen as a natural degradation of the body over time.[101] When poor farm residents are described as "cranky" or cantankerous, issues of chronic pain and the discomfort of cancers, rotting teeth, arthritis, and a host of other conditions should be considered. Emily Abel suggests that in some institutions, depression in residents could have hastened their death by weakening their immune systems.[102] Essayist Elaine Scarry notes that physical suffering can render people inarticulate or unable to express themselves using recognizable language. For those who were constantly uncomfortable, the sparse accommodations probably made things worse. Don Darling, who spent his childhood at a poor farm in Kansas, recalled attempts to make the terminally ill "as comfortable as possible and allowed to die with dignity. Even in the midst of the depression, it was a kinder, gentler America."[103]

Some poor farms began transferring terminal residents to other facilities during the 1920s, both for their own comfort and to alleviate the labor required by a dying resident. Matrons, responsible for the nursing care, did not always have the tools to abate the discomfort or suffering of the dying. Morgan County moved residents in these circumstances including a 1925 case when an elderly man who fell on ice was taken to the hospital where he died instead of remaining at the farm, a change of practice compared to previous decades.[104] This was not always possible for African American residents if medical facilities refused them admission, leaving them to the poor farm or with no assistance at all.

For those who died at the poor farm most counties ensured respectful if hasty burials, sometimes with services—even without a minister—so that other residents could pay their respects. Most were interred in the farm cemetery or a public cemetery, but bodies were claimed by relatives or friends as well. Michigan and Colorado made it policy to use unclaimed poor farm bodies as medical school cadavers, which added to fears for elderly poor farm residents.[105] One minister called that policy "a stain on Michigan; a criminal act."[106] Ohio law dictated that infectious bodies and those of "strangers or travelers" were not permitted to be donated, but those bodies unclaimed or considered "tramps" by officials could be sent to medical schools. It does not seem as though the laws about medical schools were consistently followed. Counties sometimes granted veterans and their relatives funds for private burials.[107] A few Kansas counties paid the superintendent $3 per burial and one specified that grave markers of a specific dimension were mandatory.[108] Even in death, expenses were tightly managed. In Michigan one superintendent noted that they paid an undertaker $20 and clergy $2 per death. Some of the expense was offset with "a little something" residents left before they died, or that some friend had deposited for them to pay their expenses. Providing someone a final dignity of a burial was considerably easier than caring for them in the final weeks, months, or years of their life.[109] Those who might not have been able to provide care to the living could pay respects to the dead.

While poor farm funerals were not remarkable events and most grave markers were a number only, sometimes the loss was keenly felt and commemorated. When "Badger," a little person and long-time gardener at Dane County's poor farm, became sick suddenly and died in early 1882, Superintendent J. S. Meyers oversaw the arrangements personally. His coffin was made by George Schroeder, who worked alongside him in the garden, and the residents and staff attended his on-site memorial service. Meyers recorded his death with sadness and provided a dignified burial. The deaths of longtime poor farm residents received newspaper notices as well. Even if they did not rate a full obituary, simple announcements such as "Harvey Case died at the infirmary this morning. He was about 80 years old and had been in the infirmary fourteen years. He formerly resided in Milton Center" ensured deaths were publicly recognized.[110]

Poor farm cemeteries are frequently the only remaining artifact of the institutions left in communities. Because most of the people buried in these locations did not receive a grave marker and records linking people to burials are spotty, they are sites of community contestation. Counties across the country have taken steps to commemorate and maintain poor farm cemeteries, placing markers, signage, or memorials. Others, however, are located on private property or have been buried under or relocated for development. In Summit County, Ohio, for example, an untold number of bodies were moved by the county from the first site of the poor farm, while others were apparently left behind and now lie unmarked in a local park, where they were the subject of an archaeological surveying project in 2017.

The inability to self-support in older age was a menacing specter for the elderly. State and local officials worried about the "respectable" old people who lived in poor farms. The idea of being sent to the poor farm by one's own children was used as the ultimate threat. Older people living in poor farms gave up independence, social functions, and familiar environments when they moved to the institution. Stanislas Keenan, who helped manage a poor farm in Michigan, took special note of the residents with "snow white locks, and faces deeply seamed with sadness and sorrow," who found comfort at the poor farm. He castigated friends and children who grew tired of them or wished them dead.[111]

Interestingly, not everyone found the poor farm to be a fearful end. C. J. Johnston's family managed a county infirmary for many years, and his notions surrounding the elderly are reflective:

> It might be unfair for me to say that the infirmary was a happy place, because I was young and not a patient. I am sure it was not an unhappy place or a place where people were generally held against their will. No doubt many would have preferred to be with their children or somewhere else but not many had a choice other than to be where they were. . . . My impression is that they did what they wanted to do and were not forced to do anything. Some men just hung around the barns and the animals probably as they had done all their lives. Some were depressed but any of them, except those in the [insane] ward, could have walked away. It was a warm, clean, comfortable home for many. When my father reached his last years he one time said that mother and all his friends were gone and that he was alone and ready to join them but in the meantime he thought he would be happier if he could go to the county farm. He did not get to go, but there is no doubt that he thought of it as a friendly comfortable place.[112]

Most older people did not think of the poor farm as a happy place, but as Johnston notes, it did serve as a type of home. Although counties could not solve the problems of poverty among the elderly, they frequently recognized the connections between old age, poverty, and dependence, and the aging of their residents primed them for the changes on the horizon.[113] As the elderly poor increasingly represented the majority of poor farm residents, their health concerns pushed institutions to focus on issues of public health care, with infirmaries, public hospitals, and eventually nursing homes evolving from poor farm foundations. It made less sense to keep a population of aging residents out on a farm. Luise Baun experienced these changes as an elderly, sick woman with no immediate family. She died at the Erie County Infirmary in 1962 at a time when the institution was transitioning into a nursing and long-term care facility. Her extended family ensured a decent burial and had her headstone marked "Aunt Luise Baun." The county provided her a home after her lifetime of work, and cared for her in her final illness, at the age of eighty-six, having outlived all the members of the family she once served.

7 Poor Farms and Health Care

"The reason why they are poor is because they have had a great deal of sickness."

—Dr. M. Sabia, *Proceedings of the Annual Convention, Michigan,* 1907, 8

Lewis Price was close to 100 years old, blind, senile, with swollen feet and legs when he came under the care of poor farm physician T. O. Hardesty. Hardesty recorded his warm recollections of Price shortly after his death: "money he had none; clothes he did not need; family was all dead; had no relations; had plenty friends for which he was thankful; could not see and could not read; but could sing and pray and that was enough for him." In the days before he died, Price had gone to a local hospital but returned to the farm to rest and, in all likelihood, die. Price said that he was "ready to go," never complaining, always faithful and thankful that friends sent him things for his comfort. When he died, "white friends" paid the funeral expenses.[1] Although they stepped up to ensure some comfort and a respectable burial, caring for the sick took time and resources that people lacked or reserved for family. The friends who buried Lewis Price did not nurse him; instead the county was responsible for his care.

Sickness and poverty are inextricably linked. While homelessness ranked as the leading primary reason for poor farm admission, in 1903 Homer Folks noted that sickness "is always one of the leading causes" of destitution and is "usually *the* leading cause." As a result, he suggested that it was time to consider the residents of poor farms "more nearly related to hospital patients than paupers" and asked, "At what age of chronicity of disease does it become appropriate to apply the term pauper to a patient?"[2] People waited until an illness became severe to pursue medical treatment. Sickness or injury could decimate what little savings people had and doubled their suffering by making them unable to support their families, the result of which could be going to the poor farm. But not all workplace accidents and illnesses equaled permanent dependency. In many cases people were able to rejoin the workforce if they had family support while recuperating.[3] The poor farm served as both hospital and shelter for the chronically sick and terminally ill in the same way it did for vagrants injured in bar fights, transients who fell off trains, injured laborers, and many others. This dual purpose contributed to the initial growth of poor farms, and saved counties money on relief costs by centrally locating those in need of health care.

The connection between health care and poor farms was so strong that some institutions, such as those in Ohio and California, were called county infirmaries or hospitals, although such a name did not always honestly represent the type of care provided. County infirmaries in Ohio, for example, were poor farms, not hospitals, but the title was intended to destigmatize the institution. Reformer Mary Vida Clark supported the name change, believing it might then be possible to segregate the chronically ill from the acute cases and provide the proper type of nursing and medical care.[4] As another supporter of using the term "infirmaries" said, "The almshouse today is recognized as an infirmary and hospital rather than as a place of segregation of the non-productive element of society."[5] The long-hoped-for goals of separating the poor from the aged and infirm and creating hospitals out of poor farms were not universally adopted.

While brick multistory structures were common in the Midwest, and wood frame cottages common in the South, large wooden buildings were popular in the West, like this one in Tuolumne County, California, which combined a poorhouse and hospital. Photo from the collection of the author.

Poor farms served a public healthcare function but typically did so without being a hospital.

The role of poor farms as providers of health care was also affected by the overall wellbeing of rural people. Although rural idealism touted the countryside as beneficial and healthy, men like Liberty Hyde Bailey urged improvements to rural health care, noting, "It is pitiable that so many of the good country population are lost from neglect, and antiquated treatment of disease." This was not a new problem, which is why poor farms and counties regularly faced the financial burdens associated with residents in need of medical care. Because poor farms were typically in rural areas, the fact that rural places were underserved by doctors, nurses, and medical facilities contributed to the use of the poor farm for health care. While there were fewer epidemics because the population density was lower than in cities, rural people had more chronic illnesses and impairments.[6] The isolation of rural communities when it came to health care was one of items of concern raised by the Country Life Movement. Reformer Kenyon Butterfield claimed, "The sanitary conditions, from the public point of view, are not good in the average open country. This must have considerable effect in the long run upon the health of the family."[7] The National Health Study completed in the 1920s found that nearly a fifth of the population had a chronic disease or impairment, such as a permanent handicap from disease or accident, and that low-income groups were at higher risk for a long-term disability. The study made a definitive connection between chronic illness, disability, unemployment, and dependency. If its findings were representative of the nation at large, at least 2 percent of the population had a "permanent orthopedic impairment," which the report labeled "A National Problem."[8]

As detailed in chapter 1, poor farms were supposed to reduce the cost of paying doctors for individual visits by consolidating some patients in an institution. Doctor's bills in particular were unpredictable and cumbersome: during the winter of 1870, Illinois resident Mary Ann Throckmorton received eighteen doctor's visits within two weeks. They cost seventy-five cents each. Dr. J. L Gebhard was dispatched by county officials to tend to Eliza Bagget, who later died from her sickness, thirty-two times in a single month. He earned $24 just for her case.[9] Sometimes officials bargained with doctors for reduced fees, not in the spirit of aid "grudgingly given," but as an indication of the sheer immensity of expenses of medical relief. Van Wert County, Ohio, paid for more than 400 doctors' visits in a single year, and other counties paid medical bills for conditions ranging from "lung fever" to "lingering sickness" to "crippled."[10] Cedar County, Iowa, doctors received on average 50 percent of their requested fees from the county between 1866 and 1885.[11] Since counties and townships were already paying for health care among the poor as direct aid, it is no wonder that officials perceived that poor farms resulted in financial savings. Although an 1891 NCCC meeting attendee referred to public provisions for health care as "practically socialistic," they were a large and standard part of many counties' relief expenses.[12]

Like the elderly, sick people were usually cared for at home by family. Nineteenth-century diseases incapacitated people but did not necessarily bring death quickly. The strain, expense, and time invested in taking care of the sick placed financial and emotional burdens on family for weeks, months, or even years. As historian Emily Abel established, the burden of that care usually fell on women. Although it did not necessarily interrupt wage labor for rural women, it did conflict with domestic chores and created more of them, including increased laundry, the need for more water, cooking for a specific diet, and the physical burdens of lifting or moving people.[13] Hiring nurses was financially impossible for most families, and few hospitals existed in the nineteenth century; in 1873 there were only 120 hospitals, most of them charitable and located in cities. Their numbers increased drastically over time: by 1909 more there were more than 4,000.[14] However, they were not evenly distributed, leaving rural areas profoundly underserved. Counties frequently used a section of the poor farm building—part of a floor or wing—or a building on the grounds, as the local hospital, which continued the affiliation between public health care and provisions for the poor.[15]

Abel provided a stark example that helps explain why people relied on poor farms to alleviate the burden of caring for sick relatives. In the 1880s Sarah Gillespie recorded a vivid account of her mother Emily's four-year-long illness, which began when she was only forty-six years old. Emily believed that "tensions and conflicts could produce disease" and that "loving solicitude could restore health." This idea must have been painful for those with no one to provide affectionate care. Sarah struggled to balance her job as a teacher with worrying about her mother's feet and leg pain that left her bedridden. Sarah eventually quit her job and took on the tasks of cleaning up "vomit, excreta, and blood." She lifted her mother, injuring her own back.[16] Her mother's sickness had been exacerbated by a difficult marriage and enormous amounts of farm work. Without Sarah to care for her, she might have been taken to the county home, but compassion came with costs both physical and financial for Sarah. Some women in Sarah's position went to the poor farm to continue nursing family. In Butte County, California, a sixteen-year-old daughter came to the county hospital/poor farm with her tubercular mother, because the facility did not have enough staff to give her the "close care which her helpless condition demanded."[17]

The challenges faced by Gillespie help explain why some families used the poor farm as an alternative to home care. When round-the-clock care became too difficult, too expensive, or simply not feasible, families turned to their local relief system. Not everyone was able to dedicate hours each day to medical care, nor afford the doctors' expenses related to illness, even with the help of direct aid. Migrations away from kin networks relinquished family-based care to other social structures.[18] The erosion of familial obligation was a long-term change that substantially increased the need for public care at a time when poor farms proliferated. A public institution made sense as the venue through which health care for the poor was distributed.

Nursing Care

One of the distinctions between hospital care and poor farms serving as sites of health care had to do with the professionalization of staff. Most poor farms employed a doctor, but the day-to-day tasks of caring for the sick and recuperating fell to employees, who were frequently farmers, farm hands, maids, and matrons. In 1881, Octave Thanet asked a superintendent's daughter why the poor farm had no doctor, to which she replied, "oh, pa's quite a good doctor."[19] The lack of a dedicated healthcare staff meant that conditions for sick residents could be dreadful, leaving bedridden residents to languish in "uncared-for beds with ragged bedding."[20] Critics charged that the worse patients smelled and the more helpless they were, the more likely they were to be moved to an isolated area as opposed to receiving increased, more hygienic care.

Poor farms kept ingredients on hand to perform their own medical services without a doctor present. These home remedies, common during the nineteenth century, could be passed down through families, provided from books, or received from other sources. One "recipe book" of sorts at an Illinois poor farm provided categorized treatments with ingredients and measurements. Toothaches had three different possible cures, including one for a wax that combined paraffin, burgundy pitch, and clove oil. Tooth Ache Cotton required spermaceti, crystal carbolic acid, hydrochloric acid, and cotton. The directions instructed the user to melt the spermaceti, add the carbolic acid and then the hydrochloric acid; stir until the solution was made and immerse layers of cotton. After they soaked through, they needed to hang to dry. Small pieces could then be snipped off and placed in the tooth cavity. The section on camphorated oil began by saying it was "good for hundred things where an application of oil and camphor can be used." Other notes included using digitalis for heart trouble, a shampoo recipe, and "a good all-around salve" that used beeswax, mutton suet, lard, resin, and olive oil.[21] The responsibility of making these tinctures and salves would probably have fallen to the matron.

According to Superintendent J. S. Meyers, tending to the sick required "two or three hours of my time every day."[22] The Dane County institution had more than fifty residents, but no one on staff specifically listed as a nurse, which suggests that all employees pitched in on the task. Meyers and his wife lost a child to cholera infantum during his tenure at the farm, and even with the grief and planning for the funeral, he had sick residents to care for. On the day his daughter died, he reported that he "administered medicine all day to more or less of [all] the paupers some of whom are very bad with dysentery." Two days later, he wrote in large, bold letters "Our Babe Buried," and explained that there was "not much work done to the interest of the county, except the waiting on the sick who need almost constant care." Even when farming stopped, the healthcare needs of the institution could not.[23] At the end of the month, Meyers finally noted that the sick were getting better. In 1883, when the asylum opened on the same property, the county appointed C. K. Jayne as the official physician. Jayne had worked at the poor farm intermittently for at least a few years, having attended personally to Meyers on occasion. He noted that much of his effort had been in visiting the chronic insane and helping them stay healthy.[24] Meyers was not the only superintendent with these obligations. Kansas visitors found a superintendent tube-feeding a resident, and another who ordered the sedation of sick residents without a doctor's permission.[25]

The tasks associated with nursing the sick could be burdensome and odious. In Kansas, where some superintendents were paid per resident, a few counties increased the per diem rate from $2 to $3 when a person required "medical aid and nursing."[26] Such nursing was needed for one Wisconsin resident's final days: "taken away for burial. His leg had decayed so that the bone below the knee was entirely severed and pieces of bone came out. He was a very offensive case. Worst case ever had for stench."[27] The person must have suffered dreadfully, but it was the distress of those caring for him that was recorded. At the Michigan superintendent's conference, at least one speaker recommended that superintendents "take a little interest" in the needs of sick and elderly residents and ensure even the sick got a shave and a bath each week. Lauding the care at one facility, the superintendent claimed, "We never allow a sick or feebleminded patient to lie in a mussed bed." That this deserved special note is telling about what happened elsewhere. Residents at this poor farm were fortunate that their superintendent believed in doing "all that can be done to relieve suffering . . . every keeper or matron has some inmates that are bad and hard to get along with, but we should treat them kindly and care for them when sick."[28]

The issue of suffering also applied to those for whom chronic pain was an issue. Records describing many poor farm residents as "crippled" suggest the possible pain and discomfort many of them lived with constantly. During the early 1900s more than seventy institutions existed to serve children with physical disabilities, but there were virtually none for adults. As a result, formerly institutionalized children sometimes came to poor farms as adults with disabilities and represented one of the most common types of long-term resident.[29] At one burial excavation, archaeologists discovered remains of poor farm residents that showed infantile malnutrition, arthritis, horrible tooth decay, and one set of remains they described as "a poor man, aged, practically toothless, with a very bad left leg and stiff back, seems almost a parody of an inhabitant of an almshouse."[30] The Collins family of Ohio had such problems. David Collins tried to support his wife and five children as a farm laborer, but one child was sick with rickets, indicating malnutrition. His wife became ill later that year, and she died shortly after the children were admitted to the farm in December 1880. While the other children were placed out, Lydia, the oldest with rickets, stayed at the poor farm through at least 1910, suggesting that she might have been permanently physically disabled as a result of the disease. During 1880 when she and her siblings were admitted, there was a Civil War veteran with scurvy, who later lived for a time at the home for disabled soldiers. His registration highlights the health problems that no doubt sent him to the poor farm: chronic diarrhea causing a rectal problem, and scurvy that affected his gums and teeth.[31] A lifetime of malnutrition or hard work could leave people physically wrecked, injuries caused debilitation, congenital problems affected the ability of people to make a living as a laborer, and an issue in childhood could compound health problems as people aged. Pain management was not a specialty of poor farms.[32] A Kansas man who was "badly afflicted" with sore eyes spent nine years at the poor farm before hanging himself at a nearby vacant house. The superintendent recorded, "His eyes did not hurt him anymore."[33]

An interesting partnership for better nursing care existed briefly in King County, Washington, where a group of nuns was placed in charge of health care at the county poor farm for multiple years. Initially, the women nursed residents on the farm property, but by the early 1880s they moved the patients to town. One sister, hinting at an anti-Catholic backlash, recorded that "people were so prejudiced that they prevented the sick from coming to us. The name 'poor house' prevented some from coming, as they regarded poverty a disgrace. . . . There are those who, under the pretext of saving the county money, or to make a name for themselves and be elected to an office, have no use for us." In 1886, the county decided to move people back to the farm and the sisters were not rehired. They were distressed and noted, "We deplored this decision because our poor and elderly patients would have to leave us and once more be taken care of by Protestants." Religious affiliations aside, it is likely the nursing experience of these women benefited the comfort of their patients.[34]

Nursing the sick was grueling, physically challenging, and dirty. Among the ailments listed for the residents under the care of matron Charlotte Farmer in 1880 were paralysis, syphilis, heart disease, and scurvy. Farmer did not have any hired girls living on-site during the census enumeration that year, although her husband had a farm hand. And she had three young children to tend.[35] The health issues of the residents mentioned were more chronic in nature, but acute cases also arrived regularly. Historian of health care Charles Rosenberg describes nursing during this time as "emptying bedpans, cleaning and cooking, changing sheets, and removing vomit and bloodstains." It is no wonder that many poor farms employed servants to help with these tasks, and it is not hard to understand why many of them were short-term employees.[36] A 1926 report from a Virginia poor farm noted that a patient with an amputated foot received all his aftercare from the matron because the doctor thought his trip to the farm too lengthy.[37]

Concentrations of people also meant that contagious diseases quickly swept through poor farms. Admitting a family of five with typhoid to the poor farm sick house in the 1890s, a Nebraska matron worried she would carry it to her own family living in the main building. The disease eventually killed all five family members, but the matron's children survived because she isolated herself with the dying family, a dangerous and selfless act made possible in part because of the separate structure on the grounds.[38] In January 1898, all twenty new intakes at the Summit County Infirmary were listed as sick or helpless.[39] The strain this placed on institutional resources could be immense. Although the county employed a staff at this time, the institution housed a hundred or more people.[40] The sheer volume of tasks for employees did not go unnoticed. One critic explained that a matron had "not the time to attend properly to nursing the sick, even if she had the knowledge and experience. Nurses are rarely found on the staffs of almshouses of less than one hundred inmates, where they are it is mostly because of the insane patients. . . . Consequently the matron is chiefly, often solely, responsible for the care of inmates in illness, a responsibility which, considering the usual age of the patients, may mean life or death."[41] Rare was the poor farm that had a trained nurse, an issue that remained a glaring deficit of the institutions well into the 1920s.[42]

Nursing gradually professionalized during the late nineteenth century, and as it did so, distinctions emerged between the job of nursing family members, "working class hired nurses" or practical nurses, and graduate nurses with specific training. According to nursing historian Patricia D'Antonio, the hiring of nurses demonstrated a desire to help the local poor and take responsibility for their care.[43] Nursing in poor farms, typically a low-paying job, did not attract highly trained nurses so much as it attracted local women in need of wages. As health care professionalized and poor farms became more medicalized, larger poor farms were more likely to have professionally trained nurses on hand. Will County, Illinois, and Allen County, Indiana, both institutions with close to or more than 100 residents, employed nurses by the early 1900s.

In California, where counties combined the hospital and poor farm, medical staff handled the nursing needs of the poor farm. One matron was a graduate nurse. She handled all the regular domestic duties including cooking, cleaning, and the care of two paralyzed residents. This was feasible because there were just four residents at the institution.[44] Women considered practical nurses found an array of cases to keep them busy. Butte County, California, employed a practical nurse for day-to-day care, and a graduate nurse was called out for specific, chronic cases.[45] The ailment list at that institution included hearing trouble, broken bones, rheumatism, paralysis, female trouble, asthma, TB, varicose veins, kidney trouble, bad cold, bowel trouble, flu, and sore hand.[46] Amador County employed a farmer for the superintendent and his wife as matron, who was noted as having "no medical training—is a good housewife." A nurse was on duty in the infirmary building at night.[47] The slight separation of staff responsibilities provided some degree of professionalized care.

As poor farms and public hospitals blended their purposes, more nurses appeared on poor farm staffs, and it became the norm for those poor farms that remained open into the mid-twentieth century. Frances Pickett worked at the Jackson, Michigan, County Poor Farm between 1960 and 1965. She was a registered nurse and helped the residents transition from the poor farm to the new county medical facility in town. "We had to vacate the home in a hurry," she said. "We moved 90-plus patients during a winter blizzard. . . . I was so full of compassion and pity for them. They were such wonderful souls." Pickett specifically remembered that "one of them had been a superintendent of schools. He took to drinking and ended up living and dying at the poor farm." Pickett also recalled a fifty-two-year-old patient named Billy who had Down Syndrome. When his mother died there was no one left to care for him, and Pickett recalled the heart-wrenching scene: "Billy was sitting there waiting for his mother to wake up. But she was dead, [and] we pleaded with him to come live with us."[48] Her job, like that of poor farm employees of previous decades, was to help a variety of residents.

Poor Farm Physicians

The practice of hiring a poor farm doctor resembled that of hiring a superintendent: physicians submitted bids to county officials. Dr. G. G. Craig narrowly won his job in 1876 when officials decided an "old school" doctor was preferable, although the local paper applauded the runner-up Dr. Lawrence, claiming the votes he got were "a flattering completement [sic] to an excellent young man and a deserving physician." Craig won the township contract to care for both jail inmates and the poor, sending another conflicting message about the criminality of poverty.[49] Doctors who took on the task of serving the poor farm performed no small job, and it was not considered a particularly prestigious position.[50] One critic noted, "The country doctor has usually been some man who needed the practice so badly that he would under-bid every other physician in the county for the work." But a more sympathetic observer noted that rural doctors "are obliged to work much harder for their $800 a year than do their city brethren who earn $1,200."[51]

The dismissive attitude related to the way that doctors were paid by counties for their efforts.[52] Counties preferred to pay a yearly contracted amount instead of a per visit fee, but the medical community believed contract medicine lessened the reputation of physicians. Per visit billing added up quickly and was difficult to budget in advance. After paying by the visit to Dr. Charles R. Fox, who received $10 in 1884 to care for poor farm resident Rachel Smith, Kaufman County, Texas, hired Dr. W. H. Pyle to care for all thirty-three residents during the year. Pyle was a well-known local figure who served as a surgeon in the Confederate Army and later as a state senator. Although the institution was free of contagion, he noted chronic diseases such as phthisis and consumption, two persons suffering from opium addiction, a death from heart disease, and "that most of the infirm residing at the Poor Farm suffered from broken down constitutions, or general lack of health." Pyle claimed, "I have done what is in my power to mitigate the sufferings of these unfortunates—and smooth their pathway to the tomb."[53] Physicians treating the poor had to worry that doing so would alienate better-paying clientele, and the care received under county funds may not have been quite as attentive as that provided to a privately paying patient. Pyle, however, seems to have been one poor farm doctor who came with a prominent reputation.[54]

Accepting an annual contract for poor farm doctoring could be particularly challenging if there was an outbreak of illness or many ailing residents. Contract doctors could spend more than they made traveling back and forth. For more regular medical care, Alexander Johnson recommended that doctors routinely come to the institution at least once a week for the benefit of the residents, and be paid based on a monthly or yearly fee, with pharmaceuticals paid for on a case-by-case basis.[55] Dr. O. M. Vaughn of Michigan, who was himself a supervisor of the poor, complained that no able-bodied man would do "an indefinite amount of work for a definite amount of money." Yet that is potentially what poor farm doctoring entailed if on a yearly contract.[56] Because the incomes of doctors could be limited by a contract as opposed to fee-per-visit or fee-per-case, doctors' organizations came to oppose contracts like those offered by counties.

By the early 1900s, county doctors could expect more compensation for their efforts, but Dr. James N. Plumb of York County, Nebraska, had to sue county officials after they refused to pay him for his services during a smallpox epidemic. Plumb received pay for serving both the poor farm and the county jail, but during 1908 and 1909 he was called upon to "attend, quarantine, and fumigate 132 cases of smallpox." The county refused to pay him, claiming that as a member of the county board of health, he could not be paid for services. Plumb successfully made the case that his work during the epidemic was in his capacity as a private doctor and not as a member of the board of health. His settlement of $790 was supported on appeal and was well beyond the $5 per month he typically received from the board.[57] Mississippi permitted reimbursements to doctors for their care of the indigent, but counties did not always honor those claims, and lawsuits were filed as a result. Elizabeth Wisner described the case of a doctor who provided almost $100 worth of care but because the patient had not officially been declared a pauper, the doctor was not paid for his services.[58]

Dr. T. O. Hardesty left behind a compelling record of his time as the farm doctor between 1908 and 1915, which details the types of health care provided at poor farms. Hardesty averaged approximately thirty-five visits per year on which he saw multiple residents. He also maintained detailed records on some patients, as discussed in chapter 5, using a preprinted form labeled "medical examination and record." On it, there were more than two dozen questions about physical and mental health, as well as family history. Patients were weighed, measured, asked about their history with measles, syphilis, dropsy, and other issues. The doctor noted whether they drank and used tobacco products, whether they belonged to a religion, and if they had any education. In February 1913, Hardesty reported one patient, "complaining, griping in general," who was very dirty. He was given a prescription for a cough. By April the man could not leave his room and in May his feet and hands were swollen; he continued to be very dirty and smelled bad. In July the note read "some better but not good." He died in 1915 of various causes and was buried at the poor farm, despite having many relatives listed on his health history.

Hardesty detailed other problems as well. In 1913, a seventy-year-old resident originally from Portugal who did not speak English was dealing with sleepwalking and occasional paralysis, hurting himself because of frequent falls. He lived at the poor farm for five years before his death. The language barrier and his condition combined to make a difficult case. Hardesty noted that at least one resident with "deformed" back, arms, hips, and legs had lived there since 1889, and remained until his death in 1926. Burns, paralysis, and acute emergencies like the nosebleed of a resident who was deaf and disabled all sent the doctor to the farm. It is not hard to imagine that some residents might have enjoyed the personalized attention of a doctor's visit. The man with the nosebleed had a note on his record that said "Always wants something. Nothing doing."[59]

Hardesty regularly recorded his opinions about his poor farm patients. He sympathized with residents like Lewis Price, described at the opening of this chapter, but labeled a forty-year-old woman an "idiot" while noting his suspicion (without documenting evidence) that she had both tuberculosis and gonorrhea. Hardesty noted that a tubercular man with a drinking problem had been left at the farm even though he had family nearby. One of the older residents was described as senile and irritable. To reduce the burden of caring for older dementia patients, the county transferred many of them to a state asylum. One of those men had the added complication of a prostate problem that caused incontinence, a condition staff members were probably glad to be rid of. Some of the reactions recorded by Hardesty were not uncommon among poor farm doctors. Dr. William Sisler visited the Summit County Poor Farm approximately once a week in the 1880s and was paid $300 annually. He claimed that "No one can be there long without becoming disgusted, for during meal times he will there see the maimed, epileptic, etc. . . . but there was no filth so far as I could see."[60] It is unclear how successfully he cared for those residents he found disgusting to look at, but he reported little serious illness during the year.

Despite criticisms that "the physicians in the farming country are general practitioners, commonly out of close touch with specialists and experts," what doctors at poor farms needed was general expertise.[61] Their multifaceted knowledge also helped facilitate corrections and improvements at the institutions in part because they were frequent visitors. Dr. M. Sabin of Michigan encouraged modern heating and lighting in poor farms because "overcrowded rooms, superheated with red hot stoves are no longer allowable. . . . The old man or lady with decaying bodies and decaying minds often do not heed the terrible state they are in; but, unless strict care is taken by those having charge, the abundant food and heat of the old poor house will only kindle to action the hot-bed of disease." It was not enough, according to Sabin, to make people comfortable: their care must not be complicit in hastening their deaths.[62] In an 1872 attempt to help residents, Illinois physician Dr. L. Gillet reported to county officials a paralyzed man had hair that was "one mass of vermin," and that residents told him "that they are never furnished any soap for washing themselves with. The slops from the kitchen are thrown on the ground within six feet of the well that supplies water to the pauper department. The privies are filthy beyond description and a disgrace to any public charity." He also worried about the connection between bad-quality food and the health of residents, saying:

> "The food placed on the table most of the time for the paupers is not good, healthy food. Sometimes the dinners are good enough, both as to quality and quantity . . . and sometimes it is not fit for any one to eat. The miserable compound of rye and cheap molasses furnished for breakfast as a substitute for coffee is sickening to drink, and produces debility and consequent disease. The invariable supper for the four months that I have been in attendance has been mush and sour milk. Sometimes as an especial favor, the sour milk has been changed to butter milk."[63]

Sangamon County officials took doctors' opinions seriously, making a few improvements in response. Two years earlier when they discussed moving the farm the doctor had voiced his disapproval.[64]

Doctors like Gillet who were less than pleased with provisions for residents could be instrumental in improvements by explaining how diet contributed to bad health. Poor farm physician Dr. W. J. Underwood, who visited his institution weekly, noted, "the inmates were fed and clothed fairly—sufficient amount of food, but not the right quality, my opinion of feeding paupers being on a more expensive plan." He tried to fix this, requesting extra food for sick patients, "no matter at what cost." Underwood's feedback eventually helped remove the poor farm superintendent and matron from their positions.[65] Healthier food for residents was directly tied to medical expenses, and the number of visits doctors had to make to the institutions. If they were paid on contract, it was more financially beneficial to doctors to make fewer trips to the institutions, thus their efforts to improve health through food. Doctors also noted when good food contributed to overall health. Dr. Jayne of Dane County, Wisconsin, noted that "food is furnished in abundance, and is at all times prepared in the best manner." Among the items consumed were butter, eggs, cheese, beef, pork, and fish, fruit "of all sorts," hominy, grits, rice, sugar, syrup, coffee, and tea.[66]

Alexander Johnson hoped that poor farm doctors would give opinions on the worthiness of the sick-poor and the ability of residents to labor, noting that in addition to weighing in on their capabilities, a doctor could be useful in verifying a superintendent's decision to dismiss a resident who he considered healthy enough to leave or keep a person he considered too sick to go.[67] In actuality, poor farm doctors did this sparingly if at all, but they occasionally made related suggestions. Dr. George Palmer used the Sangamon County Poor Farm as a study site about poverty, disease, and their causes. Although initially there to study tuberculosis, he quickly became fascinated by what had driven the more than one hundred residents to the farm in the first place. He concluded that many of them were there because of old age but learned from the residents that some of them had living family, who he believed should be induced to provide for their care outside the institution. When he asked about rehabilitating some of the residents so that they might leave, more than half told him that they "wanted to stay where they were, under the friendly roof of the poorhouse." He concluded that "this does not imply hopeless pauperism, however. Sick, neglected, weak and despondent—of course, they want to stay in some place, even in the poorhouse, where they are not eternally ordered to move on by the police; viewed with suspicion or fear by self-respecting citizens or in constant danger of arrest for vagrancy." His beliefs about this issue were proven apt during the move to close poor farms down after the Depression.[68]

Palmer developed a sympathy of sorts for the residents that he met, noting that some "worked hard and . . . made an honest living before their eyesight failed and they became almost blind. We label these men as paupers and do not stop to question if a simple operation for cataract would not restore them to useful occupation." Of their chronic illnesses and struggles he said, "the average superintendent knows nothing of the deadly weariness of this disease; the weariness that invades every muscle of the body; which makes work impossible; which prompts men of higher moral fiber to drink whiskey or seek other stimulation." He went on to explain in greater detail the benefits of providing better treatment to poor farm residents, noting that those who classified residents as "lazy devils" also "begrudged our poorhouse food, when, as a matter of fact, he [the poor farm resident] ought to have, and at public expense, better food than we have ever thought of giving him. With fresh air, milk, eggs, nourishing food, intelligent treatment and perfect rest, this man can get well and resume a place in the world." For Palmer, good care might spur rehabilitation, while, "with ordinary almshouse care and almshouse fare, we are signing his death warrant while we are guaranteeing his prolonged dependence upon public charity." He also identified how health problems compounded if not managed, reporting, "one Illinois county has a contract with a dentist to pull the teeth of poor farm inmates. There is no provision for saving teeth. If the inmate is writhing with toothache, he must take his choice; lose a good tooth on contract, or grin and bear the pain. The supervisors can see no reason why a pauper should want to save his teeth or why he should be permitted to do so. And yet a cheap filling would cost little more than the primitive and mutilating operation of extraction."[69]

While Dr. Palmer and many others were figuring out ways to help poor farm residents, a few doctors were decidedly less ethical, none more disturbingly so than Dr. Alvin Fouser of Summit County, Ohio. In 1887, prosecutors charged him with grave robbing from the poor farm cemetery. The initial arrest took place while the institution was already under investigation for the rape and sub-sequent pregnancy of Nellie Towner (see chapter 5). Evidence suggested Fouser paid to have bodies "resurrected," then moved to a nearby location where they were boxed, labeled as glass, and shipped to nearby medical schools.[70] Local rumors said that few bodies made it into the ground during his six years on the job, but modern efforts to survey the site indicate that at the very least there were dozens of graves dug. The accusations against Fouser were all the more sinister because there were suggestions that he hastened death to make $5 per body.[71] Hired man George Keck claimed that Fouser was called to treat a female resident but then denied there was anything wrong with her; she died later that night. Keck and other staff members believed Fouser's subpar doctoring was sanctioned by the superintendent and matron.[72] When asked by reporters for a comment on his arrest, the doctor claimed that while there was certainly body stealing going on in "every cemetery in the country," he was not responsible.[73]

In the end, Superintendent Hamlin and his wife lost their positions, but not before being publicly scolded for having "given too little attention to the infirm, insane, sick and helpless. They probably thought that they had performed their duties when they had cast their own responsibilities upon cheap labor or ir-responsible paupers. For days at a time, the matron has not visited the insane departments. Sick inmates have died, we believe, from want of proper care and attention." Furthermore, investigators noted that the practice of keeping sick residents in the "crazy house" with its single attendant was wholly unacceptable.[74] Fouser faced additional accusations from residents who said he privately charged them for care even though he was paid by the county, and that he neglected their distress and pain intentionally.[75] One man's family refused Fouser's attempt to get money from them, insulting his skills by saying that they "thought it a steep bill for a poor doctor."[76] Robert Freer claimed he waited ten days in great pain without treatment and that he considered suing Dr. Fouser, but "found it would not do any good and dropped it." Two other men said that he failed to recommend a special diet for their issues, and that they went long periods of time without seeing him.

Fouser testified on his own behalf regarding the charges of resident mistreatment, claiming he did not prescribe medicine in cases where he believed it would do no good. He accused Freer of being a hypochondriac. Fouser took issue with reports of inordinately high numbers of deaths at the institution during his tenure, specifying that "'Colored Sam' was reported as having died . . . he is not dead yet." He gave a detailed list of the causes of deaths: he blamed a Dr. Belden for performing an operation that caused a fatality, claimed that three of the deaths were sick infants, one man had been found dead in bed, another fell from his seat at the table, and one man was found dead in his cell. Although there had been no epidemic, residents had "considerable malaria, also typhoid fever and smallpox." For all these patients he had the assistance of one hired nurse. With the accusations and the body-snatching case, state charity investigators recommended that he be released from his role as infirmary doctor because "he does not show a proper consideration for the feelings of the poor unfortunates who are compelled to accept his services. They think he has no sympathy for their misfortunes. Where the patient has no faith in his physician, satisfactory results cannot be attained . . . we therefore think that a change of physician is desirable." They urged the county to rethink its medical contracts altogether. Chronic patients needed the same services afforded those who had acute illnesses, and awarding the contract to the lowest bid was strongly condemned.[77] The charges against Fouser were eventually dropped and he kept his medical license, in part because a county official apparently paid for a subpoenaed witness to leave town. Despite the publicity surrounding the body-snatching and mistreatment scandals, he later served two terms as county coroner and continued to practice medicine in the Akron area.[78]

Fouser was not the only doctor helping to give poor farms bad reputations for health care. Reporter James Oppenheim published complaints from residents in a New York institution who said, "The doctor doesn't believe in doctoring old, worn-out people, he says they don't need medicine. It will get their stomachs out of order." This would have affected a large number of residents, since reports in 1889 and again in 1910 specifically linked ill health with a vast majority of older almshouse residents.[79] Another resident said that a nurse saved his life after neglect from the doctor. On his visits, Oppenheim claimed to see residents self-medicating or left profoundly helpless and bedridden without medical attention or any nursing care at all, including a tubercular man left alone in an isolated area for days at a time, who eventually died before efforts by the visitors could assist him.[80] Withholding medical care for African American residents appears to have happened at a number of institutions, reflecting a general disregard for their wellbeing. A "well-liked" African American poor farm resident in Texas named Nollie lived in the jail out back, probably as a form of racial segregation. He suffered silently with a rectal fistula before the discomfort became too severe and he reported it to the superintendent. By that point, the cancerous tumor was advanced and there was no treatment that could be provided by a doctor. It is hard to imagine Nollie's misery, but the poor farm mourned his loss on the farm because he had taken charge of the hogs during his years at the institution.[81] Rob Quals, an elderly Black man who died at the Cannon County, Tennessee, Poor Farm, had no cause of death recorded on his death certificate, which read, "not known, didn't have any doctor." Other white residents did not have a similar notation. In 1930, a Black man in Illinois in the final stages of stomach cancer was taken to a poor farm instead of the local hospital. He remained alive only two days after his admission, perhaps because the local hospital was not willing to admit a Black patient for end-of-life care.[82]

One of the most challenging times for poor farm doctors and employees was during an outbreak of illness that affected both residents and staff. In 1891, "la grippe" hit Wisconsin, and the Dane County Poor Farm and Asylum struggled with sickness as a result. There were deaths at both institutions, and Dr. Jayne was continually on-site. Some asylum residents were moved to the poor farm to expedite care. Superintendent Meyers believed it was the first epidemic trouble in his tenure and lauded staff and Jayne for their efforts, saying, "Both institutions were attacked about the same time, and for nearly or about three months every employee well enough to work knew little of rest except during the hours of sleep. Most of those who were strong enough to pull through are to-day well and happy. Seldom missing meals."[83] County officials chose between isolating poor farms from the contagion or using them to host the sick. It was not uncommon to utilize space at poor farms or on the grounds as quarantine areas during disease outbreaks, as was the case in 1900 when tents were placed on-site at the Kaufman County Poor Farm for a smallpox quarantine.[84] An Ohio matron marked the week of December 11, 1918, as "flu week," and after that no one except officials visited the farm until June the following year, leaving the residents without visitors or entertainments.[85]

Poor farms were useful as quarantine sites because there was space outside for tents and outbuildings to convert in an emergency, but contagious diseases posed dangers to residents. Dr. Arthur Robinson of Michigan urged superintendents and county officials to find ways to isolate those who were contagious. He did not simply mean in the house, but also on the farm itself. "If your tubercular inmates are ranging at large over your farms, about the dooryards, it is only a matter of a short time when your stock are going to become infected," he noted. He blamed behavior for the unplanned spread of the disease, saying, "They expectorate anywhere, and in the county infirmaries the most of them will expectorate on the floors . . . this cannot help but infect the stock." Robinson recommended an entirely separate building with plenty of fresh air and sunlight, along with good care for the patients and concern for the financial cost of lost barnyard stock.[86] Robinson urged these changes in the years following a Progressive Era public health effort, headed in large part by Homer Folks, to educate people about the contagious nature of tuberculosis and destigmatize reporting. Folks successfully lobbied for New York counties to open their own sanitariums to isolate patients and cope with hospital overcrowding. Most counties did not have their own sanitariums, but doctors working in public health conveyed the message to states and counties, urging better poor farm practices and eventually the formation of state health departments.[87]

Being fatally ill at the poor farm meant that while a doctor might visit regularly to try and abate pain, there was no promise of a pain-free death. Stories of helpless, terminally ill people being transferred from hospitals to almshouses did nothing to improve the reputation of poor farms.[88] Records show poor farms sending the very ill to hospitals occasionally, but Emily Abel noted a reverse trend among hospitals to return ill patients who would not improve in order to keep their death rates low, and avoid the inefficiencies of caring for patients who took up time and resources. The poor farm did not afford much separation between the living and the dying.[89] Likewise, custodial, long-term chronic cases at poor farms drained already limited staff resources who could not supply the daily medical care that their conditions deserved.[90] Increasingly by the early twentieth century, poor farms and almshouses had large numbers of residents in need of specialized medical care, but many lacked the means to provide more than rudimentary assistance.[91]

Katz and Abel assert that many patients in the almshouse died without medical attention. While evidence indicates that some counties requested doctors to be present regularly, and that staff tried to comfort those in their final days, deaths at poor farms were neither medicalized nor compatible with the nineteenth-century idea of a "good death."[92] As Emily Williams Smith remembered, "Residents stayed until they felt better, many stayed until they died." The twentieth century saw a transition in the role of medical personnel in the process of dying, but many Americans continued to die surrounded by family. Poor farm residents might have lacked family, but, like Lewis Price, they typically spent their last moments in bed in their usual room.

Increasing Oversight

The development of state boards of health in the early twentieth century created a system of oversight for institutions that provided health care. Setting an optimistic tone, one report claimed, "Now that the eyes of the state authorities are turned on them [poor farms], there is every indication that great improvement will be made in their condition. There is great need of improvement in many of them."[93] It is not surprising that during the Progressive Era, reformers believed that better state supervision of local institutions would make a marked difference. The type of centralization, record keeping, and expertise consolidated in state boards appealed to reformers. In many places, new state boards of health took over for the state boards of charity, providing some expertise and more authority on the best practices of institution building, including segregated spaces for the sick.[94] Construction recommendations made in the early 1900s requested that beds in the infirmary section of an almshouse should number between 10 to 12 percent of the total institution population, separate sick wards for men and women, and entirely separate infirmary buildings at the larger institutions.[95]

The desire to create comprehensive social welfare at the county level was a nationally discussed issue, but locally those ideas did not necessarily transfer. While places were rationalizing the interactions between institutions and using social workers to investigate cases, rural areas lacked this personnel, and county officials were responsible for moving people between institutions as best they could for the proper type of care.[96] One Florida official noted that in Duval County (Jacksonville), "the county infirmary, the county hospital, the county tuberculosis sanitarium, must be brought into harmony, and related to the family case work basis of social work." Boulder County, Colorado, sold the poor farm and built a combination hospital/poorhouse on twenty acres. The property, although smaller in acreage and less focused on agriculture, still came with barns, poultry houses, and a massive orchard.[97]

Issues of health care became remained problematic for local governments. Alabama, which constantly struggled with provisions for the sick and poor, claimed in an 1897 report that even though the county institutions should really be hospitals, "nothing could be further from accurate."[98] An agent from the Missouri Board of Charities and Corrections argued for public health care to "be accepted as an essential, as much so as public education . . . let us offer to everyone hospital service." Optimistically, this would lead to "only temporary dependency, and the almshouse, with its stigma, with its random policy and its slip-shod methods, will give way to the hospital-home where the poor will receive care embodying the principles of modern science, efficiency, prevention and economy."[99] Universal health care as a way to combat poverty never materialized, but other states including North Dakota made efforts to combine their poor farms with hospitals to give residents more targeted care.[100]

Missouri officials were not alone in their optimism: the amount of commentary linking the rise of medical care to the demise of the poor farm was considerable. As Francis Bardwell from Massachusetts said in 1917, "I am swinging to the idea that the present conditions are such that the infirmary is gradually taking the place of the almshouse. That is but natural; the poor farm succeeded the workhouse, the almshouse or home for the aged succeeded the poor farm, and now the hospital or infirmary is bound to succeed the almshouse."[101] But the much-hoped for improvements were slow to appear; poor farms continued as healthcare sites in part because counties had no alternatives. No national or statewide system of health care developed. The Union County, Illinois, Poor Farm doubled as the local hospital, with county officials even staying there from time to time because of "chills and fever," "sore throat," and "epilepsy."[102] The most progress reformers could show was the expansion of state health boards and nursing services and clinics to rural counties. Better solutions only arrived with federal funding in the Sheppard-Towner Act of 1921, the New Deal, and Great Society programs.

States that did begin the process, such as California, moved toward county hospitals with an almshouse component, instead of the other way around.[103] It was not always an easy marriage; county officials worried that if the health care was free or almost free, people would use "any little excuse to put up to the county doctor to get in, until work opens up again." Most California poor farms handled the connection of poor farm and hospital as best they could, accepting small fees from people if they wanted to contribute, resulting in most of the patients being "old bachelors" who needed a place to stay.[104] Alameda County, California, rationalized its admission protocols in the 1920s and emphasized hospital care over poor farm provisions. The county's process was notable for the involvement of both social workers and medical personnel. Once a social worker approved someone for admission, doctors then determined if the person went to the hospital ward or the infirmary. Infirmary admissions were met by the steward or assistant, assigned quarters, and given the policies and procedures. The new resident went through an interview, recording basic information and trying to determine how they might best be utilized at the infirmary. This was exactly what reformers had hoped for decades earlier.[105] California also innovated by using nursing school students to provide staff in the larger county hospitals.[106]

The hospitalization of poor farms in California was not necessarily duplicated, but during the 1920s North Carolina began constructing new institutions like the Wake County Hospital with a better eye toward public health.[107] Rowan County established an equipped operating room at the behest of Mary Linton, the county superintendent of public welfare. Oklahoma also had a county institution provide "a large fully equipped operating room, and the county doctor is a skilled surgeon. . . . The county employs a trained nurse who is superintendent of the hospital as well as the farm. In addition they have three trained nurses."[108] Exceptionally large institutions, like the Wayne County, Michigan, Infirmary (known locally as "Eloise"), served as asylum, hospital, and almshouse for the growing metro area around Detroit. By the Depression, the institution had 900 acres of farmland, housed more than 8,000 people annually and was a city unto itself, complete with a train station, general store, bakery, dairy herd, piggery, power plant, and what officials claimed was the largest industrial kitchen in the nation. Thousands of the residents were patients of either the hospital or the psychiatric units, and medical staff numbered in the hundreds. The facility was one of the first in the nation to use X-rays for diagnostics and provided opportunities for research and innovative treatments.[109] Connecticut, too, reported some of its largest almshouses were being "hospitalized." The smallest hospitalized almshouse, in Waterbury, housed more than 150 residents. There was a graduate nurse serving as matron, and she had help from some residents who cooked, cleaned, and pitched in on the farm. Some were even paid small amounts for their efforts. In larger facilities, ambulatory patients were separated from chronic cases, which made for reportedly good conditions.

The increased presence of nurses, doctors, and staff in these more medically attuned institutions, referred to by one study as a "trend toward scientific and humane care for the destitute poor," was a hint of what was to come.[110] Chronic diseases of old age and senility were the most common in those almshouses undergoing a conversion to hospital and long-term nursing care. The *Atlantic Medical Journal* published an article claiming that residents deserved "the most skilled care" and "sympathetic understanding" from physicians. They recommended converting not just the buildings to hospitals, but referring to them as such. The efforts to professionalize health care can be seen in their goal to "place the professional service of these institutions in the hands of physicians skilled not only in their profession but with the idealism to regard a public hospital as a public utility." This subtle dig at the management and use of county resources reflected the changing realities and goals of reformers.[111] Most poor farms would not directly transition in to public hospitals, despite the link between poor farms and public health. They were far more likely to evolve in to nursing homes instead.[112]

During the 1920s when infirmary wards or buildings were added on to almshouses, they featured modern amenities and were designed with health care in mind; however, as with the history of all poor farms the progress of these improvements was uneven. Pennsylvania did a specific study about the healthcare needs of its almshouse residents during the 1920s and discovered that approximately 30 percent of those surveyed needed careful diagnosis and intensive long-term medical care, 27 percent needed good nursing, and the remainder needed mostly shelter and food. In other words, their daily needs were more suited toward long-term care as opposed to hospitalization. While some of the larger institutions in the state provided a medical staff, many others continued to rely on the matron, her staff, or healthy residents to provide care for the sick. At minimum, the state report recommended a graduate nurse on every staff, recognizing that "the inmates no longer present a problem of farm management, but a distinct hospital problem." But this foreshadowed developing problems: people still needed help, health care increased expenses, and the farm had diminished in importance—making the poor farm seem somewhat obsolete. To "hospitalize the almshouse" required not improvements to farm equipment but instead a full-time doctor, laboratory and operating space, a nursing staff, and perhaps most challenging in older buildings—an elevator. These changes proved prohibitively difficult to implement and expensive for counties across the country.[113]

As noted by the efforts of Dr. Hardesty in chapter 5, poor farms became more common sites of medical research during the twentieth century. Describing the prospects for this type of study, a Michigan employee described his charges as "a miscellaneous congregation made up of persons from nearly every quarter of the globe, good, bad, and indifferent. Interesting alike to the student of psychology and sociology but affording the latter a problem as enigmatical of solution as any riddle ever propounded by the Grecian Sphinx."[114] In 1913, Joseph W. Schereschewsky from the United States Public Health Service visited the Knox County Poor Farm in Tennessee to investigate institutional cases of trachoma, a severe bacterial eye infection that could cause blindness. He found sixty poor farm residents, 28 percent of whom had trachoma. Some claimed to have had the issue since childhood, and Schereschewsky believed that the disease was the cause of at least one person's admission.[115] Apparently the managers of the poor farm were not well acquainted with the disease and agreed to consider his recommendations for better sanitation, which included individual towels and separate beds.

Between 1900 and 1930 the problem of balancing poor relief with health care and long-term care worsened because the healthcare needs of residents increased alongside the aging population. The general decline of infectious disease increased life expectancy considerably, for both men and women during the first half of the twentieth century, which saw a marked increase in the number of people who reached their sixties and seventies. It also enlarged the number of people who needed long-term health care, both of which put additional pressures on poor farms.[116] Department of Public Health officials in Massachusetts studied chronic disease in the 1920s. They discovered that people with untreated cancer, for example, lived an average of twenty-one months, people with heart disease between seven and nine years, and those with forms of rheumatism survived more than fourteen years. While they did not intend for this information to directly relate to poor farms, their conclusions explain why people ended up in institutions with long-term healthcare needs, especially since they noted that poor people were at "much higher risk" and their care was a "significant factor in public welfare expenditures."[117] In 1908, representatives at the NCCC connected the idea of pensions for the elderly with poor farm healthcare issues, hoping to alleviate their use of poor farms. But at least one dissenter noted that far from pensions eliminating poor farms, a payment would do little for the many elderly people who were both poor and sick.[118]

Despite incremental improvements for the sick-poor, at the start of the Depression people could either avoid seeing a doctor, go into debt to pay for medical expenses, or seek aid, which could mean going to the poor farm. Rural areas typically lacked medical charities, although some benefitted from traveling public health nurses, such as those initially funded by the Sheppard-Towner Act. Unfortunately for sick adults, much of the emphasis on early public health nursing was on maternal and infant health.[119] Helen Munson studied the condition of poor farms at the start of the Great Depression and found that in twenty-seven almshouses in three states, approximately 62 percent of the population was over sixty-five years old. The chronically ill patient, who did not have a place at hospitals in the early twentieth century because they were designed to cure rather than continually care, wound up with inadequate, or at least amateur care. Munson identified poor farms as filled with chronic patients whose needs were incompatible with the goals of hospitals to cure or "fix" what ailed people and send them on their way. This was not necessarily a new situation, but it garnered more attention and concern as poor farm expenses increased because of the growing number of elderly and chronically ill patients.[120] The continued lack of health care in many areas led one critic to claim that the "policy of leaving to localities and states the entire responsibility for providing even nominal public health facilities and services had failed in large measure."[121] Unfortunately, Munson used the eugenic reports from the 1920s for her statistics, but her general point was that new solutions were needed for both health care and care of the elderly.[122]

The health care provided by poor farms was initially intended as a cost-saving measure that reflected the burdensome and unpredictable direct relief expenses for the sick. Contract doctors and the staff of poor farms provided a majority of the care, with mixed results. Doctors both improved care at poor farms and used them as sites of research and study. Although poor farms handled acute issues, epidemics, and end-of-life care, the increasing numbers of residents with chronic conditions played a part in altering poor farms and encouraged the medicalization of some institutions. The solution for this aging population of poor farm residents came in the transition to long-term nursing facilities, but this took time, involved new licensing, a larger number of trained nurses, which poor farms always lacked, and more money than counties typically invested in aid. If pensions, nursing homes, and public hospitals were to be the answer to decades of inconsistent poor farm care, counties would need new sources of funding. The Depression and its aftermath generated the early steps through which the transition away from poor farms took place. However, the quality of care improved based on the ability of patients to pay for nicer amenities, which left the typical poor farm resident with limited options.[123]

8 Crisis and Transition

"Rural poverty has existed in considerable magnitude in the United
States for a long time. The depression served to reveal the areas in
which this poverty was most prevalent and most nearly chronic."
—Carl Cleveland Taylor, Helen Wheeler, and Ellis Lore Kirkpatrick,
Disadvantaged Classes in American Agriculture, 1938, 1

During the 1920s, state officials in North Carolina began advocating for the
construction of new, long-term nursing and healthcare facilities as replacements for some of the dilapidated poor farms. When the day came to move
residents into their new facility, "they were led to look forward to moving into
the new home as an event in their lives. Finally the day came. Each inmate was
moved to his or her own small room. . . . One old negro man . . . had his first
experience with a bath tub and enjoyed it so much that he did not want to get
out. . . . The inmate is led to feel a responsibility for that room and to take pride
in keeping it in order."[1] These residents made what would become a familiar
transition: going from a poor farm built in the nineteenth century to a modern
facility designed with health and elder care in mind. The policies enacted during
the Depression of the 1930s increased the number of poor farm residents who
experienced similar changes.

Poor farms took on new relevance as the relief needs of people during the
Depression increased, following a multidecade increase in public and private
spending on aid. In 1913, welfare spending totaled $180 million. On the eve
of the Depression in 1929, it was $750 million. That increase does not mark
the "development of a social consciousness" or a quadrupling in the number
of people on relief, but a change in the amount spent per person.[2] In 1913, 9.7
million people received some form of aid, and by 1929 that number had grown
to approximately 12.2 million. The spending per person increased from $18.50
to $62.50. No single program accounts for the change; many states continued
to limit the amount of mother's aid and federal programs continued to assist
veterans and Indian reservations. Much of the spending went to institutional
care, which included more than 70,000 people living in 2,000 poor farms and
almshouses.[3]

Some of the added expenses came as a result of substantial improvements at many poor farms, both in terms of care provided and structural upgrades such as those for health care. The 1910s and 1920s marked a watershed of spending but also an apex in the number of poor farms in operation. Expansion also took place in county and state governance, with welfare boards replacing poor farm directors, and more professionalized state oversight. New positions such as county superintendent of public welfare began handling poor relief, serving as the state agent in the county, dealing with parole and delinquency, and even placed-out children.[4]

At the onset of the Great Depression, poor farms were being pulled in two directions—some had recently made financially costly improvements for the future, while others were being phased out in favor of alternatives. Despite the overwhelming need for relief, the number of poor farms open and operating dramatically declined during the 1930s. The financial crisis altered the landscape of locally controlled relief.[5] Those institutions still open during the Depression saw their populations increase, but the federalization of aid programs and their partnerships with state instead of local governments resulted in a power shift. Local officials began making decisions about their poor farm based on available state and federal funding, resulting in closures and dwindling poor farm populations. The policies implemented during the Depression did not eliminate the need for institutional care, nor, as historian Jeff Singleton points out, was that the goal. Instead, the intention was to modernize relief and remove it from local control. This process ended the intimacy of relief that had long been a part of communities.[6] Poor farm residents were not eligible for federal money under the Social Security Act, and to receive federal funding, county institutions needed to evolve toward hospitals or nursing homes. In addition, the modernizations needed for farming increased expenses, resulting in more money spent to care for fewer people. The farms became liabilities instead of investments. This combination of issues did not suddenly shutter all poor farms, but it did chip away at their numbers. The confluence of new policies, changing resident needs, and greater expenses alongside the increasing irrelevance of pairing a farm with an institution all helped to displace the poor farm as the fundamental institution.

The Depression

Even before the Depression, there were signs that confidence in institutions as effective and affordable methods for providing relief was wavering. In a 1904 report, R. W. Wolston, chairman of the Poor Farm Committee from Galveston, Texas, noted that inside the county farm were "two elderly white women, two elderly negro women, two white men and one Mexican, all of whom could care for themselves nicely if pensioned by the county at $5 monthly." The residents reported they were comfortable and had plenty to eat, but county officials wanted the land rented and the institution shuttered. Officials approved the pensions, then began determining where the seven residents would go.[7] Ahead of their time, the Galveston officials were less focused on pensions supporting the residents independently, and more concerned about the burden of cost associated with institutional care for so few people. A 1925 Bureau of Labor supported their decision, reiterating that poor farms, especially the smaller institutions, were an expensive way to take care of people. Minnesota did its own study two years later and, in a clear indication that the demographics of poor farms contributed to the increased costs, determined that old age pensions would be more fiscally advantageous. Reformers and experts cited cheaper food costs as an additional savings over maintaining a farm.[8] This multipoint critique encompassed many of the reasons for the decreasing popularity of poor farms, but replacement ideas reverted to previous methods. When the short-lived Searcy County, Arkansas, Poor Farm closed, the matron placed the residents in other housing in a fashion similar to boarding out, and she took sixty-seven-year-old Bill Ortman home with her. She built him a little house on her property where he worked on her farm until his death.[9] Such personalized solutions faded as relief became more bureaucratized.

The farm component, once a selling feature for poor farms as investments, increasingly prompted criticism instead. In her study of Massachusetts town farms, Heli Meltsner found by the 1930s most had small gardens and sometimes chicken and egg production, but large-scale farming was a thing of the past.[10] Some counties in Kansas leased out their land as early as the 1910s, using those funds to pay for direct relief. The farm depression of the 1920s reduced property tax revenue in Kansas, which made it more difficult for counties to fund poor relief and made land rent a welcome addition.[11] For counties that kept their farms into the start of the 1930s, the institutions became entangled in the increasingly complicated issues of financial hardship, declining agricultural profits, and federalizing aid.

The Depression put new pressures on poor farms to operate as efficiently as possible. The Brookings Institute determined in the early 1930s that the rural poor were "the poorest of America's poor." The average income of the almost six million farm families was only $1,240—well below the estimated $3,000 needed to support a family of five. Poor farms struggled with an influx of people whose poverty crossed a threshold from poor at home to poor and homeless, and those still open reported a population increase during the early years of the 1930s.[12] The crisis also affected families trying to support relatives. In 1936, a telegram from New York arrived at the Dane County, Wisconsin, Poor Farm. It read in part: "do not know what to do my husband has been out of work for some time please see that he has a deasent [*sic*] burial and keep cost as reasonable as you can sending me the bill I will find some way to pay it promptly." The sender had been notified that her father, a resident of the institution, had died. She was neither able to care for him in life, nor knew how she would help him in death.[13]

Productive farms tried to increase output to meet the demand inside institutions and make money for counties. The Kaufman County, Texas, Poor Farm was used in the Farm Demonstration Program; McLean County, Illinois, tried raising pheasants and hosted farmers for "alfalfa days"; Dane County, Wisconsin, officials were given permission from the extension service to use the corn and hogs produced in excess of their Agricultural Adjustment Act quotas at the institution instead of destroying them.[14] More common were the problems of too many mouths to feed without enough funds or farm production to do so. The Franklin County Infirmary in Columbus, Ohio, experienced an outbreak of illness in 1937, seemingly as a result of trying to stretch spoiled food. The institution reported at least 2 deaths and between 80 and 120 residents ill from food poisoning at a Sunday dinner where ham salad sandwiches (ground boiled ham and mayonnaise) were served. The doctor had to call in two additional physicians to help with the cases.[15] The increases in institutional populations varied, but in some places it was overwhelming: Calhoun County, Michigan, housed around 100 residents prior to the Depression, but by 1938 had more than 400. Few institutions could comfortably absorb that many people. Iron County saw a similar problem, as mining jobs disappeared and hundreds of people found themselves homeless. Farm production could not keep pace, which undermined the reason for having a farm in the first place.[16]

The economic crisis hit transient laborers, always a large component of the agricultural economy and the poor farm population, hard. The workforce participation of older men steadily declined between 1870 and 1930, and they were more likely to work for shorter periods of time if their unemployment lasted longer than six months. In other words, long-term unemployment "increased the chances that an elderly person would leave the labor force, sooner rather than later" and increased the likelihood that they would need care at public expense.[17] In California, researchers and officials made comparisons between poor farm residents and their peers. In San Jose, researchers noted that male poor farm residents were two times more likely to be unskilled laborers than those gainfully employed; this made them "unable to overcome sufficiently to achieve levels of income that provided a margin for maintenance in old age." The study again found that a lack of land ownership played a role in poor farm residency: "those inmates who had been farmers, lost their holdings late in life, had few remaining assets, and were too old to begin life anew." The study subjects were no better or worse educated, nor did they leave jobs more than gainfully employed people. Poor farm residents were, however, more likely to be single, and researchers believed this contributed to their destitution. Those with few family connections and no children struggled when they aged and work was scarce. The study concluded that these factors meant they "came to their last years without the aid and comfort that children and families often provide."[18] The labor market, not the generational struggles of poverty, kept many of these men from engaging in heteronormative behaviors of the time and excluded them from regular employment as they aged and became less physically able.

In Cass County, North Dakota, officials tried to use a variety of Fargo charities and county funds to keep people in their own homes, but this did not help their large population of transient farm laborers.[19] County officials threatened to move an old man to the poor farm to guilt his adult children into taking care of him. They also thought it might be possible to build barracks for the newly poor on the poor farm property, which housed between 80 and 100 mostly elderly men, but that idea was not acted on because officials worried it would be demoralizing for families.[20] State reports at the time observed, "poverty is no indication of the need for grouping people together. . . . It seems probably that many almshouse inmates could be given adequate relief in the community at less expense."[21] That change in attitude marked a sharp departure from the concerns about direct aid that helped create poor farms in the first place. The crisis forced counties to take stock of expenses related to the poor farm. One solution was to focus more attention on residency requirements, which could eliminate transients from institutions. Ohio, for example, required six months of county residency to qualify for aid, so if someone moved and then became dependent, county officials billed the county of previous residency. Given the mobility of some of the poor during the 1930s, claiming residency was a significant issue. Dozens of letters sent between county commissioners and superintendents across the state requested reimbursements for doctors' bills, poor farm stays, and other aid.[22]

Getting reimbursed by other counties required a specific accounting of how much each person cost per day, but valuations were done in a variety of ways depending on the audience and motivation. In the 1920s, some states calculated their poor farm per person expense using the value of the acreage instead of the total number of people supported over time by that land. Kansas indicated that at its smallest poor farms, a property valuation of $1,200 per inmate was accurate. At least one county, farming more than 200 acres, cared for only two people. That meant that based on their calculations $13,000 worth of land was dedicated to two individuals, but since the county put any profits from the institution into the general fund, that assessment was not entirely fair. Regardless, it made a compelling statistic with an eye to reducing the number of poor farms and articulating over concerns about efficiency.[23] The range of poor farm populations during the

1930s, as measured by Kansas, demonstrates how variable their use had become. A majority of Kansas poor farms housed fewer than 30 residents; the smallest consisted of 2 residents and 1 employee; the largest housed 208 people and employed 28 people. One county had forty residents but only one employee.[24] The measurement of per capita spending is a better indicator of actual expense, and it declined with the size of the institution: the larger the number of residents, the smaller the per diem expense. On average, counties in the state spent $.57 per day per poor farm resident. This amount did not support decent accommodations; reports indicated some institutions were infested with bed bugs, failed to provide proper bedding, and needed better lighting. State visitors assessed that the larger poor farms located in or near urban centers fared better in terms of their conditions.[25] Smaller poor farms were also not nimble enough to respond quickly to new disasters, and counties did not have money to open new poor farms in response. Three Kansas Dust Bowl counties, for example, had institutions that were so small that they could not be scaled up in time to assist with the environmental and economic crisis at hand, leaving county officials paying out increasing amounts of direct aid. Coalitions of public and private relief desperately tried to meet community needs.[26]

The national financial crisis laid bare the problems with poor farms in the twentieth century. Grace Browning noted that poor farms were in a difficult position: "Those who need institutional care are physically unable to help with the farm work and need the services of nurses rather than those of farmers." Emil Frankel agreed, saying that while farms made sense in the nineteenth century under the theory that residents would contribute, the practice of farming at the institution and a farmer as superintendent no longer made the best sense for "the old and decrepit people we find in our almshouses today" who could not do hard farm labor.[27] That was as true in the 1930s as it had been in previous decades but now it was used as evidence of misdirected efforts.[28] As one institutional historian wrote, "The farm operation . . . had served a dual purpose of producing the bulk of the food needed by the institution, while at the same time maintaining a therapeutic program for both mental patients and indigents. Its demise was, as was so many other things, caught up in an economic situation which could no longer justify its continued operation."[29] In a decade where local areas saw their tax revenues decline dramatically, it became more difficult to defend public ownership of thousands of acres of tax-free land, a criticism that became a motivator to close poor farms. Counties using resources inefficiently, like Wake, North Carolina, with 175 of its 500 acres in production, six Texas farms with no residents but a total of 607 acres, or Virginia poor farms that had less than a fourth of their 25,000 acres farmed, drew ire from more than just the eugenicists.[30]

Firsthand Accounts

Many firsthand accounts of poor farm life come from those who lived in the institutions as children during the 1930s. Their recollections demonstrate that poor farm employment remained a valuable option for men with farming experience who needed wages to support a family. In 1933, Emily Williams Smith's father died while operating the Montana poor farm where the family had lived since the 1920s. What was a tragedy for one family proved an opportunity for the Voelkers. John Voelker remembered his parents, John and Edith, leaving their homestead at the start of the Depression, after which time the family moved frequently. Living at a poor farm might have embarrassed some high school students, but he recalled with gratitude the opportunity for his father to have a stable, paying job. As a long-time farmer, Voelker had the experience needed to manage the seventy-three acres of land that provided food, including "lots of potatoes." To increase output for the approximately fifty residents, the county rented additional land. John recalled the residents being mostly those who could do only light chores, handicapped by age or illness, and that many returned in the winter unable to find consistent employment.[31]

The Groth family took over management of an Iowa poor farm in 1931, after difficult financial circumstances brought Carl Groth back to his home county. The farm received upgrades from a WPA crew, who expanded the garden and built a canning kitchen.[32] Betty Groth Syverson had fond memories of the residents who helped curl her hair with an iron, entertained her with stories and poetry, candy, and attention. Syverson's memoir leaves an impression of mutually beneficial companionship for her family and the residents alike during a difficult time. Don Darling's parents also needed jobs during the Depression and so moved to the Dickenson County Poor Farm to help his grandparents manage the institution. He recalled there being plenty of food served, noting, "I don't remember thinking of the county farm as a poor farm. To all of us it was the county farm."[33] Likewise, the grandchildren of Herman and Lois Goldston moved to the Grayson County, Texas, farm during the Depression, where their "part time grandparents" included Red, an amputee who designed his own type of bicycle that carried the children.[34] Margaret Marsh's parents ran a Tennessee poor farm for a total of twenty-four years, including during the Depression. She recalled them being paid per resident and providing almost all the food served through either the farm, foraging, or hunting. She and her siblings grew up with "a deep compassion for poor, unfortunate people." Like Syverson, she also remembered the role New Deal programs played on the farm during that decade, as a CCC camp was built on the property to aid projects in the area.[35]

James Helmick's family went to the poor farm as residents, not employees, when his father could no longer support twelve children as a farm laborer in West Virginia. He recalled "a place to live and something to eat. Life itself was nothing. You just grew up. There wasn't really anything to do until you were old enough to work. . . . You lived with the old people. Life was boring." James's mother Lena helped with the cooking at the institution, but James did not remember the food fondly, noting that it was mostly flour based. "It wasn't too good," he said, "about the only time we ever had a special dinner was on Sundays when visitors would come out so they could see how good we were eating. The rest of the time you got a lot of stuff made out of dough—pot pies, gravy and something they called milk soup. . . . I'd never heard of it before and I don't ever want to eat it again . . . it was just blue john milk and what they called ribbles. A ribble was made out of flour. They put a little water in it and made little balls. . . . I can't eat lumpy gravy to this day." The menu probably resembled what many of the residents of the county ate during the Depression. Starch-heavy meals provided calories and a sense of fullness, if not nutrition. The family was physically separated in the institution, as he and his brothers stayed in the men's ward while the girls stayed with the other women.

Helmick's parents continued to do labor on the farm to help pay for the care of their children. His father worked in the fields and with the horses, since most residents were not capable of much labor. As the children grew up, they took on small tasks such as milking cows, moving them to pasture, and hauling water. As with so many other children coming of age in the 1930s, there was no Christmas at the poor farm. Helmick said that "Christmas was just another day in the year. We never got to go anywhere, just stayed there at the poor farm except for going to school." They walked at least two miles, in his recollection, to attend the school. The family remained at the farm until 1936, when a children's home opened and he was transferred. Shortly after the children left, their father died at the poor farm, possibly of skin cancer. His mother remained until the farm closed sometime around 1965, after which time she was transferred to another institution, eventually staying with a woman who took care of her.[36] Having lost the breadwinner and her home and place of employment, she had few options. These adults, reflecting on their childhood experiences, demonstrated that certain elements of poor farm life had not changed much from previous decades: many of the full-time residents were elderly and/or had a disability and created a sort of family with the superintendent and matron in charge.

Social Security

By the late 1930s, New Deal efforts to rationalize aid and assist targeted populations intersected with local aid and poor farms, completing what reformers had long hoped for: centralized aid programs. The federal and state partnerships that developed removed the ability of local officials to determine eligibility or make their own decisions about amounts of aid. Programs like Social Security, which were known as social insurance, were demarcated from public assistance, making one earned and its recipients deserving, and one charity and its recipients suspect. The program's two components, the contributory system and grants for state-administered funds to help people who were blind, people with disabilities, dependent children, and the poor, created a division of recipients—those who had "earned" Social Security, and those who had not. The structure of programs like Social Security demonstrated reformers' deep distrust of local officials and their dislike for the "complex, multilayered, decentralized pattern that had distinguished relief and welfare in America."[37] Although ideas like the Townsend Plan, which would have provided direct funds to people, were popular among the elderly and sometimes referenced in letters to the White House, the final version of Social Security, instead of being a universal pension program, was financed by a regressive employee tax and excluded many types of workers—including farm laborers and domestics, two common residents at poor farms.

President Franklin D. Roosevelt explained the needs of the elderly by saying, "There is no tragedy in growing old, but there is tragedy in growing old without means of support."[38] In letters to the Roosevelts and other officials, elderly people expressed fear about being sent to the poor farm. They hoped that a pension system could keep them from that fate. As one woman phrased it, "there are thousands of aged women in this great and rich country who are facing poor house or suicide, it is not their fault that they are poor." People who previously had been able to keep their home, an income-generating job, and put enough food on the table were in dire straits. The elderly knew they were at risk for being turned out by family members who could not afford to keep them; by 1940 two-thirds of older Americans relied on public relief, private charity, or help from friends and family. One woman, writing about her elderly mother, begged for assistance so she did not have to send her to other family members, claiming that "she would rather go to a poor house, than live with any of the others."[39] The period also saw an increasing number of elderly people categorized as insane so they could be sent to state asylums and hospitals, shifting the responsibility for their care to the state.[40]

Social Security could keep some elderly out of poor farms, but for those already there it threw their lives into disarray because beneficiaries could not remain in public institutions. The Roosevelt administration did not want those funds going directly into county coffers. Counties that housed many ineligible people could not close their institutions unless they funded their living expenses in boarding homes as direct aid.[41] A Kansas report from 1934 hinted at the difficult decisions to follow, estimating that while 40 percent of poor farm residents might live independently on a pension, 30 percent of poor farm residents required constant medical care.[42] Some residents turned down their benefits in order to stay, while others were forced into different accommodations because counties wanted to take advantage of the savings provided. Housing and care had to be located for people before they left the poor farm. By 1940, the first year they were made available, only 222,000 people were receiving old-age benefits.[43] Poor farm residents under the age of sixty-five were ineligible as were those with disabilities who could not live alone.

By the 1940s, the effects of Social Security were changing poor farms. Summit County, Ohio, which once housed more than one hundred residents, had between twenty and thirty residents in their facility in the years after the Social Security Act passed.[44] Cass County, North Dakota, saw most of its poor farm residents leave by the late 1930s because they were receiving Social Security.[45] The same happened in Cleburn, Arkansas, which then sold its $400 investment in poor farm land and netted over $2,000.[46] The poor farm population in Will County, Illinois, diminished by approximately ten people every six months after the passage of the Social Security Act. For a large farm of more than 200 residents this did not mean closure, but by 1941 the population had declined to 119 residents. In 1935 an optimistic newspaper story heralded "Good Bye to the Poor Farm," "an institution which has smelled to heaven for a hundred years is on its way out. The sweep of old age pensions can hardly have any other effect." The article made a comparison between the "radical step in social progress" that the poor farm had once represented—that of community responsibility for the poor—and how by comparison the New Deal programs seemed "a mild step." This was how many advocates of pensions viewed the poor farm; it made an excellent foil with its reputation as an indiscriminate dumping ground.[47]

There was a way to keep poor farms open without residents rejecting Social Security, but it required some legal maneuvering. Approximately one-third of Kansas counties with poor farms decided to lease them to private individuals so that residents could receive Social Security funds and pay for their own care. Management would pay the county rent on the land and institution. Residents in these facilities indicated that they were "better satisfied with the new arrangement . . . they were more independent, since they had the satisfaction of managing their living expenses."[48] However, in 1940 the Social Security Administration ruled that the leasing arrangement of county-owned institutions did not satisfy the conditions of the law. Most of the leased institutions closed or were sold following that decision.

In Oklahoma, approximately half of the elderly poor farm residents who applied for public aid under Social Security received it. Residents hesitant to leave an institution that had provided stability and a comforting routine "debated endlessly" whether to accept Social Security if it meant leaving.[49] Staff from the Department of Public Welfare helped almost 700 poor farm residents and Social Security recipients relocate by visiting each county poor farm to discuss the transition. Many of those people filed relief applications under the Oklahoma

Social Security Act in 1936–37.[50] Some residents requested furnished rooms near a town, church, or a friend. A case worker recalled that "one of our cases was a little old lady by the name of Miss H. She was declared incompetent in 1921 and was placed at the county poor farm at that time. She was always able to assist with the work and seemed to enjoy it. She has never known any home except the poor farm and was very pleased when I put her in the car and brought her to town. She was placed in a home that is right on a busy street and she spends most of her time looking out of the windows watching the people and cars go by. She seems quite happy and has adjusted herself nicely in a different home and entirely different surroundings."[51] Finding such alternatives required the time and resources of social workers.

Small boarding facilities were established to take care of people, creating an almost cyclical return to a previous version of relief where public funds were paid to individuals to house the dependent. Comanche County, Oklahoma, closed its poor farm by moving people to other facilities, but many rural counties faced a shortage of private options such as boarding homes, and their hospital was overrun by long-term patients that were previously at the poor farm. The county considered remodeling the poor farm for use as a nursing home as a result. Others were taken in by relatives, who were more likely to help when compensated.

The hesitation of poor farm residents to leave, either because non-institutional life was challenging or because they were used to life on the farm, was common.[52] One example from Kansas is instructive:

> A.B. is sixty-two years old and has been in the county home off and on for a number of years and was on the county farm before it was moved (1920). He has two children, and I understand they are both married and they do not have enough room for him in their homes. His face is disfigured to such an extent that he is rather shy about meeting people. I think this fact contributes largely to his wishing to remain at the county home. His physical condition also has made it impossible for him to be employed, as he does not have much strength to do heavy types of work. However, he assists in various chores around the home and does some work such as mowing lawns and making gardens. He is left free to come and go as he pleases.[53]

For this man, the semi-isolation of the poor farm was a benefit. Even with challenges that made it difficult for some residents to leave, by the end of the 1930s many counties were making plans to close institutions or transition to hospitals and nursing homes. Despite its reputation as a place older people did not want to end up, those who lived there also feared the unknown and some had grown truly attached to their home. Institutional employees in Washington recalled that long-time resident James Berry "knew it was now time for him to go. After looking at the car for awhile he rushed to his room to pick up his belongings by the dresser. As he was bending over his bed he had a severe cerebral hemorrhage. He lived long enough to receive the sacrament of the sick but never recovered consciousness. How sad for all our house! His funeral was held in the little chapel he loved so much." Berry's death saved him from having to leave the institutional home he had come to appreciate.[54]

Alabama officials also decided to place as many poor farm residents as possible on to Social Security, closing thirty-one institutions, which left only thirteen open by 1938; by 1951 the state only had two poor farms remaining.[55] Closures continued nationwide throughout the 1940s. As an Illinois institution prepared to shut its doors in 1944, one resident wondered about her fate. The reporter noted, "After 18 years in one place the roots of life have descended deep in to the soil." The paper called the poor farm "an outstanding monument to the folly of an obvious impossibility" but that was not how long-time residents felt about what had become their home.[56] Illinois further diminished poor farm eligibility when it passed the Public Assistance Code in 1949, handing relief over to county welfare departments and prohibiting poor farms from taking in those who were poor but otherwise physically healthy.[57]

The need for a poor farm–like institution or publicly funded institutional care did not go away with the advent of federalized pensions, nor did for-profit entities provide all the services needed.[58] Social Security provided the means for private businesses and individuals to profit from caring for the elderly, but privatizing care did not benefit everyone equally. Companies did not race to regions with smaller populations because volume helped profit margins; as with poor farms, the more people in the institution the lower the per person cost. This meant that rural counties were frequently left with a difficult issue: they had no private facility where Social Security clients could go, and they had a poor farm that did not meet the needs of an older and infirm population.[59]

Not every county closed its poor farm. Even after a destructive fire in 1946, which left Grayson County, Texas, residents wandering around "like lost children, sitting disconsolate under the trees and grouped together recounting their experiences," the county went to substantial lengths to rebuild. The county combined the insurance money with revenue from an auction on city lots that included an old jail. The $17,000 raised from the auction combined with the $15,000 from the insurance policy was enough to rebuild a smaller main building and some cabins which housed around twenty-five people. Local groups donated beds, bedding, and clothing.[60] The poor farm did not close until a decision was made to use the property for a nursing home in the late 1950s.

Those Who Remained

Moving poor farm residents to long-term nursing facilities resulted in a changing landscape for care. At the start of the 1940s, Minnesota still had more than 1,200 residents living in its twenty-one poor farms. But at the end of the decade only eleven institutions remained, and half were licensed by the state as care facilities, which meant they had been modernized with hot water, a telephone, and consistent heating, among other requirements. Three served metropolitan counties, and while most residents were over sixty-five, there were still exceptions reminiscent of earlier poor farms; one housed a seven-year-old girl who had been placed with the matron because officials feared her parents would interfere at a foster home. Those counties that kept poor farms open continued to help people in acute distress. During World War II, the Crawford County, Indiana, Infirmary provided shelter for a family of five children whose mother was admitted to the state asylum, and whose father was in the navy. He was discharged because of this hardship and came to reclaim them, but the month in between was no doubt a strange one. Earlier in the war a widow arrived with her five children and they stayed a month before departing.[61]

Adults with disabilities were one of the groups remaining in poor farms. According to one superintendent, these younger people had "institutional disabilities." During a labor shortage, like the one experienced during World War II, he believed some of them could help on local farms.[62] In Kansas, although half the poor farms closed by the 1940s, the most common residents were those with physical and/or cognitive disabilities.[63] The push to close poor farms moved more people with disabilities into state facilities, sometimes with devastating results when states then tried to cut costs. At poor farms these residents had regularly contributed based on their skills and preferences, remained close to any local family members, and had the company of other residents and employees. In 2014, *New York Times* reporter Dan Barry revealed a thirty-year pattern of businesses in Iowa and South Carolina using dozens of developmentally disabled men from Texas state-run institutions for a program that stripped them of their wages, isolated them from family, and left them living in squalor. Many of the men reported being forced to work difficult jobs for long hours without proper health care or bathroom breaks. Company owners bragged that their program had saved the state of Texas $100 million in institutional care.[64]

The continued expansion of federal funds for welfare programs encouraged counties to adapt their poor farm properties into public nursing homes. In many cases they opened on the same property, and occasionally in the same buildings that once housed the poor farm.[65] According to Violet Fischer, "in Kansas, the changing of the name of poor house or poor farm to county home represented a sincere desire on the part of many . . . to change from the old system of poor house care to furnishing a real home for aged persons who could not be cared for in the community." As Fischer pointed out however, a name change does not necessarily change the type of care being provided. At least two counties got started early, receiving new buildings constructed by the WPA on the same grounds as the old poor farm. That was true in Oregon as well, where the WPA built doctors' housing on-site at Multnomah and made other improvements to the main building.[66] Discrepancies continued, however, and a 1940 Ohio study noted that the rural poor in that state had a death rate approximately 10 percent higher than more prosperous areas. A lack of preventative medicine in poor rural regions of the state was strongly suggested as the variable. As other related studies showed, nutritional deficiencies, chronic illness, a lack of sanitation, and "remedial defects" were "baneful symptoms of rural life wherever it is impoverished."[67] There was a serious need for health care and institutional care, but in underserved areas public resources were not replaced by private enterprise—even those eligible for Social Security funds. When private facilities opened, they were sometimes more restrictive on behavior and no less isolated from the larger community than poor farms. Privately operated facilities discriminated based on race, and in Virginia at least a few appear to have refused admission to African American residents, leaving them in the poor farm.[68]

It was not just federal intervention that altered local social welfare. Farms, too, were transforming. As historian Deborah Fitzgerald points out, modernizations in technology and agriculture happened regionally, but eventually created an entirely new system. This mattered on poor farms: it was not easy to convince officials to spend large amounts of money on more acres, equipment, chemicals, and hybrid seed while taking care of a smaller number of people. These were all changes farmers made if they wanted to remain in industrializing agriculture. Towns in Vermont reported closures to their farms between 1938 and 1966, with the larger institutions taking the longest to close because of the number of people who needed other accommodations, and because of the investments that had been made to the farms in previous decades. Montpelier and Battleboro ran dairies on-site, and the milk was sold or given to the poor, making those farm closures detrimental to more people.[69] Innovations were not the only upheaval: the relationships farmers had to systems such as banking and insurance, extension agents, implements dealers, and their dwindling need for animals and laborers all changed after World War II. In this way, counties in the business of operating a farm had more to worry about than yields and expenses: they truly needed a farmer-turned-businessman to manage their institutional property.[70] It was less financially risky to retain ownership of the land, rent it to a farmer, and benefit from the proceeds without an institution attached. In Kansas, at least six counties did so, and another kept two small buildings on the property that poor people could stay in if need be. Kansas law dictated that selling poor farm land needed to be put to a popular vote, but counties continued to see the land as an investment and treated it as such.[71]

A change to the Social Security Act in 1950 allowing people in public institutions to receive funds created a resurgence of county institutions. The poor farms that remained in operation, had been privately leased, or transitioned to county nursing homes were now eligible for additional funds. Some places renovated their old buildings to meet new requirements and renamed them things like "Green Acres Nursing Home." In Chisago County, Minnesota, the county added on to the poor farm building and still did not have enough space to meet the demand. Dodge and Koochiching Counties resumed control of their institutions from private leases, and five other counties made the poor farm-to-nursing home conversion.[72] Fayette County, Iowa, added 140 beds in the 1950s and focused on nursing care but kept the farm. Most residents were elderly, but a seventeen-year-old accident victim received care there as well.[73]

Building conversions were popular options, but if poor farms were ill-suited for nursing homes because of their multistory/no elevator design, they were even worse for conversions to county hospitals, which received an infusion of federal funds from the Hill-Burton Act. After its passage in 1946, federal funds were spent on new healthcare facilities in underserved areas, including 40 percent of the counties that lacked hospitals.[74] Because of the design issues and their locations outside of towns, few poor farms made that transition despite the great need for those facilities. It was not practical to force ambulances and doctors to go outside of town, so county hospitals were more likely to be built in towns. Places did try: Billings, Montana, obtained a large Victorian-style house and moved it to the poor farm property, which still had barns and a dairy herd, to use as a county hospital. Years later, the hospital was moved into the brick building once used as the main residence at the farm, and eventually that building became the county nursing home. Nurse Helena Heider remembered several Japanese men who made the transition between institutions, including, "little deaf-mute Junior created beautiful flowers of paper orange wrappers and gave each freely. . . . Tonaka loved gardening. . . . Y loved cleaning and window washing." It was not until the 1960s that a new nursing home was built and the outbuildings sold or destroyed. The Barrien County, Michigan, Poor Farm became the Barrien County Hospital and Infirmary, and later the Barrien General Hospital Center after an infusion of funds for new buildings.[75]

Older people contended with inadequate Social Security benefits and limited old-age assistance to cover costs related to health care. The problems prompted additional legislation during the 1960s, including the Kerr-Mills rider on the Social Security Bill of 1960 and Medicare in 1965. These allowed states to provide vastly different amounts of funding for poor, sick, and elderly recipients, reminiscent of inequitable poor farm expenditures. Medical reimbursements ranged from $0.19 to $44 and capped rates for day and month-long hospital and nursing home stays below the cost of average expenses.[76]

The End of an Era

As poor farms closed and buildings fell into disuse, counties frequently retained ownership of the one thing that continued to appreciate: the farmland. Faced

Large institutions frequently operated substantial farms. The Los Angeles County Poor Farm in Downey averaged more than 700 residents a day, possessed more than 400 acres, and had a herd of 150 Holstein-Friesians that produced around 150 gallons of milk a day. Photo courtesy of the Security Pacific National Bank Collection, Los Angeles Public Library.

with decisions about whether to farm, rent, or sell, county officials made diverse choices. The Pendleton, West Virginia, County Farm closed in 1965, and the 402-acre farm was immediately put up for sale. The land brought $74,600 and the other items, such as livestock and furnishings, sold for an additional $16,750.[77] The Kaufman County, Texas, property was first divided in 1972 when fifty-seven acres were sold for $143,000. Fulton County, Ohio, tore down its multistory, gothic-style poor farm building, and utilized some of the land for a variety of county activities. The dairy cows and cattle at the Franklin County, Ohio, Infirmary were sold in 1956 and farming stopped altogether in 1960, "after it was discovered that the residents are usually too feeble to do heavy work and food could be bought more cheaply than it could be raised." The property still houses a nursing facility in addition to an industrial park and various county offices.[78]

This trend of turning poor farm land into multiuse space for counties happened across the country. County fairgrounds, airports, dumps, animal shelters, parks, public safety buildings, water treatment plants, and mental health facilities all sit on former poor farm land across the country.[79] Farming also remained in a few places. Alamakee County, Iowa, retained 325 acres until the 1990s, having sold its dairy herd in the 1980s. Records in Iowa indicate that at least one county proposed using its poor farm land for a prison complex. In McClean, Illinois, officials noted that other counties had made the conversion from a poor farm to a nursing home and they wanted to do the same, but the old building could not make the switch. The 256-acre farm, however, continued to generate income through rent. When they did finally sell the property in 1973, it brought between $2,000 and $2,750 per acre for a total of almost a million dollars.[80] For many counties, the land purchased for the poor farm really was a good investment.

Some counties were not quick to destroy the buildings but did try to unload the financial burden of maintaining large and old structures. In the 1970s, Davis County, Iowa, and Defiance County, Ohio, built single-story nursing homes in front of their old poor farm buildings to meet code standards. In Dodge County, Nebraska, the county decided to give the poor farm building to the renters who farmed the land and in the 1950s, voters decided to sell the land and house. Most of the graves of the thirty-three people buried in the poor farm plot were moved to town before the sale was completed. The house became unlivable by the 1960s and the buildings were destroyed by a tornado and dismantled.[81]

Shifting to prioritize health care did not necessarily sever the connection between poor farms and newer county facilities, in part because there were residents who made the transition. Employees in two Ohio counties went back into the old poor farm ledgers, still on-site, to make handwritten entries for nursing home residents who had started at the poor farm. Special comments included "she showed tremendous courage throughout her illness," and "was a joy to know and will be greatly missed by residents and employees." They placed obituarial notes including burials, but also noted how long the person lived in county care.[82] Dora Robinette lived at the Paulding County Poor Farm from 1930 until record keeping at the nursing home in the poor farm ledger ceased in 1990. She was joined in the 1940s by two siblings. When she died in 2010, her obituary noted that she was the last resident of the old Paulding County Home and that she had worked for PC Workshops, which helped employ disabled adults.[83]

For people who once relied on poor farms, some of whom made the move to public nursing facilities, the change was not as life-altering as reformers had hoped. Although the stated intention of nursing homes was to provide better, more focused care for the elderly, criticisms of poor farms followed the new institutions. The "loss of independence, individuality, self-esteem and domestic and social ties which institutionalization brought" continued in the new facilities. A description from the early twentieth century of "rows of inmates on their beds staring at nothing, lost in distant memories or trapped by present pains and fear" describes many nursing homes of the twenty-first century as well.[84] S. Stanley Clifton, a graduate student who studied Minnesota nursing homes during the late 1940s, determined that residents had failing memories, ill health, hearing trouble, and depression. They lacked activities and association with their communities. Some of them lived in a "close to vegetative" state and spent much of their time sitting alone. Residents were not taken outside for activities or trips because it was a hassle for staff. One doctor commented that nursing homes should be real homes, not "places where groups of old people just sit around waiting to die."[85]

In Summit County, Ohio, some of the reasons people came to the county hospital and nursing home echoed poor farm admissions. During the 1950s, residents had health issues such as senility, cancer, diabetes, heart ailments, and broken bones. At least two people checked in because of malnutrition. Some recovered and were transferred to family or other institutions, and some died in county care. A man sent by the Salvation Army killed himself. A handful of intakes were listed as transients and were released "to the road" while others simply walked away. As in previous decades, the jail, the hospital, and the county nursing home moved people back and forth occasionally.[86]

The Depression began a long-term decline in the use of poor farms for local social welfare. Even though there was enormous need, poor farm care was no longer considered suitable for children or young families. The older people and those with disabilities who remained were not all eligible for Social Security, but the program did allow many counties to move residents out and close the doors to the farm. The expenses of modern farming also came to bear on poor farms; with rising costs and land values, it made fiscal sense for counties to rent or repurpose their land instead of investing in agricultural technology. The two most common replacements for poor farms were public hospitals and nursing homes, but neither institution was entirely charitable. There was no true successor to poor farms.

Epilogue

As an increasing number of poor farm properties crumble, are torn down, or simply fall into even greater obscurity, there are small but concerted efforts to save what is left of this aspect of history. Websites, local history groups, and genealogists are committed to preserving community memory and what remains of poor farms. In Missouri, a team of graduate students and local volunteers studied a poor farm cemetery site in Pulaski County, demarcating what they believe to be at least 151 unmarked graves. Another project took place in Akron, Ohio, during the summer of 2017 when students surveyed the poor farm graveyard-turned-park, and the institution was featured in a recent local documentary. Erie County, New York, has been the site of numerous academic excavations. In Oregon, a local brewpub and hotel occupy the former Multnomah County Home. In Dodge County, Nebraska, a small portion of the original property was converted to a homestead site where today it serves as an animal sanctuary. Some of Arkansas's poor farm cemeteries have been placed on the National Register of Historic Places. A variety of buildings from Connecticut town farms remain across the state, including some used as private homes. Poor farms also house county historical societies from the barrier islands of Virginia to the Midwest and beyond. Hundreds of local newspapers have written stories about their county farms, and countless websites offer additional information.[1]

Others, however, have not been so lucky. County buildings and other developments have been constructed over the old sites of many institutions. The gradual decline of the massive Wayne County, Michigan, operation began in 1958 when farm operations ceased. The psychiatric branch of the institution closed in 1973. A new public hospital was built in Detroit, eventually shuttering the farm hospital in 1984. The land has been parceled off for various uses including a golf course, strip malls, and condominiums.[2] The crumbling remains of others still stand, and cemetery restoration efforts sometimes conflict with private property. Coles County, Illinois, profited from the rented farmland but when county officials tried sell the remaining poor farm land and buildings, they neglected to establish what would be done with the more than sixty marked graves in the cemetery.[3] The main buildings were eventually sold and rebranded as a nursing facility called Ashmore Estates, which was later condemned. The structure was then purchased for use as a residence but was sold again in 2006, this time for use as a haunted house. Constant vandalism was an ongoing problem. In the 2010s, the building was featured on television programs about haunted buildings, and in 2017 it had been renovated enough to charge $50 per person to "investigate" paranormal activity.[4] The angle of haunted poor farms is a popular one. The Randolph County Infirmary in Indiana has also been featured on television shows and runs haunted tours through a private owner.

That these institutions be remembered for the services they provided is important in a nation where each generation is said to rediscover poverty. Poor farms provide physical evidence of publicly funded aid that was given regardless of worthiness and a time when communities accepted a shared responsibility for those in need. As people learn about these institutions for the first time via newspaper stories and historical preservation, the tone is decidedly mixed. A 2017 newspaper story in California claimed that the San Mateo County Poor Farm and Hospital required residents to grow their own vegetables, eat roadkill delivered by the sheriff's deputies, and was labeled a "disgrace to modern civilization" by state inspectors.[5]

Although most poor farms ceased operation, a few quietly stayed open in form and function, serving a population of people not unlike those of the past. In 1978, residents in Washington, Iowa, still lived at the poor farm, attended classes at the YMCA, and made crafts. In 1984, a local newspaper in Oklahoma wrote about the twenty residents living at its county home. Institutional administrator Mary Thomas explained that despite the proliferation of government programs, some people still fell through the cracks. She mentioned the case of a forty-one-year-old woman without family who, upon her release from a hospital, had nowhere else to go. In the winter, just as 100 years previously, "we get a lot of frozen feet cases" from people who prefer to be on their own for all but the coldest days. This institution received $340,000 from the county for twenty employees and to cover the health care of those in residence. The county had considered other options for the building, like a juvenile detention center and a rehab facility, but residents echoed voices of the past, saying, "I don't have any other place to go, so I've adjusted to it." Another resident said, "I get good care here. Everything's provided for, the housekeeper keeps things spotless. My daughter takes me shopping sometimes, and I have a friend who comes by and takes me out for an ice cream cone. I keep busy knitting. I just love to knit, can just lose myself in it like some people can reading." She said that although she got depressed sometimes, she was grateful for the care.[6] John Strasser's family were some of the final caretakers of the Coshocton County Infirmary; during the 1970s it was still a farm, and one of the only remaining institutions of its type. It employed a full-time cook, a part-time helper, and his mother, who did the nursing. Strasser remembered, "It was a good home to those people and they almost never had a cross word for one another."[7]

Robert and Renee Guilliams were the last managers of the Coshocton County Infirmary, where Ed Sweeney once lived. In 1975 they worked for a year at the original institution while a new nursing home was built. During its final year the 150-year-old building housed forty-five residents. They rang a buzzer at night if they needed help, and did some chores including chopping wood for the boiler and helping with the laundry. There were two kitchen employees and two aides, but only the Guilliamses lived on-site. "When we began our time at the home," Robert said, "the only support financially was from local funds. Most residents had no Social Security or other income." Guilliams noted that many of the residents had lived there a long time and had formed a family of sorts. They knew how the institution routine operated, helped each other, and enjoyed events like Wednesday movie nights. As had been done for more than 100 years, residents received their health care at the institution, and the county contracted a doctor to come once a month for visits and prescriptions. Otherwise, the nursing care and medicine dispensing were done by the superintendent, matron, and aides. Because the Guilliamses' jobs also transferred, he went from being a farmer to an "administrator of an intermediate health care facility." He and his wife served in that capacity until 2004, by which time the institution was privately owned. He noted, "I am only one of a few people in the country who has had the experience of being a superintendent of a county home, and then seeing it transition to a health care facility, and being the administrator of that facility . . . it was as if time had stood still for those people in that setting."[8]

Although the many jobs of poor farms—sheltering abused women, homeless children, the elderly, disabled people, and those in need of health care—are still necessary today, only a handful of poor farms remain open in the twenty-first century. The last remaining poor farm in Massachusetts housed four residents, and in 2005 the Easthampton institution transitioned into housing and social services, but with no meals, washing, or supervision provided by staff.[9] In Ohio, among those still operating county homes as of 2020 were Washington and Medina Counties. The farms, while no longer tied to feeding the residents, remain as park space, the site of county buildings, and rented farmland. The few dozen residents are adults who need assisted living at public expense. Medina County provides not only live-in care for county residents who qualify, but also adult day-care for a small daily fee.

The variety of styles in architecture and design were particular to each county, so officials could select what they felt best represented the tenor of their county. The Washington County, Ohio, Home outside Marietta still houses residents, although the structure has been modified. Photo from the collection of the author.

Failings of those institutions intended to replace poor farms can be seen nationwide. Rural hospitals, which fill a role once occupied by poor farms, face daunting obstacles in the twenty-first century. Between 2010 and 2019, more than 100 closed, and another 430 were considered at risk of closure. A University of Washington study indicated that rural hospital closures can increase regional mortality rates by as much as 5.9 percent. The lack of health care in rural areas tends to affect the poorest residents more, since overcoming the problem requires costly and time-consuming transportation. The closures were more numerous in states that refused Medicaid expansion as part of the Affordable Care Act, where rural populations were more likely to lack health insurance.[10] There are no other public facilities to compensate for the losses.

Other services once fulfilled by poor farms also failed to meet their aspirational intentions. One of the goals of Social Security was to extend the time of independence for the elderly, but the issues associated with healthcare needs made this difficult. Elderly people face abuse, neglect, and abandonment, and the privatization of nursing-home care has resulted in a shortage of facilities willing to take those on public funding. In the best circumstances are those who have the resources to afford services. Not even private facilities equal safety, as was the case in 2017 when at least fourteen nursing home residents died in Florida during Hurricane Irma because employees failed to evacuate the institution after a power outage.[11] A 2001 report by the Special Investigations Division for the House Government Reform Committee found that between 1999 and 2001, 30 percent of nursing homes in the United States—5,283 locations—were cited for almost 9,000 instances of abuse. More than 1,600 of those violations caused "actual harm to residents" or placed them "in immediate jeopardy of death or serious injury." Some of the offenses outlined in the report involved residents being restrained to beds. Others noted horrible bug infestations and bed sores. Approximately two-thirds of all the nursing facilities in the country are for-profit ventures.[12] In 2018, reports surfaced of Medicaid patients being evicted from nursing homes, with no arrangements for those who were removed.[13] Group settings continue to be vectors for contagious disease, and nursing homes accounted for 45 percent of all COVID deaths in 2020. The Centers for Disease Control noted that outbreaks of COVID were more likely to happen in nursing homes with the lowest state quality ratings.[14] The circumstances have resulted in the deaths of tens of thousands of elderly residents, all of whom died without family present, notified now via phone instead of telegram.

Although the poor farm was not a modern solution to the problems of poverty, some of its replacements have fared badly. The evolution of welfare involved state, federal, and private partnerships, reducing the expense burden on local communities but diminishing their power and control. Cuts to state funding for mental health care, institutional care, federal cuts to food assistance, and rising costs of health care have made vulnerable many of the same types people who received care at poor farms. Food insecurity stalks approximately 11 percent of US households.[15] Cuts to mental healthcare services and the closure of state institutions has resulted in jails returning to their nineteenth-century role as welfare institution. The use of incarceration as a social service remains racially discriminatory and costly both in financial resources and for those jailed as a result of the criminalization of poverty. In 2019, Travis County, Texas, reported that the 250 most expensive homeless cases cost the county about $223,000 in medical, jail, shelter, and other costs.[16] The politicized emphasis on dependency as a fault or character flaw, and the demands for drug testing, means testing, or employment in order to receive direct aid have placed tens of millions of people in vulnerable circumstances. Poor farms were not a panacea for social ills, but neither was removing them from the landscape of welfare.

Appendix

The census data that exists for cumulative poor farm and almshouse totals is the only nationwide data available, but it was not always consistently taken nor were the same data points routinely used, so this information, while useful, should be considered cautiously. The census collections contain additional demographic information about poor farm populations.

Single-Day Census Data Reported by State, 1880, 1890, 1903

1880		1890		1903	
Alabama	514	Alabama	623	Alabama	761
Arizona	4	Arizona	23	Arizona	146
Arkansas	105	Arkansas	223	Arkansas	575
California	1,594	California	2,600	California	4,140
Colorado	46	Colorado	87	Colorado	398
Connecticut	1,418	Connecticut	1,438	Connecticut	2,067
Dakota	0				
Delaware	387	Delaware	299	Delaware	278
DC	184	DC	221	DC	230
Florida	45	Florida	24	Florida	124
Georgia	550	Georgia	901	Georgia	1,032
Idaho	7	Idaho	20	Idaho	70
Illinois	3,684	Illinois	5,395	Illinois	5,635
Indiana	3,052	Indiana	2,927	Indiana	3,120
Iowa	1,165	Iowa	1,621	Iowa	2,019
Kansas	355	Kansas	593	Kansas	780
Kentucky	1,366	Kentucky	1,578	Kentucky	1,678
Louisiana	0	Louisiana	122	Louisiana	149
Maine	1,505	Maine	1,161	Maine	1,152
Maryland	1,187	Maryland	1,599	Maryland	1,633
Massachusetts	4,533	Massachusetts	4,725	Massachusetts	5,934
Michigan	1,746	Michigan	1,916	Michigan	2,594
Minnesota	227	Minnesota	365	Minnesota	547

1880		1890		1903	
Mississippi	345	Mississippi	494	Mississippi	517
Missouri	1,477	Missouri	2,378	Missouri	2,465
Montana	0	Montana	132	Montana	314
Nebraska	113	Nebraska	291	Nebraska	464
Nevada	95	Nevada	43	Nevada	171
New Hampshire	1,198	New Hampshire	1,143	New Hampshire	1,140
New Jersey	2,462	New Jersey	2,718	New Jersey	1,936
New Mexico	0	New Mexico	1	New Mexico	0
New York	12,452	New York	10,272	New York	10,793
North Carolina	1,275	North Carolina	1,493	North Carolina	1,519
		North Dakota	35	North Dakota	184
Ohio	6,974	Ohio	7,400	Ohio	8,172
		Oklahoma	0	Oklahoma	52
Oregon	51	Oregon	99	Oregon	257
Pennsylvania	9,184	Pennsylvania	8,653	Pennsylvania	9,054
Rhode Island	526	Rhode Island	490	Rhode Island	788
South Carolina	519	South Carolina	578	South Carolina	686
		South Dakota	53	South Dakota	159
Tennessee	1,136	Tennessee	1,545	Tennessee	1,812
Texas	210	Texas	464	Texas	913
Utah	0	Utah	62	Utah	184
Vermont	6,565	Vermont	543	Vermont	414
Virginia	2,117	Virginia	2,193	Virginia	1,915
Washington	11	Washington	71	Washington	257
West Virginia	711	West Virginia	792	West Virginia	881
Wisconsin	1,018	Wisconsin	2,641	Wisconsin	1,606
Wyoming	0				

TOTALS AND BREAKDOWN BY GENDER/FOREIGN BORN 1880, 1890, 1903, 1910

1880

Total on single day: 66,203

Men: 35,564

Women: 30,639

Foreign Born: 22,883

1890

Total on single day: 73,045

Men: 40,741

Women: 32,304

Foreign Born: 37,045

1903

Total Single Day: 81,764

Men: 52,444

Women: 29,320

Foreign Born: 39,559

1910

Total Single Day: 84,198

Men: 57,949

Women: 27,149

Foreign Born: 44,254

Notes

Introduction

1. Brown County, IL, County Farm Records, 1878–1937, ACPL; US Census 1900, Emma Frisbee, Buchanan, Missouri, St. Joseph Ward 09.

2. Brown County, IL, County Farm Records; US Census 1920, 1940, Lee Hardin, Brown County, Illinois; US WWII draft Registration Cards, 1942, Lee Hardin. See also Rose, *No Right to Be Idle*, 1. The asylum changed its name in 1909 to the Lincoln State School and Colony.

3. Warner, *American Charities*, 140.

4. US Census, *Paupers in Almshouses in 1890*, 852.

5. Hoffbeck, "Remember the Poor," 226.

6. Brenmer, *Discovery of Poverty*, 48; see also Erie County Infirmary, 1856, ACPL. Early rules at this institution included three meals a day for working and two for those who did not, strict wakeup and bedtimes, and no Sunday visiting.

7. Herndon, "'Who Died an Expense to This Town,'" 135.

8. Trattner, *From Poor Law to Welfare State*, 60.

9. Krainz, *Delivering Aid*, 12; Zunz, *Philanthropy in America*, 250.

10. Evans, *The American Poorfarm and Its Inmates*, 54. See also Green, *This Business of Relief*, 163.

11. Isenberg, *White Trash*, 21; Morgan, *American Slavery, American Freedom*, 326; Horn, *Damnation Island*, 110.

12. Altschuler and Saltzgaber, "The Limits of Responsibility," 515; Foucault, *Discipline and Punish*, pt. 4.

13. Brown, "Poor Relief in a Wisconsin County," 94.

14. Miller, *Anatomy of Disgust*, 206, 220.

15. Katz, *In the Shadow*, 25.

16. Marshall, "Shaping Poor Relief," 562; Arrom, *Containing the Poor*, 7.

17. Katz, *In the Shadow*, 13.

18. Marshall, "Shaping Poor Relief," 563.

19. Katz, *In the Shadow*, 3. Archaeology at poor farm cemeteries has provided interesting evidence about the nutrition and laboring lives of poor farm residents. See Sutter, "Dental Pathologies," 190.

20. Ziliak, "Pauper Fiction in Economic Science," 172; Kujawa, "The American Poorhouse in Historical Perspective," 46; See also Klebaner, *Public Poor Relief in America*.

21. Katz, *In the Shadow*, 86–87; Ziliak, "Pauper Fiction in Economic Science," 173; Hoffer, *Counties in Transition*, 85.

22. Mintz and Kellogg, *Domestic Revolutions*, 107. See also Goldberg, *Citizens and Paupers*, 326.

23. Roediger, *Wages of Whiteness*, 49; Katz, *In the Shadow*, 3.

24. Katz, *In the Shadow*, 11.

25. Piven and Cloward, *Regulating the Poor*, 30–31. Piven and Cloward connect the changing English rural labor markets to a desire to quell and contain any unrest those changes caused.

26. Bourque, "Poor Relief 'Without Violating the Rights of Humanity,'" 189.

27. Nash, "Poverty and Politics in Early American History," 15.

28. Herndon, "'Who Died an Expense to This Town,'" 142. I do not mean a demographic reflection: the composition of relief recipients privileged the white and native-born.

29. For samplings of the ages of residents during the 1860s see Brown, "Poor Relief in a Wisconsin County," 96–99. See also Tuten, "Regulating the Poor in Alabama," 56.

30. This change over time can be seen in countless ledgers, but one outstanding example is the Certificates for Relief, Fayette County Home, OHC, 1896–97, 1914–18, 1919–20, 1920–23, 1923–25.

31. Wagner, *Ordinary People*, 774.

32. Piven and Cloward, *Regulating the Poor*, 68.

33. Wagner, *The Poorhouse*, 40–41; Goldberg, *Citizens and Paupers*, 3. I disagree with Wagner's assertion that poor farms required people to "reform their characters" as part of receiving aid. No records I examined required such a promise, either implied or specific, in direct aid or indoor relief.

34. Trattner, *From Poor Law to Welfare State*, 57–61.

35. Meltsner, *Poorhouses of Massachusetts*, 25–26.

36. Vale, *From the Puritans to the Projects*, 95–96.

37. US Census, *Special Report on Almshouses*, 1904, 47.

38. The state facilities in Massachusetts are an outstanding example of this, built to house a few hundred people, many of them ended up with more than one thousand residents. See also Hirota, *Expelling the Poor*, 122–23. Hirota discusses the deportation of institutionalized immigrants; while I did not find evidence of counties doing this via poor farms, they regularly sent people elsewhere.

39. Davies, *Main Street Blues*, 47; Fox, *Three Worlds of Relief*, 71.

40. Fox, *Three Worlds of Relief*, 53. States in the South typically had provisions in state constitutions for the care of the poor, but Louisiana lagged behind others, only adding

a proviso in 1880. In 1928 the state permitted buildings for the poor to be placed on the property with district prisons. See Wisner, *Public Welfare in Louisiana*, 29–31.

41. Crowther, *Workhouse System*, 6.

42. For a discussion of family history and census records see Smith, "The Meanings of Family and Household," 421–56.

43. Mustakeem, *Slavery at Sea*, intro.

44. Patterson, *America's Struggle against Poverty*, 18.

45. Naldrett, *The Poorhouses and Poor Farms of Michigan*, 161.

46. Nelson, *Farm and Factory*, 29.

47. Poor farm child residents of note include sharpshooter Annie Oakley, and teacher of the blind Annie Sullivan.

48. Piven and Cloward, *Regulating the Poor*, 56–57.

49. Hough, *Rural Unwed Mothers*, 26; See also Trattner, *From Poor Law to Welfare State*, 96–97.

50. Fraser and Gordon, "A Genealogy of Dependency," 309–36; Kittay, "Dependence, Equality, and Welfare," 32–43.

51. Klages, *Woeful Afflictions*, 2.

52. Craig, "Prevention of Pauperism," 121; Jones, *American Hungers*, 72–74.

53. Hoyt, *Causes of Pauperism*, 195; Jones, *American Hungers*, 94; Miller, *Anatomy of Disgust*, 34.

54. Poppendieck, *Breadlines Knee-Deep in Wheat*, 21; Katz, *In the Shadow*, 88.

55. Johnson, *Almshouse Construction and Management*, 7.

56. Rosenberg, "From Almshouse to Hospital," 108–54; Wisner, *Social Welfare in the South*, 116.

57. Johnston, *I Was Raised at the Poor Farm*, 1.

58. Daley and Pittman-Munke, "Over the Hill to the Poor Farm," 2. Similar changes happened in England. See Crowther, *Workhouse System*, 88; Reed, *History of Kossuth County, Iowa*, 248. Wagner also wrestles with the issue of names and how much significance they held to the purpose of the institution. See Wagner, *The Poorhouse*, ch. 3.

59. US Census, *Paupers in Almshouses in 1890*, 2.

60. US Census, *Paupers in Almshouses, 1910*, table 1.

61. Cahill, *Federal Fathers and Mothers*, 39.

Chapter 1. *The Founding of Community Institutions*

1. Buchanan County, Missouri, Poor Farm Records, WSHS, 3; US Census 1870, P. King, Center Twp., Buchanan County, MO. Her name is given variously as Paulina, Perlina, Polina.

2. *The History of Polk County, Iowa*, 453–54.

3. Elia and Wesolowsky, eds., *Archaeological Excavations at the Uxbridge Almshouse*, 50; Gillin, *History of Poor Relief Legislation*, 12. Lockley, *Welfare and Charity in the Antebellum South*, ch. 1. According to Lockley, in 1829, almost half the counties in Virginia and North Carolina had poorhouses, and by the start of the Civil War that number reached almost 80 percent. Some of these closed only to open again in a different location.

4. Johnson, *Almshouse Construction and Management*, 9. In 1890 the census reported 2,373 almshouses. In 1900 that number increased to 2,476.

5. Stanley, "Beggars Can't Be Choosers," 1272–80.

6. *Board of State Charities Secretary's Report, Massachusetts*, 1871, 44.

7. Thanet, "The Indoor Pauper," 751.

8. Deutsch, *The Mentally Ill in America*, 118.

9. Massac County Poor Farm and Pauper Fund Records, Abraham Lincoln Presidential Library, Springfield, IL. Massac County is located on the Ohio River across from Paducah, KY.

10. *Rock Island Daily Argus*, March 5, 1873, 1; Rexroad, *The Poor Farm of Pendleton County*, 9.

11. Oldt, *History of Dubuque County, Iowa*, 405.

12. Smith, "Poor Relief at the St. Joseph County Poor Asylum," 182. See also Hoffbeck, "Remember the Poor," 229; Freeman, "Indigent Care in Texas," 40.

13. McCormick, "Poverty's Monument." In *Social Welfare in the South*, 41, Wisner describes an 1897 Arkansas pauper auction that may have created a similar sort of poorhouse/boardinghouse situation.

14. Morrow County Home, Minutes of the Infirmary Directors, 1862–1889, OHC; *NCCC Proceedings*, 1888, 360; Holt, "'Over the Hill to the Poorhouse,'" 9.

15. McClure, *More Than a Roof*, 90; *NCCC Proceedings*, 1889, 158; 1893, 314.

16. *NCCC Proceedings*, 1897, 403–4.

17. Wallenstein, *From Slave South to New South*, 146.

18. Shifflett, *Patronage and Poverty*, 201.

19. *NCCC Proceedings*, 1889, 171; Cottrell, "The Poor Farm System in Texas," 171–73.

20. O'Nale, *Scott County, Arkansas*.

21. Unpublished notes from Jenny Barker-Devine; Morgan County Poor Farm, Ledger, 1848–68, IRAD.

22. Defiance County Home, Directors Ledger, June 20, 1910, CAC-BGSU.

23. Minnesota provides an exception. In 1864 the state government required counties build a poor farm or provide a suitable substitute if the number of poor was so small that officials could not justify the expense. See McClure, *More Than a Roof*, 20.

24. Holt, "'Over the Hill to the Poorhouse,'" 4.

25. Keenan, *History of Eloise*, 369–70.

26. *History of Mills County, Iowa*, 419.

27. Alexander, *History of Chickasaw and Howard Counties*, 389.

28. *Annual Report of the Bureau of Labor and Industry for 1899*, 376.

29. McClure, *More Than a Roof*, 22.

30. O'Nale, *Scott County, Arkansas*.

31. McClure, *More Than a Roof*, 17–28.

32. McClure, "An Unlamented Era," 369.

33. *NCCC Proceedings*, 1900, 154.

34. Elia and Wesolowski, eds., *Archaeological Excavations at the Uxbridge Almshouse*, 55; Hamm, "Study of the Influence."

35. McClure, "An Unlamented Era," 367.

36. *Public Documents of the State of Wisconsin*, 117.

37. "For the Destitute," *Southern Illinoisan*, April 21, 2013.

38. *Poor Relief in North Carolina*, 11.

39. McClure, *More Than a Roof*, 101–5. Hennepin County reported that although a state law prohibited saloonkeepers from serving inmates of state institutions, and county commissioners had threated to blacklist drinkers, their poor farm residents were being treated to drinks at nearby saloons.

40. *Second Annual Report of the Ohio Board of State Charities for the Year 1877*, 138.

41. McClure, *More Than a Roof*, 22–23, 82.

42. Rexroad, *The Poor Farm of Pendleton County*, 1–10.

43. Hoyt, *Causes of Pauperism*, 56.

44. *Findlay Jeffersonian*, February 16, 1877, 3.

45. Letchworth, "Poorhouse Administration," 341.

46. Johnson, *Almshouse Construction and Management*, 242.

47. Yanni, "Linear Plan for Insane Asylums," 24; "Coles County Poor Farm," *Charleston [IL] Journal Gazette and Times Courier*, October, 19, 2009.

48. *NCSW Proceedings*, 1918, 262.

49. Marshall, "Shaping Poor Relief," 569–70; List of property, Dade County, Poor Farm, March 1893, ACPL.

50. McClure, *More Than a Roof*, 28.

51. Marshall, "Shaping Poor Relief," 571.

52. Franklin Sanborn, "The Management of Almshouses in New England," *NCCC Proceedings*, 1884.

53. Defiance County Home, Board of Directors Minutes, January 1, 1913–1927, CAC-BGSU.

54. Letter from Edna White, October 4, 1920, Colusa County, Board of Charities and Corrections Records, County Files, CSA; *Proceedings of the Annual Convention, Michigan*, 1917, 41.

55. Fox, *Three Worlds of Relief*, 58–59.

56. Wisner, *Social Welfare in the South*, 43; Westerfield, *Road to the Poorhouse*, 179.

57. *Study of a Group of Almshouses*, 57.

58. Johnson, *Almshouse Construction and Management*, 62.

59. *Zanesville Times Recorder*, March 15, 1927.

60. Dane County Hospital and Home Records, Annual Report, 1887, 6.

61. *Austin American Statesman*, April 27, 1893.

62. Henderson County, Illinois, Poor Farm and Jail, ACPL. This county farm continued to struggle with various issues including a tornado and fire.

63. McLennan, *Crisis of Imprisonment*, 26–27.

64. Oshinsky, "*Worse Than Slavery*," 41–42; Curtin, *Black Prisoners and Their World*, 67. See also Lichtenstein, *Twice the Work of Free Labor*, chs. 3, 4.

65. Lockley, *Welfare and Charity*, 39.

66. Hoffer, *Counties in Transition*, 86. See also Gonaver, *The Peculiar Institution*, 4.

67. Kennedy, *Ohio Poor Law*, 49.

68. Herndon, "'Who Died an Expense to This Town,'" 137

69. *Proceedings of the Annual Convention, Michigan*, 1909, 18–19. Joan Jensen briefly describes an early poor farm founding and its relation to women in the community in her work *Loosening the Bonds*, 63–68.

70. *Annual Report of the Board of State Charities of Indiana*, 1922, 128.

71. *Rock Island Daily Argus*, May 30, 1873, 2.

72. *Rock Island Daily Argus*, December 16, 1887, 2.

73. Directors of the Wood County Poor Farm, *Commemorative Historical and Biographical Record of Wood County*, 993, 1028, 1312.

74. "The St. Louis County Poor Farm." *Zenith City Press*, http://zenithcity.com/archive/historic-architecture/the-st-louis-county-poor-farm/.

75. Wyandot County Board of Commissioners, Infirmary Minutes, 1909, CAC-BGSU.

76. Wood County Board of Commissioners, Infirmary Directors Minutes, January 1877, CAC-BGSU.

77. Wood County Board of Commissioners, Correspondence, April 16, 1886, CAC, BGSU; Wood County Board of Commissioners, Infirmary Minutes, 1893–October 1894, CAC-BGSU.

78. Bourque, "Poor Relief 'Without Violating the Rights of Humanity,'" 201; Hoffbeck, "Prairie Paupers," 47–48.

79. Certificates for Relief, Fayette County, Ohio, OHC, 1910–19.

80. Goldie West, Dade County, Poor Farm, December 1894, ACPL.

81. Kennedy, *Ohio Poor Law*, 42.

82. Searcy County, Arkansas, History, ACPL.

83. *Proceedings of the Board of Supervisors of the County of Niagara, 1912*, 300.

84. Wood County Board of Commissioners, Minutes, 1905, CAC-BGSU; US Census 1910, Mary R. Lonergan, Jackson, Seneca, OH.

85. Wood County Board of Commissioners, Minutes, April 1882, CAC-BGSU; Birk, *Fostering on the Farm*, 95–96.

86. "Taxation in Ohio."

87. Hoffer, *Counties in Transition*, 88. The rest came from contributions on behalf of residents to one large institution in the survey.

88. Dane County Hospital and Home Records, Superintendent's Report, 1875, box 1, WHSA.

89. Wallis, "American Government Finance," 62.

90. Wallenstein, *From Slave South to New South*, 194.

91. *Pubic Poor Relief in North Carolina*, 50.

92. Frankel, *Poor Relief in Pennsylvania*, 17–18.

93. *Proceedings of the Annual Convention, Michigan*, 1916, 22.

94. *NCCC Proceedings*, 1901, 38.

95. Ratcliffe, "Some Illinois County Poor Relief Records," 462.

96. *NCCC Proceedings*, 1898, 32.

97. Brown County, Illinois, County Farm Records, ACPL; *Coshocton Democrat Message*, April 20, 1904.

98. *Proceedings of the Board of Supervisors of the County of Niagara, 1912*, 300.

99. *Coshocton Daily Times*, September 1, 1909; Coshocton County, Ohio, Infirmary, ACPL, 121; US Census 1880, Coshocton, Coshocton County, OH.

100. Landis, *Rural Social Welfare Services*, 16–17. Klebaner, *Public Poor Relief in America*, 238–42.

101. Those first nine states were: New York, Rhode Island, Pennsylvania, Massachusetts, Illinois, Ohio, Kansas, Wisconsin, and Michigan. Location and time altered the names by which the groups were called.

102. Wisner, *Social Welfare in the South*, 125.

103. McClure, "An Unlamented Era," 370.

104. Olmsted, *Handbook for Visitors to the Poorhouse*, 107.

105. *Stark County Democrat*, April 11, 1878, 3.

106. *NCCC Proceedings*, 1888, 357.

107. *Annual Report of the Board of State Charities of Indiana*, 1922, 129–31.

108. McClure, *More Than a Roof*, 81; McClure, "An Unlamented Era," 373.

109. Oppenheim, "He's Only a Pauper," 214–15.

110. McClure, *More Than a Roof*, 99.

111. Olmsted, *Handbook for Visitors to the Poorhouse*, 53.

112. Ordronaux, *Questions Relating to Poorhouses, Hospitals, and Insane Asylums*.

113. Williams, *The Poor Farm of Grayson County*, 14–15.

114. *NCCC Proceedings*, 1890, 73.

115. Warner, *American Charities*, 168. See also Wuthnow, *American Misfits*, 28–29.

116. Hoffman, "The Depression of the Nineties," 144.

117. *NCCC Proceedings*, 1896, 55, 37.

118. Marshall, "Shaping Poor Relief," 292.

119. Ottawa County Home, Annual Reports, 1890s, CAC-BGSU.

120. Certificates of relief, Fayette County Home, 1896–97, 1914–24, OHC. Ruth Wallis Herndon points out that African Americans were less likely to receive direct aid in the eighteenth century as well. See Herndon, "'Who Died an Expense to This Town,'" 135.

121. *NCCC Proceedings*, 1897, 391–94.

122. Kennedy, *Ohio Poor Law*, 46.

123. McKinley inaugural address quoted in White, *The United States and the Problem of Recovery*, 66.

124. Rothman, *Discovery of the Asylum*, 185.

125. Annual Report of the Bureau of Labor and Industry for 1899, 368.

126. Trattner, *From Poor Law to Welfare State*, 90.

127. Folks, "Problems in Administration of Municipal Charities," 77.

128. Katz, *Poverty and Policy in American History*, 91.

129. Johnson, *Almshouse Construction and Management*, 2–3.

130. *NCCC Proceedings*, 1896, 63–64.

131. Brown, "Poor Relief in a Wisconsin County," 94.

132. Wood County Board of Commissioners, Directors Minutes, February 5, 1906, CAC-BGSU.

133. Colusa County, Board of Charities and Corrections Records, Colusa County Hospital, June 19, 1925; October 27, 1919, CSA.

134. Morgan County Poor Farm, Almshouse Register, IRAD. See also Squillance, "Life on the Morgan County Poor Farm."

135. Morgan County Poor Farm, Almshouse Register, IRAD.

136. *Annual Report of the Board of State Charities, Ohio, 1899*, 28.

137. *A Study of Kansas Poor Farms*, 40.

Chapter 2. Populations and Conditions

1. Morgan County Poor Farm, medical records, IRAD.

2. See US Census, *Paupers in Almshouses*, 1910, Length of Stay/Discharges, for statistics available about departures. In 1910 approximately 30 percent of poor farm users stayed less than one year and approximately 30 percent had been admitted previously.

3. Frost, "Death of the Hired Man."

4. Butterfield, "Rural Life and the Family," 236; Nordin and Scott, *From Prairie Farmer to Entrepreneur*, 47.

5. James, "A Golden Age?" 960.

6. Hatton and Williamson, "Wage Gaps between Farm and City," 384–85.

7. Schob, *Hired Hands and Plowboys*, 89.

8. DePastino, *Citizen Hobo*, 9–10; *Chillicothe Gazette*, September 17, 1909. Estimates for seasonal unemployment across all industries range between 20 and 25 percent of all northern wage earners. DePastino also points out that the term "unemployment" was not used in print until 1887.

9. Ann Ellis Papers, box 1, folder 15, OHC.

10. Rosenbloom, "Extent of the Labor Market in the United States," 290.

11. Taylor, Wheeler, and Kirkpatrick, *Disadvantaged Classes*, 3.

12. Iceland, *Poverty in America*, 13; Hoyt, *Causes of Pauperism*, 197.

13. Crowther, *Workhouse System*, 1.

14. This oft-quoted passage is from a Charles Burroughs speech in 1834; see Iceland, *Poverty in America*, 12.

15. Katz, *In the Shadow of the Poorhouse*, 4.

16. Taylor, Wheeler, and Kirkpatrick, *Disadvantaged Classes*, 1.

17. Some African American associations developed to address needs within their own communities across the rural South because of their exclusion from white-only groups. See Shifflett, *Patronage and Poverty*, 210–11; Beito, *From Mutual Aid to the Welfare State*; Sharpless, *Fertile Ground, Narrow Choices*, 197–200; Barron, "Staying Down on the Farm," 327–44.

18. Nordin and Scott, *From Prairie Farmer to Entrepreneur*, 9, 25.

19. *NCCC Proceedings*, 1900, 116–120.

20. Moen, "Rural Nonfarm Households," 57; Atack and Bateman, *To Their Own Soil*; Effland, "When Rural Does Not Equal Agricultural."

21. Higbie, *Indispensable Outcasts*, intro.; Naldrett, *Poorhouses and Poor Farms of Michigan*, 161. Margaret Tennant reported a similar type of symbiosis between rural landowners and transients using seasonal charity in New Zealand, *Paupers and Providers*, 22.

22. Kusmer notes that in some places where there was highly physical work available, like the logging areas around Minneapolis, the average age of homeless men was younger. Kusmer, *Down and Out*, 117–21; Higbie, "Rural Work, Household Subsistence," 54, 62.

23. Permits to enter Yavapai County Hospital and Poor Farm, 1897–1989, ACPL.

24. Higbie, "Rural Work, Household Subsistence," 52.

25. Kessler-Harris, "Treating the Male as 'Other,'" 197. See Elia and Wesolowski, *Archaeological Excavations at the Uxbridge Almshouse*, 65. The town specifically used outdoor relief to keep families out of institutions.

26. *NCCC Proceedings*, 1894, 119; Roediger, *Wages of Whiteness*, 46–48; Nelson, *Farm and Factory*, 15.

27. Hays appears to have been married with children earlier in his life. *History of Allamakee County, Iowa*, 365.

28. US Census 1870, John White, Acadia Precinct, Morgan County, IL; US Census 1880, Morgan County.

29. *NCCC Proceedings*, 1903, 401.

30. Williams, *The Poor Farm of Greyson County*, 70–71.

31. Higbie, *Indispensable Outcasts*, 42.

32. Smith, "Poor Relief," 192.

33. Kusmer, *Down and Out*, 54, 69.

34. Editorial, *Annals of Iowa*, 227–28.

35. *NCCC Proceedings*, 1897, 359–60.

36. Will County Poor Farm, Register, September 29, 1888, Joliet Area Historical Museum. He was forty-three.

37. Higbie, *Indispensable Outcasts*, 32–35; Schob, *Hired Hands and Plowboys*, 231, 108; DePastino, *Citizen Hobo*, 15.

38. Keenan, *History of Eloise*, 433.

39. Kusmer, *Down and Out*, 70.

40. Wagner, *Ordinary People*, 186; Kusmer, *Down and Out*, 68.

41. Hoyt, *Causes of Pauperism*, 12–13.

42. Dane County Hospital and Home Records, Titus Journal, November 2–3, 1879, box 4, folder 4, WHSL.

43. Crawford County, Inmates, ACPL; Westerfield, *Road to the Poorhouse*, 217.

44. *Dayton Daily News*, August 31, 1952, 5.

45. Parsons, *Manhood Lost*, 3, 37.

46. Freeman, "Indigent Care in Texas," 41.

47. Wyandot County Board of Commissioners, Infirmary Register, CAC-BGSU, 76.

48. Gillin, *History of Poor Relief Legislation*, 90.

49. Wyandot County Board of Commissioners, Infirmary Register, CAC-BGSU, 95.

50. *NCCC Proceedings*, 1889, 249.

51. Warner, *American Charities*, 37–38; Hoyt, *Causes of Pauperism*, 17.

52. *Study of a Group of Almshouses*, 9.

53. Monkkonen, *The Dangerous Class*, 152.

54. Grant, "Blueprints for Co-operative Communities," 75. See also Gorman, "Confederate Pensions as Social Welfare," 29.

55. Hatton and Williamson, "Wage Gaps between Farm and City," 381–408.

56. Shifflett, *Patronage and Poverty*, 217–18; Olsson, *Agrarian Crossings*, 18. There are some disagreements among economic historians about the unemployment rate during the 1890s, with estimates ranging between 10 and 20 percent. See Carter, "The Great Depression of the 1890s."

57. *NCCC Proceedings*, 1889, 208; Wray, *Not Quite White*, 58–59.

58. Hatton and Williamson, "What Explains Wage Gaps between Farm and City?" 268; Shifflett, *Patronage and Poverty*, 129.

59. Ross, "Farm Tenancy in Iowa," 37. See also Nash, "Poverty and Politics," 5; Taylor, Wheeler, and Kirkpatrick, *Disadvantaged Classes*, 37–38.

60. Friedberger, "The Farm Family and the Inheritance Process," 7.

61. Schob, *Hired Hands and Plowboys*, 271. See also Winters, "Agricultural Tenancy in the Nineteenth-Century Middle West," 128–53.

62. Patterson, *America's Struggle against Poverty*, 8; Keenan, *History of Eloise*, 434.

63. Cooke, "In Praise of Peasants," 6–7; Iceland, *Poverty in America*, 14.

64. *Springfield [IL] Evening News*, November 11, 1905.

65. "Employment in Poorhouses," *NCCC Proceedings*, 1889, 197.

66. Johnson, *Almshouse Construction and Management*, 79.

67. Dane County Hospital and Home Records, Inmate Register, 1894, box 4, WHSL.

68. Dane County Hospital and Home Records, Inmate Register, 1893, box 4, WHSL.

69. Searcy County, Arkansas, History, n.p., ACPL; Rose, *No Right to Be Idle*, 20.

70. Thanet, "The Indoor Pauper," 757.

71. Good, *Black Swamp Farm*, 183–84. When Good wrote his memoir and local history in 1967, the Van Wert County Infirmary was still in operation.

72. *NCCC Proceedings*, 1889, 203; *Akron Beacon Journal*, June 29, 1895.

73. Populist platform quoted in Patterson, *America's Struggle against Poverty*, 32.

74. *NCCC Proceedings*, 1889, 203.

75. Warner, *American Charities*, 47–50.

76. US Census, 1880, 1890, 1903, 1910.

77. Krainz, *Delivering Aid*, 40, 109.

78. US Census, *Special Report on Almshouses*, 1904, 8.

79. US Census, *Special Report on Almshouses*, 1904, 13.

80. US Census, *Special Report on Almshouses*, 1904, 15.

81. Cottrell, "The Poor Farm System in Texas," 178; "Life Down on the Travis County Poor Farm," *Austin American Statesman*, September 25, 2018.

82. *Denison [TX] Sunday Gazetteer*, March 2, 1884.

83. Wallenstein, *From Slave South to New South*, 246.

84. "Life on the Farm," Medford [OR] *Mail Tribune*, April 21, 2011.

85. US Census, *Special Report on Almshouses*, 1904.

86. Thanet, "The Indoor Pauper," 750.

87. *Summit County Beacon*, June 7, 1882.

88. Johnson, *Almshouse Construction and Management*, 23.

89. *NCCC Proceedings*, 1893, 284–93.

90. Grob, *Mental Illness and American Society*, 76.

91. *Charleston [IL] Daily Courier*, August 12, 1911.

92. Kincade, Coshocton County, Ohio, Infirmary, 73.

93. O'Conner, *Poverty Knowledge*, 18.

94. *Proceedings of the Annual Convention, Michigan*, 1908, 10.

95. James Cotner, https://www.findagrave.com/memorial/41331389; *County Home for the Friendless, Cape Girardeau County, MO*.

96. *Fremont [OH] News-Messenger*, June 8, 1927; the issue of contempt and indifference is explained clearly in Miller, *Anatomy of Disgust*, 33.

97. *Wilmington [OH] News Journal*, April 13, 1927.

98. Church and Chappell, *History of Buchanan County, Iowa*, 357.

99. Frankel, *Poor Relief in Pennsylvania*, 120–21.

100. Frankel, *Poor Relief in Pennsylvania*, 123.

101. Miller, *Anatomy of Disgust*, 8.

102. Johnson, *Almshouse Construction and Management*, 113, 136–38; *Study of a Group of Almshouses*, 12–13.

103. *Proceedings of the Annual Convention, Michigan*, 1908, 10; Miller, *Anatomy of Disgust*, 218. Miller asserts that one of the differences between disgust and contempt are sensory issues related to smell, ugly sights, bodily functions, etc.

104. Johnson, Almshouse *Construction and Management*, 221–22.

105. *Study of a Group of Almshouses*, 37.

106. *Study of a Group of Almshouses*, 22.

107. *Study of a Group of Almshouses*, 42.

108. Will County Poor Farm, inventory of stock and property, Joliet Area Historical Museum. See also Woehle, "Lessons from Yellow Medicine County," 18–25.

109. Handson and Hull, eds., *Past Harvests*, 14–16.

110. Letter, June 6, 1923, Alameda County Board of Charities and Corrections Records, Industrial Home and Infirmary, Social Welfare Collection, CSA.

111. "Recommendations for the Development of Industrial and Home Features of the Alameda County Industrial Home and Infirmary, Board of Charities and Corrections Records County Infirmary," June 6, 1923, Alameda County Board of Charities and Corrections Records, Industrial Home and Infirmary, Social Welfare Collection, CSA.

112. Amador County Hospital, visit report, June 25, 1923, Alameda County Board of Charities and Corrections Records, Industrial Home and Infirmary, Social Welfare Collection, CSA.

113. Williams, *The Poor Farm of Grayson County*, 93.

114. *Coshocton Morning Tribune*, August 24, 1911.

115. *Coshocton Morning Tribune*, July 28, 1916.

116. Murray, *The Poor House and County Farm of Cannon County, Tennessee*, 93; US Census 1910, Georgie McFanen, Cannon County, Woodbury Twp., TN; Rexroad, *The Poor Farm of Pendleton County*.

117. Iroquois County Poor Farm, "Green Acres," Record of Inmates, newspaper clipping, ACPL.

118. *Coshocton Morning Tribune*, September 27, 1948; *Coshocton Daily Times*, August 6, 1913.

119. Searcy County, Arkansas, History, n.p., ACPL.

120. *Marion [IL] Daily Republican*, January 15, 1925, 6.

121. *Coshocton Morning Tribune*, January 10, 1929.

122. *Zanesville Times Recorder*, July 13, 1927.

123. Sweeney, *Poorhouse Sweeney*, x.

124. Sweeney, *Poorhouse Sweeney*, 33.

125. Sweeney, *Poorhouse Sweeney*, 93.

126. *Proceedings of the Annual Convention, Michigan*, 1910, 10–11.

127. *Coshocton Tribune*, May 11, 1927. He is not known to have published again.

128. *Detroit Free Press*, June 19, 1927, 90.

129. *Dayton Daily News*, June 12, 1927. Little is known about Edward Sweeney's early life. His draft registration for World War I shows him in the infirmary but fails to list any physical disqualifiers. In 1930 he lived with his elderly mother and brother-in-law but was also enumerated at the poor farm, as was the case in 1940. He died in 1957. His obituary did not mention his published work but noted he had been a barber by trade.

130. *NCCC Proceedings*, 1890, 100–101.

131. *NCCC Proceedings*, 1903, 386–37.

132. Fairfield County Board of Commissioners, Visitors Register, 1883–98, OHC.

133. Miron, *Prisons, Asylums, and the Public*, 7, 32, 164.

134. Defiance County Home, Visitor's Register; Williams County Board of Commissioners and County Home, Visitor's Register, CAC-BGSU.

135. Fairfield County Home, Visitor's Register, OHC; Kincade, Coshocton County, Ohio, Infirmary, 235, ACPL.

136. Johnson, *Almshouse Construction and Management*, 54–56.

137. *Coshocton Democratic Standard*, December 30, 1898.

138. Burns, *History of Blount County, Tennessee*; Margaret Marsh unpublished narrative. Marsh was interviewed by historian Melissa Walker in 1994 and provided her with written recollections.

139. Sauk County Annual Reports of the Superintendents of the Poor and the Trustees, WHSL.

140. *Rock Island Daily Argus*, October 15, 1873, 2.

141. Johnston, *I Was Raised at the Poor Farm*, 17.

142. Kincade, Coshocton County, Ohio, Infirmary, 230–34, ACPL.

Chapter 3. Farming for the County

1. Dane County Hospital and Home Records, Titus Journal, WHSL.

2. Historian David Rothman (*Discovery of the Asylum*) pinpointed this structure for institutions in the early nineteenth century as well, when superintendents were sometimes referred to as "keepers" of the poor.

3. Brown, "Poor Relief," 87.

4. Bourque, "Creation of the Almshouse," 62.

5. Johnson, *Almshouse Construction and Management*, 48–49.

6. Hoffer, *Counties in Transition*, 75.

7. Gillin, *History of Poor Relief*, 329.

8. *Study of a Group of Almshouses*, 8.

9. McKinniss, "Standards of Administration of the Almshouse," 261.

10. Ann Ellis Papers, OHC.

11. *NCCC Proceedings*, 1900, 113–14.

12. *Study of a Group of Almshouses*, 8.

13. Meltsner, *Poorhouses of Massachusetts*, 37.

14. Limbaugh, "On the Margins of Prosperity," 221.

15. Defiance County Board of Directors Minutes, January 1, 1913, CAC-BGSU; Willets, *Workers of the Nation*, 1047.

16. *Biennial Report of the State Board of Corrections and Charities*, 1884, 206.

17. *Annual Report of the Bureau of Labor and Industry for 1899*, 377.

18. *Biennial Report of the State Board of Corrections and Charities*, 1884, 224; McClure, "An Unlamented Era," 372.

19. Rexroad, *Poor Farm of Pendleton County*; Willets, *Workers of the Nation*, 1047; "Salaries in 1901," *Doing the Pan . . .*, https://panam1901.org/visiting/salaries.htm.

20. Holt, "'Over the Hill to the Poorhouse,'" 6.

21. Brammer, "A Home for the Homeless," 45–50. These wages were comparable with those for jobs such as tinsmiths and blacksmiths, respectively. Willets, *Workers of the Nation*, 1047.

22. Cottrell, "The Poor Farm System in Texas," 176.

23. Dade County, Poor Farm 1885–1901, March 1893–1895, ACPL.

24. Smith, "Poor Relief," 187.

25. *NCCC Proceedings*, 1908, 396. Hoffbeck also noted examples of this from North Dakota in "Prairie Paupers," 180.

26. *NCCC Proceedings*, 1888, 332; Annual Report Kansas Bureau of Labor, 1899, 378; Defiance County Home, Directors Minutes, 1869, CAC-BGSU.

27. *NCCC Proceedings*, 1899, 240.

28. Kincade, Coshocton County, Ohio, Infirmary, 70, ACPL.

29. *Study of a Group of Almshouses*, 19–20. Alger, *Jed: The Poorhouse Boy*, 17.

30. *Annual Report of the Bureau of Labor and Industry for 1899*, 403.

31. Krainz, *Delivering Aid*, 131; *Study of a Group of Almshouses*, 47.

32. *Study of a Group of Almshouses*, 56.

33. Butte County, Board of Charities and Corrections Records, County Files, 1916 report, CSA.

34. *Public Poor Relief in North Carolina*, 7. By the report's own tally, most also had a couple of cows and some chickens.

35. Frankel, *Poor Relief in Pennsylvania*, 28.

36. *Public Poor Relief in North Carolina*, 9.

37. *Public Poor Relief in North Carolina*, 11.

38. Wood County Board of Commissioners, County Home, Meeting Minutes, 1870–79, CAC-BGSU.

39. Wood County of Commissioners, County Home, Infirmary Records, 1879–81, CAC-BGSU.

40. Dade County, Poor Farm, March 1893, ACPL.

41. *NCCC Proceedings*, 1887, 42. In 2018 the average value of an acre of farmland in Iowa was $7,432, making the twenty-first-century value of the poor farms more than $121 million. George C. Ford, "Iowa Farmland Values Rise," *Cedar Rapids [IA] Gazette*, December 12, 2019.

42. *NCCC Proceedings*, 1900, 126.

43. Brown, "Poor Relief," 91.

44. Putnam County Home, CAC-BGSU; Stuart, *History of Franklin County Iowa*, 138.

45. Sauk County Annual Report of the Superintendents of the Poor and Trustees, 1912, WHSL.

46. Licking County Board of Commissioners, Records, 1904–1912, OHC; Neth, *Preserving the Family Farm*, 231.

47. Naldrett, *Poorhouses and Poor Farms of Michigan*, 148; Fulton County Home and Board of Commissioners, Minutes, March 1919, CAC-BGSU; Keenan, *History of Eloise*, 403–4.

48. Johnston, *I Was Raised at the Poor Farm*, 10.

49. Summit County Infirmary, Board of Infirmary Directors, Record of Orders or Auditors, 1907–12, vols. 1, 2, UAL.

50. *Proceedings of the Annual Convention of the State Association of Superintendents of the Poor, Michigan*, 1919, 102.

51. Ottawa County Home, Minutes, September 7, 1901, CAC-BGSU.

52. Wood County Board of Commissioners, County Home, Annual Reports, CAC-BGSU.

53. Brown, "Poor Relief," 103.

54. Wood County Board of Commissioners, County Home, Minutes, 1920, CAC-BGSU.

55. Fulton County Home and Board of Commissioners, Board of Directors Minutes, 1892–94, CAC-BGSU.

56. Summit County Infirmary, Auditors Docket, vol. 2, UAL.

57. Krainz, *Delivering Aid*, 117; McKinniss, "Standards of Administration of the Almshouse," 259.

58. *Austin American Statesman*, July 13, 1903.

59. *El Paso Herald*, July 6, 1916.

60. *El Paso Herald*, August 20, 1921.

61. Summit County Infirmary, Minutes, vol. 1, 1883–1914, UAL.

62. Summit County Infirmary, Board of Infirmary Directors, Record of Orders 1907–12, vol. 1, UAL.

63. Krainz, *Delivering Aid*, 115.

64. Johnson, *Almshouse Construction and Management*, 224–26.

65. Ellis, "Purchase of Supplies for County Infirmaries," 107.

66. Ruswick, *Almost Worthy*, 273.

67. Garman and Russo, "'A Disregard of Every Sentiment,'" 132–33.

68. *Coshocton Democratic Standard*, April 12, 1901; Kincade, Coshocton County, Ohio, Infirmary, 104, ACPL.

69. *Henry County, Ohio: A Collection of Historical Sketches and Family Histories*, vi.

70. *Summit County Beacon*, June 7, 1885; July 5, 1882.

71. *Summit County Beacon*, March 2, 1882, 6. In addition to the resignations of the Hamlins, a new asylum building was completed and renovations in the main building were made.

72. "Report of the Grand Jury," January 21, 1916, Henry County Genealogical Services, http://www.hcgs.net/1916gj.html.

73. "Grand Jury Report," 1919, Henry County Genealogical Services, http://www.hcgs.net/1919gj.html.

74. Ann Ellis Papers, OHC.

75. Olson, "'Halt, Blind, Lame, Sick, and Lazy,'" 163; see also Elia and Wesolowski, eds., *Archaeological Excavations at the Uxbridge Almshouse*, 71.

76. Dane County Hospital and Home Records, Annual Report of Superintendents of the Poor, 1871–74, box 1, WHSL.

77. Schob, *Hired Hands and Plowboys*, 172; US Census 1893, Naturalization Records, Christopher Krassow, Wood County, OH; US Census 1910, Wood County, Portage Twp., OH. The average 1909 farm worker wage was estimated to be $23 with board and $28 without. See US Bureau of Labor Statistics, *Monthly Labor Review*, 60.

78. Schob, *Hired Hands and Plowboys*, 159; Putnam County Home, Commissioner Records, CAC-BGSU.

79. US Census 1930, Estella Frantz, Blanchard Twp., Putnam County, OH.

80. "Saginaw County Farm."

81. Johnston, *I Was Raised at the Poor Farm*, 14.

82. Higbie, *Indispensable Outcasts*, 47.

83. Dane County Hospital and Home Records, Titus Journal, 1879, WHSL; Wysocki, *Digging Up the Dirt*, 21. Farm laborers on average in 1880 made $15 a month in the West North Central region. See *Historical Statistics of the United States*, 1:163.

84. Summit County, Putnam County Infirmary Directors Minutes, July 5, 1898, CAC-BGSU; Census 1880, 1900, 1910, Liberty, Greensburg, and Ottawa Twps., Putnam County, OH.

85. Dane County Hospital and Home Records, Titus Journal, September 11, 1878, WHSL.

86. Kincade, Coshocton County, Ohio, Infirmary, 176, ACPL.

87. Sauk County Annual Reports of the Superintendents of the Poor and Trustees, 1918, 5, WHSL.

88. Sauk County Annual Reports of the Superintendents of the Poor and Trustees, 1919, 17, WHSL. The Christensons previously worked at the state hospital for the insane.

89. Sauk County Annual Reports Annual Reports of the Superintendents of the Poor and Trustees, 1920, 16–17, WHSL.

90. *NCCC Proceedings*, 1896, 269.

91. Meseraull, "The Administration of Almshouses," 265–67.

92. Ernest Bicknell, "Poor Asylum Discipline," *NCCC Proceedings*, 1896, 271.

93. Garman and Russo, "'A Disregard of Every Sentiment.'"

94. Tuten, "Regulating the Poor in Alabama," 42.

95. Buchanan County, Iowa, Records, Minutes of Meetings, ACPL; *Annual Report of the Bureau of Labor and Industry for 1899*, 406.

96. *Proceedings of the Annual Convention, Michigan*, 1910, 9–10.

97. Erie County Infirmary, 1856, ACPL.

98. Sturtevant, "Ottawa County Community Haven," 13–17.

99. Price, *History of Clayton County, Iowa*, 219–20.

100. *Elyria [OH] Weekly Chronicle*, August 16, 1902.

101. *Annual Report of the Bureau of Labor and Industry for 1899*, 405; *Saline County Journal*, August 5, 1880, 3. Worth's wife and six children lived on their farm the year he died, and the census enumerator wrote his name down in their household but crossed it out. His occupation had been listed as pauper. He is also missing from the family's 1870 enumeration. See US Census 1880, Saline County, Liberty Twp., KS. Worth's case is not the only reported shooting of a resident by a superintendent. In the mid-1870s, Davis County, Iowa, Superintendent E. B. Townsend apparently shot a man in the leg, for which he was censured but not fired.

102. "Infirmary Site Was Antique Store," *Ottawa [MI] Herald*, August 11, 2016.

103. Dane County Hospital and Home Records, Titus Journal, WHSL.

104. *Annual Report of the Bureau of Labor and Industry for 1899*, 379–80.

105. Fulton County Home and Board of Commissioners, Fulton County Infirmary Annual Reports, CAC-BGSU; Krainz, *Delivering Aid*, 133.

106. Wood County Board of Commissioners, County Home, Wood County Infirmary Annual Reports, 1894–95, CAC-BGSU.

107. Wood County Board of Commissioners, County Home, Wood County Infirmary Annual Reports, 1904, CAC-BGSU.

108. McClure, "An Unlamented Era," 372.

109. Letter, June 6, 1923, Alameda County, Board of Charities and Corrections Records, Industrial Home and Infirmary, Social Welfare Collection, CSA.

110. Frankel, *Poor Relief in Pennsylvania*, 33.

111. *NCCC Proceedings*, 1897, 263.

112. Dane County Hospital and Home Records, Titus Journal, 1877, WHSL.

113. Williams, *The Poor Farm of Grayson County*, 9.

114. Dane County Hospital and Home Records, Annual Report, 1887, 6, box 1, WHSL.

115. *NCCC Proceedings*, 1899, 148.

116. Warner, *American Charities*, 160–61.

117. Dane County Hospital and Home Records, Titus Journal, September 10, 1879, WHSL.

118. Hoffer, *Counties in Transition*, 77.

119. See US Census, *Special Report on Almshouses*, 1904, 41–49.

120. Dane County Hospital and Home Records, Titus Journal, December 31, 1877. His surviving journal begins in 1877.

121. Dane County Hospital and Home Records, Titus Journal, May 1878.

122. Wagner mentions an incident of county officials using garden space as their own personal property: see *The Poorhouse*, 95.

123. Dane County Hospital and Home Records, Titus Journal, September 13, 1879, WHSL.

124. Dane County Hospital and Home Records, Annual Report Superintendents of the Poor, 1883, box 1, WHSL.

125. Dane County Hospital and Home Records, Trustees Report, 1887, box 2, WHSL.

126. Dobbs, *History of Gage County*, 727.

127. In the 1940s residents of the poor farm almost lost their pet dogs when someone complained about the animals. A volunteer saved the animals by buying licenses for

the pets. The complainant was apparently Ellis, who then worked at the TB hospital on the grounds. See Ann Ellis Papers, Clippings file, 2–27–41, OHC.

128. US Census 1910, Salem Twp., Wyandot County, OH.

129. *Coshocton Age*, April 4, 1885; Kincade, Coshocton County, Ohio, Infirmary, 81, ACPL.

130. Summit County Infirmary, Board of Directors Record of Orders, 1907–12, UAL; US Census 1910, Summit County, Portage Twp., District 0197, OH.

131. Wysocki, *Digging Up the Dirt*, 42–45.

132. *Study of a Group of Almshouses*, 39.

133. "Back in Time: Washington County Poor Farm," *Stillwater Gazette*, April 24, 2015.

134. Dane County Hospital and Home Records, Annual Report, 1892, 1, WHSL.

135. A year after resigning, Meyers briefly returned to the institution after a fire caused damage and injured the new superintendent.

Chapter 4. Poor Farm Women

1. Dane County Hospital and Home Records, Register, 1885, box 2, WHSL.

2. *Wisconsin State Journal*, September 12, 1884; January 31, 1885. It is not clear what happened to Johanna and Fred Antleman after her stay at the farm; her headstone has no date. For an account of the shooting see *Watertown [WI] News*, July 16, 1884. Another Wisconsin domestic abuse case resulted in a lynching, see Pederson, "Gender, Justice, and a Wisconsin Lynching," 65–82.

3. Abramowitz, "The Family Ethic," 121–35.

4. Walsh, "Gendering Mobility," 382; Bose, "Household Resources and U.S. Women's Work," 480.

5. Cahill, *Federal Fathers and Mothers*, 65–66; King, *Women, Welfare, and Local Politics*, ch. 2. In England women served as guardians of the poor by the late nineteenth century and prior to that served in an advisory visiting capacity. See also Gamber, *The Boardinghouse in Nineteenth-Century America*, 8–10; Daniels, "Intimate Violence, Then and Now," 9.

6. Cahill, *Federal Fathers and Mothers*, 90.

7. Corbit, *History of Jones County, Iowa*, 104; Borque, "Creation of the Almshouse," 62.

8. "The Almshouse," *NCCC Proceedings*, 1900.

9. Stewart, *Cost of American Almshouses*, 39.

10. *NCCC Proceedings*, 1884, 298.

11. *Fremont [OH] News-Messenger*, June 8, 1927.

12. *Summit County Beacon*, March 2, 1887, 6.

13. Dane County Hospital and Home Records, Governor's message and biennial report, Wisconsin, 1875, box 13, WHSL. Viola Titus later worked as the matron for a state institution. Crawford County, Inmates, 5, ACPL. Ida Scott died in 1899, and her husband went on to work at a state asylum, where their two children lived with him on-site.

14. Wysocki, *Digging Up the Dirt*, 46.

15. Williams County Board of Commissioners and County Home, Minutes, 1895, CAC-BGSU.

16. *Study of a Group of Almshouses*, 9.

17. Strasser, *Never Done*, 151–52.

18. US Census 1870, Eliza Plummer, Adams County, Liberty Twp., OH.

19. Fox, "Selling the Mechanized Household," 25.

20. Wyandot County Board of Commissioners, County Home, Inventory, 1897, 1905, CAC-BGSU.

21. *Coshocton Tribune*, November 19, 1934.

22. Johnson, *Almshouse Construction and Management*, 51.

23. "Matron Dead on Basement Floor," *Evening Star Auburn [IN]*, October 31, 1933.

24. *Proceedings of the Annual Convention, Michigan*, 1917, 16.

25. Wood County Board of Commissioners, County Home, Minutes, CAC-BGSU; US Census 1940, Wood County, Center Twp., OH; Persons, "Women's Work and Wages in the United States," 208.

26. "Sangamon County Poor Farm."

27. Dade County Minutes, May 1894, WHSL.

28. Thanet, "The Indoor Pauper," 755.

29. Brammer, "A Home for the Homeless," 45–50.

30. Unpublished narrative of Margaret Marsh. Marsh was interviewed by historian Melissa Walker in 1994 and provided her with written recollections.

31. Emily Williams Smith, Interview, MHSRC.

32. Drawbridge, *Unforgotten Truth*, ch. 13; Miller, *Anatomy of Disgust*, 199.

33. See Mennel, "'The Family System of Common Farmers,'" 298.

34. *NCCC Proceedings*, 1900, 157; Miller, *Anatomy of Disgust*, 136.

35. Wood County Board of Commissioners, County Home, Accounts, 1892, CAC-BGSU; https://www.findagrave.com/cgi-bin/fg.cgi?page=gr&GRid=111346587&ref=acom.

36. Erie County Infirmary, ACPL; Bell, *Historical Archaeology at the Hudson Poor Farm Cemetery*, 23; Crawford County, Inmates, 2–4, ACPL.

37. Meltsner, *Poorhouses of Massachusetts*, 37, 129.

38. *Annual Report of the Bureau of Labor and Industry for 1899*, 381.

39. Colusa County Board of Charities and Corrections Records, Reports, 1916–25, CSA.

40. *Poor Relief in North Carolina*, 14.

41. US Census 1870, Summit County, Portage Twp., OH; US Civil War Pension Index, Julia/George Glines.

42. *Summit County Beacon*, June 7, 1882

43. *Summit County Beacon*, July 5, 1882; US Census 1900, Summit County, Akron Ward 5, OH.

44. Summit County Infirmary, Board of Infirmary Directors Record of Orders and Auditors, 1907–12, vol. 1, UAL.

45. Jensen, "'I'd Rather Be Dancing,'" 5.

46. Sweeney, *Poorhouse Sweeney*, 104–6.

47. US Census 1880, Jane Gordon, Dane County, Verona Twp., WI; US Census 1870, Thomas Gordon, Dane County, Verona Twp., WI.

48. Wisconsin State Census 1905, Edward Offerdahl, Springdale, WI; US Census 1910, Josephine Thompson, Dane County, Springdale Twp., WI.

49. Willets, *Workers of the Nation*, 1047; Fraundorf, "Relative Earnings of Native and Foreign Born Women," 214. Fraundorf places the average annual wages for white women between $122 and $138 at this time.

50. Putnam County Home, Monthly Finances 1924–25, CAC-BGSU; US Census 1910, 1920, 1930, Riley Twp., Putnam County, OH.

51. *Proceedings of the Annual Convention, Michigan*, 1909, 23.

52. Greenwald, "From Hired Hand to Day Worker," 62; Roberts, "Her Real Sphere?"

53. US Census 1910, Summit County Almshouse, Summit County, Portage Twp. West Precinct, OH.

54. US Census 1900, Ida Ritchie, Summit County, Portage Twp. West Precinct, OH; US Census 1920, Ada Ruff, Summit County, Akron Ward 4, OH; US Census 1930, Ada Ruff, Stark County, Washington Twp., OH; Ada M. Ruff, https://www.findagrave.com/cgi-bin/fg.cgi?page=gr&GRid=63290770&ref=acom.

55. Kessler-Harris, *Out to Work*, 113.

56. Dudden, *Serving Women*, 75–76; Dubinsky, *Improper Advances*, 52. Dubinsky notes the danger of sexual assaults to women working in service in a private household.

57. References to Amelia Antleman's court case come from the journal of E. P. Titus between May 1881 and February 1882 (Dane County Hospital and Home Records, Titus Journal, WSHL). According to the docket, there were two bastardy cases under review during that time period, and one of the men, Peter Hansen, lived in Amelia's neighborhood. He was later listed as her daughter's father in legal papers.

58. Holland, *Murder and Mayhem*, 136.

59. *Summit County Beacon*, August 3, 1887, 5. She gave their names as Elwin, Joseph, and William Henry, who had been sold in Independence, Texas, in 1848, and taken to Arkansas by someone named Cornelius Lane. She believed the boys were later sold by Mrs. Lane.

60. *Akron Daily Democrat*, July 2, 1894. Exhaustion appears as a reason for admission/death in some other records. See also Chamberlin, "Emasculated by Trauma," 360.

61. Abramovitz, *Regulating the Lives of Women*, 156–58.

62. *NCCC Proceedings*, 1900, 126.

63. *NCCC Proceedings*, 1905, 594; *Poor Relief in North Carolina*, 18.

64. Roberts Smith, *Almshouse Women*, 15–16.

65. See Jones, *American Hungers*, pt, 2.

66. Roberts Smith, *Almshouse Women*, 20; Westerfield, *Road to the Poorhouse*, 199; Brown County Illinois, County Farm Records, Annotated Register, Mrs. Eckle Rabet, December 1882, ACPL.

67. Scadron, *On Their Own*, 306.

68. Tennant, *Paupers and Providers*, 150.

69. See Katz, *Poverty and Policy*, 76–77, 122–23.

70. Pleck, *Domestic Tyranny*, 7.

71. Rowe and Marietta, "Personal Violence in a 'Peaceable Kingdom,'" 25, 34.

72. Spencer-Wood, "Feminist Theoretical Perspectives on the Archaeology of Poverty," 110–35. Stansell described the assistance given to abused women in tenements as a "moral economy," and although the level of intimacy in a community that allowed a woman to use a poor farm to escape was much different, it still demonstrated a marked willingness

to intervene in a morally repugnant situation. See Dubinsky, *Improper Advances*, 122; Stansell, *City of Women*, 55–62.

73. *NCCC Proceedings*, 1879, 189; Johnson, *Almshouse Construction and Management*, 231.

74. *NCCC Proceedings*, 1879, 193, 197.

75. Will County Poor Farm, Registers, Joliet Area Historical Museum.

76. Williams, *The Poor Farm of Grayson County*, 60–61.

77. Sturtevant, "Ottawa County Community Haven," 15.

78. US Census 1880, 1910, Sarah Amelia Vogt Otto, Defiance, OH; Defiance County Home, Directors Minutes, 1881, CAC-BGSU.

79. *NCCC Proceedings*, 1889, 197.

80. Kincade, Coshocton County, Ohio, Infirmary, 171, ACPL.

81. Olmsted, *Handbook for Visitors to the Poorhouse*, 61.

82. Johnson, *Almshouse Construction and Management*, 124; *Chillicothe Gazette*, March 30, 1895. See also Wulf, "Gender and the Political Economy of Poor Relief," 163–88.

83. Thanet, "The Indoor Pauper," 764. Thanet was the nom de plume for Alice French, who was best known for fiction writing.

84. *NCCC Proceedings*, 1896, 25–26.

85. Warner, *American Charities*, 144.

86. Birk, *Fostering on the Farm*, ch. 2.

87. *Poor Relief in North Carolina*, 18.

88. *A Study of Kansas Poor Farms*, 4.

89. Hardin County Home, Infirmary Record, CAC-BGSU; US Census 1880, Emma Watson, Logan County, OH.

90. *Study of a Group of Almshouses*, 58.

91. The first Crittenton Home opened in 1883 in New York City to assist prostitutes, and as they expanded they served large cities in rural states like Little Rock and Omaha. See Kunzel, "The Professionalization of Benevolence," 23–25. The Homes for the Friendless had organizations in Nebraska, Kansas, Illinois, and other states. See Lock, "'As Independent as We Wished,'" 138–51; Erby, "The Hull Baby Case," 192–95.

92. Kunzel, *Fallen Women, Problem Girls*, 18–23, 30; Morton, "Fallen Women, Federated Charities, and Maternity Homes," 63.

93. Green, *This Business of Relief*, 167.

94. Hough, *Rural Unwed Mothers*, 32.

95. Kunzel, *Fallen Women, Problem Girls*, 67–68.

96. Jensen, "The Death of Rosa," 1–12.

97. Green, "Infanticide and Infant Abandonment." Green notes that the Richmond Almshouse was the largest regional provider of African American health care and saw more than one thousand babies born between 1885 and 1907.

98. Will County Poor Farm, Register, 1888, Joliet Area Historical Museum.

99. Ladd-Taylor, *Mother Work*, 21–28.

100. Dane County Hospital and Home Records, loose note, box 4, WHSL.

101. Hough, *Rural Unwed Mothers*, 78.

102. Dane County Hospital and Home Records, Titus Journal; *Wisconsin Journal*, June 7, 1880.

103. The maternity of the child was unclear. In 1900, a nine-year-old girl is living with sixty-three-year-old-Richards and his sixty-seven-year-old wife, and she is listed as his daughter. See US Census 1900, Julius Richards, Wood County, Montgomery Twp., OH.

104. US Census 1870, Henderson, IL, Twp. 11, range 5.

105. Henderson County Poor Farm and Jail, Annotated Register, ACPL.

106. Henderson County Poor Farm and Jail, Annotated Register, ACPL.

107. *Rock Island Argus*, January 8, 1902, 2. The fate of Emma Rathburn's youngest child is unknown, but her two sons grew up at a local children's home. In 1920 the young men were still together, living as boarders in Muscatine, Iowa, and working as farm laborers. See US Census 1910, Franklin and Herbert P. Rathburn, Rock Island County, Rock Island Twp., IA; US Census 1920, Muscatine County, City of Muscatine, IA.

108. Brown County, Illinois, County Farm Records, 1879–1927; US Census 1920, Marjorie Ellen Butler Spicer, Brown County, Elkhorn Twp., IL.

109. Dane County Hospital and Home Records, Ledger, box 4, WHSL; Registration of Marriage, William B. Price and Emma Jane Beard, December 28, 1877, Wisconsin Vital Records.

110. Crawford County, Inmates, ACPL.

111. Loewen, *Sundown Towns*, 103–4; Crawford County, Inmates, ACPL.

112. Goodwin, "An Experiment in Paid Motherhood," 326.

113. Ladd-Taylor, *Mother Work*, 136–42. See also Gordon, *Heroes of Their Own Lives*, 66, 102.

114. Gooden, "Local Discretion and Welfare Policy," 81. Gooden points out that the application in Virginia for mother's pension was eleven pages long. Nationwide, 96 percent of mother's aid was given to white women.

115. Krainz, *Delivering Aid*, 149; Ladd-Taylor, *Mother Work*, 147–51; Gordon, *Pitied But Not Entitled*, 191.

116. Goodwin, "An Experiment in Paid Motherhood," 332–33; Carter, "Legal Aspects of Widowhood and Aging," 286–87.

117. Ofman, "A Rural View of Mothers' Pensions," 101–6.

118. *Infirmary Records, Morgan County, Ohio, 1843–1900*.

119. Williams County Board of Commissioners and County Home, Infirmary Board of Directors Minutes, August 22, 1901, CAC-BGSU. Their recent residence in a neighboring county might account for why the assets were seized.

120. Butte County, Board of Charities and Corrections Records, March 23, 1929, CSA.

121. Ruswisk, "Just Poor Enough," 272–73. Ruswick located women who chose homelessness in Indianapolis over a stay at the poor farm. In 1881, Marion County's infirmary was investigated for mismanagement and abuse by the superintendent and doctor. May, "The 'Problem of Duty,'" 40–45.

122. Will County Poor Farm, Register, Joliet Area Historical Museum.

123. Buchanan County, Iowa, Records, Minutes of Meetings March 1876, ACPL.

124. Wright, *A Report on Marriage and Divorce*, 170; Hunt, *Marriage and Divorce 1867–1906*, 12–24; Mintz and Kellogg, *Domestic Revolutions*, 109; Sturtevant, "Ottawa County Community Haven," 14–15. See also May, *Great Expectations*, 104; Cvrcek, "U.S. Marital Disruptions," 143–45.

125. Schwartzberg, "'Lots of Them Did That,'" 574–76. Between 1860 and 1920, the rate of divorce increased considerably, from 1.2 per 1,000 marriages to 7.7. See O'Neill, *Divorce in the Progressive Era*, 20; Igra, *Wives without Husbands*, ch. 1; Roth, "Spousal Murder in Northern New England," 69.

126. *Garrett [IN] Clipper*, December 27, 1900, 2. Her first husband was Alonzo C. Rupert, for whom there is a death record in 1905.

127. US Census 1900, Minnie Rupert, Defiance County, Washington Twp., OH; see also Defiance County Home, Infirmary Directors Minutes, March 6, 1899, CAC-BGSU.

128. *Argos [IN] Reflector*, September 11, 1902, 4.

129. Crawford County, Inmates, ACPL.

Chapter 5. *The Poor Farm and Mental Health Care*

1. Ken Wyatt, "Peek through Time: Jackson County Poor Farm," *Jackson [MI] Citizen Patriot*, November 26, 1911.

2. Gollaher, *Voice for the Mad*, 206.

3. Tiffany, *Life of Dorothea Lynde Dix*, 81.

4. Klages, *Woeful Affliction*, 4, 202; Wagner, *Miracle Worker*, 35–36.

5. Schweik, *Ugly Laws*, 5; Rose, *No Right to Be Idle*, 33.

6. "Clinton County Poor Farm."

7. Rose, *No Right to Be Idle*, 33.

8. Farreras, "Clara Harrison Town," 271–81; Noll, *Feebleminded in Our Midst*, 4. Contemporary terms considered appropriate to describe the range of conditions formerly called "insane" include psychiatric disability, speech disorders, mental disability, learning disability, developmental disability, congenital disability, and adventitious disability. See Schweik, *Ugly Laws*, 11; "How to Refer to People with Disabilities"; and "Respectful Disability Language."

9. Coleborne, *Madness in the Family*, 154–55; Warner, *American Charities*, 281; Yoakum, *Care of the Feebleminded*, 16.

10. *NCCC Proceedings*, 1903, 238.

11. *Summit County Beacon*, August 10, 1887, 5.

12. Fisher, *In the Beginning There Was Land*.

13. Thanet, "The Indoor Pauper," 753. See also Wright, Moran, and Gouglas, "Confinement of the Insane," 115–25.

14. Johnston, *I Was Raised at the Poor Farm*, 19; Ann Ellis Papers, box 1, folder 19, OHC.

15. *Summit County Beacon*, February 16, 1887, 5.

16. Thanet, "The Indoor Pauper," 757; Schweik, *Ugly Laws*; Miller, *Anatomy of Disgust*, 82.

17. *Summit County Beacon*, November 19, 1887, 1.

18. Brown, "Poor Relief," 101; *Annual Report of the Board of State Charities, Ohio, 1899*, 31.

19. Franklin County Poor Farm Records, 1885, 9, OHC.

20. Brown County, Illinois, County Farm Records, ACPL.

21. Salmon, "Insane in a County Poor Farm," 32.

22. *Coshocton Daily Age*, December 6, 1879.

23. *Summit County Beacon*, June 2, 1882.

24. Dix voiced concerns about the vulnerability of "insane" women (and men) in poor farms. The documents make clear that Towner was not capable of giving consent and that officials considered this a rape, which is why I have used the term.

25. *Summit County Beacon*, February 16, 1887, 5.

26. *Summit County Beacon*, February 9, 1887.

27. *Summit County Beacon*, January 12, 1887, 2.

28. *Summit County Beacon*, February 16, 1887, 5.

29. Holland, *Murder and Mayhem*, 120–24, 141.

30. Holland, *Murder and Mayhem*, 133.

31. *Summit County Beacon*, August 3, 1887, 5. Although I am uncertain about the fate of her child, I believe he kept the last name Towner, and was eventually placed out to work as a servant on a nearby farm. The man seemingly lived a normal life, serving in World War I, marrying, and having children.

32. US Census 1900, Nellie Towner, Summit County, Portage Twp., OH; US Census 1910, Stark County, Perry Twp., OH.

33. Brown County, Illinois, County Farm Records, *Brown County Republican*, June 7, 1894, ACPL.

34. Drawbridge, *Unforgotten Truth*.

35. Johnston, *I Was Raised at the Poor Farm*, 21–22; Ann Ellis Papers, box 1, folder 19, OHC.

36. *NCCC Proceedings*, 1890, 336–37.

37. Salmon, "Insane in a County Poor Farm," 25–33. It appears that Salmon was talking about Grayson County, Texas.

38. *Journal Register Springfield [IL]*, September 27, 1944; "Sangamon County Poor Farm."

39. *Summit County Beacon*, June 4, 1886, 2.

40. Will County Poor Farm, Ledgers, January 27, 1891, May 1892, Joliet Area History Museum.

41. Cottrell, "The Poor Farm System in Texas," 176.

42. Ann Ellis Papers, box 1, folder 19, OHC; Emily Williams Smith, Interview, MHSRC.

43. Kincade, Coshocton County, Ohio, Infirmary, 231, ACPL.

44. *Proceedings of the Annual Convention, Michigan*, 1907, 30.

45. *Annual Report of the Bureau of Labor and Industry for 1899*, 415–16.

46. Rothman, *Conscience and Convenience*, 29.

47. In Michigan, Wayne County constructed its own asylum as a result of this problem. See Keenan, History of *Eloise*, 134.

48. Bryan, *Asylum Doctor*, 32.

49. Warner, *American Charities*, 153.

50. Gonaver, *The Peculiar Institution*, 165.

51. Yoakum, *Care of the Feebleminded*, 119, 20, 48. Like his peers, Yoakum supported his assertions with photographs.

52. Hoyt, *Causes of Pauperism*, 17.

53. *Summit County Beacon*, March 2, 1887, 6. See *NCCC Proceedings*, 1888, 335; Deutsch, *The Mentally Ill in America*, 251.

54. Gillespie, *History of Clay County, Iowa*, 130.

55. *Fremont [OH] News-Messenger*, June 8, 1927.

56. Grob, *Mental Illness and American Society*, 10; Rose, *No Right to Be Idle*, 43.

57. Quoted in Trent, *Inventing the Feeble Mind*, 79.

58. Floyd, *From Institutions to Independence*, ch. 1.

59. Williams, *The Poor Farm of Grayson County*, 73; Yoakum, *Care of the Feebleminded*, 128–32.

60. Yoakum, *Care of the Feebleminded*, 122.

61. Bryan, *Asylum Doctor*, 60.

62. Tomes and Gamwell, *Madness in America*, 56; Bryan, *Asylum Doctor*, 59.

63. Gollaher, *Voice for the Mad*, 168–69.

64. *Rock Island Daily Argus*, June 14, 1877, 1; Grob, "Mental Health Policy in America," 7–12.

65. Iowa, for example, made arrangements for people under the age of forty-six to be eligible for care at the feebleminded school, after which they had to be moved elsewhere. See Gillin, *History of Poor Relief Legislation*, 239; Trent, *Inventing the Feeble Mind*, 65–69.

66. Friedberger, "The Decision to Institutionalize," 403; Trent, *Inventing the Feeble Mind*, 63.

67. Tuten, "Regulating the Poor," 45–46.

68. Schneider and Deutsch, *History of Public Welfare in New York State*, 91–94; Holt, "'Over the Hill to the Poorhouse,'" 8.

69. Annual Report *of the Bureau of Labor and Industry for 1899*, 374.

70. Trent, *Inventing the Feeble Mind*, 100.

71. *NCCC Proceedings*, 1888, 339.

72. Ferguson, *Abandoned to Their Fate*, 40–41, 76–77.

73. Ebert and Trattner, "The County Mental Institution," 837.

74. Dane County Hospital and Home Records, Titus Journal, 1883, WHSL.

75. Brown, "Poor Relief," 100.

76. Dane County Hospital and Home Records, Titus Journal, 1881–1883, WHSL.

77. Johnson, *Almshouse Construction and Management*, 126–28.

78. Dane County Hospital and Home Records, Annual Report, 1883, box 1, WHSL.

79. Dane County Hospital and Home Records, Annual Report, 1883, box 1, WHSL; Nielsen, "Incompetent and Insane," 181–86.

80. Keenan, *History of Eloise*, 157.

81. Dodge County Poor Farm and Asylum, Annual Report for 1907, WHSL. Sauk County claimed it had 100 asylum residents able to do a day's worth of work but did not provide the same information for its poor farm residents.

82. Sauk County Asylum Annual Reports of the Superintendents of the Poor and Trustees, 1912, 1913, WHSL.

83. *NCCC Proceedings*, 1896, 185.

84. Warner, *American Charities*, 159.

85. Wagner, *The Poorhouse*, 53; *A Study of Kansas Poor Farms*, 4.

86. Johnson, *Almshouse Construction and Management*, 214.

87. *Proceedings of the Annual Convention, Michigan*, 1919, 107–11.

88. *Study of a Group of Almshouses*, 59; Rose, *No Right to Be Idle*, 74.

89. Defiance County Home, Infirmary Ledgers, CAC-BGSU.

90. Wray, *Not Quite White*, 68.

91. Trent, *Inventing the Feeble Mind*, 74; Rose, *No Right to Be Idle*, 72.

92. *NCCC Proceedings*, 1896, 221–25; Hoyt, *Causes of Pauperism*.

93. Ernest Bicknell, "Feeble-Mindedness as an Inheritance," *NCCC Proceedings*, 1896, 219.

94. Blackmar, "The Smoky Pilgrims," 61–64; *A Study of Kansas Poor Farms*, 38. Doctors used versions of the Binet-Simon Test on poor farm residents, in which a majority rated as either "retarded" or "moronic." Out of seventy-three exams given, forty-eight of them tested with mental ages younger than ten years old.

95. Sessions, *The Feebleminded in the Rural County of Ohio*, 8–10. Countywide the study determined that almost 500 of the 50,000 residents were intellectually disabled. Studies took place in Iowa, Minnesota, Ohio, and New York as well. While not widely discussed, officials occasionally referenced sodomy, bestiality, and homosexuality in institutional populations. *NCCC Proceedings*, 1899, 256.

96. Wray, *Not Quite White*, 87–88.

97. Finlayson, "The Dack Family," 210–22; *NCSW Proceedings*, 1920, 404. In Mississippi the Ellisville State School did not open until 1921, and until 1928 held only male residents. With no state option, it is possible that many of the small poor farms in Mississippi held a larger percentage of "feebleminded" residents than was typical elsewhere.

98. Blackmar, "The Smoky Pilgrims," 58. This rural panic expanded to Canada where Karen Dubinsky found at least one town fighting back against erroneous claims that their community was the site of many cases of "idiocy, incest, adultery, frightful deformities, insanity, and abject poverty." See Dubinsky, *Improper Advances*, 160.

99. Evans, *The American Poorfarm*, 15.

100. Rosenberg, *The 4-H Harvest*, 23, 29; Farland, "Modernist Versions of Pastoral," 905–36.

101. Evans, *The American Poorfarm*, 32.

102. Evans, *The American Poorfarm*, 65–66.

103. Naldrett, *Poorhouses and Poor Farms of Michigan*, 115–16; Ladd-Taylor, *Fixing the Poor*, ch. 3; Dorr, *Segregation's Science*, 3. Dorr claims that eugenics gained popularity in the South in part because it helped explain southern rural poverty and expunged the upper classes of responsibility. Ira Caldwell quoted in Lombardo, "From Better Babies to the Bunglers," 59. Erskine Caldwell was castigated for revealing the existence of crippling poverty in the South in his writing: see also Caldwell and Bourke-White, *You Have Seen Their Faces*. Feebleminded institutions were locations of implementation for involuntary sterilization laws that started in Indiana in 1907. At least 60,000 Americans were sterilized, 61 percent of them women. See Noll, "Care and Control of the Feebleminded," 57–80.

104. Stevens and Stevens, *Welfare Medicine in America*, 5.

105. Scandinavian countries also tried to link poverty, intellectual disability, and state-sponsored sterilization. See Broberg and Roll-Hansen, *Eugenics and the Welfare State*, 59; Schoen, *Choice and Coercion*, intro.; Reske, "Policing the 'Wayward Woman,'" 14–27.

106. Kline, *Building a Better Race*, 32–40.

107. Rosenberg, *The 4-H Harvest*, 318–20; Goddard, *Feeblemindedness*, 171–85.

108. Quoted in Elks, "Visual Rhetoric," 18.

109. Nielsen, "Historical Thinking and Disability History."

110. Morgan County Poor Farm, Medical Records, IRAD; Elks, "Visual Rhetoric," 103.

111. Isenberg, *White Trash*, 196–98.

112. Morgan County Poor Farm, Medical Records, IRAD.

113. Elks, "Visual Rhetoric," 25, 51; Schweik, *Ugly Laws*, 26–27, 34.

114. Elks, "Visual Rhetoric," 103.

Chapter 6. Old Age and Poor Farm Residency

1. The Hawthorne line from *The House of the Seven Gables* is discussed in Jones, *American Hungers*, 22.

2. Erie County, Ohio, Infirmary, CAC-BGSU. US Census 1930, 1940, Julius Frank, Sandusky City, OH; *Sandusky City Directory*, 1916, 1920, Luise Baun; *Sandusky Register*, September 26, 1962.

3. McClure, *More Than a Roof*, 31.

4. Haber and Gratton, *Old Age and the Search for Security*, 59.

5. Folks, "Disease and Dependence," 298; Dahlin, "From Poorhouse to Pension," 73–74.

6. Roberts Smith, *Almshouse Women*, 35; Levstik, "Life among the Lowly," 86.

7. Dahlin, "From Poorhouse to Pension," 27–28.

8. Hareven, "Life-Course Transitions and Kin Assistance," 114–15.

9. Adams, *Transformation of Rural Life*, 92; Leonard, *History of Union County*, 180.

10. Smith, "Life Course, Norms, and the Family System," 294; Gratton, "Emptying the Nest," 335.

11. Dahlin, "From Poorhouse to Pension," 11.

12. Courts could distribute property of the institutionalized, but supervisors of the poor complained it should default to the county. See *Proceedings of the Annual Convention, Michigan*, 1907, 19.

13. Quoted in Young, "Over the Hill to the Poor Farm, 18.

14. Haber and Gratton, *Old Age and the Search for Security*, 23.

15. Dahlin, "From Poorhouse to Pension," 39; US Census, *Special Report on Almshouses*, 1904, Age of Inmates.

16. Haber, *Beyond Sixty-five*, 29.

17. Fleming, Evans, and Chutka, "History of Old Age in America," 917.

18. Atack and Bateman, "Egalitarianism, Inequality, and Age," 85.

19. *Study of a Group of Almshouses*, 62–63.

20. *Dayton Daily News*, August 31, 1952.

21. Landis, *Rural Social Welfare Services*, 16–17.

22. *NCCC Proceedings*, 1903, 481.

23. Good, *Black Swamp Farm*, 183–84.

24. Ann Ellis Papers, box 1, folder 19, OHC.

25. Lieberman, "Institutionalization of the Aged," 330–36. Other studies indicated older people saw institutionalization as a prelude to death, and associated it with abandonment by their children, fear, dread, and rejection.

26. *Lancaster [OH] Eagle Gazette*, December 17, 1927.

27. Johnson, *Almshouse Construction and Management*, 108.

28. Flynt, *Poor But Proud*, 185–86.

29. *Billings Gazette*, July 4, 1913.

30. Folks, "Disease and Dependence," 299.

31. Dade County, Poor Farm, August 1894, ACPL.

32. Moen, "Rural Nonfarm Households," 69–71. See also Salamon, *Prairie Patrimony*, 132–34.

33. Haber and Gratton, *Old Age and the Search for Security*, 7–8, 30–31; Smith, "A Community-Based Sample of the Older Population," 67–68.

34. Wood, *Retiring Men*, 72–74.

35. Smith, "Life Course, Norms, and the Family System," 288, 292.

36. Arcury, "Rural Elderly Household Life-Course Transitions," 62.

37. Dahlin, "From Poorhouse to Pension," 62.

38. *Study of a Group of Almshouses*, 11.

39. Ruggles, "Transformation of American Family Structure," 114.

40. See Watkins, Menken, and Bongaarts, "Demographic Foundations of Family Change," 346–58.

41. Dahlin, "From Poorhouse to Pension," 58. Additional examples can be found in Olson, "Halt, Blind, Lame, Sick, and Lazy" 131–32.

42. Erie County Infirmary, 1901, ACPL.

43. Fayette County Board of Commissioners, Certificates of relief, 1896–97, 1914–24, OHC.

44. McClure, *More Than a Roof*, 30; Dahlin, "From Poorhouse to Pension," 70–71.

45. "Pathetic Tales," *Journal Register Springfield*, September 27, 1944.

46. Preble County Home, Register, OHC; US Census 1880, Joseph Clark, Preble County, Winchester Twp., OH; US Census 1870, 1860, 1850, Preble County, Gratis Twp., OH.

47. Haber, *Beyond Sixty-five*, 86.

48. Ruggles, "Transformation of American Family Structure," 122–25; Krainz, *Delivering Aid*, ch. 1.

49. Chadsey, "Out from the Poor House."

50. Morgan County Poor Farm, Register, IRAD.

51. US Census 1920, Nan Stone, Searcy County, Calf Creek Twp., AR; Searcy County, Arkansas, History, n.p., ACPL.

52. Crawford County, Inmates, ACPL.

53. *NCSW Proceedings*, 258.

54. Carleton, *Farm Ballads*, 56.

55. *Chillicothe Gazette*, August 30, 1902.

56. *NCCC Proceedings*, 1900, 154.

57. Frankel, *Poor Relief in Pennsylvania*, 44.

58. Olmsted, *Handbook for Visitors to the Poorhouse*, 83.

59. Westerfield, *Road to the Poorhouse*, 231–32.

60. Johnston, *I Was Raised at the Poor Farm*, 21; Searcy County, Arkansas, History, n.p., ACPL.

61. Crawford County, Inmates, ACPL.

62. US Census 1920, Minnie Meek, Henry County, Henry Twp., IN; US Census 1880, Minnie Meek, Henry County, New Castle Twp., IN.

63. Frost, "Death of the Hired Man."

64. Rose, *No Right to Be Idle*, 112; Haber and Gratton, *Old Age and the Search for Security*, 102; Tennant, *Paupers and Providers*, 146.

65. Dahlin, "From Poorhouse to Pension," 70–71; Gratton, "The Poverty of Impoverishment Theory," 42.

66. Weiler, "Industrial Scrap Heap," 65.

67. Brents, "Policy Intellectuals, Class Struggle, and the Construction of Old Age," 1251–60; Dahlin, "From Poorhouse to Pension," 55.

68. McClure, *More Than a Roof*, 127.

69. Rose, *No Right to Be Idle*, 138, 150; Holdren, *Injury Impoverished*, 177.

70. Ruggles, "Multigenerational Families in Nineteenth-Century America," 140.

71. Morgan County Poor Farm, Register, IRAD; US Census 1880, Martin Hoag, Schedules of Defective, Dependent, and Delinquent Classes, Morgan County, IL; US Census 1900, Martin Hoag, Morgan County, Jacksonville, IL.

72. Wood County Board of Commissioners, County Home, Minutes, Infirmary Directors, 1893, CAC-BGSU; US Census 1880, Harvey Case, Wood County, Milton Twp., OH; US Census 1900, Wood County, Center Twp., OH.

73. Dane County Hospital and Home Records, Inmate Register, 136, box 5, WHSL.

74. Fairfield County Board of Commissioners, Certificates of Relief, 1896–97, 1914–24, OHC.

75. Frankel, *Poor Relief in Pennsylvania*, 113.

76. Kincade, Coshocton County, Ohio, Infirmary, 72.

77. Haber and Gratton, *Old Age and the Search for Security*, 58–89, 134; see also Quadagno and Meyer, "Organized Labor, State Structures, and Social Policy Development," 184–87; Wood, *Retiring Men*, 84; Achenbaum, "Social Security Entitlements," 162.

78. Quadagno, "Transformation of Old Age Security," 141; Stevens and Stevens, *Welfare Medicine in America*, 6.

79. Dahlin, "From Poorhouse to Pensions," 61; Lauters, *More Than a Farmer's Wife*, 72.

80. Weiler, "Religion, Ethnicity, and the Development of Private Homes for the Aged."

81. Haber and Gratton, "Old Age, Public Welfare, and Race," 265–72. See also Haber, "The Old Folks at Home," 242–43; Weiler, "Religion, Ethnicity, and the Development of Private Homes for the Aged."

82. Letter from C. O. Driscoll, June 14, 1862, Inventory of the Military Department, Adjutant General, Indian War Papers, CSA.

83. *Report of the Commissioners of the Iowa Soldiers' Home*, 9.

84. Donovan, "The Harder Heroism of the Hospital," 163–64.

85. *Springfield Evening News*, November 11, 1905.

86. Dahlin, "From Poorhouse to Pension," 168, 384; Averell, *Inspection of the State Homes for Disabled Soldiers*, 139.

87. Donovan, "The Harder Heroism of the Hospital," 164–79, 197–98.

88. Williams, *The Poor Farm of Grayson County*, 103; Syverson, *How I Grew Up Rich on the Poor Farm*, 48.

89. *Study of a Group of Almshouses*, 11.

90. Johnson, *Almshouse Construction and Management*, 28.

91. Williams, *The Poor Farm of Grayson County*, 103.

92. Henry County Board of Commissioners, Infirmary Registers, 1870–1980, CAC-CGSU; US Census 1900, 1880, Joshua Wheeler, Henry County, Napoleon, OH.

93. Brown County, Illinois, County Farm Records, 1879–1927, ACPL; US Census 1920, Julia Hendricks, Pike County, Griggsville, IL; Illinois Statewide Death Index.

94. Henry County Board of Commissioners, Infirmary Registers, 1886, CAC-BGSU.

95. Nielsen, *Disability History*, xvi.

96. Nielsen, *Disability History*, 89.

97. Auburn [IN] *Evening Star*, October 17, 1929.

98. Frankel, *Poor Relief in Pennsylvania*, 31.

99. Ann Ellis Papers, box 1, folder 22, clippings, OHC.

100. Frankel, *Poor Relief in Pennsylvania*, 23.

101. Haber, "Geriatrics: A Specialty in Search of Specialists," 66.

102. Abel, *The Inevitable Hour*, 80; Haber and Gratton, "Old Age, Public Welfare, and Race," 270.

103. Roth, "The (Historical) Body in Pain"; Scarry, *The Body in Pain*, 54–60; Darling, "The Poor Farm Revisited," 2.

104. Morgan County Poor Farm, Medical Records, IRAD.

105. Keenan cites the various laws in *History of Eloise*, 421–22; "The Friendless Dead," *Ann Arbor Chronicle*, October 1, 1913.

106. *Proceedings of the Annual Convention, Michigan*, 1909, 27.

107. Kennedy, *Ohio Poor Law*, 54–55.

108. *Annual Report of the Bureau of Labor and Industry for 1899*, 395.

109. *Proceedings of the Annual Convention, Michigan*, 1909, 24. See also Farrell, *Inventing the American Way of Death*, 108.

110. *Daily Sentinel* (Wood County, OH), February 24, 1921.

111. Keenan, History of *Eloise*, 434.

112. Johnston, *I Was Raised at the Poor Farm* 30.

113. McClure, *More Than a Roof*, 132.

Chapter 7. Poor Farms and Health Care

1. Morgan County Poor Farm, Medical Records Book, 47, IRAD.

2. Folks, "Disease and Dependence," 297–98.

3. Rose, *No Right to Be Idle*, 121. Rose notes the decline in businesses that rehired injured workers.

4. *Annual Report of the Bureau of Labor and Industry for 1899*, 416.

5. *NCCC Proceedings*, 1903, 376.

6. Grob, *The Deadly Truth*, 220. In World War I and II rural men were rejected from service for health issues more than those from cities and towns.

7. Butterfield, "Rural Life and the Family," 237; Apple, "'Much Instruction Needed Here,'" 109.

8. Grob, *The Deadly Truth*, 231.

9. Massac County Poor Farm and Pauper Fund Records, Abraham Lincoln Presidential Library; Bailey, "Rural Development in Relation to Social Welfare," 86; see also Marshall, "Shaping Poor Relief," 562–68.

10. Williams County Board of Commissioners and County Home, Infirmary Register, 1882, CAC-BGSU.

11. Olson, "Halt, Blind, Lame, Sick, and Lazy," 152; Stevens and Stevens, *Welfare Medicine in America*, 5.

12. *NCCC Proceedings*, 1891, 40.

13. Abel, "Man, Woman, and Chore Boy," 187–88.

14. Abel, "Family Caregiving in the Nineteenth Century," 576.

15. Abel, *Who Cares for the Elderly*, 49.

16. Abel, "Family Caregiving in the Nineteenth Century," 595.

17. Butte County, Board of Charities and Corrections Records, County Files, November 28, 1926, CSA.

18. Abel, "Man, Woman, and Chore Boy," 190–92.

19. Thanet, "The Indoor Pauper," 754.

20. *Study of a Group of Almshouses*, 44–45.

21. Morgan County Poor Farm, Medical Records, IRAD.

22. Dane County Hospital and Home Records, Titus Journal, November 14, 1879, WHSL.

23. Dane County Hospital and Home Records, Titus Journal, September 16, 1880, WHSL.

24. Dane County Hospital and Home Records, Physicians Report, Dane County Annual Report, 1883, WHSL.

25. *A Study of Kansas Poor Farms*, 32.

26. *Annual Report of the Bureau of Labor and Industry for 1899*, 395.

27. Dane County Hospital and Home Records, Register, 130, box 5, WHSL.

28. *Proceedings of the Annual Convention, Michigan*, 1917, 16.

29. Linker, *War's Waste*, 47–48.

30. Elia and Wesolowski, *Archaeological Excavations at the Uxbridge Almshouse*, 120.

31. US Census 1880, Wood County, Center Twp., OH; Board of Commissioners, County Home, Resident Census, 1880–81, CAC-BGSU.

32. Estimates suggest that in 1930, one in ten rural southerners were permanently disabled or too ill to function normally. See Roberts, *Farm Securities Administration*, intro.

33. *Annual Report of the Bureau of Labor and Industry for 1899*, 405.

34. Mitchell, "King County Poor Farm," 11–13.

35. US Census 1880, Wood County, Center Twp., OH.

36. Rosenberg, *The Care of Strangers*, 214.

37. James, *Disappearance of the County Almshouse in Virginia*, 24.

38. Drawbridge, *Unforgotten Truth*, ch. 7.

39. Summit County Infirmary, Register of Inmates, 1897, UAL.

40. US Census 1910, Della A. Statler, Summit County, Portage Twp., OH.

41. Stewart, *Cost of American Almshouses*, 39–40.

42. Marshall, "Shaping Poor Relief," 572. Evans, *The American Poorfarm*, 44. Marshall located at least one antebellum poor farm that hired a nurse.

43. D'Antonio, *American Nursing*, 7.

44. Munson, "The Care of the Sick," 1229.

45. Butte County, Board of Charities and Corrections Records, Hospital, November 28, 1926, CSA.

46. Butte County, Board of Charities and Corrections Records, Hospital, January 1924, CSA.

47. Amador County, Board of Charities and Corrections Records, Social Welfare Files, June 1923, CSA.

48. "Peek through Time," *Jackson [MI] Citizen Patriot*, November 26, 2011.

49. Rock Island *Daily Argus*, May 3, 1876, 2.

50. Rosenberg, *The Care of Strangers*, 322–23.

51. Gillin, *History of Poor Relief*, 285; Willets, *Workers of the Nation*, 893.

52. Ratcliffe, "Some Illinois County Poor Relief Records," 469.

53. US Census 1880, William H. Pyle, Kaufman County, town of Kaufman, TX; "Kaufman County's 'Poor Farm,'" Dallas Morning News, October 3, 2019.

54. Stevens and Stevens, *Welfare Medicine in America*, xviii.

55. Johnson, *Almshouse Cost and Management*, 119.

56. *Proceedings of the Annual Convention, Michigan*, 1905, 16. Counties also negotiated contracts for doctors to do outdoor relief visits. See also Hoffman, *The Wages of Sickness*, ch. 1.

57. "Nebraska Supreme Court, Plumb v. York County," 2153–54.

58. Wisner, *Social Welfare in the South*, 41–42.

59. Morgan County Poor Farm, Medical Records, IRAD.

60. *Summit County Beacon*, June 7, 1882, 4.

61. Bailey, "Rural Development in Relation to Social Welfare," 86.

62. *Proceedings of the Annual Convention, Michigan*, 1908, 22.

63. "Sangamon County Poor Farm."

64. Sangamon County Poor Farm, Proceedings of Board of Supervisors, June 10, 1870, University of Illinois Springfield Archives.

65. *Summit County Beacon*, June 7, 1882.

66. Dane County Hospital and Home Records, Annual Reports, 1882, 1883, WSHL.

67. Johnson, *Almshouse Cost and Management*, 117–19.

68. Palmer, "Why Is the Pauper," 15.

69. Palmer, "Why Is the Pauper," 15.

70. *Akron City Times*, January 26, 1887.

71. Holland, *Murder and Mayhem*, 117.

72. *Summit County Beacon*, February 9, 1887, 4.

73. *Summit County Beacon*, January 26, 1887, 2.

74. *Summit County Beacon*, March 2, 1887, 6.

75. *Summit County Beacon*, February 9, 1887, 4.

76. *Summit County Beacon*, February 16, 1887, 5.

77. *Summit County Beacon*, March 2, 1887, 6.

78. *Akron Beacon Journal*, September 7, 1929, 1.

79. Dahlin, "From Poorhouse to Pension," 50–51.

80. Oppenheim, "He's Only a Pauper."

81. Williams, *The Poor Farm of Grayson County*, 122.

82. Murray, *The Poor House and County Farm*, 100; Morgan County Poor Farm, Medical Records, IRAD.

83. Dane County Hospital and Home Records, Annual Report, 1891, 5, WSHL.

84. "Kaufman County Historical Commission to Host Living History Day at Poor Farm," https://www.cedarcreeklake.com/news--entertainment--Kaufman-County-Historical-Commission-to-host-Living-History-Day-at-Poor-Farm/402.

85. Defiance County Home, Register, 1918, CAC-BGSU. Women from the local WCTU chapter normally made regular visits to the institution.

86. *Proceedings of the Annual Convention, Michigan*, 1910, 7–8.

87. Trattner, "Homer Folks and the Public Health Movement," 419.

88. Abel, *The Inevitable Hour*, 33–34, 76.

89. Abel, *The Inevitable Hour*, 42–46.

90. *Study of a Group of Almshouses*, 17.

91. Schneider and Deutsch, *History of Public Welfare in New York State*, 280–82.

92. Abel, *The Inevitable Hour*, 23–24, 33.

93. *NCCC Proceedings*, 1887, 38.

94. NCCC Proceedings, 1887, 71.

95. Johnson, *Almshouse Construction and Management*, 25.

96. "The Status of Social Work in Rural Communities," *NCSW Proceedings*, 1919, 83–90. See also "The County as a Unit in Charity Administration," *NCSW Proceedings*, 1919, 241–44.

97. *NCSW Proceedings*, 1918, 248; Krainz, *Delivering Aid*, 120.

98. *NCCC Proceedings*, 1897, 376.

99. *NCSW Proceedings*, 1918, 265.

100. Hoffbeck, "Prairie Paupers," 124.

101. Bardwell, "Standards of Almshouse Administration," 364.

102. Adams, *Transformation of Rural Life*, 119, 92; Leonard, *History of Union County*, 108–9.

103. Johnson, *Almshouse Cost and Management*, 117.

104. Butte County, Board of Charities and Corrections Records, November 14, 1922, County Files, CSA.

105. Alameda County, Board of Charities and Corrections Records, Industrial Home and Infirmary, CSA.

106. W. A. Gates, "County Hospitals," 594. See also Tennant, *Paupers and Providers*, 158.

107. *Poor Relief in North Carolina*, 39.

108. Browning, "Effect of a Social Security Assistance Program," 64.

109. Ibbotson, *Eloise*, 8.

110. *Study of a Group of Almshouses*, 28–33.

111. Frankel, *Poor Relief in Pennsylvania*, 45.

112. Abel, "A Terrible and Exhausting Struggle," 483.

113. Frankel, *Poor Relief in Pennsylvania*, 36–39.

114. Keenan, *History of Eloise*, 431.

115. Schereschewsky, "Trachoma," 1853–54.

116. Grob, *The Deadly Truth*, 200, 217–20.

117. Grob, *The Deadly Truth*, 227–28. See also Wagner, *The Poorhouse*, ch. 6.

118. *NCCC Proceedings*, 1908, 219.

119. Apple, "'Much Instruction Needed Here,'" 97–99.

120. Munson, "Care of the Sick," 1228.

121. Stevens and Stevens, *Medical Welfare in America*, 14.

122. Munson, "Care of the Sick," 1228.

123. Abel, *Who Cares for the Elderly*, 127–29; Schell, "Origins of Geriatric Nursing," 203–16.

Chapter 8. Crisis and Transition

1. *Poor Relief in North Carolina*, 13–14.

2. *Study of a Group of Almshouses*, 6.

3. Engerman and Gallman, eds., *Cambridge Economic History of the United States*, 2:280; US Census, *Paupers in Almshouses, 1923*, 3.

4. Stevenson, *Public Welfare Administration*, 87–88.

5. Freeman, "Indigent Care in Texas," 46; McClure, *More Than a Roof*, 232–33.

6. Singleton, *The American Dole*, 175.

7. *Galveston Daily News*, December 15, 1904.

8. *NCCC Proceedings*, 1900, 154–55.

9. Searcy County, Arkansas, History, n.p., ACPL.

10. Meltsner, *Poorhouses of Massachusetts*, 79.

11. Holt, "'Over the Hill to the Poorhouse,'" 11.

12. Patterson, *America's Struggle against Poverty*, 16.

13. Dane County Hospital and Home Records, telegram, box 4, folder 4, WHSL.

14. Dane County Hospital and Home Records, box 4, folder 4, WHSL.

15. *Marysville [OH] Journal Tribune*, June 7, 8, 1937; Ann Ellis Papers, OHC.

16. Naldrett, *Poorhouses and Poor Farms of Michigan*, 45, 93.

17. Margo, "Labor Force Participation of Older Americans in 1900," 420.

18. Anderson and Davidson, "County Poor Farm Inmates," 232–36.

19. Danbom, *Going It Alone*, 28–31, 73–74.

20. Danbom, *Going It Alone*, 95, 107.

21. *A Study of Kansas Poor Farms*, 19.

22. Records of transactions concerning indigents, Franklin County Home, 1892–1895, OHC.

23. *A Study of Kansas Poor Farms*, 7.

24. *A Study of Kansas Poor Farms*, 18.

25. *A Study of Kansas Poor Farms*, 31.

26. Riney-Kehrberg, *Rooted in Dust*, 68–69.

27. Frankel, *Poor Relief in Pennsylvania*, 29.

28. Browning, "Effect of a Social Security Assistance Program," 66.

29. Clark and Keenan, *A History of the Wayne County Infirmary*, 83.

30. *NCCC Proceedings*, 1890, 342; Freeman, "Indigent Care in Texas," 50; Shifflett, *Patronage and Poverty*, 202–3.

31. John W. Voelker, reminiscence, MHSRC.

32. Syverson, *How I Grew Up Rich on the Poor Farm*, ch. 1.

33. Darling, "The Poor Farm Revisited."

34. Williams, *The Poor Farm of Grayson County*, 17.

35. Margaret Marsh, unpublished narrative. Marsh was interviewed by historian Melissa Walker in 1994 and provided her with written recollections.

36. Rexroad, *The Poor Farm of Pendleton County*, 36; US Census 1930, James R. Helmick, Pendleton County, Mill Run Twp., WV.

37. Katz, *In the Shadow of the Poorhouse*, 247.

38. Quoted in Dauber, *The Sympathetic State*, 125.

39. McElvaine, *Down and Out in the Great Depression*, 98–103; Mintz and Kellogg, *Domestic Revolutions*, 140. See also Klein, *For All These Rights*, 67.

40. Grob, *The Mad among Us*, 122. For a fictionalized account of poor farm residency during this time see Favor, *The Edgefielders*.

41. Browning, "Effect of a Social Security Assistance Program," 62.

42. *A Study of Kansas Poor Farms*, 45.

43. Achenbaum, "Social Security Entitlements," 168; Mintz and Kellogg, *Domestic Revolutions*, 148.

44. Summit County Infirmary, box 1, loose volume 1, UAL.

45. Danbom, *Going It Alone*, 97.

46. Cothren, "Arkansas Listings in the National Register of Historic Places," 163–67.

47. *Dayton Daily News*, July 8, 1935.

48. Fischer, "Kansas Homes after the Social Security Act," 445.

49. McClure, "An Unlamented Era," 378.

50. Browning, "Effect of a Social Security Assistance Program," 51–52.

51. Fischer, "Kansas Homes after the Social Security Act," 450–51.

52. Browning, "Effect of a Social Security Assistance Program," 58–60; Fischer, "Kansas Homes after the Social Security Act," 444.

53. Fischer, "Kansas Homes after the Social Security Act," 458.

54. Mitchell, "King County Poor Farm," 13.

55. Flynt, *Poor but Proud*, 185, 318; Tuten, "Regulating the Poor," 55.

56. "Pathetic Tales," *Journal Register Springfield*, September 27, 1944.

57. "For the Destitute," *Southern Illinoisan*, April 21, 1913.

58. Thiede et al., "A Demographic Deficit?" 49–52.

59. The Midwest and West were the regions most likely to have rural counties served by government-operated nursing homes, and female residents outnumbered men. Ballou, "Nonprofit and Government Nursing Homes," 248.

60. Williams, *The Poor Farm of Grayson County*, 20; "A History of the Grayson County Poor Farm," *Sherman [TX] Herald Democrat*, April 20, 2014.

61. Crawford County, Inmates, ACPL.

62. McClure, *More Than a Roof*, 186–93.

63. Fischer, "Kansas Homes after the Social Security Act," 456.

64. Barry, *The Boys in the Bunkhouse*, 28.

65. McClure, *More Than a Roof*, 147.

66. Fischer, "Kansas Homes after the Social Security Act," 453–54.

67. Kolb and Brunner, *A Study of Rural Society*, 412.

68. Hoffer has limited statistics from 1927 that indicate that two counties had opened old folks' homes in addition to poor farms. The poor farms admitted both white and Black residents, but the old folks' homes appeared to have had no African American residents. *Counties in Transition*, 82.

69. Hoffbeck, "Remember the Poor," 236.

70. Fitzgerald, *Every Farm a Factory*, 11–17.

71. Fischer, "Kansas Homes after the Social Security Act," 448–49.

72. McClure, *More Than a Roof*, 217.

73. Moeller, ed., *Out of the Midwest*.

74. Schuman, "A Bygone Era." By 1975, the legislation was responsible for funding almost one-third of hospitals in the United States. See Thomas, "The Hill-Burton Act and Civil Rights," 823–70.

75. *Billings Gazette*, September 2, 1996, 5; Naldrett, *The Poorhouses and Poor Farms of Michigan*, 41.

76. Stevens and Stevens, *Medical Welfare in America*, 26–27; Ward, *Out in the Rural*, 167–68.

77. *Pendleton Times*, October 7, 1965.

78. Ann Ellis Papers, box 1, folder 15, OHC.

79. Buxton, "Bullitt County Poor Farm"; "The St. Louis County Poor Farm."

80. Poor Farm Collection, *Pantagraph*, September 21, 1951 and May 28, 1973, box 1, McClean County Museum of History.

81. Drawbridge, *Unforgotten Truth*, n.p. See also "The Old Poor Farm."

82. Defiance County Home, Register, CAC-BGSU.

83. Paulding County Home, Register, CAC-BGSU.

84. Dahlin, "From Poorhouse to Pension," 45–46.

85. McClure, *More Than a Roof*, 195–96.

86. Summit County Infirmary, Records, 1940–60, UAL. Most of these records are closed because of HIPAA regulations, but a composite of admissions and the income statements are open.

Epilogue

1. Askin, "Oregon's Forgotten Public Social Welfare Institutions," ch. 6; Westerfield, *The Road to the Poorhouse*, 299–302.

2. Ibbotson, *Eloise*, 8.

3. "County Selling Ashmore Estates in Auction," *Charleston [IL] Times Courier*, July 8, 1998; "County Still Responsible," *Charleston [IL] Journal Gazette*, July 21, 2001; Poor Farm Makes Money for Coles County," *Charleston [IL] Times Courier*, January 2, 1980.

4. "Ashmore Estates," http://www.ashmoreestates.net/; "Keep Out . . . until Halloween," *Charleston [IL] Times Courier*, August 31, 2006.

5. Shirley Burgett and Michael Svanevik, "Matters Historical: Memories of the Peninsula's Great Horse Farms," *San Jose Mercury News*, August 30, 2017.

6. Gypsy H. Gilmore, "The County Home: There's Just Not Many Living at the 'Poor Farm' These Days," *The Oklahoman*, July 1, 1984, reprinted at: http://newsok.com/article/2073411.

7. Kincade, Coshocton County, Ohio, Infirmary, 235–36.

8. Kincade, Coshocton County, Ohio, Infirmary, 237–39.

9. See Meltsner, *Poorhouses of Massachusetts*, 139.

10. Phil McCausland, "Rural Hospital Closings Cause Mortality Rates to Rise," *NBC News*, September 6, 2019, https://www.nbcnews.com/news/us-news/rural-hospital -closings-cause-mortality-rates-rise-study-finds-n1048046.

11. "Florida Nursing Home Hurricane Deaths Ruled Homicides," *CBS News*, November 23, 2017, https://www.cbsnews.com/news/hollywood-hills-florida-nursing-home-deaths -hurricane-irma-homicides/

12. "Abuse of Residents of Long Term Care Facilities," National Center on Elder Abuse, https://ncea.acl.gov/NCEA/media/Publication/ResearchBriefLTCF.pdf. See also David Ruppe, "Elderly Abused at 1 in 3 Nursing Homes," *ABC News*, January 7, 2006, http://abcnews.go.com/US/story?id=92689&page=1.

13. David Frank, "Feds Seek to Stop Illegal Nursing Home Evictions," *AARP*, January 11, 2018, https://www.aarp.org/caregiving/financial-legal/info-2018/nursing-home -evictions-fd/.

14. Bui et al., "Association between CMS Quality Ratings and COVID-19 Outbreaks in Nursing Homes."

15. "Food Security and Nutritional Assistance," USDA Economic Research Service, December 16, 2020, https://www.ers.usda.gov/data-products/ag-and-food-statistics- charting-the-essentials/food-security-and-nutrition-assistance/.

16. "Street Fight: Inside Austin's Bitter Brawl," *Texas Monthly* (November 2019): 56.

Bibliography

Archival Collections

Abraham Lincoln Presidential Library, Springfield, IL
    Massac County Poor Farm and Pauper Fund Records
Allen County Public Library Genealogy Center (ACPL), Fort Wayne, IN
    Brown County, Illinois, County Farm Records
    Buchanan County, Iowa, Records
    Coshocton County, Ohio, Infirmary, assembled by Glen Kincade
    Crawford County, Inmates
    Dade County, Poor Farm 1885–1901, transcribed by Goldie West
    Erie County Infirmary, transcribed by Katherine Huss Wunderly, 1991
    Henderson County, Illinois, Poor Farm and Jail, transcribed by Carolyn Cooper
    Iroquois County Poor Farm, "Green Acres," Record of Inmates
    Permits to enter Yavapai County Hospital and Poor Farm, 1897–1989
    Searcy County, Arkansas, History, compiled by Edward and Maurice Tudor
California State Archives (CSA), Sacramento, CA
    Alameda County, Board of Charities and Corrections Records
    Amador County, Board of Charities and Corrections Records
    Butte County, Board of Charities and Corrections Records
    Colusa County, Board of Charities and Corrections Records
Center for Archival Collections, Bowling Green State University, OH (CAC-BGSU)
    Defiance County Home
    Erie County, Ohio, Infirmary
    Fulton County Home and Board of Commissioners
    Hardin County Home
    Henry County Board of Commissioners
    Ottawa County Home
    Paulding County Home

Putnam County Home
Van Wert County Home
Williams County Board of Commissioners and County Home
Wood County Board of Commissioners, County Home
Wyandot County Board of Commissioners, County Home
Illinois Regional Archives Depository (IRAD), Springfield, IL
Morgan County Poor Farm
Joliet Area Historical Museum, Joliet, IL
Will County Poor Farm
McLean County Museum of History, Bloomington, IL
Poor Farm Collection
Montana Historical Society Research Center (MHSRC), Helena, MT
Emily Williams Smith, interview, 1990
John W. Voelker, reminiscence, 1932–1937
Ohio History Center (OHC), Columbus, OH
Ann Ellis Papers
Fairfield County Board of Commissioners
Fayette County Home
Franklin County Home
Licking County Board of Commissioners
Morrow County Home
Preble County Home
University of Akron Libraries Archival Services (UAL), OH
Summit County Infirmary
University of Illinois Springfield Archives/Special Collections/Sangamon Valley Collection, Lincoln Library
Sangamon County Poor Farm
Wisconsin State Historical Society Library and Archive (WSHL)
Buchanan County, Missouri, Poor Farm Records
Dade County, Missouri, Minutes
Dane County Hospital and Home Records
Dodge County Poor Farm and Asylum
Fond Du Lac Reports of the Board of Trustees
Sauk County Annual Reports of the Superintendents of the Poor and Trustees

Newspapers and Periodicals

Akron Beacon Journal
Akron City Times
Argos [IN] Reflector
Austin American Statesman
Billings Gazette
Charities
Charleston [IL] Daily Courier

Charleston [IL] Journal Gazette
Charleston [IL] Journal Gazette and Times Courier
Charleston [IL] Times Courier
Chillicothe Gazette
Coshocton Daily Age
Coshocton Daily Times
Coshocton Democratic Standard
Coshocton Morning Tribune
Daily Sentinel (Wood County, OH)
Dallas News
Dayton Daily News
Denison [TX] Sunday Gazetteer
Detroit Free Press
El Paso Herald
Evening Star Auburn [IN]
Findlay Jeffersonian
Fremont [OH] News-Messenger
Galveston Daily News
Garrett [IN] Clipper
Jackson [MI] Citizen Patriot
Journal Register Springfield (Illinois)
Lancaster [OH] Eagle Gazette
Marion [IL] Daily Republican
Marysville [OH] Journal Tribune
Medford [OR] Mail Tribune
The Oklahoman
Pendleton Times
Rock Island Daily Argus
Saline County Journal
San Jose Mercury News
Scribner's Magazine
Sherman [TX] Herald Democrat
Southern Illinoisan
Springfield [IL] Evening News
Stark County Democrat
Stillwater Gazette
Summit County Beacon
The Survey http://www.gutenberg.org/files/43625/43625-h/43625-h.htm
Watertown [WI] News
Wilmington [OH] News Journal
Wisconsin State Journal
Zanesville Times Recorder
Zenith City [MN] Press

Published Primary Sources

Annual Report of the Board of State Charities of Indiana. Indianapolis, 1922.

Annual Report of the Board of State Charities, Ohio, 1899. Columbus: L. D. Myers, 1899.

Annual Report of the Bureau of Labor and Industry for 1899. Topeka, 1899.

Averell, William W. *An Inspection of the State Homes for Disabled Soldiers and Sailors of the United States.* Washington, DC: GPO, 1889.

Bailey, E.H.S. *A Dietary Study of Some Kansas Institutions under Control of the State Board of Administration.* Topeka: B. P. Walker, 1921.

Bailey, Liberty Hyde. "Rural Development in Relation to Social Welfare." *NCCC Proceedings,* 1908.

Bardwell, Francis. "Standards of Almshouse Administration." *Proceedings of the National Conference for Social Work, 1917.* Chicago: NCSW, 1917.

Biennial Report of the State Board of Corrections and Charities. St. Paul, MN: Pioneer Press, 1884.

Board of State Charities Secretary's Report, Massachusetts, 1871. Boston: Wright and Potter, 1872.

Butterfield, Kenyon. "Rural Life and the Family." *American Economic Association Quarterly* 10:1 (1909): 233–38.

Chadsey, John N. "Out from the Poor House." Canaan, NY: Chadsey & Smith, 1879. https://www.loc.gov/resource/sm1879.10915.0/?sp=3.

County Home for the Friendless, Cape Girardeau County, Missouri, 1874–1956. Jackson, MO: Cape Girardeau County Genealogical Society, 1981.

Craig, Oscar. "The Prevention of Pauperism." *Scribner's Magazine* 14 (1893).

Danielson, Florence, and Charles Davenport. *The Hill Folk: Report on a Rural Community of Hereditary Defectives.* Cold Spring Harbor, NY: Press of the New Era, 1912.

Dugdale, Robert L. *The Jukes: A Study in Crime, Pauperism, Disease, and Heredity.* New York: Putnam, 1877.

Ellis, Otis. "Purchase of Supplies for County Infirmaries—Right and Wrong Methods." *Ohio Bulletin of Charities and Corrections* 7 (1901).

Evans, Harry. *The American Poorfarm and Its Inmates.* Des Moines, 1926.

Frankel, Emil. *Poor Relief in Pennsylvania.* Harrisburg: Pennsylvania Department of Welfare, 1925.

Folks, Homer. "Disease and Dependence." *The Survey* 11 (1903).

———. "Problems in Administration of Municipal Charities." *Annals of the American Academy of Political and Social Science* (March 1904).

Gates, W. A. "County Hospitals." *NCCC Proceedings,* 1905.

Goddard, Henry. *Feeblemindedness: Its Causes and Consequences.* New York: Macmillan, 1914.

Governor's Message and Biennial Report. Madison, WI, 1875.

Historical Statistics of the United States: Colonial Times to 1970. Washington, DC: US Department of Commerce, 1975.

Hoffer, Frank William. *Counties in Transition: A Study of Public and Private Welfare Administration in Virginia.* Charlottesville: University of Virginia Institute for Research in the Social Sciences, 1929.

Hoyt, Charles. *The Causes of Pauperism*. Troy, NY: Parmenter, 1877.

Hunt, William C. *Marriage and Divorce 1867–1906*. Washington, DC: GPO, 1909.

Illinois Statewide Death Index, Pre-1916. Illinois State Archives. https://www.cyber driveillinois.com/departments/archives/databases/death.html.

Infirmary Records, Morgan County, Ohio, 1843–1900. Transcribed by Ruth Hart and Eleanor Jones. McConnelsville, OH: Morgan County Genealogical Society, 1997.

James, Arthur. *The Disappearance of the County Almshouse in Virginia: Back from "Over the Hill."* Richmond, 1926.

Johnson, Alexander. *The Almshouse Construction and Management*. New York: Charities Publication Committee, 1911.

Johnston, Carl C. *I Was Raised at the Poor Farm*. West Lafayette, IN, 1986.

Letchworth, William P. "Poorhouse Administration, and the Proper Provision for the Dependent Classes." *The Sanitarian* 16 (June 1886): 333–43.

McCormick, Mildred. "Poverty's Monument: The Poorhouse." *Springhouse Magazine Online*. http://www.springhousemagazine.com/poorhouse.htm.

McKinniss, Clyde. "Standards of Administration of the Almshouse." *Proceedings of the NCSW* 45 (1918).

Meseraull, S. I. "The Administration of Almshouses." *Proceedings of the NCSW* 45 (1918).

"Nebraska Supreme Court. Extra Compensation Allowed to County Physician for Unusual Services during an Epidemic. Plumb v. York County, 146 N. W. Rep., 938. April 3, 1914." *Public Health Reports (1896–1970)* 29:33 (1914).

Olmsted, Frederick Law. *Handbook for Visitors to the Poorhouse*. New York, G. P. Putnam's Sons, 1888.

Oppenheim, James. "He's Only a Pauper, Whom Nobody Owns!" *American Magazine* 70 (1910).

Ordronaux, John. *Questions Relating to Poorhouses, Hospitals, and Insane Asylums*. New York: State Charities Aid Association, 1874.

Palmer, George T. "Why Is the Pauper." *The Survey* 30:1 (April 5, 1913).

Poor Relief in North Carolina. Special Bulletin no. 4. Raleigh: North Carolina State Board of Charities and Public Welfare, 1925.

Proceedings of the Annual Convention of the State Superintendents of the Poor, Michigan. Lansing: Wynkoop, Hallenbeck, Crawford, Co., 1905–1919.

Proceedings of the Board of Supervisors of the County of Niagara, 1912. Lockport, NY, 1912.

Proceedings of the National Conference of Charities and Corrections (*NCCC Proceedings*).

Proceedings of the National Conference for Social Work (*NCSW Proceedings*).

Public Documents of the State of Wisconsin. Madison: Democrat Printing, 1885.

Report of the Commissioners of the Iowa Soldiers' Home. Des Moines: State Printer, 1888.

Roberts Smith, Mary. *Almshouse Women: A Study of Two Hundred and Twenty-eight Women in the City and County Almshouse of San Francisco*. Palo Alto: Stanford University Press, 1896.

Salmon, Thomas. "Insane in a County Poor Farm." *Mental Hygiene* 1:1 (1917): 25–33.

Schereschewsky, Joseph W. "Trachoma: Prevalence in Knox County, Tenn." *Public Health Reports* 28:36 (September 5, 1913).

Second Annual Report of the Ohio Board of State Charities for the Year 1877. Columbus: Nevins & Myers, 1878.

Sessions, Mina. *The Feebleminded in the Rural County of Ohio.* Columbus: Ohio State University, 1918.

Stewart, Estelle. *The Cost of American Almshouses.* Bulletin of the US Bureau of Labor Statistics, no. 386. Washington, DC: GPO, 1925.

Study of a Group of Almshouses in Connecticut, New Jersey, New York, and Pennsylvania. New York: National Women's Department, National Civil Federation, 1927.

A Study of Kansas Poor Farms. Topeka: Kansas Emergency Relief Committee, 1935.

Sweeney, Ed. *Poorhouse Sweeney.* New York: Boni and Liveright, 1927.

Syverson, Betty Groth. *How I Grew Up Rich on the Poor Farm.* N.p., 1997.

Taylor, Carl Cleveland, Helen Wheeler, and Ellis Lore Kirkpatrick. *Disadvantaged Classes in American Agriculture.* Washington, DC: USDA, 1938.

Thanet, Octave. "The Indoor Pauper: A Study." *Atlantic Monthly* (June 1881).

US Bureau of Labor Statistics. *Monthly Labor Review.* Washington, DC: GPO, 1939.

US Census. Manuscript Census, 1870, 1880, 1890, 1900, 1910, 1920, 1930, 1940. Accessed via Ancestry.com.

———. *Paupers in Almshouses in 1890.* Bulletin 154, July 8, 1891.

———. *Paupers in Almshouses.* Bulletin 120, 1910.

———. *Paupers in Almshouses, 1923.* Washington, D.C.: GPO, 1925.

———. Schedules of Defective, Dependent, and Delinquent Classes, 1880. Accessed via Ancestry.com.

———. *Special Report on Almshouses.* Washington, DC, 1904.

Warner, Amos G. *American Charities.* New York: Thomas Crowell & Co., 1894.

Wisconsin State Census, 1885, 1895, 1905. Accessed via Ancestry.com.

Wisconsin Wills and Probate. Accessed via Ancestry.com.

Wright, Carroll Davidson. *A Report on Marriage and Divorce in the United States, 1867–1886.* Washington, DC: GPO, 1889.

Secondary Sources

Abel, Emily. "Family Caregiving in the Nineteenth Century: Emily Hawley Gillespie and Sarah Gillespie, 1858–1888." *Bulletin of the History of Medicine* 68:4 (1994): 573–99.

———. *The Inevitable Hour: A History of Caring for Dying Patients in America.* Baltimore: Johns Hopkins University Press, 2013.

———. "Man, Woman, and Chore Boy: Transformations in the Antagonistic Demands of Work and Care on Women in the Nineteenth and Twentieth Centuries." *Milbank Quarterly* 73:2 (1995): 187–211.

———. "A Terrible and Exhausting Struggle: Family Caregiving during the Transformation of Medicine." *Journal of the History of Medicine and Allied Sciences* 50:4 (October 1995): 478–506.

———. *Who Cares for the Elderly: Public Policy and the Experiences of Adult Daughters.* Philadelphia: Temple University Press, 1991.

Abramowitz, Mimi. "The Family Ethic: The Female Pauper and Public Aid, Pre-1900." *Social Service Review* 59:1 (1985): 121–35.

———. *Regulating the Lives of Women: Social Welfare Policy from Colonial Times to the Present.* Boston: South End Press, 1996.

"Abuse of Residents of Long Term Care Facilities." National Center on Elder Abuse Research Brief. https://ncea.acl.gov/docs/Abuse-of-Residents-of-Long-Term-Care-Facilities-(2012)_1.pdf

Achenbaum, W. Andrew. "Social Security Entitlements as a Measure of Modern American Life." In *Growing Old in a Bureaucratic Society*, ed. David Van Tassel and Peter N. Stearns, 156–92. New York: Praeger, 1986.

———. "W(H)ither Social Welfare History." *Journal of Social History* 24:1 (1990): 135–41.

Adams, Jane. *The Transformation of Rural Life: Southern Illinois, 1890–1990*. Chapel Hill: University of North Carolina Press, 2000.

Alexander, W. E. *History of Chickasaw and Howard Counties*. Decorah, IA: Western Pub., 1883.

Alger, Horatio. *Jed: The Poorhouse Boy*. Philadelphia: John C. Winston Co., 1899.

Altschuler, Glenn C., and Jan M. Saltzgaber. "The Limits of Responsibility: Social Welfare and Local Government in Seneca County, New York 1860–1875." *Journal of Social History* 21:3 (Spring 1988): 515–37.

Anderson, H. Dewey, and Percy E. Davidson. "County Poor Farm Inmates Compared with Their Brothers and the Working Population of the Same Community." *Social Forces* 16:2 (1937): 231–37.

Apple, Rima D. "'Much Instruction Needed Here': The Work of Nurses in Rural Wisconsin during the Depression." *Nursing History Review* 15 (2007): 95–111.

Arcury, Thomas. "Rural Elderly Household Life-Course Transitions, 1900 and 1980 Compared." *Journal of Family History* 11:1 (1986): 55–75.

Arrom, Silvia Marina. *Containing the Poor: The Mexico City Poor House, 1774–1871*. Durham, NC: Duke University Press, 2000.

Askin, Timothy B. "Oregon's Forgotten Public Social Welfare Institutions: The Oregon State Hospital and the Multnomah County Poor Farm as Case Studies in the Challenge of Preserving Stigmatized Places." MS thesis, University of Oregon, 2010.

Atack, Jeremy, and Fred Bateman. "Egalitarianism, Inequality, and Age: The Rural North in 1860." *Journal of Economic History* 41:1 (1981): 85–93.

———. *To Their Own Soil: Agriculture in the Antebellum North*. Ames: Iowa State University Press, 1987.

Ballou, Jeffery. "Do Nonprofit and Government Nursing Homes Enter Unprofitable Markets?" *Economic Inquiry* 46:2 (April 2008): 241–60.

Barron, Hal S. "Staying Down on the Farm: Social Processes of Settled Rural Life in the Nineteenth-Century North." In *The Countryside in the Age of Capitalist Transformation*, ed. Steven Hahn and Jonathan Prude, 327–44. Chapel Hill: University of North Carolina Press, 1985.

Barry, Dan. *The Boys in the Bunkhouse: Servitude and Salvation in the Heartland*. New York: Harper Perennial, 2017.

Beito, David T. *From Mutual Aid to the Welfare State: Fraternal Societies and Social Services, 1890–1967*. Chapel Hill: University of North Carolina Press, 2000.

Bell, Edward. *Historical Archaeology at the Hudson Poor Farm Cemetery*. Boston: Massachusetts Historical Commission, 1993.

Ben-Moche, Liat, Chris Chapman, and Allison Carey, eds. *Disability Incarcerated: Imprisonment and Disability in the United States and Canada*. New York: Palgrave Macmillan, 2014.

Birk, Megan. *Fostering on the Farm: Child Placement in the Rural Midwest.* Urbana: University of Illinois Press, 2015.

Blackmar, Frank. "The Smoky Pilgrims." In *White Trash: The Eugenic Family Studies, 1877–1919,* ed. Nicole Hahn Rafter, 55–65. Boston: Northeastern University Press, 1988.

Bose, Christine E. "Household Resources and U.S. Women's Work: Factors Affecting Gainful Employment at the Turn of the Century." *American Sociological Review* 49 (1984): 474–90.

Bourque, Monique. "The Creation of the Almshouse: Institutions as Solutions to the Problem of Poverty." *Journal of the Lancaster County Historical Society* 102:2 (2000): 56–81.

———. "Poor Relief 'Without Violating the Rights of Humanity': Almshouse Administration in the Philadelphia Region, 1790–1860." In *Down and Out in Early America,* ed. Billy Smith, 163–88. University Park: Penn State University Press, 2004.

Brammer, Richard. "A Home for the Homeless: Remembering the Pleasants County Poor Farm." *Goldenseal* 20:3 (Fall 1994): 45–50.

Brenmer, Robert H. *The Discovery of Poverty in the United States.* New York: Transaction, 1992.

Brents, Barbara. "Policy Intellectuals, Class Struggle, and the Construction of Old Age." *Social Science and Medicine* 23:12 (1986): 1251–60.

Broberg, Gunnar, and Nils Roll-Hansen. *Eugenics and the Welfare State: Sterilization Policy in Denmark, Sweden, Norway, and Finland.* East Lansing: Michigan State University Press, 1996.

Brown, Elizabeth Gaspar. "Poor Relief in a Wisconsin County, 1846–1866: Administration and Recipients." *American Journal of Legal History* 20:2 (April 1976): 79–117.

Browning, Grace. "The Effect of a Social Security Assistance Program on the Poor Farms of a Western State." *Social Service Review* 12:1 (1938): 51–68.

Brownlee, Kimberly. "Treatment of the Mentally Ill in Northwest Ohio: The Lucas County Infirmary and Poor Farm and the Toledo State Hospital." *Northwest Ohio History* 79:1 (Fall 2011): 1–14.

Bryan, Charles S. *Asylum Doctor: James Woods Babcock and the Red Plague of Pellagra.* Columbia: University of South Carolina Press, 2014.

Bui, David P., Isaac See, Elizabeth M. Hesse, et al. "Association between CMS Quality Ratings and COVID-19 Outbreaks in Nursing Homes." *Morbidity and Mortality Weekly Report,* September 18, 2020.

Burns, Inez. *History of Blount County, Tennessee: From War Trail to Landing Strip, 1795–1955.* Nashville: Tennessee Historical Commission, 1957.

Buxton, Daniel. "Bullitt County Poor Farm." *Bullitt County History.* http://www.bullitt countyhistory.com/bchistory/poorfarm.html.

Cahill, Cathleen. *Federal Fathers and Mothers: A Social History of the United States Indian Service, 1869–1933.* Chapel Hill: University of North Carolina Press, 2011.

Caldwell, Erskine, and Margaret Bourke-White. *You Have Seen Their Faces.* New York: Viking Press, 1937.

Carleton, Will. *Farm Ballads.* New York: Harper and Brothers, 1882.

———. *Farm Legends.* Toronto: Rose-Belford Publishing Co., 1875.

Carter, Helen S. "Legal Aspects of Widowhood and Aging." In *On Their Own: Widows and Widowhood in the American Southwest, 1848–1939*, ed. Arlene Scadron, 271–300. Urbana: University of Illinois Press, 1988.

Carter, Susan. "The Great Depression of the 1890s: New Suggestive Estimates for the Unemployment Rate, 1890–1905." *Research in Economic History* 14:1 (1992): 347–87.

Chamberlin, Sheena Eagan. "Emasculated by Trauma: A Social History of Post-Traumatic Stress Disorder, Stigma, and Masculinity." *Journal of American Culture* 35:4 (November 2012): 358–65.

Church, Harry, and Katharyn Joella Chappell. *History of Buchanan County, Iowa, and Its People*. Chicago: S. J. Clarke, 1914.

Clark, Alvin C, and Stanislas Keenan. *A History of the Wayne County Infirmary, Psychiatric, and General Hospital Complex at Eloise, Michigan, 1832–1982*. N.p.: Wayne County General Hospital Anniversary Committee, 1982.

"Clinton County Poor Farm." Clinton County IAGenWeb Project. http://iagenweb.org/clinton/places/waterford/poorfarm.htm.

Coleborne, Catharine. *Madness in the Family: Insanity and Institutions in the Australasian World, 1860–1914*. New York: Palgrave, 2010.

Cooke, Andrew. "In Praise of Peasants: Ways of Seeing the Rural Poor in the Work of James Agee, Walker Evans, John Berger, and Jean Mohr." PhD diss., University of Iowa, 2013.

Corbit, Robert McClain, ed. *History of Jones County, Iowa, Past and Present*. Chicago: S. J. Clarke, 1910.

Cothren, Zackery A. "Arkansas Listings in the National Register of Historic Places: Poorhouse Cemeteries." *Arkansas Historical Quarterly* 65:2 (Summer 2006): 163–67.

Cottrell, Debbie Mauldin. "The Poor Farm System in Texas." *Southwestern Historical Quarterly* 93:2 (October 1989): 169–90.

Crowther, M. A. *The Workhouse System, 1834–1929: The History of an English Social Institution*. Athens: University of Georgia Press, 1982.

Curtin, Mary Ellen. *Black Prisoners and Their World, Alabama, 1865–1900*. Charlottesville: University Press of Virginia, 2000.

Cvrcek, Tomas. "U.S. Marital Disruptions and Their Economic and Social Correlates, 1860–1948." *Journal of Family History* 36:2 (2011): 142–58.

Dahlin, Michel R. "From Poorhouse to Pension: The Changing View of Old Age in America, 1890–1929." PhD diss., Stanford University, 1982.

D'Antonio, Patricia. *American Nursing: A History of Knowledge, Authority, and the Meaning of Work*. Baltimore: Johns Hopkins University Press, 2010.

Daley, Michael, and Peggy Pittman-Munke. "Over the Hill to the Poor Farm: Rural History Almost Forgotten." *Contemporary Rural Social Work* 8:2 (December 2016): 1–17.

Danbom, David. *Going It Alone: Fargo Grapples with the Great Depression*. St. Paul: Minnesota Historical Society Press, 2005.

Daniels, Christine. "Intimate Violence, Then and Now." In *Over the Threshold: Intimate Violence in Early America*, ed. Christine Daniels and Michael V. Kennedy, 3–21. New York: Routledge, 2014.

Darling, Don. "The Poor Farm Revisited." *Rural Heritage* 14:4 (Winter 1989): 1–2.

Dauber, Michele Landis. *The Sympathetic State: Disaster Relief and the Origins of the American Welfare State*. Chicago: University of Chicago Press, 2013.

Davies, Richard O. *Main Street Blues: The Decline of Small-Town America*. Columbus: Ohio State University Press, 1998.

DePastino, Todd. *Citizen Hobo: How a Century of Homelessness Shaped America*. Chicago: University of Chicago Press, 2003.

Deutsch, Albert. *The Mentally Ill in America: A History of Their Care and Treatment from Colonial Times*. New York: Columbia University Press, 1965.

Directors of the Wood County Poor Farm. *Commemorative Historical and Biographical Record of Wood County*. Chicago: J. H. Beers, 1897.

Dobbs, Hugh Jackson. *History of Gage County, Nebraska: A Narrative of the Past*. Lincoln: Western Publishing, 1918.

Donovan, Brian Edward. "The Harder Heroism of the Hospital: Union Veterans and the Creation of Disability, 1862–1910." PhD diss., University of Iowa, 2015.

Dorr, Gregory Michael. *Segregation's Science: Eugenics and Society in Virginia*. Charlottesville: University of Virginia Press, 2008.

Drawbridge, Kathy. *The Unforgotten Truth of the Life and Times at the Dodge County Poor Farm*. N.p., 2007.

Driscoll, Betty. *History of the Gratiot County Poor Farm*. New Era, MI: N.p., 2005.

Dubinsky, Karen. *Improper Advances: Rape and Heterosexual Conflict in Ontario, 1880–1929*. Chicago: University of Chicago Press, 1993.

Dudden, Faye E. *Serving Women: Household Service in Nineteenth-Century America*. Middletown, CT: Wesleyan University Press, 1983.

Ebert, Thomas, and Walter I. Trattner. "The County Mental Institution: Did It Do What It Was Designed to Do?" *Social Science Quarterly* 71:4 (1990): 835–47.

Editorial. *Annals of Iowa* 8:3 (October 1907): 227–28.

Effland, Anne. "When Rural Does Not Equal Agricultural." *Agricultural History* 74:2 (Spring 2000): 489–501.

Eggleston, Edward. *The Hoosier Schoolmaster*. New York: Grosset and Dunlap, 1871.

Eichengreen, Barry, and Henry A. Gemery. "The Earnings of Skilled and Unskilled Immigrants at the End of the Nineteenth Century." *Journal of Economic History* 46:2 (June 1986): 441–54.

Elia, Ricardo J., and Al B. Wesolowsky, eds. *Archaeological Excavations at the Uxbridge Almshouse Burial Ground in Uxbridge*. Oxford: BAR International Series, 1991.

Elks, Martin. "Visual Rhetoric: Photographs of the Feebleminded during the Eugenics Era, 1900–1930." PhD diss., Syracuse University, 1992.

Elliot, Samuel H. *New England's Chattels; or, Life in the Northern Poor-house*. New York: H. Dayton, 1858.

Engerman, Stanley, and Robert Gallman, eds. *The Cambridge Economic History of the United States*, vol. 2. Cambridge: Cambridge University Press, 2000.

Engle Lang, Gladys. ed. *Old Age in America*. New York: H. W. Wilson, 1961.

Erby, Kelly. "The Hull Baby Case and Women in 1870s Kansas." *Kansas History* 40:3 (2017): 187–202.

Farland, Maria. "Modernist Versions of Pastoral: Poetic Inspiration, Scientific Expertise, and the 'Degenerate Farmer.'" *American Literary History* 19:4 (Winter 2007): 905–36.

Farley, Douglas, ed. *A Poorhouse Trilogy*. Buffalo, NY: People's Ink Press, 2015.

Farrell, James J. *Inventing the American Way of Death, 1830–1920*. Philadelphia: Temple University Press, 1980.

Farreras, Ingrid G. "Clara Harrison Town and the Origins of the First Institutional Commitment Law for the Feebleminded." *History of Psychology* 17:4 (2014): 271–81.

Favor, Judith Wright. *The Edgefielders*. N.p.: CreateSpace, 2013.

Ferguson, Philip M. *Abandoned to Their Fate: Social Policy and Practice toward Severely Disabled Persons, 1820–1920*. Philadelphia: Temple University Press, 1994.

Figart, Deborah M., Ellen Mutari, and Marilyn Power. *Living Wages, Equal Wages: Gender and Labor Market Policies in the United States*. London: Routledge, 2002.

Finlayson, Anna Wendt. "The Dack Family: A Study in Heredity Lack of Emotional Control." In *White Trash: The Eugenic Family Studies, 1877–1919*, ed. Nicole Hahn Rafter, 210–14. Boston: Northeastern University Press, 1988.

Fischer, Violet. "Kansas Homes after the Social Security Act." *Social Service Review* 17 (1943): 442–65.

Fisher, Kathy. *In the Beginning There Was Land: A History of Washington County, Iowa*. Washington: Washington County Historical Society, 1978.

Fitzgerald, Deborah. *Every Farm a Factory: The Industrial Ideal in American Agriculture*. New Haven: Yale University Press, 2003.

Fleming, Kevin C., Jonathan M. Evans, and Darryl S. Chutka. "A Cultural and Economic History of Old Age in America." *Mayo Clinic Proceedings* (July 2003): 914–21.

"Florida Nursing Home Hurricane Deaths Ruled Homicides." *CBS News*, November 23, 2017. https://www.cbsnews.com/news/hollywood-hills-florida-nursing-home-deaths -hurricane-irma-homicides/.

Floyd, Barbara, ed. *From Institutions to Independence: A History of People with Disabilities in Northwest Ohio*. Toledo: University of Toledo Press, 2010.

Flynt, Wayne. *Poor but Proud: Alabama's Poor Whites*. Tuscaloosa: University of Alabama Press, 1989.

Foucault, Michel. *Discipline and Punish: The Birth of the Prison*. Translated by Alan Sheridan. New York: Pantheon Press, 1978.

Fox, Bonnie J. "Selling the Mechanized Household: 70 Years of Ads in *Ladies' Home Journal*." *Gender & Society* 4:1 (1990): 25–40.

Fox, Cybelle. *Three Worlds of Relief: Race, Immigration, and the American Welfare State from the Progressive Era to the New Deal*. Princeton, NJ: Princeton University Press, 2012.

Fraser, Nancy, and Linda Gordon. "A Genealogy of Dependency: Tracing a Keyword of the U.S. Welfare State." *Signs: Journal of Women in Culture and Society* 19:2 (1994): 309–36.

Fraundorf, Martha Norby. "Relative Earnings of Native and Foreign Born Women." *Explorations in Economic History* 15:2 (April 1978): 211–20.

Freedman, Estelle. *Their Sisters' Keepers: Women's Prison Reform in America, 1830–1930*. Ann Arbor: University of Michigan Press, 1984.

Freeman, Martha Doty. "Indigent Care in Texas: A Study of Poor Farms and Outdoor Relief." *Index of Texas Archaeology: Open Access Gray Literature from the Lone Star State* (2008).

Freeman, Ruth, and Patricia Klaus. "Blessed or Not? The New Spinster in England and the United States in the Late Nineteenth and Early Twentieth Centuries." *Journal of Family History* 9:4 (1984): 394–414.

Friedberger, Mark. "The Decision to Institutionalize: Families with Exceptional Children in 1900." *Journal of Family History* 6:4 (1981): 369–409.

———. *Farm Families and Change in 20th Century America*. Lexington: University Press of Kentucky, 1988.

———. "The Farm Family and the Inheritance Process: Evidence from the Corn Belt, 1870–1950." *Agricultural History* 57:1 (1983): 1–13.

Frost, Robert. "Death of the Hired Man." https://www.poetryfoundation.org/poems/44261/the-death-of-the-hired-man.

———. "A Servant to Servants." https://www.poetryverse.com/robert-frost-poems/a-servant-to-servants.

Gamber, Wendy. *The Boardinghouse in Nineteenth-Century America*. Baltimore: Johns Hopkins University Press, 2007.

Gans, Herbert J. "Positive Functions of the Underserving Poor: Uses of the Underclass in America." *Politics and Society* 22:3 (1994): 269–83.

Garman, James C., and Paul R. Russo. "'A Disregard of Every Sentiment of Humanity': The Town Farm and Class Realignment in Nineteenth-Century Rural New England." *Historical Archaeology* 33:1 (1999): 118–35.

Garton, Stephen. *Out of Luck: Poor Australians and Social Welfare, 1788–1988*. Sydney: Allen & Unwin, 1990.

Gillin, John Lewis. *History of Poor Relief Legislation in Iowa*. Iowa City: State Historical Society of Iowa, 1914.

Gillespie, Samuel. *History of Clay County, Iowa, from Its Earliest Settlement to 1909*. Chicago: S. J. Clarke, 1909.

Goldberg, Chad Alan. *Citizens and Paupers: Relief, Rights, and Race, from the Freedmen's Bureau to Workfare*. Chicago: University of Chicago Press, 2007.

Gollaher, David. *Voice for the Mad: The Life of Dorothea Dix*. New York: Free Press, 1995.

Gonaver, Wendy. *The Peculiar Institution and the Making of Modern Psychiatry, 1840–1880*. Chapel Hill: University of North Carolina Press, 2019.

Good, Howard. *Black Swamp Farm*. Columbus: Ohio State University Press, 1967.

Gooden, Susan T. "Local Discretion and Welfare Policy: The Case of Virginia (1911–1970)." *Southern Studies* 6:4 (1995): 79–110.

Goodwin, Joanne L. "An Experiment in Paid Motherhood: The Implementation of Mothers' Pensions in Early Twentieth-Century Chicago." *Gender & History* 4:3 (1992): 323–42.

Gordon, Linda. *Heroes of Their Own Lives: The Politics and History of Family Violence*. Urbana: University of Illinois Press, 2002.

———. *Pitied But Not Entitled: Single Mothers and the History of Welfare*. Cambridge, MA: Harvard University Press, 1994.

Gorman, Kathleen. "Confederate Pensions as Social Welfare." In *Before the New Deal: Social Welfare in the South, 1830–1930*, ed. Elna Green, 24–39. Athens: University of Georgia Press, 1999.

Grant, H. Roger. "Blueprints for Co-operative Communities: The Labor Exchange and Colorado Cooperative Company." *Journal of the West* 13:3 (1974): 74–82.

Gratton, Brian. "Emptying the Nest: Older Men in the United States, 1880–2000." *Population & Development Review* 36:2 (June 2010): 331–56.

———. "The Poverty of Impoverishment Theory: The Economic Well-Being of the Elderly, 1890–1950." *Journal of Economic History* 56:1 (1996): 39–62.

Green, Elna. *Before the New Deal: Social Welfare in the New South, 1880–1930.* Athens: University of Georgia Press, 1999.

———. "Infanticide and Infant Abandonment in the New South: Richmond, Virginia, 1865–1915." *Journal of Family History* 22:2 (1999): 187–212.

———. *This Business of Relief: Confronting Poverty in a Southern City, 1740–1940.* Athens: University of Georgia Press, 2003.

Greenwald, Maurine Weiner. "From Hired Hand to Day Worker: Household Labor in the United States, 1800–1920." *International Labor and Working Class History* 27 (Spring 1985): 60–71.

Grob, Gerald. *The Deadly Truth: A History of Disease in America.* Cambridge, MA: Harvard University Press, 2005.

———. "Mental Health Policy in America: Myths and Realities." *Health Affairs* 11:3 (Fall 1992): 7–22.

———. *Mental Illness and American Society, 1875–1940.* Princeton, NJ: Princeton University Press, 1987.

———. *The Mad among Us: A History of the Care of America's Mentally Ill.* New York: Free Press, 1994.

Grossberg, Michael. "From Feebleminded to Mentally Retarded: Child Protection and the Changing Place of Disabled Children in the Mid-Twentieth-Century United States." *Paedagogica Historica* 47:2 (2001): 729–47.

Haber, Carole. *Beyond Sixty-five: The Dilemma of Old Age in America's Past.* Cambridge: Cambridge University Press, 1983.

———. "Geriatrics: A Specialty in Search of Specialists." In *Old Age in a Bureaucratic Society,* ed. David Van Tassel and Peter N. Stearns, 66–84. Westport, CT: Greenwood Press, 1986.

———. "The Old Folks at Home: The Development of Institutionalized Care for the Aged in Nineteenth-Century Philadelphia." *Pennsylvania Magazine of History* 101:2 (1977): 240–57.

Haber, Carole, and Brian Gratton. *Old Age and the Search for Security.* Bloomington: Indiana University Press, 1993.

———. "Old Age, Public Welfare, and Race: The Case of Charleston, South Carolina, 1800–1949." *Journal of Social History* 21:2 (1987): 263–79.

Hacker, Jacob S. "Bringing the Welfare State Back In: The Promise (and Perils) of the New Social Welfare History." *Journal of Policy History* 17:1 (2005): 125–54.

Hall Kelly, Patricia, and Steven Ruggles. "'Restless in the Midst of Their Prosperity': New Evidence on the Internal Migration of Americans, 1850–2000." *Journal of American History* 91:3 (December 2004): 829–46.

Hamilton, Charles V. "Social Policy and the Welfare of Black Americans: From Rights to Resources." *Political Science Quarterly* 101:2 (1986): 239–55.

Hamm, Dorothy Ann. "A Study of the Influence of Public Assistance Legislation on the Almshouse Population in Mississippi." MA thesis, Tulane University, 1947.

Handson, Cameron, and Heather Hull, eds. *Past Harvests: A History of Floyd County to 1996*. Floyd, VA: Floyd County Historical Society. 1996.

Hareven, Tamara. "Life-Course Transitions and Kin Assistance." In *Old Age in a Bureaucratic Society*, ed. David Van Tassel and Peter N. Stearns, 110–25. Westport, CT: Greenwood Press, 1986.

Hatton, Timothy J., and Jeffrey G. Williamson. "Wage Gaps between Farm and City: Michigan in the 1890s." *Explorations in Economic History* 28:4 (1991): 381–408.

———. "What Explains Wage Gaps between Farm and City? Exploring the Todaro Model with American Evidence, 1890–1941." *Economic Development and Cultural Change* 40:2 (1992): 267–95.

Henry County, Ohio: A Collection of Historical Sketches and Family Histories. Napoleon, OH: Henry County Historical Society, 1976.

Herman, Bernard. "The Development of the Charitable Landscape." *Journal of the Lancaster County Historical Society* 102:2 (June 2000): 114–34.

Herndon, Ruth Wallis. *Unwelcome Americans: Living on the Margin in Early New England*. Philadelphia: University of Pennsylvania Press, 2001.

———. "'Who Died an Expense to This Town': Poor Relief in Eighteenth-Century Rhode Island." In *Down and Out in Early America*, ed. Billy G. Smith, 135–62. University Park: Penn State University Press, 2004.

Higbie, Frank Tobias. *Indispensable Outcasts: Hobo Workers and Community in the American Midwest, 1880–1930*. Urbana: University of Illinois Press, 2003.

———. "Rural Work, Household Subsistence, and the North American Working Class: A View from the Midwest." *International Labor and Working Class History* 65 (Spring 2004): 50–76.

"Hill-Burton Free and Reduced-Cost Health Care." Health Resources and Services Administration. https://www.hrsa.gov/get-health-care/affordable/hill-burton/index.html.

Hirota, Hidetaka. *Expelling the Poor: Atlantic Seaboard States and the Nineteenth-Century Origins of American Immigration Policy*. Oxford: Oxford University Press, 2017.

History of Allamakee County, Iowa. Waukon, IA: Allamakee County, Iowa, Heritage Book Committee, 1990.

History of Mills County, Iowa. Des Moines: State Historical Company, 1881.

History of Polk County, Iowa. Des Moines: Birdsall, Williams, & Co, 1880.

Hoffbeck, Steven R. "Prairie Paupers: North Dakota Poor Farms, 1879–1973." PhD diss., University of North Dakota, 1992.

———. "Remember the Poor." *Vermont History* 57:4 (1989): 226–40.

Hoffman, Beatrix. *The Wages of Sickness: The Politics of Health Insurance in Progressive America*. Chapel Hill: University of North Carolina Press, 2001.

Hoffman, Charles. "The Depression of the Nineties." *Journal of Economic History* 16:2 (June 1956): 137–64.

Holdren, Nate. *Injury Impoverished: Workplace Accidents, Capitalism, and Law in the Progressive Era*. New York: Cambridge University Press, 2020.

Holland, Jeri. *Murder and Mayhem in Akron and Summit County*. N.p.: CreateSpace, 2012.

Holt, Marilyn Irvin. "'Over the Hill to the Poorhouse': Kansas Poor Relief." *Kansas History* 39:1 (Spring 2016): 2–15.

Hooks, Christopher. "Inside Austin's Bitter Brawl Over Homelessness." *Texas Monthly* (November 2019).

Horn, Stacy. *Damnation Island: Poor, Sick, Mad, and Criminal in 19th Century New York.* Chapel Hill: Algonquin Books, 2018.

Hough, Mazie. *Rural Unwed Mothers: An American Experience 1870–1950.* London: Pickerington and Chatto, 2010.

Howe, Edward T., and Donald J. Reeb. "The Historical Evolution of State and Local Tax Systems." *Social Science Quarterly* 78:1 (March 1997): 109–21.

"How to Refer to People with Disabilities." National Center for Biotechnology Information. https://www.ncbi.nlm.nih.gov/books/NBK64884/.

Ibbotson, Patricia. *Eloise: Poorhouse, Farm, Asylum, and Hospital, 1839–1984.* Charleston, SC: Arcadia Publishing, 2002.

Iceland, John. *Poverty in America: A Handbook.* Berkeley: University of California Press, 2003.

Igra, Anna R. *Wives without Husbands: Marriage, Desertion, and Welfare in New York, 1900–1935.* Chapel Hill: University of North Carolina Press, 2007.

Isenberg, Nancy. *White Trash: The 400-Year Untold History of Class in America.* New York: Viking, 2016.

James, John A. "A Golden Age? Unemployment and the American Labor Market, 1880–1910." *Journal of Economic History* 63:4 (2003): 959–94.

Jensen, Joan. "The Death of Rosa: Sexuality in Rural America." *Agricultural History* 67:4 (1993): 1–12.

———. "'I'd Rather Be Dancing': Wisconsin Women Moving On." *Frontiers: A Journal of Women Studies* 22:1 (2001): 1–21.

———. *Loosening the Bonds: Mid-Atlantic Farm Women, 1750–1850.* New Haven: Yale University Press, 1986.

Jones, Gavin. *American Hungers: The Problem of Poverty in US Literature, 1840–1945.* Princeton, NJ: Princeton University Press, 2008.

Katz, Michael. *In the Shadow of the Poorhouse: A Social History of Welfare in America.* New York: Basic Books, 1996.

———. "Poorhouses and the Origins of the Public Old Age Home." *Milbank Quarterly* 62:1 (1984): 110–40.

———. *Poverty and Policy in American History.* New York: Academic Press, 1983.

Keenan, Stanislas. *History of Eloise: Wayne County House, Wayne County Asylum.* Detroit: Thomas Smith Press, 1913.

Kennedy, Aileen E. *The Ohio Poor Law and Its Administration.* Chicago: University of Chicago Press, 1934.

Kessler-Harris, Alice. *Gendering Labor History.* Urbana: University of Illinois Press, 2007.

———. *Out to Work: A History of Wage-Earning Women in the United States.* New York: Oxford University Press, 1982.

———. "Treating the Male as 'Other': Redefining the Parameters of Labor History." *Labor History* 34:2 (1993): 190–204.

King, Steven. *Women, Welfare, and Local Politics, 1880–1920*. Brighton: Sussex Academic Press, 2006.

Kittay, Eva Feder. "Dependence, Equality, and Welfare." *Feminist Studies* 24:1 (1998): 32–44.

Klages, Mary. *Woeful Afflictions: Disability and Sentimentality in Victorian America*. Philadelphia: University of Pennsylvania Press, 1999.

Klebaner, Benjamin J. "Poverty and Its Relief in American Thought, 1815–1861." *Social Service Review* 38:4 (December 1964): 382–99.

———. *Public Poor Relief in America, 1790–1860*. New York: Arno Press, 1976.

Klein, Jennifer. *For All These Rights: Business, Labor, and the Shaping of America's Public-Private Welfare State*. Princeton, NJ: Princeton University Press, 2003.

Kline, Ronald. *Consumers in the Country: Technology and Social Change in Rural America*. Baltimore: Johns Hopkins University Press, 2000.

Kline, Wendy. *Building a Better Race: Gender, Sexuality, and Eugenics from the Turn of the Century to the Baby Boom*. Berkeley: University of California Press, 2005.

Kolb, John H., and Edmund de S Brunner. *A Study of Rural Society*. Westport, CT: Greenwood Press, 1971.

Koppelberger, G. *A History of the Winnebago County Poor Farm*. Oshkosh, WI: N.p., 1985.

Krainz, Thomas. *Delivering Aid: Implementing Progressive Era Welfare in the American West*. Albuquerque: University of New Mexico Press, 2005.

Kujawa, Loretta M. "The American Poorhouse in Historical Perspective." MA thesis, Roosevelt University, 2009.

Kunzel, Regina. *Fallen Women, Problem Girls: Unmarried Mothers and the Professionalization of Social Work, 1890–1945*. New Haven: Yale University Press, 1993.

———. "The Professionalization of Benevolence: Evangelicals and Social Workers in the Florence Crittenton Homes, 1915–1945." *Social History* 22:1 (1988): 21–43.

Kusmer, Kenneth. *Down and Out, on the Road: The Homeless in American History*. Oxford: Oxford University Press, 2002.

Ladd-Taylor, Molly. *Fixing the Poor: Eugenic Sterilization and Child Welfare in the Twentieth Century*. Baltimore: Johns Hopkins University Press, 2017.

———. *Mother Work: Women, Child Welfare, and the State, 1890–1930*. Urbana: University of Illinois Press, 1994.

Landis, Benson Y. *Rural Social Welfare Services*. New York: Columbia University Press, 1949.

Lauters, Amy Mattson. *More Than a Farmer's Wife: Voices of American Farm Women, 1910–1960*. Columbia: University of Missouri Press, 2009.

Leonard, Lulu. *History of Union County*. Anna, IL: N.p., 1942.

Levstik, Frank. "Life among the Lowly: An Early View of an Ohio Poor House." *Ohio History* 88:1 (1979): 84–88.

Lichtenstein, Alex. *Twice the Work of Free Labor: The Political Economy of Convict Labor in the New South*. London: Verso, 1996.

Lieberman, Morton A. "Institutionalization of the Aged: Effects on Behavior." *Journal of Gerontology* 24:3 (1969): 330–40.

Limbaugh, Ronald H. "On the Margins of Prosperity: The Mortimore Family in Oregon." *Oregon Historical Quarterly* 106:2 (2005): 204–31.

Linker, Beth. *War's Waste: Rehabilitation in World War I America*. Chicago: University of Chicago Press, 2011.

Lock, William D. "'As Independent as We Wished': Elizabeth Scott and Alice Fish of Blaine County, Nebraska." *Nebraska History* 82 (2001): 138–51.

Lockley, Timothy James. *Welfare and Charity in the Antebellum South*. Gainesville: University Press of Florida, 2007.

Loewen, James. *Sundown Towns: A Hidden Dimension of American Racism*. New York: New Press, 2005.

Lombardo, Paul A. "From Better Babies to the Bunglers: Eugenics on Tobacco Road." In *A Century of Eugenics in America*, edited by Paul A. Lombardo, 45–67. Bloomington: Indiana University Press, 2011.

Los Angeles County Poor Farm: Photographs, Written Historical and Descriptive Data, Field Records. Washington, DC: Historic American Buildings Survey, n.d.

Margo, Robert. "The Labor Force Participation of Older Americans in 1900: Further Results." *Explorations in Economic History* 30 (1993): 409–23.

Marshall, Joan E. "Shaping Poor Relief for the Sick-Poor in Indiana's Pioneering Era, Tippecanoe County, Indiana, 1826–1846." *Social Service Review* 74:4 (December 2000): 560–88.

May, Elaine Tyler. *Great Expectations: Marriage and Divorce in Post-Victorian America*. Chicago: University of Chicago Press, 1980.

May, Martha. "The 'Problem of Duty': Family Desertion in the Progressive Era." *Social Service Review* 62:1 (1988): 40–60.

McCabe, Carol. "Over the Hill to the Poorhouse." *Early American Homes* 29:2 (1998): 36–39.

McCausland, Phil. "Rural Hospital Closings Cause Mortality Rates to Rise." *NBC News*, September 6, 2019. https://www.nbcnews.com/news/us-news/rural-hospital-closings-cause-mortality-rates-rise-study-finds-n1048046.

McClure, Ethel. *More Than a Roof: The Development of Minnesota Poor Farms and Homes for the Aged*. St. Paul: Minnesota Historical Society, 1968.

———. "An Unlamented Era: County Poor Farms in Minnesota." *Minnesota History* (December 1963): 365–77.

McElvaine, Robert S., ed. *Down and Out in the Great Depression: Letters from the Forgotten Man*. Chapel Hill: University of North Carolina Press, 1983.

McLennan, Rebecca M. *The Crisis of Imprisonment: Protest, Politics, and the Making of the American Penal State, 1776–1941*. Cambridge: Cambridge University Press, 2008.

Meltsner, Heli. *The Poorhouses of Massachusetts: A Cultural and Architectural History*. Jefferson, NC: McFarland, 2012.

Mennel, Robert. "'The Family System of Common Farmers': The Early Years of Ohio's Reform Farm, 1858–1884." *Ohio History* 89:3 (Spring 1980): 279–322.

Miller, William Ian. *The Anatomy of Disgust*. Cambridge, MA: Harvard University Press, 1997.

Mintz, Steven, and Susan Kellogg. *Domestic Revolutions: A Social History of American Family Life*. New York: Free Press, 1988.

Miron, Janet. *Prisons, Asylums, and the Public: Institutional Visiting in the Nineteenth Century*. Toronto: University of Toronto Press, 2011.

Mitchell, Terri. "The King County Poor Farm." *Columbia* 16:2 (Summer 2002): 8–14.

Moeller, Helen, ed. *Out of the Midwest: A Portrait*. Marceline, MO: Walsworth Publishing, 1976.

Moen, Jon. "Rural Nonfarm Households: Leaving the Farm and the Retirement of Older Men, 1860–1980." *Social Science History* 18:1 (Spring 1994): 55–75.

Monkkonen, Eric. *The Dangerous Class: Crime and Poverty in Columbus, Ohio, 1860–1885*. Cambridge, MA: Harvard University Press, 1975.

Morgan, Edmund. *American Slavery, American Freedom*. New York: W. W. Norton, 1975.

Morton, Marian J. *And Sin No More: Social Policy and Unwed Mothers in Cleveland, 1855–1990*. Columbus: Ohio State University Press, 1993.

———. "Fallen Women, Federated Charities, and Maternity Homes, 1913–1973." *Social Service Review* 62 (March 1988): 61–82.

Munson, Helen. "The Care of the Sick, in Almshouses." *American Journal of Nursing* 30:10 (1930): 1226–30.

Murray, R. L. *The Poor House and County Farm of Cannon County, Tennessee*. N.p.: CreateSpace, 2017.

Mustakeem, Sowande' M. *Slavery at Sea: Terror, Sex, and Sickness in the Middle Passage*. Urbana: University of Illinois Press, 2016.

Naldrett, Alan. *The Poorhouses and Poor Farms of Michigan*. N.p., 2019.

Nash, Gary. "Poverty and Politics in Early American History." In *Down and Out in Early America*, ed. Billy Smith, 1–37. University Park: Penn State University Press, 2004.

Nelson, Daniel. *Farm and Factory: Workers in the Midwest, 1880–1990*. Bloomington: Indiana University Press, 1995.

Neth, Mary. *Preserving the Family Farm: Women, Community, and the Foundations of Agribusiness in the Midwest, 1900–1940*. Baltimore: Johns Hopkins University Press, 1995.

Nielsen, Kim. *A Disability History of the United States*. Boston: Beacon Press, 2012.

———. "Historical Thinking and Disability History." *Disability Studies Quarterly* 28:3 (2008). https://dsq-sds.org/article/view/107/107.

———. "Incompetent and Insane: Labor, Ability, and Citizenship in Nineteenth and Early Twentieth Century United States." *Rethinking History* 23:2 (2019): 175–88.

Noll, Steven. "Care and Control of the Feebleminded: Florida Farm Colony, 1920–1945." *Florida Historical Quarterly* 69:1 (1990): 57–80.

———. *Feebleminded in Our Midst: Institutions for the Mentally Retarded in the South, 1900–1940*. Chapel Hill: University of North Carolina Press, 1995.

Nordin, Dennis S., and Roy V. Scott. *From Prairie Farmer to Entrepreneur: The Transformation of Midwestern Agriculture*. Bloomington: Indiana University Press, 2005.

O'Conner, Alice. *Poverty Knowledge: Social Science, Social Policy, and the Poor in Twentieth-Century U.S. History*. Princeton, NJ: Princeton University Press, 2002.

Ofman, Kay Walters. "A Rural View of Mothers' Pensions: Allegan County, Michigan, Mother's Pension Program, 1913–1928." *Social Service Review* 70:1 (March 1996): 98–119.

"The Old Poor Farm." https://www.theoldpoorfarm.com/history.html.

Oldt, Franklin T. *History of Dubuque County, Iowa*. Chicago: Goodspeed Historical Association, 1911.

Olson, Marilyn. "'Halt, Blind, Lame, Sick, and Lazy': Care of the Poor in Cedar County, Iowa." *Annals of Iowa* 69 (2010): 131–72.

Olsson, Tore. *Agrarian Crossings: Reformers and the Remaking of the US and Mexican Countryside*. Princeton, NJ: Princeton University Press, 2017.

O'Nale, John P. *Scott County, Arkansas: Its Courthouses, Jails, Poor Farm, and Paupers*. Waldron, AR: Scott County Historical and Genealogical Society, 2003.

O'Neill, William. *Divorce in the Progressive Era*. New Haven: Yale University Press, 1967.

Oshinsky, David. *"Worse Than Slavery": Parchman Farm and the Ordeal of Jim Crow Justice*, New York: Free Press, 1996.

Park, Deborah Carter, and J. David Wood. "Poor Relief and the County House of Refuge System in Ontario, 1880–1911." *Journal of Historical Geography* 18:4 (October 1992): 439–55.

Parsons, Elaine Frantz. *Manhood Lost: Fallen Drunkards and Redeeming Women in the Nineteenth-Century United States*. Baltimore: Johns Hopkins University Press, 2003.

Patterson, James T. *America's Struggle against Poverty, 1900–1994*. Cambridge, MA: Harvard University Press, 1994.

Pederson, Jane. "Gender, Justice, and a Wisconsin Lynching, 1889–1890." *Agricultural History* 67:2 (Spring 1993): 65–82.

Persons, C. E. "Women's Work and Wages in the United States." *Quarterly Journal of Economics* 29:2 (1915): 201–34.

Piven, Francis Fox, and Richard Cloward. *Regulating the Poor: The Function of Public Welfare*. New York: Vintage Press, 1993.

Pleck, Elizabeth. *Domestic Tyranny: The Making of Social Policy against Family Violence from Colonial Times to Present*. Oxford: Oxford University Press, 1987.

Poppendieck, Janet. *Breadlines Knee-Deep in Wheat: Food Assistance in the Great Depression*. Berkeley: University of California Press, 2014.

Price, Rialto E. *History of Clayton County, Iowa*. Chicago: Robert O. Law Co., 1916.

Quadagno, Jill. "The Transformation of Old Age Security." In *Old Age in a Bureaucratic Society: The Elderly, the Experts, and the State in American Society*, ed. David Van Tassel and Peter Stearns, 129–55. Westport, CT: Greenwood Press, 1986.

Quadagno, Jill, and Madonna Harrington Meyer. "Organized Labor, State Structures, and Social Policy Development: A Case Study of Old Age Assistance in Ohio, 1916–1940." *Social Problems* 36:2 (1989): 181–97.

Ratcliffe, S. C. "Some Illinois County Poor Relief Records 1837–1860." *Social Service Review* 3:3 (1929): 460–75.

Reed, Benjamin F. *History of Kossuth County, Iowa*. Chicago: S. J. Clarke, 1913.

Reske, Phyllis E. "Policing the 'Wayward Woman': Eugenics in Wisconsin's Involuntary Sterilization Program." *Wisconsin Magazine of History* 97:1 (2013): 14–27.

"Respectful Disability Language." National Youth Leadership Network. http://www .aucd.org/docs/add/sa_summits/Language%20Doc.pdf.

Rexroad, William D. *The Poor Farm of Pendleton County*. Hutchinson, KS: Dolphin Publications, 2009.

Riney-Kehrberg, Pamela. *Rooted in Dust: Surviving Drought and Depression in Southwestern Kansas*. Lawrence: University Press of Kansas, 1994.

Roberts, Charles Kenneth. *The Farm Securities Administration and Rural Rehabilitation in the South*. Knoxville: University of Tennessee Press, 2015.

Roberts, Evan Warwick. "Her Real Sphere? Married Women's Labor Force Participation in the United States, 1860–1940." PhD diss., University of Minnesota, 2007.

Roediger, David. *Wages of Whiteness: Race and the Making of the American Working Class*. London: Verso, 2007.

Rose, Sarah F. *No Right to Be Idle: The Invention of Disability, 1840s–1930s*. Chapel Hill: University of North Carolina Press, 2017.

Rosenberg, Charles E. *The Care of Strangers: The Rise of America's Hospital System*. Baltimore: Johns Hopkins University Press, 1995.

———. "From Almshouse to Hospital: The Shaping of Philadelphia General Hospital." *Milbank Memorial Fund Quarterly, Health and Society* 60:1 (1982): 108–54.

Rosenberg, Gabriel. *The 4-H Harvest: Sexuality and the State in Rural America*. Philadelphia: University of Pennsylvania Press, 2016.

Rosenbloom, Joshua. "The Extent of the Labor Market in the United States, 1870–1914." *Social Science History* 22:3 (1998): 287–318.

Ross, Earl D. "Farm Tenancy in Iowa." *Annals of Iowa* 31 (1951): 36–40.

Roth, Cassia. "The (Historical) Body in Pain." *Nursing Clio* blog, April 9, 2019. https:// nursingclio.org/2019/04/09/the-historical-body-in-pain/.

Roth, Randolph A. "Spousal Murder in Northern New England, 1776–1865." In *Over the Threshold: Intimate Violence in Early America*, ed. Christine Daniels and Michael V. Kennedy, 65–93. New York: Routledge, 1999.

Rothman, David. *Conscience and Convenience: The Asylum and Its Alternatives in Progressive America*. New York: Routledge, 1980.

———. *The Discovery of the Asylum: Social Order and Disorder in the New Republic*. Boston: Little,Brown, 1971.

Rowe, G. S., and Jack D. Marietta. "Personal Violence in a 'Peaceable Kingdom' Pennsylvania, 1682–1801." In *Over the Threshold: Intimate Violence in Early America*, ed. Christine Daniels and Michael V. Kennedy, 22–44. New York: Routledge, 2014.

Ruggles, Steven. "Multigenerational Families in Nineteenth-Century America." *Continuity and Change* 18:1 (2003): 139–65.

———. "The Transformation of American Family Structure." *American Historical Review* 99:1 (1994): 103–28.

Ruppe, David. "Elderly Abused at 1 in 3 Nursing Homes." *ABC News*, January 7, 2006. http://abcnews.go.com/US/story?id=92689&page=1.

Ruswick, Brent. *Almost Worthy: The Poor, Paupers, and the Science of Charity in America, 1877–1917*. Bloomington: Indiana University Press, 2012.

———. "Just Poor Enough: Gilded Age Charity Applicants Respond to Charity Investigators." *Journal of the Gilded Age and Progressive Era* 10:3 (2011): 265–87.

"Saginaw County Farm." Saginaw Genealogical Society. http://www.sgsmi.org/county-farm.html.

Salamon, Sonya. *Prairie Patrimony: Family, Farming, and Community in the Midwest.* Chapel Hill: University of North Carolina Press, 1995.

"Sangamon County Poor Farm." Sagamon County Historical Society. http://sangamoncountyhistory.org/wp/?p=6763.

Scadron, Arlene, ed. *On Their Own: Widows and Widowhood in the American Southwest, 1848–1939.* Urbana: University of Illinois Press, 1988.

Scarry, Elaine. *The Body in Pain: The Making and Unmaking of the World.* Oxford: Oxford University Press, 1987.

Schell, Ellen. "The Origins of Geriatric Nursing: The Chronically Ill Elderly in Almshouses and Nursing Homes, 1900–1950." *Nursing History Review* 1 (1993): 203–16.

Schneider, David M., and Albert Deutsch. *The History of Public Welfare in New York State, 1867–1940.* Chicago: University of Chicago Press, 1941.

Schob, David E. *Hired Hands and Plowboys: Farm Labor in the Midwest, 1815–1860.* Urbana: University of Illinois Press, 1975.

Schoen, Johanna. *Choice and Coercion: Birth Control, Sterilization, and Abortion in Public Health and Welfare.* Chapel Hill: University of North Carolina Press, 2005.

Schuman, John Henning. "A Bygone Era: When Bipartisanship Led to Health Care Transformation." *NPR*, October 2, 2016. https://www.npr.org/sections/health-shots/2016/10/02/495775518/a-bygone-era-when-bipartisanship-led-to-health-care-transformation.

Schwartzberg, Beverly. "'Lots of Them Did That': Desertion, Bigamy, and Marital Fluidity in Late Nineteenth-Century America." *Journal of Social History* 37:3 (2004): 573–600.

Schweik, Susan M. *The Ugly Laws: Disability in Public.* New York: New York University Press, 2009.

Sharpless, Rebecca. *Fertile Ground, Narrow Choices: Women on Texas Cotton Farms, 1900–1940.* Chapel Hill: University of North Carolina Press, 1999.

Shifflett, Crandall A. *Patronage and Poverty in the Tobacco South: Louisa County, Virginia, 1860–1900.* Knoxville: University of Tennessee Press, 1982.

Singleton, Jeff. *The American Dole: Unemployment Relief and the Welfare State in the Great Depression.* Westport, CT: Greenwood Press, 2000.

Skocpol, Theda. *Protecting Soldiers and Mothers: The Political Origins of Social Policy in the United States.* Cambridge, MA: Belknap Press of Harvard University Press, 1995.

Smith, Bruce. "Poor Relief at the St. Joseph County Poor Asylum, 1877–1891." *Indiana Magazine of History* 86:2 (1990): 178–96.

Smith, Daniel Scott. "A Community-Based Sample of the Older Population from the 1880 and 1900 United States Manuscript Census." *Historical Methods* 11:2 (1978): 67–74.

———. "Female Householding in Late Eighteenth-Century America and the Problem of Poverty." *Journal of Social History* 28:1 (1994): 83–108.

———. "Life Course, Norms, and the Family System." *Journal of Family History* 4:3 (1979): 285–98.

———. "The Meanings of Family and Household: Change and Continuity in the Mirror of the American Census." *Population and Development Review* 18:3 (1992): 421–56.

Spencer-Wood, Suzanne M. "Feminist Theoretical Perspectives on the Archaeology of Poverty: Gendering Institutional Lifeways in the Northeastern United States from the Eighteenth Century through the Nineteenth Century." *Historical Archaeology* 44:4 (2010): 110–35.

Squillace, Joe. "Life on the Morgan County Poor Farm: Christian Benevolence in Early Social Services." *Journal of the Illinois Historical Society* 112:2 (Summer 2019): 163–86.

Stanley, Amy Dru. "Beggars Can't Be Choosers: Compulsion and Contract in Postbellum America." *Journal of American History* 78:4 (1992): 1265–93.

Stansell, Christine. *City of Women: Sex and Class in New York, 1789–1860*. Urbana: University of Illinois Press, 1987.

Stevens, Robert, and Rosemary Stevens. *Welfare Medicine in America: A Case Study of Medicaid*. New York: Free Press, 1974.

Stevenson, Marietta. *Public Welfare Administration*. New York: Macmillan, 1938.

Stillman, E. B. *Past and Present of Greene County, Iowa*. Chicago: S. J. Clarke, 1907.

"The St. Louis County Poor Farm." *Zenith City Press*. http://zenithcity.com/archive/historic-architecture/the-st-louis-county-poor-farm/.

Strasser, Susan. *Never Done: A History of American Housework*. New York: Pantheon, 1982.

Stuart, I. L. *History of Franklin County, Iowa*. Chicago: S. J. Clarke, 1914.

Sturtevant, Deborah. "Ottawa County Community Haven: A Poor Farm Withstands the Test of Time." *Michigan History Magazine* 76:5 (Fall 1992): 13–17.

Sutter, Richard. "Dental Pathologies among Inmates at the Monroe County Poorhouse." In *Bodies of Evidence: Reconstructing History through Skeletal Analysis*, ed. Anne Grauer. 185–96. New York: Wiley-Liss, 1995.

"Taxation in Ohio." Ohio Department of Taxation. http://www.tax.ohio.gov/portals/0/taxeducation/history/taxation%20in%20ohio_history.pdf.

Tennant, Margaret. *Paupers and Providers: Charitable Aid in New Zealand*. Wellington: Allen & Unwin, 1989.

Thiede, Brian, David L. Brown, Scott R. Sanders, Nina Glasgow, and Laszlo J. Kulcsar. "A Demographic Deficit?: Local Population Aging and Access to Services in Rural America, 1900–2010." *Rural Sociology* 82:1 (2017): 44–74.

Thomas, Karen Kruse. "The Hill-Burton Act and Civil Rights: Expanding Hospital Care for Black Southerners, 1939–1960." *Journal of Southern History* 72:4 (2006): 823–70.

Tiffany, Francis. *The Life of Dorothea Lynde Dix*. Cambridge, MA: Riverside Press, 1890.

Tomes, Nancy, and Lynn Gamwell. *Madness in America: Cultural and Medical Perceptions of Mental Illness before 1914*. Ithaca, NY: Cornell University Press, 1995.

Trattner, Walter. *From Poor Law to Welfare State: A History of Social Welfare in America*. New York: Free Press, 1999.

———. "Homer Folks and the Public Health Movement." *Social Service Review* 40:4 (1966): 410–28.

Trent, James. *Inventing the Feeble Mind: A History of Mental Retardation in the United States*. Berkeley: University of California Press, 1994.

Tuten, James H. "Regulating the Poor in Alabama." In *Before the New Deal: Social Welfare in the South, 1830–1930*, ed. Elna Green, 40–60. Athens: University of Georgia Press, 1999.

Vale, Lawrence J. *From the Puritans to the Projects: Public Housing and Public Neighbors*. Cambridge, MA: Harvard University Press, 2000.

Wagner, David. *The Miracle Worker and the Transcendentalist: Annie Sullivan, Franklin Sanborn, and the Education of Helen Keller.* New York: Routledge, 2011.

———. *Ordinary People: In and Out of Poverty in the Gilded Age.* Boulder, CO: Paradigm Publishing, 2008.

———. *The Poorhouse: America's Forgotten Institution.* Lanham, MD: Rowman & Littlefield, 2005.

Wallenstein, Peter. *From Slave South to New South: Public Policy in Nineteenth-Century Georgia.* Chapel Hill: University of North Carolina Press, 1992.

Wallis, John Joseph. "American Government Finance in the Long Run, 1790 to 1990." *Journal of Economic Perspectives* 14:1 (2000): 61–82.

Walsh, Margaret. "Gendering Mobility: Women, Work, and Automobility in the United States." *History* 93:3 (July 2008): 376–95.

Ward, Thomas J. *Out in the Rural: A Mississippi Health Center and Its War on Poverty.* New York: Oxford University Press, 2016.

Warren, Paula, and James Warren. *Transcribed Ramsey County, Minnesota Relief Records 1862–1868.* St. Paul: Warren Research and Marketing, 1990.

Watkins, Susan Cotts, Jane A. Menken, and John Bongaarts. "Demographic Foundations of Family Change." *American Sociological Review* 52:3 (1987): 346–58.

Weiler, N. Sue. "Industrial Scrap Heap: Employment Patterns and Change for the Aged in the 1920s." *Social Science History* 13:1 (1989): 65–88.

———. "Religion, Ethnicity, and the Development of Private Homes for the Aged." *Journal of American Ethnic History* 12:1 (1992): 64–91.

Westerfield, Michael. *The Road to the Poorhouse: The Windham Town Farm and the Connecticut Almshouse System.* Willimantic, CT: Ashford Press, 2017.

White, Gerald. *The United States and the Problem of Recovery after 1893.* Tuscaloosa: University of Alabama Press, 1981.

Willets, Gilson. *Workers of the Nation: An Encyclopedia of the Occupations of the American People,* vol. 2. New York: P. F. Collier, 1903.

Williams, Dusty. *The Poor Farm of Grayson County, Texas.* N.p.: CreateSpace, 2015.

Winters, Donald. "Agricultural Tenancy in the Nineteenth-Century Middle West: The Historiographical Debate." *Indiana Magazine of History* 78:2 (1982): 128–53.

Wisner, Elizabeth. *Public Welfare in Louisiana.* Chicago: University of Chicago Press, 1930.

———. *Social Welfare in the South from Colonial Times to World War I.* Baton Rouge: Louisiana State University Press, 1970.

Woehle, Ralph. "Lessons from Yellow Medicine County: Work and Custodial Service at the County Poor Farm, 1889–1935." *Journal of Sociology and Social Welfare* 24:4 (1997): 14–28.

Wood, Gregory. *Retiring Men: Manhood, Labor, and Growing Old in America, 1900–1960.* Lanham, MD: University Press of America, 2011.

Wray, Matt. *Not Quite White: White Trash and the Boundaries of Whiteness.* Durham, NC: Duke University Press, 2006.

Wright, David, Sean Moran, and Sean Gouglas. "The Confinement of the Insane in Victorian Canada: The Hamilton and Toronto Asylums, c. 1861–1891." In *The Confinement of the Insane: International Perspectives, 1800–1965,* ed. Roy Porter and David Wright, 100–128. Cambridge: Cambridge University Press, 2003.

Wulf, Karin. "Gender and the Political Economy of Poor Relief in Colonial Philadelphia." In *Down and Out in Early America*, ed. Billy Smith, 163–88. University Park: Penn State University Press, 2004.

Wuthnow, Robert. *American Misfits and the Making of Middle-Class Respectability*. Princeton, NJ: Princeton University Press, 2017.

Wysocki, Gina. *Digging Up the Dirt: The History and Mysteries of the Will County Poor Farm and Potter's Fields*. New York: iUniverse, 2009.

———. *Remembering the Paupers: A Brief History of the Will County Poor Farm and Its Cemetery*. Lockport, IL: Will County Historical Society, 2008.

Yanni, Carla. "The Linear Plan for Insane Asylums in the United States before 1866." *Journal of the Society of Architectural Historians* 62:1 (2003): 24–49.

Yoakum, C. S. *Care of the Feebleminded and Insane in Texas*. Bulletin of the University of Texas, Austin, 1914.

Young, Steve. "Over the Hill to the Poor Farm." *Vermont Life* (Spring 1990): 14–19.

Ziliak, Stephen. "Pauper Fiction in Economic Science: 'Paupers in Almshouses' and the Odd Fit of Oliver Twist." *Review of Social Economy* 60:2 (June 2002): 159–81.

Zunz, Oliver. *Philanthropy in America*. Princeton, NJ: Princeton University Press, 2012.

Index

MEGAN BIRK is a professor of history at the University of Texas Rio Grande Valley. She is the author of *Fostering on the Farm: Child Placement in the Rural Midwest.*

The University of Illinois Press
is a founding member of the
Association of University Presses.

University of Illinois Press
1325 South Oak Street
Champaign, IL 61820-6903
www.press.uillinois.edu